Theodor Fontane and the
European Context

53

Internationale Forschungen zur
Allgemeinen und
Vergleichenden Literaturwissenschaft

In Verbindung mit

Dietrich Briesemeister (Friedrich Schiller-Universität Jena) — Guillaume van Gemert (Universiteit Nijmegen) — Joachim Knape (Universität Tübingen) — Klaus Ley (Johannes Gutenberg-Universität Mainz) — John A. McCarthy (Vanderbilt University) — Manfred Pfister (Freie Universität Berlin) — Sven H. Rossel (University of Washington) — Azade Seyhan (Bryn Mawr College) — Horst Thomé (Universität Kiel)

herausgegeben von

Alberto Martino
(Universität Wien)

Redakteure:
Prof. Dr. Norbert Bachleitner. — Doz. Dr. Alfred Noe

Anschrift der Redaktion:
Institut für Vergleichende Literaturwissenschaft, Berggasse 11/5, A-1090 Wien

Theodor Fontane and the European Context

Literature, Culture and Society in Prussia and Europe

Proceedings of the Interdisciplinary Symposium at the
Institute of Germanic Studies, University of London
in March 1999

Edited by

Patricia Howe and Helen Chambers

Amsterdam - Atlanta, GA 2001

This book is published simultaneously as Volume 76 in the series PUBLICATIONS OF THE INSTITUTE OF GERMANIC STUDIES (University of London School of Advanced Study) ISBN 085457-196-5

Le papier sur lequel le présent ouvrage est imprimé remplit les prescriptions de "ISO 9706:1994, Information et documentation - Papier pour documents - Prescriptions pour la permanence".

The paper on which this book is printed meets the requirements of "ISO 9706:1994, Information and documentation - Paper for documents - Requirements for permanence".

ISBN: 90-420-1236-6
©Editions Rodopi B.V., Amsterdam-Atlanta, GA 2001
Printed in The Netherlands

Contents

Preface

Among German novelists of the nineteenth century Theodor Fontane is generally considered to be the one whose writing has the most immediate appeal for a European public because it clearly belongs to the broad tradition of European narrative realism. His novels of social life, set mainly against the background of Prussia, are sustained by his wide reading in European literature and his experience as a journalist, traveller and theatre critic, and complemented by his other writings. As the supreme novelistic chronicler of the new Germany, he plays a crucial part in moving the German novel away from the introspection and provincialityoften ascribed to it.

Yet when we read Fontane's novels it is also apparent that this is realism in a different key. While Fontane shares with Balzac, Dickens or Tolstoy a profound interest in human beings and the communities theycreate and inhabit, his novels often seem less dramatic, energetic and comprehensive than those of his European counterparts, and more muted in tone and slighter in scope. Fontane's social portraiture, as recent studies of European Realism have shown, has less to do with detailed documentation and the presentation of physical realities in texts than with registering contemporary shifts in thinking and the symbolisation and codification of personal and social life. In part, the differences may be ascribed to the relative 'lateness' of Fontane's realism, to the fact that Germany does not become a nation state until 1871, and to the fact that he writes against a background of religious, scientific and political uncertainties. The late nineteenth century sees itself as an age of transition, and comes to be marked by a sense of unease and of tension between past authority and rapid change. Many of its tensions are articulated both in the themes of Fontane's novels and in their structures. By comparison with writers of the mid-century he tends increasingly to move the focus of interest away from plot, referentiality, and the panoramic portrayal of social life. As traditional structures and strategies are appraised and revised, his narratives become more self-consciously reflective. His realism is increasingly subtle, oblique, restrained, essentially literary in its allusiveness, its use of sub-texts and codifications – the "thousand finesses"of which Fontane himself speaks.

The similarities and differences between Fontane and other writers in the realist tradition raise important questions about how realism may be understood, and is understood by its practitioners, about cultural context, literary genre and personal temperament. One aim of the essays in this volume is to ask how realism constructs and mediates values, defines identity and community, and how far Fontane engages with these issues thematically in his perception of class systems, codes of behaviour, mechanisms of repression and articulates them textually. They examine the extent to which these qualities may be explained as a matter of individual sensibilities and as an expression of the self-consciously transitional period of the late nineteenth century. A further aim is to locate Fontane's narrative fiction in its Prussian context, against the background of the new Germany and in the tradition of thinking about national literatures, about nationhood and national identity. Another aspect of this is the cultural and linguistic problems Fontane's writings may present for translators.

All the essays in the volume were first given as papers at events held at the Institute of Germanic Studies, University of London, to commemorate the centenary of Fontane's death. Most of them were first heard at an international symposium held in March 1999, from which the volume also takes its title. The other two papers, by Peter James Bowman and Godela Weiss-Sussex, were given at a one-day colloquium in December 1998 entitled *Fontane at the End of the Century*, the purpose of which was, in part, to promote the work of younger scholars. Both events owe their inspiration to Professor Charlotte Jolles, Honorary President of the Fontane Gesellschaft and Emeritus Professor of German in the University of London, who proposed the central focus on reception and comparison. These events brought together colleagues from a number of different countries and disciplines to explore issues raised at the end of the nineteenth century which have a particular interest and importance for students of cultural, intellectual and social change at the turn of the twentieth century. Their interests and expertise range over the fields of English, French, German, Irish, Italian, Norwegian, Portuguese, Russian and Spanish literatures, as well as art history, philosophy, sociology and translation theory. Some of the contributors are also writers of biography, fiction and poetry.

The essays focus mainly on novels and theatre reviews, considering them from many perspectives and producing contrasting but complementary readings. Fontane's writing is considered from the different perspectives of philosophy and sociology, in the contexts of topography and painting. He appears not only in the company of predecessors and contemporaries, such as Scott, Thackeray, Saar, Ibsen, Turgenev, but also in that of writers he has rarely if ever been seen beside, such as E. T. A. Hoffmann, Stendhal, Trollope, Beckett, Faulkner. His reception of French theatre and of Ibsen reveals new aspects of his own unsystematic poetics. Certain texts, most notably *Schach von Wuthenow* and *Effi Briest*, recur as the focus of discussion about the historical novel and the novel of adultery. The connections and crosscurrents that emerge give a sense of the dialogue that informed the symposium itself. Perhaps in consequence, the essays do not fall readily into groups, and it was felt that, following the Introduction by Rüdiger Görner and the keynote paper by Renate Böschenstein on the concept of reality in literature, this sense of dialogue would be best preserved by arranging them alphabetically.

Fontane emerges as a writer who is receptive to the voices of the past and to their modes of narration, and creative in his re-interpretation and revision of them. He transforms the nineteenth-century German novel into a form that, with all its specific cultural and personal differences, can stand beside other European novels. He also shows himself to be a 'strong precursor', albeit a different kind of precursor from those that Harold Bloom had in mind when he formulated this concept in *The Anxiety of Influence*. The citations, allusions, echoes and revisions that, paradoxically, give a porous texture to Fontane's writing as well as creating the unmistakable 'Fontane-tone', both sum up a tradition and point to new possibilities. He is not a precursor who overwhelms or creates a long shadow, but one in whose company other writers could, as the protagonist of Beckett's *Krapp's Last Tape* says of Effi Briest, 'be happy'.

There are many people and institutions to whom we owe thanks. We would like to thank the following for their generous financial contributions to the symposium: The Austrian Cultural Institute, London; The Embassy of the Federal Republic of Germany: The Embassy of Switzerland/ Pro Helvetia; The Department of German, University of Leeds. We would also like to express our gratitude to a number of people who gave generously of their time and expertise to make the symposium and the one-day colloquium possible: Professor Charlotte Jolles for inspiration and encouragement; Professor Martin Swales of University College London, our co-organiser for his generous help with both events; Professor Rudiger Görner, Director of the Institute of Germanic Studies, and the administrative staff of the Institute, for their assistance with administration; Professor John Flood, Deputy Director, and Mr William Abbey, Librarian, of the Institute of Germanic Studies, and the staff of the Arts Computing Unit of Queen Mary and Westfield College, University of London, for their patient and expert help in preparing this volume; Hugh Rorrison for the translation of the paper by Domenico Mugnolo. We would also like to thank those who gave us permission to reproduce illustrations. Their names are given in the List of Illustrations at the end of the volume.

P. H./ H. C.

Note

Unless otherwise stated references to Fontane's novels, essays and poetry are taken from *Sämtliche Werke*, edited by Edgar Gross, Kurt Schreinert et al..Munich: Nymphenburger 1959-1975, abbreviated as NFA, followed by the number of the volume and page.

References to letters and commentaries are taken from *Werke, Schriften und Briefe*, edited by Walter Keitel and Helmuth Nürnberger. Munich: Hanser 1962 ff., and are abbreviated as HFA, followed by the numbers of the part, the volume and the page.

Quotations are given in English in the body of the text with the original in a footnote. Titles of novels, dramas, poems, etc. are given in English in brackets after the original title. They are italicised only where they refer to published editions of translations. E.g. *Irrungen, Wirrungen* (*Delusions, Confusions*).

Rüdiger Görner

Fontane and the European Context: Introduction

When reading Fontane some are reminded of Montaigne and the sanity and balance of his argument; others compare the style of Fontane's *causerie* with English common sense and his prose with the poetic realism of the great Russian writers.

However appropriate such comparisons may seem, there is a strong feeling *of joie de vivre* in Fontane's writing too, yet it is always coupled with melancholy and a sense of irretrievable loss – of human values. Palmerston's Britain is just as present in Fontane's work as Bismarck's Prussia; and even an element of *italianità* appears as a pictorial quotation at the end of *Der Stechlin* (*The Stechlin*), when we glimpse Amalfi, Sorrento and Capri, where Woldemar and Armgard are spending their honeymoon, which is sadly terminated, however, by the news of Dubslav von Stechlin's death. A wreath of laurel and olive from Capri will eventually be placed on Dubslav's grave, as if to say: here rests a worldly-wise man.

One hundred years after the death of this most European and urbane of nineteenth-century German novelists, Fontane's presence in German culture is more prominent than ever. The origins of the more recent renaissance of Fontane go back to Rainer Werner Fassbinder's film version of *Effi Briest* (1972/74), with Hanna Schygulla in the title role; there are the editions of his letters, diaries, and complete works, most notably the correspondence between the writer and his wife, Emilie, which has done much to correct our view of his life-long partner, whose love, support and understanding for his caprices and tempers can only be called overwhelming.

But there is also Günter Grass's controversial novel *Ein weites Feld* (*Too Far Afield*), with its Fontane-obsessed protagonist Fonty, which has contributed to raising public awareness of Fontane.[1] Historians like Lothar Gall and Gordon A. Craig, and philosophers like the late Hans Blumenberg, regarded Fontane as an inspiration and a challenge, while theatre critics had long seen Fontane as one of them, too. After all, he was an accomplished translator of *Hamlet*, and a subtle critic who, mainly from his famous seat number twenty-three in the Royal Court Theatre in Berlin, saw and reviewed every current production – from Sophocles to Kleist, from Shakespeare to Schiller, Karl Gutzkow to Friedrich Hebbel, Henrik Ibsen to Gerhart Hauptmann. Fontane's columns on Hauptmann were instrumental in the break-through of the young dramatist.

Fontane, the lyric poet, has regained recognition during the last decade or so, assisted by Christian Friedrich Delius's ballad on German unification, *Die Birnen von Ribbeck* (The Pears of Ribbeck). The political Fontane can no longer be overlooked either, since the ground-breaking study by Charlotte Jolles (1983) and subsequent

---

1 See: Oskar Negt (ed.): Der Fall Fonty. "Ein weites Feld" von Günter Grass im Spiegel der Kritik. Göttingen: Steidl 1996.

studies by others. This writer who "wrote the way others breathe", as the famous Berlin theatre critic Friedrich Luft once put it, moved between sense, sensibility, and social scrutiny.[2]

With Thomas Mann, who ascribed to his revered predecessor a "charming sobriety", we can argue that it was obviously necessary to acquire a lot in terms of painful experience in order to have grown fully aware of Fontane's outstanding cultural significance.[3] Quite apart from his unique style and approach to storytelling, this must surely also be due to his highly accomplished way of conveying value-oriented retrospection as an indispensable precondition for progression.

Fontane's novels are about elementary, but essential questions. This explains part of the appeal that his prose continues to have for readers in our time. These are questions that purposely reduce the often artificial complexity of discourse to fundamental issues, such as: what is "humanity"? How do we relate to others? How does personal memory influence what we are doing?

The most stoic of answers to such questions was, of course, given by Dubslav von Stechlin who concludes at the end of his life:

> The self is nothing – one has to let this idea sink in completely. An eternal law is being fulfilled, nothing more. And this fulfilment, even if it's called death, shouldn't alarm us. Accepting this law calmly, that's what makes a human being moral and ennobles him.[4]

This very "law" [das Gesetzliche] was neither a reflection of Prussian nor any other state law but rather the principle of "permanence and change" ("Dauer und Wechsel") in Goethe's sense of the words, in combination with partly Kantian and partly Stoic notions of ethics; in addition, "das Gesetzliche" is an expression of the ever more urgent attempt to reconcile human ambition with the demands of nature. Fontane's last novel ends, after all, as it began – with a reference to the lake Stechlin.

Some of Fontane's own answers to such questions amounted to a plea for harmony:

> O darken not these days with shade,
> The sun's last rays shine on us still,
> How long before the light will fade,
> And on us breaks the winter's chill.[5]

---

2 Friedrich Luft: Er schrieb wie andere atmen. Zu den Briefen Theodor Fontanes. In: Die Welt, 7 November 1978.

3 "charmante Nüchternheit"; Thomas Mann to Albrecht Goes, 15 January 1954. In: Thomas Mann: Briefe III (1948-1955), ed. by Erika Mann. Frankfurt a. M.: Fischer 1979, p. 321.

4 "Das Ich ist nichts – damit muß man sich durchdringen. Ein ewig Gesetzliches vollzieht sich, weiter nichts, und dieser Vollzug, auch wenn er Tod heißt, darf uns nicht schrecken. In das Gesetzliche sich ruhig schicken, das macht den sittlichen Menschen und hebt ihn." Fontane: *Der Stechlin*, NFA, VIII, 341. Translations into English from Fontane's writings are by Patricia Howe.

5 "O trübe diese Tage nicht,/ Sie sind der letzte Sonnenschein,/ Wie lange, und es lischt das Licht,/Und unser Winter bricht herein." Balladen und Gedichte, NFA, XX, 9.

In lines like these lies the very proof of Fontane's "charming sobriety". But the essence of his often deceptively simplistic views was his relentless attack on human vanity, which he experienced in the Berlin of the *nouveaux riches* during the *Gründerzeit* in the 1880s and 1890s and, earlier in Britain, with the ascendancy of the commercial and industrial, upper middle classes. Fontane's desire to expose this vanity and show the emptiness behind it was matched in European literature of the time by Thackeray's, admittedly cruder, social satire.

The stylistic device of such "sobriety" was a prose free of ornament. Fontane's "modernism" in questions of aesthetic judgement is nowhere more obvious than in the words of art professor Cujacius, again in *Der Stechlin*, whose artistic credo comes close to Fontane's own "poetics": "There is only one salvation: to turn back, to return to the chaste line. The colourists are the misfortune of art."[6] This was the essence of what some years later in Vienna and elsewhere in the art world was to be debated vigorously, anticipating the notion of a neo-Kantian "objectivity" ("Sachlichkeit") in art. In Fontane's novels and stories colourfulness was reserved for his individual characters but not for their "line" of argument.

Admittedly, neither Flaubert, nor Dickens, nor Turgenev, for that matter, was as preoccupied with war as Fontane was. It seems that Fontane did most of his extensive writing on the Prussian Wars, or so-called "Wars of Unity" ("Einheitskriege"), in order to receive recognition from the Prussian King. His hopes were, as we know, frustrated, for Wilhelm I clearly felt that his subject from Neuruppin had not quite fulfilled his patriotic duty; Fontane's prose did not sound heroic enough to true blue ears. To some extent, however, we must nevertheless describe Fontane as the Thucydides of the Prussians, although nowadays we have little time for such bellicose extravagances as those of this first European historian.

More to the point, however, one would need to compare Fontane's writings on war with Tolstoy's early account of the war in the Caucasus and, of course, with *War and Peace*, and with, say, Thomas Hardy's novel *The Trumpet Major*. Fontane's contribution to this genre was his late but stunning début as a novelist, *Vor dem Sturm (Before the Storm)*. What becomes evident is that Fontane's authentic and fictitious historiography was informed by a poetic realism that allowed him to depict history as a landscape of time. The landmarks in this scenery were to him anecdotes and episodes that always put a question mark over any so-called achievements or preconceived ideas. What is so refreshing about reading Fontane today, apart from his compositional and stylistic art, is the absence of ideology in his prose. Whilst ideological confrontations had become the order of the day Fontane could afford to play with dogmatic convictions, thus undermining their credibility.

Fontane was concerned with three particular forces behind human or inhuman action: people's fear of ridicule; their desire to conceal their weaknesses; and their dangerously futile striving for social recognition. *Schach von Wuthenow (A Man of Honor)* is about these themes as is *Effi Briest*. In the latter novel Fontane mastered the

---

6 "Es gibt nur ein Heil: Umkehr, Rückkehr zur keuschen Linie. Die Koloristen sind das Unglück in der Kunst." Fontane: *Der Stechlin*. NFA, VIII, 221.

art of writing in the paradoxical mode of what I would like to call detached intimacy, to a point at which passion and social analysis, symbolism and "the chaste line" are but one declaration of love for the unceasing act of narrating.

Fontane internalised the European context of his writings and, at the same time, provided German literature, again, with a European significance that it had lost after Heine.

Renate Böschenstein

Fontane's Writing and the Problem of 'Reality' in Philosophy and Literature.

1

In 1959 Jorge Luis Borges wrote his poem *El otro tigre* (*The Other Tiger*).[1] In this text he describes his dream of a tiger living on the shores of the Ganges. Though he tries as far as possible to adopt the perspective of the tiger, the poet becomes aware that he is unable to evoke by his words anything but a "tiger made of symbols and of shadows". There is no possibility of evoking "the other tiger", the "true tiger" "beyond the mythologies" At last he resigns himself to the creation of a "third tiger", knowing that this one also will be only a "system of human words". In spite of this knowledge there is something forcing him into this "adventure, senseless and old."

"How real is reality? Is the world made – or invented?" Those were the headlines the journal *Die Zeit* put above the elaborate article in which, in 1997, Hans-Ulrich Gumbrecht commented on a joke made by the physicist Alan Sokal which stirred up the intellectual world.[2] In a parody written in "postmodern" jargon he had proved that even the laws of nature were nothing other than constructs depending on the given cultural context of the researcher – and this parody had been published as a serious essay in the renowned periodical *Social Text*.

The literary and the theoretical example show that the irritating stimulus that, more than a hundred years ago, pushed Stifter's painter Roderer to his desperate endeavour to represent "real reality", has lost nothing of its power, although many artists and scholars have resigned themselves to the impossibility of proving the existence of a reality outside the subject and of making statements about it.[3] "Only reality seems more real" – by this assertion, accompanied by the picture of a delicately coloured running-shoe, an advertisement praises the quality of the colours produced by certain ink jet printers. We even could say that, *mutatis mutandis*, we find ourselves in a situation which is not dissimilar to the situation in which Fontane, as a young author, started his literary production. In his time there was the turning away from the speculative and metaphysical interpretations of the world which the idealistic philosophers had imposed, a turn that he has described in vivid colours in his early

---

1 El otro tigre. Text with German translation in: Borges und ich. Gesammelte Werke, vol. 6. Munich: Hanser 1982, pp. 72-75. (In the collection 'El hacedor'. Obras completas, Buenos Aires: Emecé editores 1974). All translations into English are my own.

2 "Wie wirklich ist die Wirklichkeit ? Ist die Welt gemacht – oder erfunden?" Die Zeit 28 February 1997.

3 "die wirkliche Wirklichkeit." Adalbert Stifter: Nachkommenschaften. Gesammelte Werke in 14 Bänden, Basel, Stuttgart: Birkhäuser 1964, vol. 5, p. 259.

essay *Unsere lyrische und epische Poesie seit 1848* (Our lyrical and epic literature since 1848).[4] Presently, after many years during which the various kinds of constructivism and poststructuralism have made dominant the conception of a world that is only mentally constituted and in which objects, subjects and history are only elements of a text, we notice a new influence of philosophers who leave the 'linguistic turn' behind them. In a new 'turn' they try to revalorise the old conception of a world that exists independently of the mind and can, approximately, be recognised and described by language. I should like to concentrate here on an essay by John R. Searle, written in 1993, which seems to me typical of this new movement: *Rationality and Realism, What is at Stake?*.[5] Against philosophers like Derrida and Rorty, Searle defends the legitimacy of the intellectual tradition which he calls the "Western Rationalistic Tradition". Its basis is the acceptance of a correspondence between the mind and the external world. It strives for clarity and objectivity, acknowledges criteria for the truth of statements and has a self-critical quality. The motives for this revalorisation of the assumption that there is an external and partially understandable world are, on one hand, the moral standards of science, which, as Searle fears, are endangered by an arbitrary juxtaposition of various readings of the universe. On the other hand, however, it is the insufferable gap between philosophy and common speaking and acting that opens when the existence of a reality outside the subject is denied. Searle says:

> Realism does not function as a thesis, hypothesis, or supposition. It is, rather, the condition of the possibility of a certain set of practices, particularly linguistic practices. [6]

Kant had already called it a scandal for philosophy and common sense that the existence of the things outside us cannot be proved.[7] This scandal has stimulated, in the history of philosophy, the ups and downs of cognition theory. The efforts to span the gap between confidence in the existence and legibility of the world that is empirically perceived and insight into its uncertain character are followed by attempts to eliminate this unsolved problem by turning to other questions. Walther Zimmerli, who in 1984 presented a survey of the development of the problem of cognition over

---

4 Fontane: Unsere lyrische und epische Poesie seit 1848. Literarische Essays und Studien, NFA, XXI/1, 7-33.

5 John R.Searle: Rationality and Realism, What is at stake? In: Daedalus, Proceedings of the American Academy of Arts and Sciences 122/4, (1993), pp. 55-83. For a survey of this movement see: Thomas Bartelborth: Wissenschaftlicher Realismus. Ein Forschungsbericht. In: Information Philosophie (1997/2), pp. 18-29.

6 Searle: Rationality and Realism, What is at stake? p. 81.

7 For a detailed historical survey of the problem of "reality" see the series of articles dealing with "Realismus" and "Realität" in: Historisches Wörterbuch der Philosophie, ed. by Joachim Ritter and Karlfried Gründer, Basel: Schwabe und Co. 1992, vol. 8. The difficulty of the problem is illustrated by the fact that several articles on this subject were necessary. The article 'Subjekt/Objekt; subjektiv/objektiv' in volume 10, 1998, is also relevant for the problem, but I could not make use of it for this contribution as the volume appeared after my manuscript was finished.

the last two centuries, including the consequences for art, comes to an aporetical result:

> – The realistic assumption of the correspondence between thinking and being must be considered unfounded, as attempts to legitimise it have failed in transcendental philosophy as well as in the theory of science.
> – However, the realistic assumption is indispensable for our being and acting in the world.[8]

Searle, too, admits that the realistic conception cannot be proved, but he maintains that, given its fundamental importance, the burden of proof is on the side of the opponents.

But what is, beyond this general importance, at stake for us, as readers of literature, as readers of 'realistic' literature and as readers of Fontane? As we all know, in the past decades the question has been discussed over and over again whether texts do refer to something, and if they do, to which entities. The mainstream tendency was to attribute to texts a status of autonomy which could be proclaimed all the more easily when the reality to which they might refer was itself nothing but a mental conception. Representative of this conviction, namely that the text is autonomous, is a differentiated essay by Michael Riffaterre, *L'illusion référentielle,* the title meaning the naive reader's illusion that words could refer to 'real' entities. Without denying the existence of an external world he ends peremptorily:

> [...] the poetic text is self-sufficient; if there is an external reference, it is not to something outside it, it is not to the real – far from that. There is no external reference but to other texts.[9]

Here he speaks of poetry, but he applies this theory also to narrative texts: according to him, there is no other difference between authors like Rabelais and the surrealists, and authors like Balzac and Zola than that the former openly demonstrate the absence of reference to an outer world whereas the latter try to disguise it. Of course it is as impossible as it is unnecessary to give here a survey of the positions of the literary critics who have dealt with the problem of the reference of 'realistic' texts to the outer world, from Auerbach and Brinkmann to Robert C. Holub or Lilian Furst.[10] I would only like to outline two antithetical positions and an attempt to mediate between them. In 1969 when research on realistic literature tended to eliminate the question of

---

8 "Die realistische Annahme der Übereinstimmung von Denken und Sein erweist sich nach dem Scheitern sowohl der transzendentalen wie auch der wissenschaftstheoretischen Legitimations-versuche als grundlos. – Die realistische Annahme ist jedoch für unser Sein und Handeln in der Welt unabdingbar." Walther Zimmerli : Das vergessene Problem der Neuzeit. Realismus als nicht nur ästhetisches Konzept. In: Jahrbuch für Internationale Germanistik, 16 (1984), pp. 18-79. (p. 59).

9 "[...] le texte poétique est autosuffisant; s'il y a référence externe, ce n'est pas au réel – loin de là. Il n'y a de référence externe qu'à d'autres textes." Michael Riffaterre : L'illusion réferentielle. In: Roland Barthes et al.: Littérature et réalité. Paris: Seuil 1982, p. 118.

10 For a discussion of those positions see: Martin Swales: Studies of German Prose Fiction in the Age of European Realism. Lewiston/Queenston/Lampeter: The Edward Mellen Press 1995; Martin Swales: Epochenbuch Realismus. Romane und Erzählungen. Berlin: Erich Schmidt 1997.

reference to reality and confine itself to the description of forms and structures, Gerhard Kaiser firmly demanded that the view on extratextual reality "has to be integrated into the interpretation of the literary text" because there is no other way to point out the specificity of 'realistic' writing.[11] By contrast, at about the same time an influential critic like Preisendanz rejected the necessity of taking the concept of reality into account. He considered such an attempt as groundless because of the lack of a generally accepted conception of 'reality' which could be valid for all periods of history.[12] In my opinion, Wolfgang Iser in his book *Das Fiktive und das Imaginäre* offers a promising model of the structure of literary texts which is intended to replace the sterile opposition of 'mimesis of extratextual reality' versus 'autonomous fiction'.[13] The "fictive" that mediates as a third instance between the real and the imaginary is not "fiction" in the traditional sense but a creative force, an intentional act enabling the human being to overstep the borders of the given, pre-existing world. The modes of this act are selection, combination and self-reference; they transform the imaginary, which as such is vague and chaotic, into the new reality of the text. The great advantage of Iser's model is the stress he lays on the active nature of "fiction", insisting on the Latin root "fingere". But I must admit there is a certain omission in this theory. By the given "real" on which the "fictive" works and which forms the "fields of reference" of the latter, Iser understands "systems of meaning, social systems and 'Weltbilder' [...] as well as perhaps other texts [...]".[14] This definition neglects a difference of categories: "social systems" are "external reality" in a different way from "systems of meaning" and "Weltbilder". I cannot presume to give an answer to the unsolved question of how external reality is structured. But it may be helpful to distinguish, in a heuristic way, between four layers of "reality".

1. Material objects that can be perceived and described either by sensual observation or, in a scientific way, as an organisation of particles. Examples are a) stones, plants, animals and b) objects created by human work like houses or ships. Objects of this kind can be imagined as existing in a world without human beings (before or after history).

2. Interpreted objects. On these objects the human mind has worked by means of language, mythisation, conceptualisation. This layer of reality is the product of 'images' or 'conceptions' of reality. The objects are shaped by intersubjective interpretation which is often preceded by individual (theoretical or artistic) interpretation.

3. Complex objects that have been created and /or modified by the work of the human mind, such as cities, rites, institutions. As far as they have been materialised,

---

11 Gerhard Kaiser: Realismusforschung ohne Realismusbegriff. In: Deutsche Vierteljahrsschrift für Literaturwissenschaft und Geistesgeschichte 43, (1969), p. 159.

12 Wolfgang Preisendanz: Das Problem der Realität in der Dichtung. In: Wege zum Realismus. Zur Poetik und Erzählkunst im 19. Jahrhundert. Munich: Fink 1977, pp. 217-228.

13 Wolfgang Iser: Das Fiktive und das Imaginäre. Perspektiven literarischer Anthropologie. Frankfurt a. M.: Suhrkamp 1991.

14 Iser: Das Fiktive und das Imaginäre, p. 20.

they have been formed from objects belonging to 1. In addition, there are 'transitional objects' which we call 'constructs' the status of which is uncertain: mere mental conception or complex reality?

4.   Human beings.

To give an example: on level 1, a river is a mass of water that has taken a certain form under the impact of the surrounding ground formations. On level 2, this mass of water is interpreted by a name (Rhine), by description (big stream), by mythisation (Father Rhine), by political meaning (borderline situation). On level 3, it is integrated into a functional system (regulation, navigation). An example of a construct is the specificity of the Rhenish culture.

Among the great variety of reflexions on the referentiality of texts, there seems to be a consensus that they can only refer to the conceptions of reality existing in a certain time. I would prefer the terms 'interpreted' and 'complex' reality because they do not exclude the existence of real objects outside the human mind, implying, at the same time, that the human mind is constantly working on the objects writers are referring to. Regarding those permanent modifications and transformations, the literary text is the extreme point of a common work on reality that is mainly performed by language. Without sharing Riffaterre's view that texts refer only to texts we may nevertheless use his striking formulation that words, together with concepts, create a "mythologie du réel".[15]   Indeed the anthropomorphic character of language makes it a preform of mythology and literature. But the latter often functions as a kind of pioneer in this work, and I think this is what is really at stake: its possibility of acting on the mentality and consequently on the reality of a given time may not be sacrificed to a *l'art pour l'art* conception of writing.

Later I shall examine in what way Fontane has contributed to such action. But before this I have to ask which specific mode of the 'work on reality' typical of a certain period can be found in texts intended to be 'realistic' by their authors or understood by their readers as such. To me the 'realistic' authors seem to have in common that, unlike romantic or surrealist authors, they do not totally reject the limited and factual reality conception of their average contemporaries but, in a certain measure, respect and even share it, undermining it only partially and often indirectly. In this context another facet of the reality problem must be considered. There is a curious parallel between the new movement toward philosophical realism and 'realistic' literature: the predilection for material objects belonging to the first layer of reality as described in the above schema. Thus Hilary Putnam, one of the best-known philosophers of that movement, referring to Wittgenstein, regards trees and chairs as appropriate paradigms for what we call 'real'. This leads to much detailed research into the nature of such objects. But what is really at stake in our situation is the exploration of the reality status of those parts of the work on reality that move in a zone of transition between concept, construct and concrete external entity, such as "nation" or "collective identity". These questions are of the highest relevance for our coping with those phenomena. The motive for the writers' predilection for material objects – in the

---

15 Michael Riffaterre: L'illusion référentielle, p. 93.

evocation of which the realistic authors excel – is obvious: the congenital confidence in the reliability of sensual perception is a fundamental attitude towards the world. It is exactly in the context of his most 'non-realistic' works, the *Joseph* novels and *Der Erwählte* (*The Holy Sinner*), that Thomas Mann points out that realism is the "backbone" of art:

> What pleases us in art, is, after all, the striking recognition of real life [...].We may stylise and symbolise as much as we want to – realism is indispensable.[16]

We are aware of the profound joy small children experience when they first recognise familiar objects in drawings and photographs. This attitude is rarely destroyed, even by metaphysical or scientific insight, and if the reader encounters such objects in a text he will also have confidence in what it pretends to render otherwise. Thus Holub speaks of a "ruse" of the realistic author.[17] Well-known is Roland Barthes's witty formulation that the non-functional objects like the barometer in *Un coeur simple* say: "Nous sommes le réel".[18] Fontane was shocked when a lady who wanted to pay him a compliment on *Schach von Wuthenow* (*A Man of Honor*) said: "[...] it's so fascinating, one knows all the names of the streets."[19] Nevertheless he continued to cite such generally known local names in his novels; when he was writing *Irrungen, Wirrungen* (*Delusions, Confusions*) he even visited the streets through which Botho rides towards the cemetery where Frau Nimptsch is buried. Why did he cling to that 'Realism of Detail' which even the "Programmatic Realists" condemned as a fixation with the inessential? On the one hand, I think, he was actually fascinated by the sensually perceptible world, a fascination he shared with his contemporaries; on the other hand he could use those material elements as a sort of tool for his representation of that part of reality for which at the end of his century the term "psychical reality" was invented. Now we associate this term mainly with Freud; but originally it was introduced as a philosophical concept by the followers of Franz Brentano.[20] The term owes its creation to the effort to mark off the psychical phenomena from mere appearances, to confer on them a status as "facts of the mind". What was helpful for elaborating this status was the particularity of the German language – often mentioned in the context of the reality problem – which offers 'Wirklichkeit' as a synonym for 'reality', thus defining 'the real' by means of its dynamics and power. Freud was stimulated by Theodor Lipps, one of

---

16 " [...] das frappierende Wiedererkennen des wirklichen Lebens ist es zuletzt doch immer, was uns freut an der Kunst [...].Wir mögen stilisieren und symbolisieren so viel wir wollen, – ohne Realismus geht's nicht." Thomas Mann to Henry Hatfield, 19 November 1951. In: Thomas Mann: Briefe 1948-1955 und Nachlese, ed. by Erika Mann. Kempten: Fischer 1965, p. 231.

17 Robert C. Holub: Reflections of Realism. Paradox, Norm and Ideology in 19th Century German Prose. Detroit: Wayne State University Press 1991, p. 35.

18 Roland Barthes: L'effet de réel. In: Barthes et al.: Littérature et réalité, p. 89.

19 "[...] es ist so spannend, man kennt ja alle Straßennamen." Fontane to Emilie Fontane, 14 August, 1882. In: Emilie und Theodor Fontane, Der Ehebriefwechsel 1873-1898, ed. by Gotthard Erler with Therese Erler. Grosse Brandenburger Ausgabe, Berlin: Aufbau 1994ff., p. 276.

20 For the history of this concept see: Joachim Ritter and Karlfried Gründer: Historisches Wörterbuch der Philosophie, pp. 200-206.

Brentano's disciples. Freud's great discovery, at the end of the century, was the fact that collective representations as well as individual desires and fantasies, even and especially when they are unconscious, may exert in the psyche and consequently in the behaviour of a person, the same power as motivations based on facts or reasoning, so that they are, in this way, extremely 'real'. As we know, Fontane was among the authors whom he considered as his precursors.[21]

2

Fontane's contribution to the exploration of psychical reality began before he started writing novels. The earlier newspaper articles are, to a great extent, already texts that are artistically structured; they also contain single elements which I would like to call "crystal splinters": linguistic and visual unities forming vertical texts throughout his entire writing, a chain of texts which has to be seen together with the elaborated novels and novellas to grasp the specificity of his writing. These unities generally go beyond what one would call "motifs". Evidently Fontane was directed by his profession as a journalist towards the observation and description of single phenomena, but it seems to me that he was prepared for this task by a kind of fragmentary perception of the world similar to Lichtenberg's. A small masterpiece of such fragmentary perception of an object is the article *Ein Gang durch den leeren Glaspalast* (A Stroll through the Empty Glass Palace).[22] Fontane starts by explaining his visit to the building that was constructed in 1851 for the Great Exhibition which was now already over, offering as a motivation the human liking for autumn and churchyards. It is striking that he uses the name "Glass Palace" instead of the more current "Crystal Palace" which he employs himself in a later article.[23] In the course of his text, he circumscribes the object by a series of reflections, observations and – mainly – metaphors. He evokes the deserted building *ex negativo* by describing the life of the exhibition that has ceased to exist and has left only a few traces, such as a lonely guardian and a Melusinian lady painter with her veil "green like the sea". The dome is glittering in the midday sun like the Kohinoor, the huge diamond that fascinated the public of the day. The "glass body" itself is a "giant's corpse" without its soul, exerting the magic power of empty space. To the visitor it becomes an image of London: "deterring monotony in detail, fullest

---

21 It may be useful to distinguish, as for external reality, different layers of psychical reality. Such a distinction will be helpful to cope with the difficulties arising from the impossibility of separating, by logical reasoning, mere individual fantasies like the hallucinations produced by insanity, from the spiritual entities that exist throughout entire epochs and attain quite another status by their powerful impact on the organisation of society. Paul Daniel Schreber, in his famous description of his mental illness, makes use of this impossibility to legitimise his personal visions. He says that in "our positive religion" there are several dogmas that are "unattainable to human reason", such as the Trinity or the resurrection of the body (Denkwürdigkeiten eines Nervenkranken, ed. by Peter Heiligenthal and Reinhard Volk. Frankfurt a. M.: Syndikat 1985, p. 8). He had an intelligent precursor in E. T. A. Hoffmann's hermit Serapion, whom his visitors could not convince by their rational arguments that he was living near Berlin and not in the Thebaid desert as he believed.

22 Fontane: Ein Gang durch den leeren Glaspalast. Aus England und Schottland, NFA, XVII, 10-11.

23 Fontane: Aus England und Schottland, NFA, XVII, 587-591.

harmony of the whole". These metaphors are not immovable; the visitor lets his readers participate in his work on them. The image of the "glass body" becomes more profound through the integration of mythology: it is *not* the body of the woman Charlemagne loved and which, even in death, held him bound to itself by a spell. On the contrary, it is perishable. But at the end of the article, the swallows flying into the decaying glasshouse make it an image of rebirth as well as of destruction. This description mirrors the object not by mimesis but by reflexivity. Reading this short text, one sees a deeper meaning in the seemingly trivial metaphor of the broken glass in *Irrungen, Wirrungen*. But the text can also be read independently, not as a finished picture but as a series of signs that are an incentive for the reader's reflections. If we consider the importance of this early writing, the manifesto of realism published in 1853 becomes interesting, too, although it precedes Fontane's fictional writing by so many years. Everybody knows that Fontane was no friend of philosophical theories; nevertheless we can find in his writings implicit philosophical positions. I should like to highlight two points in his essay at which he proclaims that realism is not only the art of his time but the principle of all true art. As is well-known he stresses that realism is not the "naked" mimesis of the "world of the senses" and of "everyday life" but "the reflection of all real life, of all forces and interests" from the *infusoria* to the meditations and sentiments Goethe shaped in his *Faust*. Like his contemporaries, Fontane identifies literary "matter" with immediate reality, thus being misled by the "illusion référentielle". But it is striking that he does not include himself by using the pronoun "we" in the introductory description of the timely turn away from speculation :

> Physicians reject all conclusions and combinations, they want experience [...]; the world is tired of speculating [...].[24]

Moreover it is striking that, excepting Fouqué, he does not devalue the Romantic poets themselves, only the post-Romantic authors of the thirties. Consciously or uncon-sciously he seems to cling to the dichotomic "Weltbild" in which the empirically perceptible world is only a surface behind which a deeper reality reveals itself. Like all German realists, Fontane had been profoundly marked by this pattern as a young reader. Especially important seems to me the impact of E. T. A. Hoffmann which becomes apparent not only in the integration of single motifs but also on the level of structure. Against the criticism of his friend Merckel, Fontane defends Hoffmann as a "man of genius".[25] Through Hoffmann he was indirectly marked by the idealistic philosophy he never studied. In Hoffmann's works he could find the principle of the double structure: on one hand, the sharp observation of the outside world, on the other hand the ingenious introduction of a second world. In Hoffmann, this second world contains partly religious representations, partly pictures of sacred art, and partly

---

24 "Die Ärzte verwerfen alle Schlüsse und Kombinationen, sie wollen Erfahrungen [...] die Welt ist des Spekulierens müde [...]." Fontane: Unsere lyrische und epische Poesie. Literarische Essays und Studien, NFA, XXI/1, 7.

25 Fontane to Wilhelm von Merckel, 18 February 1858, HFA, IV, 1, 608f.

constructs of idealistic philosophy. But it also contains to a large extent figurations of the unconscious of the figures or the narrator. I shall come back to the transformation this double structure underwent in Fontane's writing.

The second interesting point in his essay is his choice of the great models of realistic writing. Deliberately deviating from current opinion, the young critic praises Lessing's *Nathan der Weise* as the "ripest fruit of an enlightened spirit", who knew "what is at stake". Fontane does not explain in detail what makes the philosophical drama, the setting and form of which are shaped in such a classical mode, a 'realistic' piece of art. Probably it is the complexity and the antagonistic structure of the characters and conflicts that Fontane is thinking of.

This testimony of the young Fontane's relation to reality is completed by another one that is non-theoretical. There is a sort of 'primary scene' of his encounter with the outside world which he tells us about in his autobiography. When he lived as a schoolboy in the Burgstraße in Berlin, he loved, on summer evenings, to look out of the window for a long time:

> In the soft evening mist to the left the image of the Great Elector arose and behind it the sluiceway of the Mühlendamm; but in front of me was the castle with its "Green Hat" and its gothic gables which here still existed, while in the river Spree itself lights without number were reflected.[26]

It is not only the looking out of a window that returns many times in Fontane's writings but also this specific pattern. He says of Edinburgh:

> On grey rocks arise grey rock houses of eight floors high up into the air, the scroll tower of St. Giles rises phantom-like over the houses, like a bridal garland of silver, and over the whole picture lies that common soft, grey veil of mist that brings to perfection the spell of this Northern city of beauty.[27]

What I would like to point out, here, is not so much Fontane's interest in history which manifests itself in his predilection for such scenes but the fact that it is a section of the world that has already been worked on, that has been interpreted, with which he communicates with such intensity. It is important that the "mist" is an essential part of that section of the world: it is the metaphor of the element of reflexivity and imagination which continues the work of interpretation that has already materialised in the buildings and monuments that are visible. If Fontane's theory yields to the illusion

---

26 "In dem leisen Abendnebel stieg nach links hin das Bild des Großen Kurfürsten auf und dahinter das Schleusenwerk des Mühlendamms, gegenüber aber lag das Schloß mit seinem 'Grünen Hut' und seinen hier noch vorhandenen gotischen Giebeln, während in der Spree selbst sich zahllose Lichter spiegelten." Fontane: Von Zwanzig bis Dreißig. Autobiographisches, NFA, XV, 111.

27 "Auf grauen Felsen steigen graue, acht Stock hohe Felsenhäuser in die Luft, phantastisch schnörkelt sich, einer silbergrauen Brautkrone nicht unähnlich, der Turm von St. Giles über die Häuser empor, und gemeinschaftlich über dem Ganzen liegt jener graue Nebelschleier, der den Zauber dieser nordischen Schönheitsstadt vollendet." Fontane: Aus England und Schottland, NFA, XVII, 198.

of immediate contact with reality, proclaimed by the trend of the time, it is abandoned
by his practice of perception.

Fontane's encounter with England and Scotland as worlds that were still unknown to
him and had to be explored, of course offers a good chance of insight into the
specificity of his experience of reality. I should like to focus upon two notes contained
in the London diaries which are now, thanks to Charlotte Jolles and Rudolf Muhs, at
our disposal, complete and accompanied by an excellent commentary. Those notes are
like orientation marks for the understanding of his future writing. On 18 May 1856, he
came back from the quay, having seen his wife on to the steamer at the end of her visit
to London, which had not turned out to be very rewarding. He writes only:

> With Schweitzer [a friend] to Bloomsbury Square, in complete silence [...] "They rode nearly
> forty miles/ And did not speak four words."[28]

In the state of deepest emotional excitement his own, spontaneous language fails, but it
is replaced by lines from a ballad preserved in memory. They belong to Strachwitz's
poem *The Heart of Douglas*. What is striking is not only the support Fontane finds in
another poet's expression but also the displacement it undergoes. In the ballad, the
faithful vassals are silent because they are in great haste. They must arrive in time to
receive from their dying king his last order: to take his heart to the Holy Land. The
meaning of Fontane's quotation cannot only be the likeness of the mere absence of
words; we can suppose that in his psychical reality the saving of the heart in a marital
crisis is at stake. Perhaps there is also an association through the motif that the rider is
"bleeding". The appearance of internalised passages of poetry in situations of crisis,
shows how deeply Fontane's inclination to intertextual writing is anchored in his
psyche. We find in Fontane the speaking silence taken over from the ballad not only as
a self-therapy but also a principle of art. A crucial point of novel-writing, much
discussed in recent literary criticism, is the question of the representation of characters
as coherent or incoherent. Fontane himself was sensitive to this problem, having been
stirred up by a review of *Ellernklipp,* in which the critic wrote that Hilde's agreement
to marry the "Heidereiter" was not compatible with her character. Fontane in a letter to
the reviewer wholly accepted this reproach.[29] He says that he might write about Hilde's
behaviour "a new psychological novella with a philosophical and didactic touch", but
in doing so he would compromise the inner law of his writing, the "ballad-like
feeling". He calls the "gaps" the living condition of the ballad, and is convinced that
"blanks and uncertainties" are, for this mode of writing, still better than "trivialities and
platitudes" by which he must mean the current psychological explanations.[30] He does

---

28 "Mit Schweitzer lautlos nach Bloomsbury Square [.] 'Sie ritten vierzig Meilen fast / Und sprachen
   Worte nicht vier.'" Theodor Fontane: Tagebücher 1852, 1855-1858, ed. by Charlotte Jolles and
   Rudolf Muhs. Tage- und Reisetagebücher 1, Grosse Brandenburger Ausgabe, Berlin: Aufbau
   1994ff., p. 120.

29 "Ein Stück Autokritik". Fontane to Theophil Zolling, 4 March 1882, NFA, XXI /1, 496.

30 Fontane speaks of "Sprünge", probably thinking of the formula "Würfe und Sprünge" by which
   Herder characterised folk poetry.

not say that characters are incoherent or unreadable. One year later, in 1883, in a conversation with Rudolf Lindau he criticises this novelist's sketching of incoherent characters. Fontane says:

> A person who has been represented for ten pages in a certain way cannot, after ten more pages, do things that contradict his past and the description of his character up until that point. [31]

Lindau defends his method – which he ascribes to his master Turgenev –, saying that in "life" such gaps can be often observed. Fontane replies that it is seldom possible for the artist to transfer matters directly from "life" into art. According to him, "life" mediates between the contrasts by a hundred small traits "in an unpretending but perceptible way". By his attitude he implicitly legitimates the new orientation of Fontane research that pays much attention to the disguised symbolism of the subtexts which the author combines with his manifest cast of characters that obeys the rules of empirical psychology. For Fontane, when he follows his ballad mode, does not confine himself to leaving gaps at the surface of the text, but develops a range of procedures that allow him to give his figures a deeper psychical dimension than would be possible on a merely rational and empirical level.

In the second London diary, there is a surprisingly violent rejection of the limited conception of reality ruling the middle of the nineteenth century. Fontane sees a performance of Shakespeare's *Winter's Tale*. While most notes are concise and factual, here we have an actual outburst of feeling. To his own astonishment he is filled with enthusiasm by the pastoral play of the fourth act. He evokes it in detail from the "joyful scenery" to the "hopping and jumping of the satyr and the fauns": "It is the first time that I learnt to understand why the most excellent minds of a whole century could rejoice in such plays". [32]

Fontane opposes the "meridional" pastoral world to the insufferable world of "money-making" that surrounds him. Diverging from his contemporaries he professes his belief in an "ideal world" of which the pastoral world is the symbol. What warrants this belief is precisely his psychic reality, the longing for a paradise. This longing is either "enigmatic reminiscence or presentiment". The lesson given to him by this play – in a genre that was particularly 'unrealistic' and abolished in his own time – he calls outright a "sermon". The heart of paradise, so he understands, is "Ruhe" ("peace") – and peace will become a leitmotif in his writing.

It is well-known that the deconstruction of money fetishism is one of the main modifications of the contemporary reality concept that Fontane tries to undertake. Surely he found a sympathetic soul in the friend who, on Christmas Day 1855, presented him with a poem telling him that he is "no great storer / Of that so-called

---

31 "Ein Charakter, der zehn Seiten lang so und so gezeichnet ist, kann zehn Seiten weiter nicht Dinge tun, die seiner Vergangenheit und seiner bis dahin gegebenen Charakterschilderung wider-sprechen." Fontane: Rudolf Lindau. Ein Besuch. Literarische Essays und Studien, NFA XXI/1, 318-329 (326).

32 "Zum erstenmal hab' ich begreifen gelernt, daß die besten Köpfe eines ganzen Jahrhunderts sich an solchen Spielen erfreuen konnten." Theodor Fontane: Tagebücher 1852, 1855-8, p. 163f.

realities [sic]", namely money.[33] But as an example of his modifying work on a construct I prefer another subject, namely his handling of the the concept of 'national characters', as the work on it is as important today as it was in his time. 'Nation' itself remains for Fontane a given entity, the reality of which he does not doubt. In this, he shares his contemporaries' view of reality. But he was intrigued throughout his life by the status of "collective characters" between phantom and reality. Of course it is impossible for me to give a survey of his reflections on this topic. I have chosen some passages of the book in which the encounter with national characteristics is presented in the context of a precarious situation, namely his stay in France as a prisoner of war.[34] The situation of the writer was precarious, too. Aware of his family roots he had often recognised in himself, traits of the assumed 'national character' from those who had recently been 'the enemies'. His origins became strikingly present when Fontane, meeting a certain prison guard, found himself face to face with a portrait of his father. The public he was writing for was emotionally rarely willing to perceive positive elements in the 'national character' of the French. Close to the beginning of the book, Fontane presents the current scheme of the clichéd representations of collective characters. He uses as a distorting mirror a contemporary children's and school book, entitled: *Peter Parley's trip round the world.* Fontane is amused by the concise style of the descriptions of the different nations – "[...] the *Turk* smokes and invokes Allah" – , but those formulas, he has to admit, correspond to the spontaneous associations evoked by the names of foreign peoples, elementary representations that are mostly visual: "a long plait, or slanted eyes, or a nose ring".[35]

In his efforts to deconstruct such perilous clichés, Fontane has – besides Flaubert with his *Dictionnaire des idées reçues* – a fellow-combatant in George Eliot. In *Adam Bede* she makes the protagonist destroy the cliché of the French as weaklings. In one of her essays, she defends the Germans against the reproach of speculative ignorance of the world. In this campaign she is very witty, introducing a typical allegorical half-construct, John Bull, who, according to her, is just beginning not to think any more that every Italian was once a little beggar who grew up to be a rascal. This change of mentality does, however, not prevent John Bull from considering himself "the supreme type of manhood".[36] How does Fontane proceed to demonstrate the absurdity of the Peter Parley principle? His first and strongest means is the confrontation with immediate experience. Fontane has always imagined that a Corsican is a "small brown fellow" who "assassinates his enemy treacherously", and consequently, he is terrified when he hears that an official whom he is to meet comes from Corsica. But this Corsican turns out to be a thin, delicate man who is full of understanding for his

---

33 Theodor Fontane: Tagebücher 1852, 1855-1858, p. 69.

34 Fontane: Kriegsgefangen. Erlebtes 1870, NFA, XVI, 7-157.

35 Fontane: Kriegsgefangen. Erlebtes 1870, NFA, XVI, 14-16. 'Peter Parley' was the pseudonym of the American author Samuel Griswold Goodrich (1793-1860). Fontane gives the title in German: "Peter Parleys Reise um die Welt, oder was zu wissen not tut. " – " [...] der *Türke* raucht und ruft Allah."

36 George Eliot: A Word for the Germans. Essays, ed. by Thomas Pinney. London: Routledge and Kegan Paul 1963, pp. 386-390.

situation. However, in the course of his narration, the author does not completely give up the Peter Parley principle. In his situation as a prisoner of war, Fontane became acquainted with a great number of Frenchmen, especially prison officials and their families as well as other prisoners. The contact with other German prisoners of war shows him a panorama of inhabitants from different German regions, mainly members of the lower classes. The word "Stämme" (tribes) that was in use in Fontane's time presupposes a sort of regional character. The soldiers themselves think and speak quite naturally in those categories. A sergeant from Pomerania regrets that he cannot transform the slow soldiers from Schleswig that he commands into straight Prussians. The author renders such opinions with a mild irony which he also applies to himself, for instance when he expresses his ambivalent feelings towards the Saxons who are intelligent but too fond of showing off their education. The most valid antidote to seduction by the Peter Parley principle, is the perception and evocation of several very individual persons. The most eminent of these is Rasumofsky, the attendant, waiting on Fontane in the fortress of Oléron, who, as a Pole, a hussar and a tailor, had developed a very original personality. The travelling prisoner assigns the landlady of the ferry inn, who, though an old woman, still combines erotic attraction with authority, to a certain group of women – but he has conceived this group from his own observations and does not think of subsuming her under the stereotype 'coquettish Frenchwoman'. When, in a particular passage of the book, he imposes on himself a general estimation of the character of the French people, he expressly presents it as a summary of his experiences with a great number of French persons, and he rejects explicitly and implicitly current German prejudices. Fontane praises the great joviality and amiability of the French which stands the test of the distressing imprisonment. Moreover, he extols their culture and education, thus deconstructing the cliché of the superiority of the German school system. What he deplores in the French is a kind of general nihilism and cynical distrust of "government, church, law": "There was no solid and noble belief in anything, neither in the things of the visible nor in the things of the invisible world".[37]

We must leave open the question whether this observation was right – what is important is the method of his reflections: in the first place, he bases them explicitly on his own perception; in the second place, his balanced judgment obeys the inner rule of his thinking and speaking which he expressed earlier in a letter to his father: namely that, after every positive utterance the opposite automatically appears in his mind.[38] It is the principle which Martin Swales, with regard to the novels, has described as "half-truths" and which has its origin in the intense desire to do justice to the ambivalence reigning in such large parts of human reality.[39] We must admit that Fontane's position with regard to the question of 'national characters' was not always as differentiated as in *Kriegsgefangen*; he was a true "realist" in partially sharing the theories and

---

37 "Ein fester, schöner Glaube existierte an nichts, weder an die Dinge der sichtbaren noch der unsichtbaren Welt." Fontane: Kriegsgefangen. Erlebtes 1870, NFA, XVI, 49.
38 Fontane to Henri Louis Fontane, 19 October 1856, HFA, IV,1 538f.
39 Martin Swales: Studies of German Prose Fiction in the Age of European Realism, p. 65ff..

categories of his contemporaries.[40] But the merit of overcoming them is therefore all the greater.

3

The means by which Fontane as a novel-writer has tried to subvert the narrow and often one-sided character of the reality conception of his time are well-known: perspectivism, evident exaggeration, the self-doubts of the narrator or withdrawal of statements by the figures. Why does he, in spite of all these tools, need the sub-texts woven out of allusions, disguised symbolism, speaking names, images, quotations, associations – the sub-texts that are in part so subtle that they have been unveiled only after several decades? On the one hand, they are necessary when tabooed subjects are to be integrated into the text – Fontane as an au...or who depends on his public, is very cautious in this respect. On the other hand, the discourse of the narrator and the figures, moving on the level of the conscious mind, is not always capable of expressing the specificity of the psychical reality and its contents. It seems strange that Fontane's novels and novellas contain few dreams, whereas many other realists – Keller, for instance – use dreams as a medium to enlarge the limited reality conception of the middle and end of the nineteenth century. But Fontane's writing itself has a structure that is partly analogous to dream. We notice that in his second review of a performance of Grillparzer's *Der Traum ein Leben* he takes back his former opinion that the dream character of what is acted on the stage diminishes its effect. Now, in 1884, he considers that what is crucial is only the "luminosity" and the "intensity" of the "beautiful appearance" of poetry.[41] If now for him the limits between 'reality' and 'dream' become blurred, as far as poetry is concerned, this change may have to do with the influence of the only philosopher in whom Fontane had a genuine interest, Schopenhauer. Unfortunately we do not know in detail the discussions on the "Schopenhauer nights" with the Wangenheims and Hofprediger Windel or the conversations with Wiesike, Schopenhauer's prophet. But Fontane certainly was familiar with the fundamental ideas and terms, as we know from quotations. This means a certain de-realisation and transparency of the empirically perceptible world. Probably the dichotomic structure of the *Weltbild* he had received from the romantic authors was reinforced, just at the moment when he began his novel writing, by the impact of Schopenhauer. In an intuitive way, Fontane has integrated into his writing several operations which the unconscious uses in structuring dreams. There is the transformation of locutions into concrete images. "People who live in glasshouses should not throw stones" – this is the situation of Gordon who blames Cécile for her past but in fact desires to seduce her himself, and consequently Fontane gives him a predilection for the "glass pavillion" of a Berlin hotel where he finally receives the

---

40 An example of this dependency is his discussion of the Danish people in his 'Reisebriefe aus Jütland'. Fontane: Unterwegs und wieder daheim, NFA, XVIII, 310-316.

41 [On] 'Franz Grillparzer: Der Traum, ein Leben'. Fontane : Causerien über Theater. Zweiter Teil, NFA, XXII/2, 311.

challenge to the duel with her husband.[42] Thus Effi walks to her rendez-vous with Crampas, who says he cannot be drowned because he is "born for the rope" along a path that is called the "Reeperbahn", "Reep" being a dialect word for rope. Another mode is displacement. It is not Cécile with her witch-like charm who receives the name of Hexel but her unattractive friend.[43] But the most important force of these dreamlike proceedings is the possibility to shape ambivalence. I should like to demonstrate this by three examples in which ambivalence means at the same time the questioning of a tabooed phenomenon which cannot be treated in the manifest text. The nineteenth century is part of the period of the glorification of maternal love that extends approximately from the end of the eighteenth century to the middle of ours.[44] 'Maternal love' was considered as a natural instinct, the absence of which was regarded as a weighty, culpable deformation. While Effi Briest is dying, her mother sits down on a "small black chair with three gold spars [Stäbchen] in its ebony back". Why this detail? Certainly it does not serve to represent "le réel". Ebony and golden decoration anticipate the coffin, but the reader knows without that hint that Effi is dying. Again a locution has been transformed into visual shape: "den Stab brechen" ("to break the rod"), which means, in medieval law, to condemn.[45] This is what Frau von Briest does when she reminds her dying daughter, incredibly cruelly, that the catastrophe of her married life was her own fault. This mother is sitting on a judge's seat, but at the same time the sentence is passed on herself. She is guilty because she has pushed Effi into a marriage which only replaced the marriage she has missed by *her* own fault. But the salient point is that Frau von Briest, as becomes evident by the whole representation of the relationship between mother and daugher throughout the novel, at the same time, really *loves* her child. This ambivalence explodes the conventional thinking in distinct oppositions and therefore can only be hinted at.

In *Schach von Wuthenow*, too, it is by hints and allusions that another and decisive reason is added to the various explanations of the protagonist's inability to accept marriage, that are proposed in the manifest text. This reason is his inclination towards homosexuality. This entire field of psychological problems is very much repressed in Fontane's writing, so that here, too, the signals are very subtle.[46] The most evident one is the allusion to the Knights Templar. "Vices of all kinds" is the periphrasis Schach

---

42 "Wer im Glashaus sitzt, darf nicht mit Steinen werfen."

43 For the function of names in sub-texts see: Renate Böschenstein: Caecilia Hexel und Adam Krippenstapel. Beobachtungen zu Fontanes Namengebung. In: Fontane Blätter (1996) 2, pp. 31-57.

44 For a historical survey of this phenomenon see: Mutter und Mütterlichkeit. Wandel und Wirksam- keit einer Phantasie in der deutschen Literatur. Festschrift für Verena Ehrich - Haefeli, ed. by Irmgard Roebling and Wolfram Mauser. Würzburg: Königshausen und Neumann 1996.

45 This strong and evocative formula has often been integrated into poetic texts. Fontane certainly knew Brentano's Lureley, a poem in which the sorceress implores her judge: "O brechet mir den Stab", in order to save her soul.

46 Consequently, as far as I can see, the question of homo-erotic elements has not been much discussed in Fontane research. An exception is Wolfgang Paulsen who analyses his friendship with Bernhard von Lepel from this perspective in Wolfgang Paulsen: Im Banne der Melusine. Theodor Fontane und sein Werk. Berne: Peter Lang 1988.

has to choose when in his conversation with young Victoire at Tempelhof he mentions the reproaches made to the Templars which led to the abolishment of the order. Schach is so enthusiastic about this order that Victoire calls him a "latterday Knight Templar", and he affirms himself that he could have lived as a member of this order. The first person to notice Schach's suicide is Ned, his small groom, who, according to Victoire is too much spoiled and becomes more and more of a "plaything". The meaning of the relationship between master and young servant becomes clearer when the death scene in Fontane's novel is compared with the death of the protagonist in Spielhagen's novel *In Reih' und Glied* which Fontane certainly had read. Spielhagen, too, is cautious in his wording but stresses much more the fervent love the young servant feels for his master who, in his last moments, tenderly smiles at him.[47] But there is a second reason for his profound aversion to marriage which is connected with the first. In the grandiose night scene at Wuthenow in which Schach is led to his negative decision, Fontane has made clear that the inability to accept married life is related to Schach's fixation on his mother. It is true that his reflections on that night do not turn to his mother but to the mockery of a society to which he will expose himself by marrying a disfigured woman, and to the emptiness of rural life into which he will be forced to flee. Nevertheless, in the scenery surrounding him, the dead mother is omnipresent.[48] She is in the half-wild park that still bears the traces of her horticultural art; she is in the portrait that reveals her to be the most beautiful woman in the family; but above all she is in the dead "arm" of the lake on which Schach is drifting in the boat she had used. The rocking movement of the current carries the emotionally confused man, who falls asleep, back into a sort of prenatal state. From this sleep Schach returns as a dead man. The circle into which he feels banned when he compulsively walks again and again around a tree is the magic circle which the *arm* of the dead mother twists about him. The author evokes archaic, mythical images of terrifying force to make the reader feel the power of psychical reality.

In *Irrungen, Wirrungen,* too, mythical images are fitted into the reality of Berlin with the street names everybody knows, in order to symbolise the psychical death of the protagonist. Botho's ride to Frau Nimptsch's grave has already been analysed as a ride into the underworld, so that I can confine myself to examining some points which confirm and radicalise that reading.[49] Consulting the Baedeker edition of those years

---

47 Friedrich Spielhagen: In Reih' und Glied. Berlin: Otto Janke 1866, vol. V, pp. 284f.
48 The first critic to point out the importance of the mother figure was Gerhard Kaiser: Schach von Wuthenow oder die Weihe der Kraft. In: Bilder lesen. Studien zu Literatur und bildender Kunst. München: Wilhelm Fink 1981, p. 137. In their differentiated essay: "Le laid c'est le beau". Liebesdiskurs und Geschlechterrolle in Fontanes Roman *Schach von Wuthenow,* Gabriele Brandstetter and Gerhard Neumann convincingly describe the Wuthenow scenery as an anticipation of death. In: Deutsche Vierteljahrsschrift für Literaturwissenschaft und Geistesgeschichte, 72 (1998), p. 266.
49 Patricia Howe: Reality and Imagination in Fontane's *Irrungen Wirrungen.* In: German Life and Letters, 38 (1985), pp. 346-356; Denys Dyer: Botho von Rienäcker lays a Wreath on Frau Nimptsch's Grave – Fontane's Narrative Mastery. In: Connections: Essays in Honour of Eda Sagarra on the Occasion of her 60th Birthday, ed. by Peter Skrine et al.. Stuttgart: Heinz 1993;

we can follow Botho's way through the then 'Rixdorf' very well, so that we can see the elements Fontane chooses from the multiple buildings and monuments which also could have invited him to transform them into signs. There is a striking analogy to the beginning of the novel: behind a wooden fence – that is to say, behind a hiding-place that does not hide – shops and pubs are to be seen and their inscriptions can be read. Is that the self-reference of a mode of writing that is not satisfied by mimesis of the empirical reality? "With growing curiosity" Botho observes the picturesque fragments of modern life. He is probably not aware of the background that opens behind them: an allegory of 'Frau Welt' who once more presents herself to him on his way into death. Places of entertainment interchange with tomb sculptures exhibited by stone-masons. This baroque allegory has received the mark of modern times by the posters promising actual attractions as well as by the predominance of publicity itself: "Miss Rosella the miracle girl" – "grave-markers at lowest prices". Fontane emphasises the 'Frau Welt' character of this passage by integrating various countries, west and east, north and south. The posters are praising "American instantaneous photography" and "Russian ball-shooting", "Swedish punch" and "Sicilian nights". At the same time this panorama is a central site where quite a few of the recurrent 'unities' in Fontane's writing come together; like Blondin the rope-dancer and Tell the archer. Certainly there are two legitimate readings of this passage: the naive interest of Botho who had once declared: "Probably this world is one of the best ones", and the lucidity of the reader who recognises the absurdity of its patchwork character.[50]

At Rixdorf, Botho makes the coachman stop at the "Rollkrug" – why not at the "Rathskeller" Baedeker recommends? Because it is a "Krug", because the house is very low, close to the ground, and because an "iron arm" is sticking out of the gable and holding an "upright gilded key". Fontane has fitted in here one of the "small myths" he prefers, the myth of the "Nobiskrug". That is the myth of the "border inn", where the dead stay for a while on their way into the other world.[51] In *Vor dem Sturm* (*Before the Storm*) Fontane had already made use of this myth, which had been wide-spread in Germany since the sixteenth century. In folklore, this inn mostly has very gloomy connotations. In *Vor dem Sturm*, Fontane splits it into a pub and a chapel-like niche

Christine Hehle: Unterweltsfahrten. Reisen als Erfahrung des Versagens im Erzählwerk Fontanes. In: Theodor Fontane. Am Ende des Jahrhunderts, ed. by Hanna Delf von Wolzogen and Helmuth Nürnberger. Würzburg: Königshausen and Neumann 2000 [forthcoming].

50 "Es ist doch wohl eine der besten Welten." Fontane: Irrungen, Wirrungen, NFA, III, 122.

51 For the history and the variations of this interesting but now widely forgotten myth see Friedrich Kluge: Etymologisches Wörterbuch der deutschen Sprache, article "Nobiskrug"; Hans Bächtold-Stäubli: Handwörterbuch des deutschen Aberglaubens, articles "Hölle", "Unsterblichkeit", "Wirtshaus"; Jacob und Wilhelm Grimm: Deutsches Wörterbuch, article "nobiskrug". The name (with its corollaries like "Nobisgat", "Nobishaus") seems to have its origin in "nobis", a synonym for "no", which was used in the thieves' language ("Rotwelsch"). An interesting modern version of the myth is Emil Barth's novella Enkel des Odysseus, (1949/50). The protagonist, a soldier in the Second World War, is aware of the meaning of his name "Nobisgat" = evil spot. He is suffering from a severe depression of which he is cured when, in an air crash, he hovers some time between life and death.

which are both called "The last farthing", and one of the characters comments on their vicinity, pointing out that the way to hell is close to the way to heaven.[52] In *Irrungen, Wirrungen* Fontane has evoked the ambivalence of the border situation between life and death by choosing only one and the same sign: St Peter's key on the bad inn signifies the possibility that heaven may be opened to the dead person. Whether, and in what sense, this is true for Botho, remains uncertain.

But who is Frau Nimptsch to whom Botho brings the wreath? Here, as in a dream, everything is overdetermined. On the surface of the text Botho is acting like a good-natured young man without social prejudices towards a hospitable and motherly old woman. On a second level her name and the atmosphere of her house make her an incarnation of the world of poetry. But in this passage her mythical dimension is at stake. Why is Lene an adoptive child? Because Frau Nimptsch, constantly watching over the fire, is a Vestal and as such has to be a virgin. But it is her maternal quality, so much stressed in the novel, that makes her ambivalent. Botho, son of a mother who, as it seems, is a very superficial person, is as much attracted by the fairy-like atmosphere of the Nimptsch house as by Lene herself. But this aura also means the seduction of death. The maternal world – as Fontane's contemporaries Bachofen, Keller, and Raabe pointed out – brings forth life but also takes it back into death. It is certainly not by chance that Fontane gives to Frau Nimptsch the same kind of coffin that Hoppenmarieken, the demon-like old woman in *Vor dem Sturm*, is buried in: yellow with blue metal-work. The everlasting flowers of the wreath the old woman had wanted not only signify perpetual memory but also the timelessness of the unconscious that binds Botho forever to the maternal world he has lived in for a short time. Botho, who has told the driver to wait at the inn on the border, returns to life – in the outside reality a living being, but in psychical reality a dead man.

I said that in his contributions to the exploration of psychical reality Fontane continues a tradition started by the Romantic authors. His art of completing the manifest texts by carefully elaborated sub-texts is one of the main instruments of this undertaking. But one problem arises that has not yet been solved. In a number of those sub-texts we find references to religion, to Christian belief. Does he evoke them only as representations in the psyche, or do they signify a reality beyond it? This is a question waiting to be answered.

As far as I know, Fontane never made any effort to perceive the true nature of a tiger and to evoke it in words. The creature he devoted his efforts to was the emblem of the nineteenth century, composed of nature and intellect, the creature that invents enigmas and is an enigma itself: the sphinx, otherwise called the human being.[53]

---

52 Fontane: Vor dem Sturm, NFA, I, 546. The vicinity of the chapel and the 'Nobiskrug' is to be found in sources of the sixteenth century.

53 I am grateful to Margaret Kehoe Winkler for her help with the English text of this article and to Gerhard Kaiser for his critical remarks.

Norbert Bachleitner

Of Grieving Girls and Suicidal Soldiers:
Theodor Fontane and Ferdinand von Saar

Documents on Fontane's reception in Austria are scarce. Even if evidence for such a
statement has never been collected systematically, we can draw our conclusions from
the materials compiled by Fontane scholarship during the last hundred years. His early
works seem to have been almost neglected by Austrian reviewers, after his death the
major papers deigned at least to print obituaries. Moreover, the major Austrian writers
of the Realist epoch, like Marie von Ebner-Eschenbach, Ferdinand von Saar, Ludwig
Anzengruber or Peter Rosegger, seem not to have noticed their Prussian colleague.[1]

Fontane himself commented upon the lack of fortune of his works in the Habsburg
Empire. During his stay in Karlsbad in 1898 he wrote to Paul Linsemann who had
favourably reviewed his *Stechlin* in the journal *Die Zeit*: "Unfortunately, you will not
win over the real Viennese for my side. 'Unfortunately' is perhaps the wrong word,
because I am un-Viennese to such a degree, that I feel almost flattered at the failure of
such a conquest."[2]

Fontane seems to have grasped intuitively the reason why his works lacked success
in Austria. Of course, it was not necessary to be Austrian or even Viennese to be
successful there, as he suggests. But instead of "un-Viennese" he could just as well
have written "Prussian". Although at the time many Austrian liberals dreamed of a
pan-German state, the deep-rooted rivalry between Vienna and Berlin, that had only
recently been renewed by the war of 1866, was not easily swept away. Some
deprecating remarks about Austria scattered here and there in Fontane's novels were
undoubtedly apt to remind readers of this rivalry.

An analysis of the image of Austria in Fontane's novels could contribute to a more
exact definition of his "Prussianness". But such an analysis is not proposed here. I
would rather compare some of his works to selected novellas of Ferdinand von Saar
without regard to questions of reception or impact. By way of this comparison I
propose to argue that, in spite of the two authors' undeniable particularities, they were
reacting to the same social problems. I will limit myself to remarks on some motifs and

---

1 An exception among these authors is Jakob Julius David who wrote an obituary in the journal *Die
   Wage* in 1898. In his obituary David declares that he has been an admirer of Fontane's for a long
   time, and he reports a meeting with the novelist in Berlin around 1891; J. J. David: Theodor Fontane.
   Die Wage, 1 (1898), No. 40, pp. 660-662.

2 "[...] den richtigen Wiener werden Sie für mich leider nicht erobern. 'Leider' - ist vielleicht falsch.
   Denn ich bin so unwienerisch, daß diese Nicht-Eroberungen mir beinah schmeicheln." Fontane to
   Paul Linsemann, 17 August 1898, HFA, IV, 4, 740. Linsemann's review appeared in *Die Zeit* on 5
   November 1898. All translations from the German into English are my own.

paradigmatic figures that show how both authors demonstrate social change and link individual histories with general history.[3] I would first like to draw your attention to an "out-moded love-story"[4] – thus the narrator qualifies the story in Saar's novella *Ginevra* which appeared in 1890.

A young ensign called Emil, whose regiment is stationed in Theresienstadt in Bohemia, attends a ball in nearby Leitmeritz, where he falls in love with Ginevra. She is the daughter of a former Italian officer who had to quit the service because he married a poor girl. Now Ginevra lives with her mother, and Emil soon becomes a regular guest in the house of the two women. In spite of the poor conditions she has to live in, Ginevra has a certain degree of education, for example she is able to read the Italian classics together with Emil. The lovers spend a harmonious time together until Emil receives the order to move to Vienna. At their parting there is tacit agreement between the partners that the liaison will soon be replaced by marriage.

In Vienna the ensign is introduced into the house of his commanding officer and his wife Lodoiska. The somewhat naive ensign falls a prey to this *femme fatale*. The correspondence with Ginevra, regular and affectionate at the beginning, dwindles and soon comes to end. The odds are clearly against a marriage with Ginevra. Emil's uncle, an influential person on whom he depends financially, would not even hear of such a union. A friend and fellow soldier of Emil's voices the same opinion when he warns him: "Watch out you don't get hooked!"[5] Finally Lodoiska reminds him of the fact that he would inevitably ruin his career by such a step. It is no surprise that a weak character like Emil follows such advice and admonitions. A few months later Ginevra visits the ensign to demand back a cross that she had given to him. She resigns herself to her destiny with a dignity which contrasts strongly with his feeling of weakness and wretchedness. In an epilogue we learn that Ginevra has married a young man who made a fortune in Egypt, whereas Emil cannot free himself of Lodoiska, although he suffers from jealousy because of her frequent erotic escapades.

Saar's story is reminiscent of Fontane's *Irrungen, Wirrungen* (*Delusions, Confusions*) (1887). On the part of Emil we observe an exaggerated obedience to social conventions. He is extremely hesitant and depends on the opinion of others. Botho von Rienäcker is also characterised by his friend and fellow soldier von Wedell

---

3   So far works by Fontane (*Schach von Wuthenow, Effi Briest*) and Saar (*Sappho, Schloß Kostenitz*) have only been compared with regard to narrative patterns in two essays by Patricia Howe: Faces and Fortunes: Ugly Heroines in Stifter's *Brigitta*, Fontane's *Schach von Wuthenow* and Saar's *Sappho*. In: German Life and Letters, 44 (1990/91), pp. 426-442; Realism and Moral Design. In: Perspectives on German Realist Writing: Eight Essays, ed. by Mark G. Ward. Lewiston/Queenston/Lampeter: The Edwin Mellen Press 1995, pp. 45-63. For a recent account of Fontane scholarship see Helen Chambers: The Changing Image of Theodor Fontane. Columbia, SC: Camden House 1997.

4   "eine veraltete Liebesgeschichte". Ferdinand von Saar: Ginevra, edited and interpreted by Stefan Schröder. Tübingen: Niemeyer 1996, p. 11.

5   "Gib acht, daß du nicht hängen bleibst." Saar: Ginevra, p. 20.

as weak and open to influences of every sort. It is quite clear that Botho would prefer to marry Lene. Even if he later defends his decision to marry Käthe von Sellenthin as reasonable, he misses Lene's simple manners and her truthfulness. Matrimonial customs, and traditional norms of class-conscious behaviour in general, are no longer self-evident; on the other hand, Botho is not really free to transgress them and to obey his natural instincts. In fact, it is the middle course that is dangerous for Fontane's lover, the course between strict observance of traditional habits and total neglect of conventions and taboos.

In both cases it is not the weakness of the lovers' characters alone that is to blame. Emil's and Botho's decisions are obviously determined by the circumstances. In Emil's case it is the norm of conduct codified by army regulations that discourages him. In the first half of the nineteenth century government still had to consent to the marriage of one of its army officers, and it usually withheld that consent in the absence of a certain amount of capital.[6] In Botho's case, it is his family, and notably his uncle, who insists on feudal and military tradition and proposes the marriage with his cousin Käthe.

Both Saar and Fontane create a dichotomy between urban and rural scene. A connection with Ginevra seems natural and unproblematic to Emil in Leitmeritz, a provincial town in Bohemia. But things and opinions change rapidly as he moves to Vienna. The same is true of Fontane who underlines the happiness of his lovers in natural surroundings, for example in the Spree valley at Hankel's Ablage. They feel totally at ease as long as they are untouched by the restrictions of society.

If we look at Lene and Ginevra, the grieving girls, similar suspicions arise: however much the narrator stresses Ginevra's love and devotion to Emil, she may be a little calculating. In fact, there are indications in the text that she, in a way, ensnares Emil. She does not stick to her role of an ethereal angel throughout the story. After Emil's untruthfulness has become clear she reacts in a rather pragmatic way. The narrator presents her as a robust and strong-willed nature, a temperament that guarantees happiness, whereas the weak will always suffer. In any case, Ginevra seems not to suffer from her disappointed hopes of marriage with Emil, whereas he, the weakling, has not surmounted the problem of his love and untruthfulness to Ginevra even a quarter of a century later, that is, at the time when he tells his story. Furthermore, he cannot refrain from comparing Ginevra to Lodoiska, the heartless seducer.

We remember that Botho also compares his wife with Lene. Käthe has a leaning towards affected and silly conversation that contrasts with Lene's candour. There is no doubt that Lene loves Botho; in this respect she steps out of the traditional role of the mistress that is prescribed for a girl in her milieu. She is disgusted by the mistresses of Botho's fellows, who regard their activities as a business to secure a living. In spite of her love for Botho, Lene is realistic enough to renounce him without much ado; it is even she who first speaks of putting an end to the liaison.

---

6 The sum necessary to obtain a marriage licence amounted to 12,000 florins; cf. Saar: Ginevra, p.180. Emil's situation is complementary to Schach von Wuthenow's: Emil would have to resign his commission if he *did* marry Ginevra, Schach risks the same consequence if he *does not* marry Victoire de Carayon.

Thus, Ginevra and Lene seem not to be grieving too long or too much. Compared with their male partners, they are emotionally strong characters. Saar cites Goethe's dictum in *Maximen und Reflexionen* about men, who chase after women and are worn out by these relationships.[7] Emil is an out-dated and decadent figure, and, in a way, we may say the same of Botho. The time they live in is not favourable for them. Emil is destined to succumb in the battle of life. Besides the influence of Darwin, the strong impact of Schopenhauer's ideas can be noticed in Saar's works. All his characters can do is to resign themselves to their fate. Their happiness is only a relative one, and it is particularly relative to the demands of society. This maxim of Saar's may also be derived from *Irrungen, Wirrungen*.

Moving from grieving girls to suicidal soldiers we will first consider Saar's novella *Leutnant Burda* (1887). The lieutenant is introduced by the narrator, a fellow soldier, as an extremely vain person, who devotes much time to the cultivation of his appearance. In addition, he is very strict about questions of honour and *esprit de corps*. His manners are perfect and, although he never speaks about such matters, he seems to be very successful with the other sex. But he is extremely particular in his choice and a declared enemy of misalliances:

> For Burda the female sex did not exist below the baroness. A young lady's noble birth was only acceptable to him if her father was a general or president of a high governmental office. Upon the mere daughters of a Hofrat he used to look down with a sort of pity. Ladies of the plutocracy could be sure of his thoroughgoing scorn.[8]

The airs he gives himself appear even more ridiculous as one learns that he is himself of humble extraction. Son of a subordinate clerk, the lieutenant is in permanent need of money. Nevertheless, he signs himself "Gf Burda", which is the usual abbreviation for Count (Graf). Asked for an explanation by his commander, he declares "Gf" to be an abbreviation of his second Christian name, Gottfried. Yet, actually, he hopes to be taken for a Count. He secretly believes that he is descended from aristocratic forebears, and he tries to obtain possession of documents which prove his noble stock.

Burda's regiment moves to Vienna, where he addresses an anonymous love poem to the youngest of the Princesses of L..., who is counted among "the most splendid figures of the aristocratic world", because he is convinced that the princess is waiting for a sign of his devotion to her.[9] A few days later Burda attends a performance of

---

7 "Er [i. e. Emil] hat sich seit jeher mit Weibern geschleppt, und da wird man, wie Goethe sagt, zuletzt abgewunden gleich Wocken." Saar: Ginevra, p. 41. "He [i.e. Emil] has always carried on with women and, as Goethe says, this leads one to be unwound like a distaff."

8 "[...] für Burda [begann] das weibliche Geschlecht erst bei der Baronesse. Den einfachen Geburtsadel einer jungen Dame ließ er nur dann gelten, wenn der betreffende Vater General oder Präsident irgend einer hohen Landesstelle war; auf gewöhnliche Hofratstöchter pflegte er mit einer Art von Mitleid herabzusehen; Damen der Plutokratie verachtete er gründlich." Ferdinand von Saar: Leutnant Burda, edited and interpreted by Veronika Kribs. Tübingen: Niemeyer 1996, p. 6.

9 Die Prinzessin gehörte "zu den blendendsten Erscheinungen der aristokratischen Frauenwelt". Saar: Leutnant Burda, p. 12.

Minna von Barnhelm in the Burgtheater since he has found out that the princess will also be there. She wears a yellow dress, which is the colour of Burda's regiment, and he takes this as a subtle sign of consent on her part. At the Imperial court ball that Burda attends in the hope of receiving another sign from his beloved, the narrator is informed by her father's adjutant that the liberties taken by Burda are no longer tolerable and are being critically observed by the ducal family of L... . But this warning is to no avail because Burda interprets it as a stratagem to discourage him against the will of the princess. On another night, when leaving the Burgtheater, Burda finds a posy of violets in the pocket of his overcoat. He believes the posy to be a token sent by the princess who had carried a similar one during the performance. But the narrator knows better: the flowers were destined for another gentleman by some coquette, and the wardrobe master put them into the lieutenant's pocket by mistake.

After Burda's regiment has moved to Bohemia, the princess visits a close friend who lives in the small town where he is stationed. In Burda's mind this coincidence is further clear proof of her love for him. From now on he lives on the alert, expecting every minute a secret messenger inviting him to negotiate a marriage to the princess. He applies for a transfer to Vienna to be near his beloved. When this transfer is declined and at the same time his search for documents relating to his aristocratic ancestry fails, he suspects an intrigue by his commander. Burda considers fighting a duel with the commander, but since this idea sounds unreasonable even to him, he tries to provoke the nephew of the commander, a cavalry captain. Anyway, members of the cavalry regiment have lately begun teasing Burda because of his haughty and ceremonious manners and nicknamed him "the enchanted prince".[10] In the event it is not the commander's nephew but one of his fellows, a certain Schorff, a notorious troublemaker, who fights the duel. Burda is severely injured and dies soon after the duel, without having changed his mind about the imaginary love affair. He dies with the posy of violets on his pillow, but a few days after Burda's funeral Princess L... becomes engaged to a certain Prince A... .

Since the outcome of the duel must have been clear even to Burda it is the equivalent of suicide. The duel is Burda's last effort to impress the princess. From the start the narrator is sceptical about Burda's project. He is amazed at "the way in which Burda explains everything to himself"[11] and finally declares him to be insane. There is no doubt that Burda falls a victim to egomania, which leads to misconceptions of reality. His misinterpretations manifest themselves partly in megalomania and partly in paranoia. As far as megalomania is concerned, exaggerated self-esteem is a common phenomenon among the Imperial officers. When Burda's regiment is stationed in Bohemia and he proposes a visit to a nearby manor, his captain replies, that such a visit could be construed as obtrusive: "One did not pay attention to these aristocrats until they had themselves taken notice of His Imperial Majesty's officers."[12]

---

10 "der verwunschene Prinz". Saar: Leutnant Burda, p. 41.

11 "Es war erstaunlich, wie Burda sich alles und jedes zurechtlegte." Saar: Leutnant Burda, p. 19.

12 "Man dürfe sich um diese Aristokraten nicht eher kümmern, als bis sie selbst von den kaiserlichen Offizieren, die wir seien, Notiz genommen." Saar: Leutnant Burda, p. 32.

In this respect Burda resembles Fontane's Schach von Wuthenow, who represents the grandeur, but also the faults and prejudices of an officer of the old style. Both characters identify themselves with the old order that is doomed to vanish. Schach shows the same exaggerated desire to distinguish himself, and like Burda he depends on society's judgement of his behaviour. Schach is vain and at the same time a weak character. "He depends pathologically, that is to an extent bordering on weakness, on society's judgement, and in particular on the judgement of his peers."[13] In Bülow's eyes Schach is the typical representative of the Prussian army, "which has replaced honour by presumption and its soul by a clockwork mechanism".[14] Both characters over-estimate the importance of honour and of the symbols of aristocratic superiority. Such an exaggerated concern for outward appearance creates vanity and make-believe that only thinly disguises a relative lack of self-esteem.

In both stories the concept of honour (*Ehre*) that has become hollow and the hero's fear of becoming ridiculous in the eyes of society suggests a parallel between individual and national history. Schach personifies the fate of Prussia just as Burda represents the decline of the Habsburg Empire. Saar left no doubt about this parallel when he wrote to Karl Emil Franzos: "I wanted to show the hollowness and futility of Burda's life – and of the entire period."[15] In both cases the fate of an individual prefigures a historical defeat that was soon to follow. In this context it is important to note, that Bülow remarks with regard to the defeat of the combined Russian and Austrian forces against Napoleon: "The vanquished are not willing to search for the reason for their defeat in the right place, that is in themselves."[16]

Schach's suicide prefigures Prussia's defeat at the battle of Jena, whereas Burda's death anticipates Austria's fate in the Crimean War and the defeats of 1859 and 1866 against Sardinia, France and Prussia, respectively, that paved the way for the assault of liberalism. Here the question arises: are the aristocratic values represented by the two officers challenged by middle-class values? Schach seems to be fascinated by the new ways of life that are current in Berlin. His disinclination to lead the life of a squire (*Junker*) in Wuthenow castle may be mentioned here. Instead, he prefers to frequent the Berlin salons only to be defeated in rhetorical duels by intellectuals like Bülow or the publisher Sander. In *Leutnant Burda* the challenge to traditional values is much more obvious. The duel is a confrontation between Burda, a representative of the old order, and a rich upstart, whom he treats with utmost scorn. In Burda's opinion his opponent Schorff is only an "impudent and arrogant plebeian".[17] The same class consciousness characterises the officers of the Gensdarmes Regiment in *Schach von*

---

13 "Er ist krankhaft abhängig, abhängig bis zur Schwäche, von dem Urteile der Menschen, speziell seiner Standesgenossen [...]." Fontane: Schach von Wuthenow, NFA, II, 288.

14 "die statt der Ehre nur noch den Dünkel und statt der Seele nur noch ein Uhrwerk hat." Fontane: Schach von Wuthenow, NFA, II, 383.

15 "Aber ich wollte damit auch das durchaus *Hohle* und *Nichtige* im Leben Burda's – ja der ganzen Zeitperiode kennzeichnen." Cited in Saar: Leutnant Burda, p. 170.

16 "Jedem Besiegten wird es schwer, den Grund seiner Niederlagen an der einzig richtigen Stelle, nämlich *in sich selbst* zu suchen [...]."Fontane: Schach von Wuthenow, NFA, II, 311.

17 "dieser freche, aufgeblasene Plebejer". Saar: Leutnant Burda, p. 44.

Wuthenow when they remark that the sleigh-ride is destined "pour les domestiques" and "pour la canaille".[18] Incidents and remarks like this are significant details in the portrait of a society that dissolves and gives way to the battle for life of each individual.

The problem of the decline of the Habsburg Empire can be traced through almost all of Saar's novellas. One notices a certain regret at the loss but, in close analogy with the ideas of Schopenhauer, Saar underlines the necessity of individual and historical events. Milieu and experience form the character of the individual who is the architect of his or her fortune. On the other hand, when Fontane mentions that Schach's stars were against him, the phrase is rhetorical rather than evocative of some sort of predestination. Fontane would hardly have agreed with Saar's determinism, which at times brings the latter's work close to naturalism.

The remarkable coincidences which make Burda believe that the princess really loves him have "a touch of design".[19] Even the sceptical narrator must admit that he is upset by the appearance of the princess in the small Bohemian town. From this time he takes a peculiar interest in the case. After Burda's death he blames himself for not having broken the spell of the lieutenant's self-deception. But he comes to the conclusion that Burda's character was in his way. "Would it have been possible to cure him of his delusion? No, it was impossible! Everything had to happen as it happened: he had, like everybody else, fallen a victim to the relentless fate that was dictated by his nature."[20]

There is another story of Saar's that may well be compared with *Schach von Wuthenow*. In *Vae victis* (1878) Saar depicts another officer of the Austrian army, who has to yield to the assault of liberalism, and particularly to the assault of science and politics.

General von Brandenberg has distinguished himself fighting under the command of Radetzky in Italy in 1848. His deeds earned him the *Theresienorden* and the title of *Freiherr*. In short, he is a product of the times when the army was at the height of its glory. Therefore, a senior clerk has given him his daughter Corona in marriage. Brandenberg adores his young wife, a strikingly beautiful, but strong-willed and cold woman. The marriage is an unhappy one because Corona rejects her husband's love. Much of this aversion is due to her contempt for military manners. To divert herself, she opens her house to the intelligentsia after the model of the Jewish salons. Among the visitors a former revolutionary of 1848 stands out; he is now a doctor of laws and a radical speaker in Parliament. Only recently he has turned against the army and proposed cuts in the military budget. The political pressure on the army leads to reforms and to dismissals of conservative officers who are no longer suited to the new

---

18 Fontane: Schach von Wuthenow, NFA, II, 336.

19 "ein[en] Schein der Absichtlichkeit". Saar: Leutnant Burda, p. 30.

20 "Wäre es überhaupt möglich gewesen, ihn von seinem Wahne zu heilen? Nein, es war nicht möglich! Es mußte alles so kommen, wie es kam: er war, wie jeder, dem unerbittlichen Schicksale seiner Natur verfallen." Saar: Leutnant Burda, p. 47.

system. Even Brandenberg admits that reforms of the army were necessary but he maintains that they should be carried out by military experts. Corona falls in love with the lawyer, who represents genius and tenacity. In her eyes he embodies a new type of hero that will replace the previous model, the soldier. Thus, she addresses the officers in her salon:

> "All of you, you are milksops compared to him. If he had chosen a military career, he would have been a great commander and he would have saved Austria from the disgrace of Magenta and Solferino. However, he has chosen another profession and he has a great future. You, on the contrary, you have none."[21]

Obviously Corona hurts her husband with such remarks, and the more so since he has just come back from the defeat on the Italian battlefields. His spirits are already broken, now he has to accept that he has become despised in his own house as well. Although Brandenberg has lost much of his self-respect, he still tries to maintain his former outward appearance in Corona's salon. In this mood he overhears a conversation between his wife and the radical lawyer. He learns that they intend to marry; in addition, the lawyer has reliable information that Brandenberg will be dismissed in the next few days.

In an interior monologue Brandenberg evaluates his situation. He foresees that the lawyer would decline a duel; if he simply shot his opponent without any warning, the latter would be celebrated as a martyr. There seems no other solution left to him but to shoot himself: "He, the latecomer, was a survival, he was alone, unloved, despised – actually he should rather spin wool!"[22] The last phrase refers to one of the lawyer's projects: he intends to deprive dismissed soldiers of their pensions which he deems undeserved. After the suicide of her husband Corona becomes the lawyer's wife. For some years the lawyer is the most influential person of his time, but then his fortunes change and he ends as a rich but forgotten man. Corona's fortune is also dubious, but the narrator stresses her strong character which makes her prepared for the battle of life.

The rivalry between Brandenberg and the doctor of laws reminds one of the opposition of Schach and Bülow. Like Brandenberg, Schach appears as the incarnation of narrow-mindedness, which relies blindly on the strength of the army. Apart from this major parallel other details might be listed to show that the two characters resemble each other more closely: for example Brandenberg's interior monologue in which he contemplates suicide much in the way that Schach does.

---

21 "Ihr alle seid, mit ihm verglichen, Weichlinge. Hätte er sich dem Militär gewidmet, er wäre ein bedeutender Feldherr geworden und würde Österreich vor der Schmach von Magenta und Solferino bewahrt haben. Indes, sein Beruf ist ein anderer, und er geht einer großen Zukunft entgegen. *Ihr* aber habt samt und sonders keine mehr." Ferdinand von Saar: Sämtliche Werke, ed. by Jakob Minor. 12 vols., Leipzig: Hesse, undated, VIII, p. 17.

22 "Er aber, der Nachgeborene, hatte sich selbst überlebt und stand nun da, einsam, ungeliebt, verachtet – und sollte eigentlich von Rechts wegen Wolle spinnen!" Saar: Sämtliche Werke, VIII, p. 36.

The salons with their climate of intellectual brilliancy and their mainly middle-class members who have excelled in various metiers are set against the world of the army officers in *Vae victis* as in *Schach von Wuthenow*. Just as Bülow is a lion of Madame von Carayon's salon so the doctor of laws distinguishes himself in Corona's circle. He represents social progess as does Bülow. Both are heralds of freedom and modernisation, and in particular, critics of the army or, more precisely, critics of the army's organisation. In both cases the army serves as a stronghold of reactionary ideas.

In *Vae victis* Saar once more symbolises general historical tendencies in the story of an individual defeat. The Brandenbergs live near the Josefstädter Glacis which was still used in the 1850s as a drill ground by the army and as a playground by children. But one could already see the scaffolding of buildings that would a few years later be part of the new Ringstrasse. Brandenberg's fate echoes the events of the year 1860 which was indeed an important year in Austrian history. One year after the defeat at Solferino the Emperor had to announce a constitution which gave more power to the *Reichsrat*, the Austrian Parliament, and thus transferred much of the political power to men like the radical lawyer.

There is no doubt, that despite the similarities that I have highlighted in this comparison, the differences between the two authors are numerous as well as important. Although Saar excels at dialogue at times, and although he tries to vary the speech of his characters to give them individuality and a social identity, he is far from achieving Fontane's differentiated representation of a rich variety of contemporary discourses and linguistic registers. Saar almost entirely lacks humour; one of the few exceptions is the episode recounting Burda's attempts at proving his noble descent. Saar prefers narrators that appear in the frames of his stories and who, since they are often biased or downright unreliable, render the narrated events ambiguous. It is true that the same applies to Fontane's writings, but I would contend that Fontane arrives at this goal by the application of polyperspectival narration. In any case, as a result, it is difficult for the reader to decide how to evaluate a given character. As a particularity in the case of Saar I would add an inclination towards the autobiographical, relating mainly to his years in the army but also to the problem of the artist living on the margins of society. The list of differences could be continued, but those mentioned may suffice to indicate that the two authors who drew pictures of similar social change differed substantially with respect to the narrative strategies they employed.

Peter James Bowman

Schach von Wuthenow: **Interpreters and Interpretants**

1. Introduction: Reading and Interpretation

A complete theory of the role of the reader in constructing the meaning of literary texts must account both for the linguistic, literary and cultural expectations which the reader brings to the text, and for those elements within the text itself, such as symbolism, narratorial suggestion and virtual readers, which prompt the external or real reader to make sense of the narrative in one way or another. One of the most interesting questions in this whole debate concerns the way the text, particularly the novel, constructs within itself an "implied" reader who influences the responses of the real reader. The formation of the implied reader by means of a variety of narrative devices ensures that novels are structured from within by their addressivity, by their status as texts to be read. If we accept that "reading" determines the very construction of the author's text, then it is but a small step to the claim that fiction, in its more self-conscious moments at least, thematises and foregrounds the process of interpretation. This argument is made by Naomi Schor: "Novels are not only about speaking and writing (*encoding*), but also about reading, and by reading I mean the *decoding* of all manner of signs and signals".[1] The idea that a fictional text contains within its fabric an "awareness" of the reader is widespread, as is evidenced by the number of appellations given to this virtual presence (implied reader, ideal reader, addressee, fictionalised audience etc.). Because this "awareness" is an inherent element in the meaning-producing structure of fiction, novels can be said to "represent and reflect upon interpretation as performance".[2] In this way, interpretation is seen "not as something that is done *to* fiction but rather as something that is done *in* fiction".[3]

Schor calls her own addition to the list of intratextual "readers" discovered by theorists the *interpretant*, and this figure is contrasted with the *interpreter* or external reader. What distinguishes the interpretant from the theoretical constructs listed above is that it is "neither supporting actor, nor theoretical construct, nor intaglio figure, but instead coextensive with the first-person narrator or main protagonist of the fiction".[4] In other words, characters and narrators (the distinction is often blurred in first-person narratives) are themselves readers in the general sense that they must comprehend their experiences so as to be able to respond appropriately, and by evaluating the success of their manner of interpretation the *interpreter*, or real reader, can develop the most appropriate reading strategy.

---

1 Naomi Schor: Fiction as Interpretation/Interpretation as Fiction. In: The Reader in the Text. Essays on Audience and Interpretation, ed. by Susan R. Suleiman and Inge Crosman. Princeton: Princeton University Press 1980, pp. 165-182 (p. 168).

2 Schor: Fiction as Interpretation/Interpretation as Fiction, p. 167.

3 Schor: Fiction as Interpretation/Interpretation as Fiction, p. 168.

4 Schor: Fiction as Interpretation/Interpretation as Fiction, p. 169.

2. Bülow as Interpretant

In Fontane's fiction, characters such as Effi Briest, Lehnert Menz, Lewin von Vitzewitz, Waldemar von Haldern, Robert von Gordon and Graf Holk all try with varying degrees of success to interpret their experiences and environment, and their well-being, sometimes their survival, depends on their interpretative competence. On the other hand, we can safely say that Fontane's narrators, none of whom are actors in the events they describe, are never interpretants in Schor's sense. Fontane employs fairly unobtrusive narrators who very rarely express opinions or judge characters in their own voice. His narrative technique is polyperspectival, and all interpreting is undertaken by the characters themselves, who try to understand and evaluate situations and other characters. *Schach von Wuthenow* (*A Man of Honor*) falls into this general pattern. The novel is made up of a conversational network in which events and characters are discussed from numerous perspectives and subjected to multiple interpretations which both complement and relativise one another. The main characters gain shape largely through descriptions made of them by others, so that external interpreters, in forming their evaluations of characters, must interpret interpretations already made.

However, *Schach von Wuthenow* also contains a feature which makes it different from the rest of Fontane's fiction. The character of Heinrich Dietrich von Bülow is quite unique in Fontane's oeuvre, in some ways making this novel an exception to the author's usual polyperspectival style. Bülow seems to have almost no role to play in the story's plot, and yet he is not a secondary character. He is fully characterised, and a large amount of textual space is devoted to his speech. Bülow seems to do nothing, but has something to say about everything. His unique status can be explained partly in terms of the efforts made by Fontane to create an authentic period flavour. Like almost all of the characters in the novel, he is based on a real historical figure. The real Bülow (1757-1807), a writer of military treatises, was a particularly important source in Fontane's research into the period in which the novel is set, that is to say the eve of Prussia's defeat at the hands of Napoleon's army at Jena in 1806. As Pierre-Paul Sagave has shown in detail, the real Bülow's writings find their way in adapted form into the fictional Bülow's long monologues, and so the critique of Prussia which he provides forms an important element in the evocation of the age.[5] All the same, the significance of this character greatly exceeds what is necessary for the purposes of historical realism. The inclusion of Bülow must have a further motivation.

Bülow's importance seems to lie largely in his role as a commentator both on general contemporary issues and on the specific events of the story. His cosmopolitanism and peripatetic existence give him the status of outside observer untainted by Prussian prejudices and the short-sighted militarism and nationalism of

---

5   Pierre-Paul Sagave: Un roman berlinois de Fontane: "Schach von Wuthenow". In: Recherches sur le roman social en Allemagne, Publications des Annales de la Faculté de Lettres: Aix-en-Provence 1960, new series 28, pp. 87-108.

the time, and his commentary generally seems to inspire respect amongst other characters. As we learn on the opening page of the story, within a few weeks of taking up residence in Berlin, Bülow and his publisher Sander have attained a position of dominance in the Carayon salon, and Prinz Louis Ferdinand clearly also admires his perspicacity. The real reader too is likely to be impressed with the progressiveness and intelligence of his opinions and the eloquence with which they are expressed. Bülow is at his most impressive when describing the social and ethical hollowness of the Prussia of 1806, and especially the state of the military machine, which is dangerously weak under its brilliant exterior. His criticism of the self-indulgent troublemaking of the pampered élite regiments and of the bourgeoisie's demeaning craving for honorific titles are particularly apt (NFA, II, 276-277, 316). Bülow's commentary is invested with all the more authority for the fact that the reader knows that his predictions of imminent and catastrophic military defeat will prove accurate within a matter of months after the time in which the narrative is set. This raises the question of why Fontane feels it necessary to include in this narrative an authoritative interpretant or *Deuter* in the form of Bülow, especially as there are no other examples in his fiction of this practice, which is in any case incompatible with his trademark polyperspectival technique. In order to account for the significance of the fictional Bülow, we must turn our attention to the main protagonist of the novel.

The Rittmeister Schach von Wuthenow is clearly the main focus of interest in this work, as its title suggests. The story concentrates on the stages, including the turning point of the seduction of Victoire, which lead to his suicide. Even when Schach is not present he is often the subject of others' discussions, and one might say that other characters, most of whom are rather static, exist only in order to shed light on him. Clearly, then, any interpretation is bound to be based on an understanding of Schach's behaviour, and yet herein lies a serious problem. Schach is in many ways a baffling character, and his suicide seems to be an extreme, almost irrational response to the situation in which he finds himself. The reaction of an early reviewer is typical of the perplexity of many readers:

> We simply do not understand him, this handsome Schach, who out of fear of the mockery of his peers, out of a false feeling of honour, dares not marry an ugly girl, although having deprived her of her virtue he is duty-bound to save her good name; and who, when his king obliges him to go ahead with this marriage, obeys, only then to put a bullet through his head immediately after the wedding. It is impossible for us to empathise with such a peculiar way of feeling, it remains opaque to us.[6]

---

6 "Wir verstehen ihn einfach nicht, diesen schönen Schach, der ein häßliches Mädchen, deren Frauenehre er widerherstellen [sic] soll, weil er selbst sie geraubt – nicht zu heiraten wagt aus Furcht vor dem Spott der Welt, aus einem falschen Gefühl der Ehre; und der, als sein König ihm die Heirat befiehlt, zwar gehorcht, aber unmittelbar nach der Hochzeit sich eine Kugel durch den Kopf schießt. Die Besonderheit seines Empfindens nachzuempfinden ist uns unmöglich, es bleibt uns incommensurabel." K. W.: Deutsche Litteraturzeitung, 4 (1883), quoted in Erläuterungen und Dokumente: Theodor Fontane, Schach von Wuthenow, ed. by Walter Wagner. Stuttgart: Reclam 1980, p. 84. Translations from *Schach von Wuthenow* and other texts are in all cases my own.

The very centrality of Schach means that bewilderment about his conduct is a serious threat to the intelligibility of the story as whole. It is this threat which naturally makes us look to Bülow, the model interpretant, to see if he can help us to be competent interpreters. Bülow's greatest significance in the story is thus as a judge of the novel's main protagonist.

Bülow speaks and writes extensively about Schach, seeing him as exemplifying the false honour of his peers in the officer corps. Bülow's first words on the subject of the handsome cavalry captain come in the third chapter, set in the drinking den 'Sala Tarone':

> "For all I know he may have his merits, but to my mind he is nothing but a pedant and a stuffed shirt, and at the same time he is the embodiment of a type of Prussian narrow-mindedness which only has three articles of belief; first article 'The Prussian state rests as securely on the shoulders of the Prussian army as the world rests on the shoulders of Atlas', second article 'The Prussian infantry charge is irresistible', and third and last, 'a battle is never lost as long as the Garde du Corps Regiment has not yet made its attack'." [7]

In the same chapter Bülow goes on to call Schach "the little man in big boots!"[8] and he makes further critical remarks about Schach in his first letter to Sander in Chapter 13. By far his most important contribution to a potential understanding of the hero's personality comes in his second letter to Sander, which forms the penultimate chapter of the novel. Bülow elucidates what might seem hard to account for in Schach's case by drawing a parallel between it and the failings of the age as a whole. His censure of Schach is of a piece with his negative appraisal of the entire Prussian élite, and he explains Schach's suicide in terms of his adherence to the cankered values of his society:

> "It [the Schach case] is entirely a product of its time, although, to be sure, with specific local features. In its causes it is a quite abnormal case, which in this shape and form could only have taken place in the capital city and residence of His Majesty the King of Prussia, or, if not there, in the ranks of our shadow of a Friederician army, an army which has replaced honour with arrogance, and whose soul is now a mere clockwork mechanism – a mechanism which shall soon enough have run down." [9]

---

7 "Er mag seine Meriten haben, meinetwegen, aber mir ist er nichts als ein Pedant und Wichtigtuer, und zugleich die Verkörperung jener preußischen Beschränktheit, die nur drei Glaubensartikel hat: erstes Hauptstück 'die Welt ruht nicht sicherer auf den Schultern des Atlas, als der preußische Staat auf den Schultern der preußischen Armee', zweites Hauptstück 'der preußische Infanterieangriff ist unwiderstehlich', und drittens und letztens, 'eine Schlacht ist nie verloren, solange das Regiment Garde du Corps nicht angegriffen hat'." Fontane: Schach von Wuthenow, NFA, II, 288.

8 "Der kleine Mann in den großen Stiefeln!" Fontane: Schach von Wuthenow, NFA, II, 289.

9 "Er [der Schach-Fall] ist durchaus Zeiterscheinung, aber, wohlverstanden, mit lokaler Begrenzung, ein in seinen Ursachen ganz abnormer Fall, der sich in dieser Art und Weise nur in Seiner Königlichen Majestät von Preußen Haupt- und Residenzstadt, oder, wenn über diese hinaus, immer nur in den Reihen unsrer nachgeborenen friedericianischen Armee zutragen konnte, einer Armee, die

The superficial notion of honour Schach shares with his society has led him, argues Bülow, to think that marriage to Victoire would disgrace him, not because of any personal or social unsuitability in his fiancée, but because her unattractive appearance exposes him to the mockery of his fellow officers. Bülow is quite uncompromising in his judgement of Schach's behaviour:

> "There you have the essence of false honour. It makes us dependent on that most volatile and capricious of things, the matchwood judgement of society, and causes us to sacrifice the most sacred commandments, the loveliest and most natural dictates of our hearts to this worship of etiquette." [10]

3. The Critical View of Schach's Tragedy

Bülow, then, is essentially a non-participating commentator in the story who seems to be invested with an exceptional authority to speak both on general issues and on specific individuals, most particularly the main protagonist. In Schor's terminology, it seems that we have an interpretant who leaves the interpreter very little to do. Certainly a good many critics are satisfied by Bülow's explanation for Schach's suicide, and assume that Fontane himself identified with the views he puts in Bülow's mouth. Conrad Wandrey repeats Bülow's point that Schach's fate is a sign of the times, and adds that Bülow explains this in Fontane's name. [11] Like Wandrey, Georg Lukács agrees with Bülow in seeing Schach as typical for his period, and in his analysis he quotes a long passage from Bülow's last letter, assuming his review of Schach's story expresses the author's purpose: "What Fontane uncovers here by literary means is the frailty of any people and social system whose morality is based on this kind of false honour". [12] Richard Brinkmann also views Schach as symptomatic of his society's infirmities, and argues that Bülow's identification of that fact makes him the author's mouthpiece. [13] Gertrude Michielsen and H. R. Klieneberger similarly adopt Bülow's view that Schach's fate is to be explained by his adherence to social prejudices, and comment that his very significance lies in the parallel between his own fate and that of Prussia shortly after his death. [14] More recently Manfred Dutschke has followed the

---

statt der Ehre nur noch den Dünkel, und statt der Seele nur noch ein Uhrwerk hat – ein Uhrwerk, das bald genug abgelaufen sein wird." Fontane: Schach von Wuthenow, NFA, II, 383.

10 "Da haben Sie das Wesen der falschen Ehre. Sie macht uns abhängig von dem Schwankendsten und Willkürlichsten, was es gibt, von dem auf Triebsand aufgebauten Urteile der Gesellschaft, und veranlaßt uns, die heiligsten Gebote, die schönsten und natürlichsten Regungen eben diesem Gesellschaftsgötzen zum Opfer zu bringen." Fontane: Schach von Wuthenow, NFA, II, 384.

11 Conrad Wandrey: Theodor Fontane. Munich: Beck 1919, p. 157.

12 Georg Lukács: German Realists in the Nineteenth Century, transl. by Jeremy Gaines and Paul Keast. London: Libris 1993, p. 326.

13 Richard Brinkmann: Theodor Fontane. Über die Verbindlichkeit des Unverbindlichen, 2nd. edition. Tübingen: Niemeyer 1977, p. 69.

14 Gertrude Michielsen: The Preparation of the Future. Techniques of Anticipation in the Novels of Theodor Fontane and Thomas Mann. Berne: Lang 1978, p. 116; H. R. Klieneberger: The Novel in

same line.[15] Benno von Wiese goes as far as to paraphrase Bülow's comments in his own argument.[16] Sagave too assumes a complete unanimity of opinion of the author and Bülow, and he takes the latter's words to be Fontane speaking in his own voice.[17] Other critics are more cautious in identifying themselves and the author with Bülow's interpretation. John Osborne sees Bülow as the author's mouthpiece, but also comments that he is often not portrayed sympathetically.[18] Gerhard Kaiser takes a critical view of the fictionalised military historian and his generalising tendencies, but nonetheless echoes his argument that Schach is a mere reflection of and parallel for the empty and fatal vanity of contemporary Prussia.[19] Walter Müller-Seidel sees Fontane's use of a real historical character in Bülow as giving greater weight to the criticisms he puts in his mouth, although he sees Lukács's view of Bülow as a figural embodiment of the authorial voice as simplistic.[20] Whether or not they remark on imperfections in Bülow's personality, then, most critics consider his understanding of Schach's character and suicide to be valid.

In what follows I would like to take issue with these views, and argue that Bülow not only fails satisfactorily to explain Schach's case, but also that his procedures of interpretation make him fundamentally ill-qualified to do so. His final letter to Sander is not an accurate explanation of what has happened. It is not even an explanation of only partial validity. Rather, Bülow's interpretative abilities can be seen to be thoroughly undermined in the text, and his final letter should be read as an example of the dangers of imposing over-simple notions of character and motivation on an individual's actions. Furthermore, Bülow is not a privileged outsider who stands above

---

England and Germany. A Comparative Study. London: Wolff 1981, p. 150f.

15 "Schachs Tragödie beruht auf einer distanzlosen Identifikation mit den Prinzipien preußischer Lebensart"; "Schach's tragedy is founded on a complete identification with the principles of the Prussian way of life." Manfred Dutschke: Geselliger Spießrutenlauf. Die Tragödie des lächerlichen Junkers Schach von Wuthenow. In: Theodor Fontane, ed. by Heinz Ludwig Arnold. Munich: text und kritik 1989, pp. 103-116 (p. 114).

16 "Bülow durchschaut später mit Recht, daß der leichtsinnige Sprachgebrauch mit dem Wort Ehre die Begriffe verwirrt hat und die wahre, die richtige Ehre damit totschlägt"; "Bülow later rightly perceives that the careless application of the term honour has confused matters and in so doing has killed true honour." Benno von Wiese: Die deutsche Novelle von Goethe bis Kafka. Interpretationen. Düsseldorf: Bagel 1962, vol. 2, p. 253f.

17 Sagave: Recherches sur le roman social en Allemagne, pp. 93, 100, 103.

18 John Osborne: *Schach von Wuthenow*. "Das rein Äußerliche bedeutet immer viel ...". In: Interpretationen: Fontanes Novellen und Romane, ed. by Christian Grawe. Stuttgart: Reclam 1991, pp. 92-112 (pp. 104f, 106f).

19 "Preußen wird an derselben Welt des Scheins zugrundegehen, an der Schach zugrundegegangen ist. Diese Welt ist schöner Schein wie Schachs Schönheit scheinhaft; sie ist von tödlicher, selbstmörderischer Egozentrik"; "Prussia will founder on the same world of appearances as Schach founders on. This world is a beautiful surface, just as Schach's beauty is only superficial; it is deadly, suicidal egocentricity." Gerhard Kaiser: *Schach von Wuthenow* oder die Weihe der Kraft. Variationen über ein Thema von Walter Müller-Seidel, zu seinem 60. Geburtstag. In: Jahrbuch der deutschen Schillergesellschaft, 22 (1978), pp. 474-495 (p. 477).

20 Walter Müller-Seidel: Theodor Fontane. Soziale Romankunst in Deutschland, 3rd edition, Stuttgart: Metzler, 1994, p. 142f.

the events leading to Schach's suicide, but is himself deeply implicated in the factors which drive the hero to take his own life. Like other characters, but to a greater degree, Bülow uses an objectifying mode of speech which forces Schach into complete isolation.

As for Schach himself, he is not, as Bülow and subsequent readers have said, typical or symptomatic of the society in which he lives, but rather radically different from it and alienated by it. This alienation is nowhere clearer than in his exchanges with Bülow, who, unwittingly to be sure, reduces him from being a participant in social speech to being an object of it. Bülow's apparently radical views and Schach's seemingly conservative conventionality should not blind us to the fact that in the speech community here depicted it is Bülow who is deeply conventional in his discursive strategies, while Schach is radical in his opposition to them. I shall consider Schach's relationship with the speech community in which he lives presently, but first I shall try to show that Bülow's view of the main protagonist and his interpretation of the final tragedy are problematised in this narrative in two related ways: first, they are exemplary in their wrongness and thus, for the reader, of cautionary value; and second, they are symptomatic of a use of language which denies the individual the possibility of maintaining an even partially autonomous identity.

4. Bülow's (Un)Fitness to Judge

Before considering the validity of Bülow's comments about both Schach's personality and the motivation for his suicide, let us examine his competence to make judgements of this sort. We have said that Fontane seems to give Bülow the role of a specially privileged interpretant or *Deuter*. However, a closer look at the way he is presented in the narrative reveals that his status is in fact far more ambiguous. The first indication of this comes on the opening page, with a lengthy description of him in the narrator's voice:

> His name was Bülow. Nonchalance was part of his genial manner, and so, with both feet stretched far in front of him and his left hand in his pocket, he thrust his right hand around him in the air, intending with such lively gesticulation to lend greater emphasis to his lecture. As his friends said, his speech always took the form of lecturing and – he spoke the whole time.[21]

The unambiguous narratorial irony of this description automatically puts the reader in a position of superiority in regard to the character described, a position from which it is difficult to take what that character might have to say entirely seriously. Narratorial description and veiled criticism of Bülow continue. The exchanges in the Carayon salon, which form the first two chapters of the novel, show his pomposity to the full.

---

21 "Sein Name war von Bülow. Nonchalance gehörte mit zur Genialität, und so focht er denn, beide Füße weit vorgestreckt und die linke Hand in der Hosentasche, mit seiner rechten in der Luft umher, um durch lebhafte Gestikulationen seinem Kathedervortrage Nachdruck zu geben. Er konnte, wie seine Freunde sagten, nur sprechen, um Vortrag zu halten, und – er sprach eigentlich immer." Fontane: Schach von Wuthenow, NFA, II, 273.

In the second chapter he is described as displaying arrogance, and is unable to tolerate being edged out of the limelight by Alvensleben. His unremitting volubility is accompanied by an unwillingness to give others any credit for their opinions, and even more striking is the dogmatism of his views, particularly on Prussian foreign policy and on Lutheranism. As Kaiser has said, Bülow is therefore implicated in the failings of the society he criticises by sharing its self-regard and ostentation.[22] Moreover, the validity of his criticism of the establishment is brought into question by his embitterment at the lack of recognition accorded to him by the Prussian state, as Schach points out (NFA, II, 298). Finally, his prediction that both Prussia and Luther are mere "episodes" whose days are numbered turns out to be wrong, despite the imminent defeat of Prussian forces at the hands of Napoleon (NFA, II, 281).

Connected with Bülow's dogmatism is his tendency to generalise, about which he is quite candid in his final letter to Sander: "You are familiar with my tendency (which I follow in this instance too) to argue from the part to the whole, but also inversely from the whole to the part, which is what generalising is about".[23] Whether he is opining that poets are always a disappointment when encountered in the flesh (NFA, II, 278), that female members of the royal family are stupid (NFA, II, 279), or that any monarch having the epithet "good" is bound to be ineffectual (NFA, II, 312f.), Bülow has a propensity to simplify and pigeonhole which should not inspire readers' confidence in his ability to account for the complex motivation leading up to Schach's suicide. Indeed, there is evidence that his judgement specifically of human nature is flawed, as when he describes the agreeable but hardly artless Frau von Carayon as having "the whole magic of truth and naturalness about her".[24] It is in the light of these interpretative weaknesses that we should consider Bülow's explanations of Schach's conduct and fate.

5. An Inaccurate Reading of Character

Those who see Bülow as a privileged interpreter within the text naturally agree with his negative view of its eponymous hero. To be sure, Schach is not without faults: he is highly class-conscious, unimaginative, petulant and, in the last analysis, lacking in courage, but a close look at the text reveals that many of the harsh criticisms made of him by Bülow are undeserved. The weight of the condemnation of Schach expressed by Bülow in the third chapter and repeated in part in his final letter is that he is a vain, self-important pedant and a stiffly conventional purveyor of outworn clichés. Turning to the first charge, it is true that Schach is conscious of his own dignity, but, although it has become a truism that he is a vain and showy character, direct evidence for this in the text is very hard to come by. Apart from by Bülow, Schach is accused of vanity by

---

22 Kaiser: *Schach von Wuthenow oder die Weihe der Kraft* , p. 492.

23 "Sie kennen meine Neigung (und dieser folg ich auch heut), aus dem Einzelnen aufs Ganze zu schließen, aber freilich auch umgekehrt aus dem Ganzen aufs Einzelne, was mit dem Generalisieren zusammenhängt." Fontane: Schach von Wuthenow, NFA, II, 382f.

24 "Den ganzen Zauber des Wahren und Natürlichen." Fontane: Schach von Wuthenow, NFA, II, 288.

Leutnant von Zieten (NFA, II, 334) and Frau von Carayon (NFA, II, 361). The weasely Zieten is such a thoroughly despicable character, driven by envious rancour to act in a craftily malicious way towards Schach, that his views can be ignored. As for Frau von Carayon's stricture, it is delivered at a moment of extreme tension following Schach's disappearance from Berlin and before the reasons for his flight are known to her; later she makes a full apology to Schach for having thought ill of him (NFA, II, 380f.). Schach's own behaviour does not reveal much in the way of self-importance, and there is no evidence at all of physical vanity. He is unfailingly kind and considerate to his subordinates, such as Krist, Mutter Kreepschen and Ordonnanz Baarsch, and is therefore held in affection by them. Schach can seem stuffy and even pompous in the salon conversations, but this is largely because he is riled by Bülow's callous cynicism and overweening manner, which he gallantly opposes with his unimaginative but consistent decency. In any case, he is nothing like as pompous and self-important as the man who accuses him of these failings. Bülow's second criticism is that Schach is an unimaginative conservative who peddles old clichés and is blind to the bankruptcy of his society. Sure enough, during the visit to Tempelhof Schach does reproduce almost verbatim one of the articles of belief previously ascribed to him by Bülow. In general, though, Schach is the one character who consistently opposes the outworn clichés and simplistic generalisations of his peers. In his sparring matches with Bülow, Schach does not pigeonhole people and reduce experiences to convenient formulae, but is rather on the conversational back foot, opposing Bülow's tendency to do just this, for example in his exasperated responses to Bülow's dismissal of Lutheranism and his belittling of the Tsar Alexander (NFA, II, 281; 312f.).

The most important part of Bülow's interpretative role is played by the letter which forms Chapter 20 of the novel, in which he attributes Schach's downfall to a false code of honour which he shares so completely with his society that he would rather die than break with it.[25] It is this congruence of Schach's self-image and the way society as a whole sees itself that allows Bülow to see in Schach's tragedy an omen for the destiny of that society. Of course, to see Schach as an example of and parable for something else is to deny him the open-endedness essential in fictional characters if we are to engage with them on their own terms. To view Schach as standing for the failings of the society in which he lives is to see him as a functional device, a mere building block in an intentional textual structure which "tells" us something. Indeed, some critics, agreeing with Bülow, make this idea explicit: in Sagave's view Fontane creates Schach as a way of analysing the spirit of the period,[26] while von Wiese and Dutschke see in

---

25 Following Bülow, von Wiese argues that Schach's sense of honour is handicapped by its purely social nature: "So wie dieses Ehrgefühl bei Schach angelegt ist, in seiner durchaus gesellschaftlichen Orientierung reicht es nicht aus, um mit einer unkonventionellen Situation fertig zu werden"; "Given the nature of this sense of honour in Schach's case, by virtue of its essentially social orientation it is inadequate to deal with an unconventional situation." Benno von Wiese: Die deutsche Novelle von Goethe bis Kafka, vol. 2, p. 247.

26 "Fontane crée son personnage afin d'analyser, en psychologue, l'esprit du temps et l'esprit de caste"; Sagave: Recherches sur le roman social en Allemagne, p. 102. Sagave's view follows that of Wandrey: "Im Gegensatz zu *Vor dem Sturm*, wo die Menschen aus sich heraus, soll Schach nur aus

him more a representative than an individual person.[27] However, it seems to me that Schach's problems stem not from despair at having to behave in a way that his peers deride, but from a complete withdrawal from the patterns of language use and communication which characterise the speech community to which he belongs. This withdrawal sets him at odds with that community well before the obligation to marry Victoire. Schach's tragedy derives not from his excessive adoption of society's values, but rather from the excessive rupture between these values and his own. Furthermore, it is his antipathy to the generalising and categorising modes of speech of other members of his social class which provokes the unwitting but orchestrated drive to quash his discursive non-conformity. In order to see how this takes place, it is necessary to take a closer look at the nature of the speech community in which Schach is situated.

6. The Speech Community and Schach

In challenging the view that Schach is a mere representative of his age, I am not suggesting that the depiction of the pre-Jena *Zeitgeist* is not central to Fontane's creative intention in *Schach von Wuthenow*. Fontane clearly goes to great lengths to portray the society and attitudes of the period. If any character *can* be considered representative of the cynical amorality and vacuous ostentation of this society, then surely it is Karl von Nostitz: "A daredevil horseman and even more daring as a ladies' cavalier and amasser of debts, he had long been one of the most popular men in the regiment".[28] Despite the noisy arrogance of men like Nostitz, the officer corps is society's idol, and Frau von Carayon and Victoire make sure they spend the spring days at their window so as not to miss the military parades that troop by.

Of particular concern for Fontane as he reconstructs this period are the speech manners and mannerisms of the dominant social class, and Eduard Engel, a contemporary reviewer, comments on the socio-linguistic accuracy of speech in the novel.[29] Leaving aside the matter of historical language features, how can we characterise the speech of characters in *Schach von Wuthenow*? Almost all of Fontane's fictional works contain ironic and irreverent characters whose idiom is amused and amusing. Here, though, this tone acquires a distinctly heartless edge, and none of

---

seiner Zeit heraus begriffen werden"; "In contrast to *Before the Storm*, where the individual human beings are to be understood in terms of their own make-up, Schach is to be understood only in terms of the period." Wandrey: Theodor Fontane, p. 157.

27   "Schach ist hier weit mehr Repräsentant als individuelle Person." Benno von Wiese: Die deutsche Novelle von Goethe bis Kafka, vol. 2, p. 240.

28 "Ein tollkühner Reiter und ein noch tollkühnerer Cour- und Schuldenmacher, war er seit lang ein Allerbeliebtester im Regiment." Fontane: Schach von Wuthenow, NFA, II, 286.

29 "Alle jene Menschen reden im Geiste ihrer Zeit, – das erstreckt sich bis auf Kleinigkeiten des Ausdrucks"; "All those people speak in accordance with the spirit of their age – and this applies to the smallest details of expression." Eduard Engel: Schach von Wuthenow. In: Das Magazin für die Literatur des In- und Auslandes, 51 (1882), quoted in Wagner: Erläuterungen und Dokumente. Theodor Fontane, Schach von Wuthenow, p. 74.

Fontane's novels contains as much malignant cynicism as this one, or as much misogynist humour. Again Nostitz is typical in his combination of innuendo and cynicism:

> "Why I played truant from the Carayons? Well, because I wanted to go to Französisch-Buchholz to see whether the storks have returned there, whether the cuckoo's call is to be heard again, and whether the schoolmaster's daughter has got the same flaxen-blonde plaits she had last year. A delightful child. I always have her show me the church, and then, as I have such a passion for old bell inscriptions, we climb up the tower. You just cannot imagine the discoveries one can make in a tower like that. The hours I spent there are amongst the happiest and most instructive I have known."[30]

The ensuing debate about the relative merits of blondes and brunettes continues in the same vein. The greatest concentration of this civilised lubricity comes in the sixth and seventh chapters, which are devoted to Prince Louis Ferdinand's soirée. It is worth noting that Bülow, despite his customary high-mindedness, gets fully into the spirit of these risqué exchanges.

Another of the most noticeable features of the dialogues in this novel is the degree of verbal ostentation in evidence. Characters often clearly feel that they are in the presence, not of interlocutors, but of an audience, and many of their extended utterances have a strong performative element, for example the Prince's "capriccio" on the varieties of female beauty in Chapter 7 (NFA, II, 319f.). The Prince's long speech also reveals another striking feature of many of the contributions to salon discussion, namely the tendency of frivolous extemporising to work itself free of any real reference to its ostensible subject and become self-generating verbal exuberance. In the Prince's mouth the phrase "la beauté du diable" ("diabolic beauty") goes through such a bewildering series of redefinitions that by the end of his philippic he has communicated precisely nothing. This spiralling of language away from meaning is, of course, a direct result of the ostentation and performativity of salon speech. Clearly, in such conversations, the content of what is said is of less importance than the virtuosity of the speaker.

Of course, we must not be fooled by the secondary importance of its subject matter into thinking that salon conversation and the officers' exchanges are mere verbal froth of no real consequence. There are in fact very significant things going on in these exchanges. Analysts of speech in Fontane's novels tend to see it in terms of sociolinguistic realism, the polyperspectival narrative technique, displays of urbane brilliance by the author, or his humane ideal of communication, but what is insufficiently noted is the subtle conversational politics which Fontane reproduces on

---

30 "Warum ich bei den Carayons geschwänzt habe? Nun, weil ich in Französich-Buchholz nachsehen wollte, ob die Störche schon wieder da sind, ob der Kuckuck schon wieder schreit und ob die Schulmeisterstochter noch so lange, flachsblonde Flechten hat, wie voriges Jahr. Ein reizendes Kind. Ich lasse mir immer die Kirche von ihr zeigen, und wir steigen dann in den Turm hinauf, weil ich eine Passion für alte Glockeninschriften habe. Sie glauben gar nicht, was sich in solchem Turme alles entziffern läßt. Ich zähle das zu meinen glücklichsten und lehrreichsten Stunden." Fontane: Schach von Wuthenow, NFA, II, 286f.

the pages of his novels. His fiction shows an acute interest in the subtle, semi-conscious or unconscious shifts of position in the continual battle for identity and recognition amongst characters. Typical for Fontane are long conversations between a number of speakers at such social occasions as dinner parties, salon gatherings and day trips. *Schach von Wuthenow* contains all three of these set social occasions, and in all three this conversational manoeuvring can be observed. These extended passages of direct speech reveal insecurity, self-assertion, and a general jockeying for position in a series of conversational power games in which identity itself is at stake, and in which the subject matter discussed is subordinated to the self-image aspired to by the speaker. Sander's exuberant excursus on May punch and the best colour for drinking glasses has less to do with his drinking habits than with the desire of a bourgeois to show that he is as accomplished and decadent a *bon viveur* as his aristocratic friends (NFA, II, 285-286). The reaction of the officers of the Gensdarmes Regiment to Zacharias Werner's play *Die Weihe der Kraft* is also typical. The officers speak about the play not because they have an opinion to express about it, but because they want to outdo one another as irreverent humorists (NFA, II, 332f.).

A sense of identity is always relational; individuals assert that identity partly by describing and making sense of their environment and those who inhabit it, and in doing so they each define and categorise all that is outside themselves. The ethical implications of this self-definition via other-definition are explored by Roland Barthes in terms of the "violence" implicit in the use of the third-person pronoun: "Whenever I say the word 'he' of someone, I always imagine a sort of murder by language".[31] A very conspicuous feature of *Schach von Wuthenow* is the quantity of speech about others it contains, especially when these objects of speech are absent. In Chapters 1, 2, 3, 6, 7 and 10 in particular, we hear characters speaking cynically and reductively about each other, and time and again perfunctory and humorous comments shade into mockery. In the context of this subjection of the human objects of discourse to the reductive attentions of the speaker, it is not surprising that personal loyalty is not a possibility. This state of affairs is candidly explained by Sander: "For just as children's balls are, in the experience of Your Majesty, in fact best in the absence of children, so friendships are best without friends. Surrogates are the only meaningful things in life, and are the very essence of wisdom".[32] Even the positively portrayed Alvensleben has some unkind things to say about his best friend Schach in the "Sala Tarone" scene (NFA, II, 287f.). In this game of claiming identity for the self by undermining the identity of others, there are bound to be winners and losers, and the clearest winner is Bülow, who is the most eloquent and witty speaker. We learn on the opening page that he "terrorises" opinion in Berlin, and he does this by being the most adroit of all the

---

31 "Disant de quelqu'un 'il', j'ai toujours en vue une sorte de meurtre par le langage." Roland Barthes: *Roland Barthes*. Paris: Seuil 1975, p. 171.

32 "Denn wenn die Kinderbälle, nach Ansicht und Erfahrung Eurer Königlichen Hoheit, eigentlich am besten ohne Kinder bestehen, so die Freundschaften am besten ohne Freunde. Die Surrogate bedeuten überhaupt alles im Leben, und sind recht eigentlich die letzte Weisheitssentenz." Fontane: *Schach von Wuthenow*, NFA, II, 318.

characters at reducing everything he discusses to cleverly formulated axioms, subjecting people and values to ridicule in the process. Not all the main characters in the novel speak in the way described, and in particular the Carayons, mother and daughter, are far less quick to categorise others and thus rob them of their open-endedness as human beings. However, this is the dominant tone of the society depicted, and one which aggressively demands acceptance and submission from its members. As Nostitz tells his fellow officers, they are "heirs to an ancient renown in the fields of military and social honour – for we have not only determined the course of battles, we have also set the tone for society".[33]

Despite the obvious unpleasantness of this discursive practice, there is no escape from its rigours, at least not for the male characters. It is in the nature of this sort of conversational exchange that individuals are constantly threatened with categorisation and must continually speak for themselves so as to avoid it. This creates a sort of compulsion to converse amongst characters which gives the impression of a competition to be heard. Only one character, Schach, sets his face against all this. The erroneousness of the view that Schach is purely a product of a vain society becomes clear when we look at his relationship with the dominant social tone of his peer group. Schach always opposes self-aggrandisement and off-hand reductiveness in speech. His barely concealed anger with Bülow in the two opening chapters has less to do with differences of opinion than with his hostility to the aggressive insolence of Bülow's breezily dismissive discussion of the Prussian state and Lutheranism. The tension between the two men threatens to get out of control in both of the first two chapters, and it is only because of the conciliatory presence of the Carayons that stronger words are not spoken. Schach's final meeting with Bülow is at the Prince's soirée, and again he cannot refrain from challenging his adversary's generalisations about the state of the Prussian army and his belittlement of Tsar Alexander. Schach is also manifestly perturbed by the cynical-humorous references to Victoire by Sander and the Prince, and speaks decently and gallantly in her defence (NFA, II, 319). Those who see in Schach only the anxious conformist forget the independence of spirit needed to defy the tone of conversation adopted and set by the Prince of Prussia. Speaking of music, Schach says "All salon virtuosity is hateful to me",[34] and this comment could also stand as a statement of his reservations about fluent but callous verbal display. That Schach is "different" from others is noted by one of the most adept practitioners of social discourse, Nostitz: "I do not have much time for him, but one thing is true, everything about him is genuine, even his stiff refinement, tedious and offensive as I find it. And in that way he is different from us. He is always himself".[35] The verdict of Alvensleben on Schach is the same: "At least he shows an honest face to the world,

---

33 "Erben eines alten Ruhmes auf dem Felde militärischer und gesellschaftlicher Ehre – denn wir haben nicht nur der Schlacht die Richtung, wir haben auch der Gesellschaft den *Ton* gegeben." Fontane: Schach von Wuthenow, NFA, II, 333.

34 "Alle Salonvirtuosität ist mir verhaßt." Fontane: Schach von Wuthenow, NFA, II, 282.

35 "Ich habe nicht viel für ihn übrig, aber das ist wahr, alles an ihm ist echt, auch seine steife Vornehmheit, so langweilig und so beleidigend ich sie finde. Und *darin* unterscheidet er sich von uns. Er ist immer er selbst." Fontane: Schach von Wuthenow, NFA, II, 289.

and not a mask".[36]

Schach's search for an alternative, "authentic" mode of existence explains, I think, the admiration for the Christian Knights Templar he expresses to Victoire at the end of the visit to Tempelhof in Chapter 4. Schach venerates the Templar movement because of its attempt to found an existence on autonomously determined terms. His desire for integrity makes him sympathise with the ultimately unsuccessful attempt of the Templars to live outside society. Victoire interprets Schach's comments as a determination never to marry, but this seems too simple a conclusion to draw from what he says (NFA, II, 386). The autonomy he wishes to retain flows from a sense of independent selfhood and a refusal to compromise himself in the hazardous process of creating and recreating identity through discursive interaction with others. Significantly, the attempt by the Templars to live outside society and structure their lives according to their own principles brought them into opposition with the established powers, and they were disbanded, a result which Schach describes as "the lot and fate of all phenomena which, even in their failings and errors, distance themselves from the mundane".[37] Schach reveres the Templars for the nobility of their ideals, and believes they were destroyed by the envy and self-interest of the dominant culture (NFA, II, 302). Both the Templars and their latterday admirer attempt to distance themselves from the turbulence and compromise of life in society, and both are brought low by society's insistence that its members collaborate in the unending interplay of language and identity, in which the individual must try not to lose, but at the same time can never be allowed to win. It is to the destruction of Schach by the speech community to which I shall now turn.

7. The Impossibility of Authenticity

The very first paragraph of the novel contains a reference to Schach by his friend and fellow officer Alvensleben, who takes the seat next to Frau von Carayon, but "while at the same time jokingly expressing his regret that the man most entitled to take up this position is absent".[38] This begins what is an unending series of comments and insinuations made by other characters about Schach, which continue unabated even after his death. Not only is he the absent subject of explicit character dissections in Chapters 3, 5, 15, 20 and 21, he is also the focus of a stream of passing judgement, ill-informed speculation and malignant suggestion. From the discussion in Sala Tarone about his relations with Frau von Carayon to the wager made by Ordonnanz Baarsch that he will not marry Victoire, Schach forms by far the most common topic of the speech of others in the novel. Even a reduction in the number of visits he makes to the

---

36 "Jedenfalls trägt er ein ehrliches Gesicht und keine Maske." Fontane: Schach von Wuthenow, NFA, II, 288.

37 "Das Los und Schicksal aller Erscheinungen, die sich, auch da noch wo sie fehlen und irren, dem Alltäglichen entziehn." Fontane: Schach von Wuthenow, NFA, II, 302.

38 "Unter gleichzeitigem scherzhaftem Bedauern darüber, daß gerade *der* fehle, dem dieser Platz in Wahrheit gebühre." Fontane: Schach von Wuthenow, NFA, II, 273.

Carayon salon is jestingly and insinuatingly remarked upon by Nostitz and Alvensleben (NFA, II, 332).

I have said that the subject matter of most salon and officer-class conversation tends to be less important than the opportunities of self-promotion for the speaker, but that Schach constitutes an exception to the general rule. The sustained concentration on him, as well as allowing speakers to define their own position against an eminent member of society, has supplementary motivation. Schach publicly distances himself from the practices of his speech community, and continually challenges its simplifications and categorisations. The community, in its turn, cannot tolerate either the implied criticism of its use of language or the attempt to live outside its constraints. Schach's seemingly stiff and haughty refusal to "join in" leads to a common response which, conscious or unconscious as it may be in the minds of individuals, serves to undermine the independence he has arrogated to himself. The distance Schach establishes between himself and others shows itself in his demeanour, and, as Victoire perceives, "it is this very formality which makes Bülow so hostile to him. Much, much more than any differences of opinion".[39] As Sander writes to Bülow, "He is far from being popular. People who try to be different never are".[40]

The malevolent attitude to Schach evident in the discussion in Sala Tarone is provoked by the recognition that, unlike his peers, he is always true to himself. This causes resentment, and so Sander, Nostitz, and Bülow, riled by his integrity, take a delight in denigrating him. A general desire to humiliate Schach has gathered momentum by the time the Gensdarmes Regiment is planning its parody of the controversial play *Die Weihe der Kraft*. Zieten's proposal that Schach play Luther in the parody is motivated by hatred for his nominee, who he knows will be discomfited by the suggestion (NFA, II, 334). Then Schach's well-considered letter arrives, in which he refuses to play any part in the plan but at the same time does not condemn it and promises discretion on the subject. Nostitz's response is ominous; he burns Schach's letter. Three chapters later, Schach is sent the caricatures which put him to flight from Berlin society to the rural idyll of his ancestral seat. Significantly, we are never told who drew the caricatures, and this uncertain authorship confirms the impression that they represent a general desire to extirpate Schach's discursive rebellion. The generalised envy and hatred behind this move are made clear by the narrative voice: "One of all too many people who envied and opposed him had seized the opportunity of giving free rein to his spiteful desires".[41]

Schach's suicide is generally understood as a consequence of his belief that he has made himself ridiculous in the eyes of his peers by being trapped into marriage with Victoire, and so forfeited his right to shine in the glittering social élite. In my reading,

---

39 "So ist es gerade dies Feierliche, was Bülow so sehr gegen ihn einnimmt. Viel, viel mehr als der Unterschied der Meinungen." Fontane: Schach von Wuthenow, NFA, II, 305.

40 "Er ist nichts weniger als beliebt. Wer den Aparten spielt, ist es nie." Fontane: Schach von Wuthenow, NFA, II, 347.

41 "Einer seiner Neider und Gegner, deren er nur zu viele hatte, hatte die Gelegenheit ergriffen, seinem boshaften Gelüst ein Genüge zu tun." Fontane: Schach von Wuthenow, NFA, II, 346.

Schach's estrangement from his social group begins well before the seduction of Victoire in Chapter 8, which is merely the catalyst giving others an opportunity to avenge his perceived snub to the norms of their speech community. Marriage is, in the militantly bachelor culture of the officer corps, the ultimate platitude, and Schach can now easily be fitted into an undignified stereotyped role. His discursive autonomy was always precarious, and depended on the fact that it was impossible to place him in any simple category. With the obligation to marry, his proud independence is shattered. The considerable degree of interior monologue and free indirect discourse which follows this blow shows Schach imagining a future for himself entirely dictated by clichés which have their source in the categorising voice of the "other". He sees his future existence as the filling out of predictable platitudes, and this is more than he can bear:

> I am hopelessly exposed to the mockery and wit of my comrades, and can picture myself living out in exemplary fashion the laughable prospect of a blissfully happy country marriage which blossoms like a violet in obscurity. I can see exactly what will happen; I shall resign my commission, take Wuthenow over again, till the soil, make improvements, grow rape or turnips, and devote myself to complete marital fidelity.[42]

Significant in such imaginings are Schach's fears of what others will say or imply. As he continues to paint the picture in his mind of a prosaic life as a country squire, he visualises himself in attendance during a visit by Prince Louis Ferdinand to a neighbouring town: "And he looks me over in my old-fashioned coat and asks me: 'how am I getting on?' And in doing so his face expresses only one thought: 'Oh God, what a mere three years can do to a person'".[43] Once he receives the caricatures, Schach knows for sure that there is no escape from brutally reductive discourses, and his increasing pessimism about a future with Victoire now takes the form of imagined remarks made about them in the light of her blighted looks:

> He could see himself in a carriage driving up to the Princes' residence to present Victoire von Carayon to them as his bride. And he could hear quite clearly how the old Princess Ferdinand whispered to her daughter, the lovely Radziwill: 'Est-elle riche?' 'Sans doute'. 'Ah, je comprends.'[44]

---

42 "Ich bin rettungslos dem Spott und Witz der Kameraden verfallen, und das Ridikül einer allerglücklichsten 'Landehe', die wie das Veilchen im Verborgenen blüht, liegt in einem wahren Musterexemplare vor mir. Ich sehe genau, wie's kommt: ich quittiere den Dienst, übernehme wieder Wuthenow, ackere, melioriere, ziehe Raps oder Rübsen, und befleißige mich einer allerehelichsten Treue." Fontane: Schach von Wuthenow, NFA, II, 344.

43 "Und er mustert mich und meinen altmodischen Rock und frägt mich: 'wie mir's gehe?' Und dabei drückt jede seiner Mienen aus: 'O Gott, was doch drei Jahre aus einem Menschen machen können.' " Fontane: Schach von Wuthenow, NFA, II, 344.

44 "Er sah sich in einem Kutschwagen bei den prinzlichen Herrschaften vorfahren, um ihnen Victoire von Carayon als seine Braut vorzustellen. Und er hörte deutlich, wie die alte Prinzeß Ferdinand ihrer Tochter, der schönen Radziwill, zuflüsterte: 'Est-elle riche?' 'Sans doute'. 'Ah, je comprends.'" Fontane: Schach von Wuthenow, NFA, II, 354.

Schach finds no meaningful refuge from the cruelty of society in Wuthenow, and the insects which plague him and prevent him from sleeping there symbolise his persecution by his peers. His defencelessness in the face of this persecution is mirrored in the narratorial structure of the novel. Once the caricatures are published, Schach makes no further contributions to conversation in direct speech, other than a few insignificant comments to his subordinates in Wuthenow, and, thereafter, the briefest of responses to the words of others. His dealings with Frau von Carayon, the King and Queen, and the wedding guests are all given in indirect speech. The unusualness of this indirect technique in Fontane makes us all the more conscious of its significance here. Whereas he had previously said a great deal in his own voice, now Schach is silenced literally by the narrator, and figuratively by the invisible but fatal destruction of his discursive autonomy by his social group.

In my view, then, the news of his engagement to Victoire and the ensuing caricatures are only a convenient means for suppressing Schach's anomalous status within his speech community, and this suppression would have occurred sooner or later anyway. Considerable steps towards rendering him ridiculous have already been taken by the insistent labelling of Schach as vain, an accusation which, though often repeated by critics, is, as I have said, not corroborated in any way by the hero's behaviour. If we look at the way these accusations of vanity arise, we can see how Schach is in a "no-win" situation. Because he refuses to put forward a convenient persona for the purposes of social intercourse, he is not less, but more susceptible to categorisation by others, and they fill the vacuum by ascribing to him, partly on the strength of his good looks and partly on the strength of his perceived haughtiness, an all-consuming vanity. Vanity, especially physical vanity and especially in a man, is one of the more laughable and humiliating of weaknesses. As Victoire ponders in her first letter: "It is said that men should not be vain, because vanity makes them ridiculous".[45] So, to label Schach as vain is to make him ridiculous, and to make him ridiculous is to punish his presumption in not playing his part in the conversational exchange. In this way, the very gesture of avoiding the categorising techniques of the speech community is nullified by being made the object of those selfsame techniques. The ability of dominant discourses to disarm and assimilate non-conforming discourses by integrating them into their own framework of reference silences Schach's language of integrity. That Schach himself is clearly aware of his vulnerability to the weapon of ridicule is revealed at several points in the text. This explains the paradox that he is both very susceptible to the judgement of others and always true to himself. The fact is that he *is* an independent spirit, but at the same time one who knows only too well that those he has opposed could, if he drops his guard, put him in categories from which it would be difficult to escape. This only serves to exacerbate the double bind in which he is caught: the attempt to maintain a dignified manner provokes the very response it seeks to avoid, namely derision. Not only is Schach labelled as vain, and thus ridiculous, but also his very fear of ridicule is seen as a form of vanity. In this way,

---

45 "Es ist ein Satz, daß Männer nicht eitel sein dürfen, weil Eitelkeit lächerlich mache." Fontane: Schach von Wuthenow, NFA, II, 306.

Schach, who chooses to avoid the social tone but who cannot avoid being the object of it, is well on the way to being subdued by it even before his engagement to Victoire plunges him irredeemably into absurdity.

8. Learning from Interpretants

To return now to Bülow's letter, we can see how its thesis of false honour characterising both Schach and his society fails to account for the way in which the hero is fundamentally alienated from his social group. It is not Schach who stands for the failings of society, but rather Bülow's letter itself, exemplifying as it does the simplistic generalising tendencies of discourse about the other in the struggle to give identity to the self. I have tried to question the explanation for Schach's tragedy provided by Bülow and echoed in the secondary literature, arguing for an interpretation which turns away from social and historical factors, and instead looks at the way this work analyses the nexus of language and self, the complex forming and unforming of identity through discursive strategies in an intersubjective environment. But what of Fontane himself? Does he explain how he means Schach to be understood and how Bülow is significant to the story? In agreeing with Bülow's interpretation critics can and do cite pronouncements made by Fontane in letters. The link made by Bülow between Schach's suicide and false honour seems to have been established in Fontane's mind well before work on the story began, as the following outline indicates:

> Contents: Vain characters who are trapped by mundane notions of honour find the mockery and laughter of society so intolerable that they choose death in preference to the fulfilling of a duty which they themselves are decent and intelligent enough to recognise as a duty, but which, because of their fear of being mocked, they are weak enough not to want to fulfil.[46]

Nearly two years later, when Fontane has written the sketch, he gives a very similar synopsis, and also more explicitly links Schach's suicide, as Bülow does in the text, with the degeneracy of the age, describing the events as "All a product of the age, its opinions, vanities and prejudices".[47] However, a comment written after Fontane had finished writing the story reveals a more differentiated picture. Fontane says he considered using a title which would have given the story a tendentious message, but then rejected the idea as too presumptuous: "If I took a different approach to this question, I could easily trumpet something about 'false honour' etc. in the title, but I cannot reconcile myself to such bravado".[48] Furthermore, as Hugo Aust has clearly

---

46 "Inhalt: Eitlen, auf die Ehre dieser Welt gestellten Naturen, ist der Spott und das Lachen der Gesellschaft derartig unerträglich, daß sie lieber den Tod wählen, als eine Pflicht erfüllen, die sie selber gut und klug genug sind als Pflicht zu erkennen, aber auch schwach genug sind aus Furcht vor Verspottung nicht erfüllen zu wollen." Fontane to Gustav Karpeles, 14 March 1880, HFA, IV, 3, 66.

47 "Alles ein Produkt der Zeit, ihrer Anschauungen, Eitelkeiten und Vorurtheile." Fontane to Julius Grosser, 31 January 1882, HFA, IV, 3, 176.

48 "Stünd ich anders zu dieser Frage, so könnt' ich leicht etwas von 'falscher Ehre' etc. in dem Titel zum Besten geben, aber zu solcher Bravade kann ich mich nicht verstehen." Fontane to Wilhelm Friedrich, 5 November 1882, HFA, IV, 3, 217.

shown, Fontane was critical of another novel using the same original anecdote, Willibald Alexis's *Ruhe ist die erste Bürgerpflicht*, for making excessively simplistic criticisms of the period and events.[49] So, even assuming that such evidence is admissible, the letters are too inconclusive to justify a reading based on Bülow's authority as an interpretant.

Having rejected Bülow's interpretation, we must see if we can gain any understanding of Schach from what other characters say about him. Frau von Carayon has many strong words to say about Schach's behaviour, but she later admits that her judgements, which were not made in full possession of the facts, were rash and unfairly recriminatory. We also have the perspectives on Schach of his fellow officers and their circle, whose inadequacy as commentators I have already examined. Then there is Victoire's friend Lisette von Perbandt, who enjoys only an epistolary existence, but who in her medium provides a page of her own diagnosis. If anything, she is more reductive than Bülow in her comments on Schach, proclaiming that "One is either a man of honour, or one is not".[50] In many ways the best interpretant is Victoire herself, especially in her letter with which the story closes (Chapter 21). She realises there can be no easy explanation for Schach's suicide, and provides a version of events which takes account of the general view but does not follow it. Victoire interprets Schach's admiration for the Templars and desire for an independent existence in the very specific sense of a wish to avoid marriage. She also thinks that the mockery to which he was subjected would not have lasted, and that Schach was aware of this; therefore she does not see this as a decisive factor in his decision to kill himself. On both counts her "reading" is different from mine. Her reconstruction of events is nevertheless ultimately more valuable than that of Bülow because of the manner in which she makes it. She is able to see that different interpretations are possible, and that no final word can be spoken on what has happened.

All this leaves readers to make what they can of the various acts of interpretation effected within the text they are reading. In Schor's terms, are the interpretants in *Schach von Wuthenow* a help or a hindrance to the interpreter? According to Schor, "the interpreter/interpretant relationship is not an easy one: the lure of narcissistic identification only makes it more difficult for the interpreter to keep his distance from the interpretant".[51] This, perhaps, is the "lure" which has led many readers to identify with Bülow's flawed understanding. However, the realisation that interpretants are as likely as not to lead us astray need not cause hermeneutic despair. After all, we can learn from interpretants' mistakes and fashion our reading accordingly. As Schor says: "Via the interpretant the author is trying to tell the interpreter something *about* interpretation and the interpreter would do well to listen and take note".[52] This is what

---

49 Hugo Aust: Theodor Fontane. "Verklärung", eine Untersuchung zum Ideengehalt seiner Werke. Bonn: Bouvier 1974, pp. 128-130.

50 "Man ist entweder ein Mann von Ehre, oder man ist es nicht." Fontane: Schach von Wuthenow, NFA, II, 324.

51 Schor: Fiction as Interpretation/Interpretation as Fiction, p. 169.

52 Schor: Fiction as Interpretation/Interpretation as Fiction, p. 170.

I have tried to do in identifying Schach as a victim of reductive social discourses and of his own futile opposition to them.

Yves Chevrel

Theodor Fontane and France : A Problematic Encounter

The broad title I have chosen for this paper, will not, I think, surprise any specialist reader of Theodor Fontane. It is obvious that one may talk of a problematic encounter between him and France, and this in at least two senses. The French origins of his family and of his wife are well known, as is the fact that he belonged to the Huguenot "colony" in Berlin. At the same time his German and Prussian patriotism is equally well known and indisputable: Fontane was always loyal to his king and emperor. He did not, however, fall into extreme nationalism, as some of his contemporaries did, and, from time to time during his life, he recalled his distant origins: "The older I get, the more the Frenchman in me comes out".[1]   There are numerous works about Fontane's French "roots". Likewise, the three very short stays he made on French soil (one of them was particularly difficult since he was a prisoner of war in November 1870), have been the subject of several studies.

If Fontane is a German writer, in the fully accepted sense of this term, one could nevertheless risk the hypothesis that his ancestors' country must have taken some interest in his work. But, as Marc Thuret showed recently at a colloquium on Fontane in Paris in October 1998, France remains to this day largely in ignorance of the work of a writer whose name is nevertheless not totally unknown to her.[2] Should one say, then, in a sentence: Fontane and France, an encounter so problematic that it could be expressed in the following manner: "Fontane and France, or How one heart does not find another"?[3]

From a strictly literary point of view, many explorations have also been attempted where it was possible. It would be fruitless, I think, to look in France for any trace of the influence of the novelist Fontane, who became known too late and was certainly the victim of the involuntary competition created by his junior and admirer, Thomas Mann. Conversely, studies of the influences on Fontane have shown that French literature was far from the centre of his preoccupations, whereas English literature or even some Scandinavian or Russian authors played a greater role in the development of his literary ideas and their implementation in his novels. One French writer, however, seems to emerge, namely Zola, and this has prompted critics who are often ideologically engaged (Hans-Heinrich Reuter among others) to attempt to show a certain progressivism on the part of Fontane. I have myself attempted to specify the ways in which one may appropriately speak of Fontane as a reader and a critic of Zola,

---

1   "Der Franzose, je älter ich werde, kommt immer mehr heraus". Fontane to Paul Schlenther, 21 December 1890, HFA, IV, 4, 79. Translations from the French are by the author. Translations from Fontane's writings are by Patricia Howe.

2   Marc Thuret: Fontane en France et en français. In: Theodor Fontane un promeneur dans le siècle, ed. by M. Thuret. Paris: Publications de l' Institut d' Allemand 1999, pp. 251-272.

3   "Fontane und Frankreich, oder Wie sich Herz zum Herzen nicht findet"...?

but by highlighting the technical rather than the ideological problems that Fontane raised in connection with Zola's work.[4] A third route has been opened in the last few years which consists in leaving aside all question of influence, all question of links between Fontane and France, and in relocating the writer in the context of European literature – this volume exemplifies this approach – and, in so doing, of trying to understand the place of an author who has been said to have restored to German literature its place in European literature. The names of Flaubert, Pérez Galdós, Ibsen, Turgenev are among those most often mentioned in this regard (it is rarer to see that of Stendhal). This route is one among those that need to be explored and the present volume should make it possible to demonstrate the European importance of Fontane: there are affinities of preoccupation which link him to many of his European contemporaries.

However, that is not the path that I will directly follow here. I would like to attempt to specify what may have been for Fontane the real circumstances of his knowledge of the French literary activity of his time, taking into account his education, his taste and, even more, the possibilities which were offered to him as a well rounded Berliner in the last third of the nineteenth century. There is a well known document which gives us an indication of Fontane's wide reading (*Belesenheit*), or rather, of the works which were in his eyes "The best books" and which answered the question "What should I read?"[5] We know that in response to two questionnaires published under those titles, in 1889 and 1894 respectively, he sent a list of seventy-one almost identical references (the few changes made from one list to the other are for present purposes unimportant). Twenty-one of these references, that is almost 30%, are foreign references, among which English authors are by far the most frequently represented. Besides three Russian authors and three Scandinavian authors, there are only two French ones: Eugène Sue, with two titles cited in German, *Die Geheimnisse von Paris, Der ewige Jude* (*The Secrets of Paris, The Eternal Jew*), and Emile Zola, with three titles, two of them cited in French, *L'Assommoir, La Faute de l'Abbé Mouret* (*Abbé Mouret's Transgression*) and one in German, *Die Eroberung von Plassans* (*The Conquest of Plassans*). Of course we do not know the circumstances which prevailed over Fontane's composition of this list, but this very limited choice may surprise us. It is likely that the mention of Eugène Sue, who was successful in Europe in the 1830s and 40s, called upon old memories, of the type linked to works read with passion during youth, but it also testifies to the persistence of the success of this author of social novels. Fontane was not the only one among the German authors questioned to have cited Eugène Sue! As for the choice of the three novels by Zola, this can be explained partly, perhaps, by the fact that, when Fontane really started reading Zola in June 1883, he did so following the reflections of Ludwig Pfau, published in an article in *Nord und Süd* in April 1880 and re-issued in a volume in 1888, which stated, in

---

4 Yves Chevrel: Fontane lecteur de Zola. In: Lectures, systèmes de lecture, ed. by J. Bessière. Université de Picardie, Paris: Presses universitaires de France 1984, pp. 53-69.

5 See: Fontane: Literarische Essays und Studien, NFA, XXI/2, 741-743 for the list of 1889 entitled "Was soll ich lesen?" and NFA, XXI/1, 497-499, for the list of 1894 "Die besten Bücher".

particular, that *The Conquest of Plassans* was among "the most outstanding" among the *Rougon-Macquart* novels already in print.[6] Should one talk of the authors absent from this list, which seem just as curious to us today? Norbert Bachleitner, in his reference work *Quellen zur Rezeption des englischen und französischen Romans in Deutschand und in Österreich im 19. Jahrhundert* reminds us judiciously that none of the thirty-five German authors who answered the questionnaire in 1889 mentioned either Stendhal or Flaubert.[7] The future author of *Effi Briest*, another novel on adultery, was thus far from being an exception in his indifference towards the author of *Madame Bovary*.

Fontane reacted to French literature like many of his fellow authors, depending, like them, on the information available to him. When he decided to read Zola, he did it in response to the article by Ludwig Pfau cited above, which he criticised, but he paid tribute to some of the choices made by a commentator whom at the same time he referred to condescendingly as "a trained aestheticist".[8] But Fontane, like all his contemporaries, could not avoid encountering the name of Zola whose works spread abundantly in Germany in translations as well as originals from 1880 on, and were widely commented upon in literary reviews and daily newspapers. The same was not true of Flaubert, who died precisely in 1880 and remained unrecognised, even virtually unknown in Germany at the end of the nineteenth century.

In one particular area, Fontane nevertheless was in greater direct contact than his fellow authors with "contemporary" French literature (the term has to be put in quotation marks). Indeed, he had to give accounts of the productions by the Französisches Theater (French Theatre) of Berlin from 1874 to 1879. The study of these articles, published in the *Vossische Zeitung*, offers an opportunity to discover what a Berlin public with knowledge of the French tongue could see, and also to compare the reactions of Fontane to those of Zola when they saw the same play. This study will be supplemented where appropriate by the study of other reviews by Fontane about the German versions of French plays performed on the stage of the Königliches Schauspielhaus (Royal Court Theatre). Fontane was the official drama critic of the "Vossin" from 1870 to 1889.

Fontane saw forty-nine French plays, or to be exact, forty-eight, since one of them was put on twice. The list of playwrights gives a sense of the idea that a Berlin spectator who understood French could gain of the French theatre. As one should expect, Victorien Sardou came at the top of the list with seven productions (it is one of his plays, *Les Vieux Garçons* (The Old Boys) which was staged twice for the re-opening on 1st January 1874 and in 1879) followed by Théodore Barrière (six plays),

---

6 "die vorzüglichsten". See: Fontane to Emilie Fontane, 13 April 1880, in Emilie und Theodor Fontane: Der Ehebriefwechsel 1873-1898, ed. by Gotthard Erler. Grosse Brandenburger Ausgabe, p. 215.

7 Norbert Bachleitner: Quellen zur Rezeption des englischen und französischen Romans in Deutschand und in Österreich in 19. Jahrhundert. Tübingen: Niemeyer, 1990, p. xv.

8 "geschulter Aesthetiker", Fontane to Emilie Fontane, 13 April 1880, in Emilie und Theodor Fontane: Der Ehebriefwechsel 1873-1898, p. 215.

Émile Augier, Alexandre Dumas *fils* and Scribe (four plays each), Meilhac and Halévy (three plays). There was no production of plays from the classical repertory and the only play which to my mind still belongs to today's repertory is *Un Caprice* (A caprice) by Alfred de Musset. In addition, most of the plays were revivals of works staged in France long before 1870 except for two: *L'Étrangère*, (The Stranger) by Alexandre Dumas *fils*, first produced in Paris in February 1876 and performed in Berlin in March 1879, and *Dora*, by Victorien Sardou, first produced in Paris in January 1877 and performed at the French Theatre in April 1879. That is why it is necessary to put the adjective "contemporary" in quotation marks.

Fontane obviously was aware of this discrepancy. As a conscientious drama critic, he knew that the French troupes invited offered proven successes and plays that had often already been staged in German, which made even more sense since the audiences of the French Theatre did not have a perfect knowledge of the language. The first review he wrote for the *Vossische Zeitung* on 3 January 1874, for the re-opening of the French Theatre stated the facts clearly. Fontane considered it unnecessary to summarise the plot of *Les Vieux Garçons*: "We will not linger over the content of the play, assuming it to be well known"; he added with his usual sense of humour: "Modern people have to know everything, and so 'as is well known' do know everything, most of all what they don't know".[9] Fontane preferred to address himself to the performance of the relatively numerous actors – the play by Sardou has fourteen characters – and to derive a few conclusions from a comparison with the acting of German actors from the Königliches Schauspielhaus. While finding that the comparison was far from being to the detriment of the latter (the more so because the French troupe was not first rate), Fontane judged that elegance ("Vornehmheit") was the quality which distinguished French actresses, and that an overall sense of composition in the scenes (as with the salon scene in the second act) characterised the French production. In addition Fontane stated:

> Admittedly our people [the German actors] can learn from them [the French actors] because such a considerable proportion of everything performed on any stage is not only French in origin, but also, without dissimulation or doubt, deliberately aims to set French figures before us.[10]

To those who thought that the coming of the French troupe was, at the least, premature – the war had only been over for three years – Fontane replied:

> Premature? If we had wanted to wait until the French changed their attitude to us, saw us as equals or even perhaps as superior, we would be waiting a long time. They will *not change*; that's what makes them French, that's to say, a charming, eminently interesting nation, equipped with

---

9 "Bei dem Inhalt des Stückes verweilen wir nicht, denselben als bekannt voraussetzend"; "Der moderne Mensch muß alles wissen und weiß deshalb 'bekanntlich' auch alles, am meisten was, was er nicht weiß." Fontane: Causerien über Theater, NFA, XXII/3, 121.

10 "Zwar können die unsrigen [= die deutschen Schauspieler] deshalb von ihnen [= den französichen] lernen, weil ein so erheblicher Bruchteil alles dessen, was unsere Bühne bringt, nicht nur französischen Ursprungs ist, sondern auch, unverhohlen und unzweifelhaft, französiche Gestalten vor uns hinstellen will". Fontane: Causerien über Theater, NFA, XXII/3, 124.

every possible merit, but also with every possible weakness. To the last of these belongs, as all the world knows, the fact that they are very vain and believe themselves to be the best, come what may. Let us let them believe it; we are in the fortunate position of being able to do so. Able to do so because we are calm and rational enough to accept *real* merits as such and to smile at imaginary or *trivial* ones – to which, in the end, all these comedies and their performances belong.[11]

This long quotation which ends the article could in fact almost summarise the way Fontane positioned himself as a critic of the French theatre.

The productions seen by Fontane moved him, indeed, very often to compare the practices and habits of both countries and further, to sketch the outlines of an "ethnopsychology" sometimes without surprise. Thus in 1877 at the end of a fairly critical review of *Nos intimes* (Our nearest and dearest), another play by Sardou, first performed in France in 1861, he thanked the director Emil Neumann "for creating that measure of stimulation and entertainment that is inseparable from French theatrical performance".[12] As this sentence implies, it appears clear that for Fontane, French contemporary theatre as he knew it did not in general go beyond providing simple amusement without any import. He considered that this theatre was marked by comic, even farcical aspects, not only because of the texts of the plays, but also because of the style of the actors, who accentuated or privileged the comic aspects of certain roles, going far beyond what a German public was accustomed to:

The French, as far as my knowledge of this subject extends, emphasise the comic, I may even say, the farcical aspects more than suits our German taste, or perhaps to be more precise, more than seems acceptable. For our aesthetic principles judge a degree more strictly than our aesthetic nerves.[13]

Did the incidental comment "as far as my knowledge extends" betray real doubts on Fontane's part, or was it a kind of precaution against those who might reproach him for understanding the French too well? Whichever may be the case, Fontane rarely failed to explain his position when he juxtaposed the traditions of both countries. A particular

---

11 "Verfrüht? Wollten wir warten, bis die Franzosen ihre innerliche Stellung zu uns änderten, uns als ebenbürtig oder wohl gar als überlegen ansähen, so würden wir lange warten. Sie werden sich *nicht ändern*; dafür sind sie eben Franzosen, d. h. eine liebenswürdige, eminent interessante, mit allen möglichen Vorzügen, aber auch mit allen möglichen Schwächen ausgerüstete Nation. Zu diesen letzteren gehört, weltbekanntermaßen, daß sie sehr eitel sind und sich, nach wie vor, für die ersten halten. Lassen wir ihnen das; wir sind in der glücklichen Lage, es zu können. Es zu können, weil wir Ruhe und Besonnenheit genug haben, *wirkliche* Vorzüge als solche gelten zu lassen, und eingebildete oder *gleichgültige* – zu denen doch zuletzt alle diese 'Comedies' und ihre Vorstellungen gehören – zu belächeln." Fontane: Causerien über Theater, NFA, XXII/3, 125.
12 "jenes Maß von Anregung und Unterhaltung zu verschaffen, das nun mal von französischen Theatervorstellungen unzertrennlich ist." Fontane: Causerien über Theater, NFA, XXII/3, 134.
13 "Die Franzosen, soweit meine Kenntnis auf diesem Gebiete reicht, betonen das Komische, ja ich muß sagen, das Possenhafte mehr, als unserem deutschen Geschmack zusagt oder richtiger vielleicht zulässig erscheint. Denn unsere Geschmacksprinzipien sitzen um einen Grade strenger zu Gericht als unsere Geschmacksnerven." Fontane: Causerien über Theater, NFA, XXII/3, 178.

occasion for this was given to him by an insignificant play *Cendrillon* (Cinderella) (1859) by Théodore Barrière, of which a German version, *Aschenbrödel*, had been staged previously. Fontane found the play "graceful", but was surprised by what he called the "cult of my mother", incomprehensible to a German public and therefore in need of explanation:

> In France, according to everything that I have not just read in books, but also been assured of by people who know about the country and its people, it happens, or at least it can happen that a daughter who has been neglected for years in the most hurtful way is transported to a seventh heaven just because she is addressed once as "my daughter" in affectionate tones: but a *German* girl's heart – as far as I know anything about them, is not to be won back so quickly and with so little effort. At least not by mothers…

and he concludes: "These are national differences. And in these matters I feel like a German."[14]

One of the interesting aspects of the study of this review is that it brings to light quite clearly the elements of Fontane's aesthetics which made his encounter with French contemporary literature really problematic. The name of Honoré de Balzac, rarely met in Fontane's writing, appeared on the occasion of the staging of *Mercadet ou le Faiseur*, (Mercadet or the Swindler) a play more or less finished, published after its author's death and adapted by Dennery. Fontane summarised the plot and regretted the outcome and specifically the fact:

> that the crooked hero of the play, who undermines the happiness of others, in order to continue his criminal way of life undisturbed, instead of getting the punishment he deserves, in the end attaining riches and honour, proves once again how easily and lightly the French take poetic justice.[15]

What is important here, is the expression "poetic justice". Fontane knew that in real society crooks sometimes triumphed but he believed that literature should not have to paint life as it was. A clear example of an aesthetic point of view rather than a moralistic one is provided by his review of *Froufrou*.

The play by Meilhac and Halévy was first produced in Paris on 30 October 1869 with a success which soon went beyond French frontiers. It showed a lively and

---

14 "anmutig";"ma mère-Cultus"; "In Frankreich, nach allem, was ich nicht bloß in Büchern gelesen, sondern auch von Land- und Leute-Kundigen vielfach versichern gehört habe, kommt es vor, oder *kann* es wenigstens vorkommen, daß eine jahrelang in kränkendster Weise zurückgesetzte Tochter durch eine bloßes zärtlich anklingendes 'ma fille' in einen Himmel voll Seligkeit versetzt wird: ein *deutsches* Mädchenherz aber, soweit ich sie kennengelernt habe, ist so schnell und unter so wenig Einsatz nicht zurückzuerobern. Wenigstens nicht durch Mütter"; "Das sind so nationale Unterschiede. Und in diesen Dingen empfind' ich deutsch". Fontane: *Causerien über Theater, NFA*, XXII/3, 194.

15 "daß [...] der schwindelhafte Held des Stückes, der das Glück anderer untergräbt, um ungestört seine verbrecherische Lebensweise fortzusetzen, anstatt der verwirkten Strafe, schließlich noch zu Geld und Ehre kommt, ist ein neuer Beweis, wie leicht es die Franzosen mit der poetischen Gerechtigkeit nehmen". Fontane: *Causerien über Theater, NFA*, XXII/3, 128.

flirtatious young girl named Froufrou who marries the man she loves and who loves her, becomes a mother, but runs away with her lover to come back to die with her husband. The play was staged all over Europe: Emilie Fontane saw it in London in May 1870, and called "a French tragedy", when the authors had chosen to present it as a "comedy".[16] After seeing the play for himself on 18 February 1877, Fontane began his review by comparing it to *Les Filles de marbre* (The marble Girls) by Théodore Barrière and Lambert Thiboust. This work, equally famous in its time and which dates from 1853 is basically only known today through the allusion made to it by Proust in *Un amour de Swann*. Commenting upon the similarity of the two plots – "Both are Parisian pictures of *mores*, in both unfaithfulness breaks a faithful heart",[17] Fontane contrasts the two plays. On one hand "*Les filles de marbre* are a reality but not a play; the heroine is not a heroine, because she doesn't inspire interest, to the extent that even her sacrifice strikes us as sad rather than tragic."[18] On the other hand "a play that moves without actually being a sentimental play. What we have here [in *Froufrou*] is real life",[19] considering the poetic means used by the authors, our critic particularly appreciated the astuteness they used:

> A particularly fine aspect of the play is the fact that Froufrou returns to her husband's home after her seducer has fallen in a duel, not so much from love but from a desire for reconciliation and from that kind of aesthetic need that is often so peculiar to gentle natures. [20]

The notion of reconciliation because of aesthetic necessity, underlined by Fontane himself is at the core of his poetics.

This explains why it is not surprising that he knew to distance himself from the successful playwrights who dominated the European stages at the time and, in the first place, the trio "Audusar", that is Augier – Dumas *fils* – Sardou. The commentaries he made concerning them are even more valuable as they can be compared in some cases to the ones made by Émile Zola.

Fontane had no difficulty in recognising that plays by Sardou:

---

16 "französisches Trauerspiel "; see: Emilie Fontane to Fontane, 18 May 1870, in: Emilie und Theodor Fontane: Der Ehebriefwechsel 1857-1871, p. 483.

17 "Beide sind Pariser Sittenbilder, in beiden bricht Untreue ein treues Herz." Fontane: Causerien über Theater, NFA, XXII/3, 150.

18 "*Les filles de marbre* sind eine Realität, aber kein Stück ; die Heldin ist keine Heldin, weil sie uns kein Interesse einflößt, so wenig, daß selbst ihr Opfer uns mehr traurig als tragisch berührt". Fontane: Causerien über Theater, NFA, XXII/3, 150.

19 "[ein] Stück, [das] rührt, ohne ein eigentliches Rührstück zu sein [...] Was sich hier [= in *Frou-frou*] gibt, ist wirkliches Leben." Fontane: Causerien über Theater, NFA, XXII/3, 150.

20 "Ein besonders feiner Zug des Stückes ist der, daß Froufrou, nachdem ihr Entführer im Duell gefallen ist, weniger aus Liebe als aus Versöhnungshang und jenem *ästhetischen Bedürfnis*, wie es weichen Naturen so oft eigen ist, in das Haus ihres Gatten zurückkehrt." Fontane: Causerien über Theater, NFA, XXII/3, 151.

have a strong family resemblance. [...] It is all praxis, recipe, routine, which is not meant to be disparaging, nor in the least to deny that what is being served up is a fine looking, tasty lobster in aspic. [...] This whole way of proceeding smacks more of craft than of art.[21]

These lines can be found in the *Vossische Zeitung* dated 26 January 1878. A few weeks later, on 11 March 1878, Zola attacked Sardou in a famous article where he used four times as a leitmotiv the sentence "But, he [= Sardou] does not have our literary esteem": the global condemnation is of the same calibre.[22] Fontane and Zola also converged in their technical judgement of the plays by Sardou. Zola: "There are always two very distinctive parts in this author's works, what I would call the frame and what I would call the plot. M. Sardou looks for the frame within current events".[23] As for the plot:

as with his preceding comedies, we have had two acts of exposition, very detailed, followed by two acts of action, very skilfully framed and ending with an outcome cobbled together in any sort of fashion in order to let the public go away with a cheerful impression.[24]

Fontane: "Sardou invents new backgrounds and gives the whole thing and its individual parts a new framework. But what is put into this framework is always the same thing."[25]

Fontane saw four plays by Émile Augier, for whom he has more esteem than for Sardou; that is also the case with Zola. One of them, *Paul Forestier*, comedy in four acts in verse, staged in Paris in January 1868 resulted in two reviews by Zola, one just after the opening night and the other in November 1876; Fontane's review is dated January 1877. Both critics agree in their appreciation of the grand scene at the end of the third act where the hero, who came to insult the woman he loved and whom he knew to be unfaithful, ends up trying to reconquer her rather brutally. But while Zola quite liked what he called "la chute de Léa" (the fall of Leah), who betrayed her lover because of hurt vanity, Fontane once again invokes German taste:

---

21 "haben eine starke Familienähnlichkeit. [...] Es is alles Praxis, Rezept, Routine, womit nichts Despektierliches gesagt, am wenigsten aber in Abrede gestellt sein soll, daß schließlich ein gut aussehender und gut schmeckender Hummeraspik aufgetragen wird. [...] Diese ganze Art zu verfahren erinnert mehr an Kunsthandwerk als an Kunst." Fontane: Causerien über Theat*er*, NFA, XXII/3, 171.

22 "Mais il [=Sardou] n'a pas notre estime littéraire." Émile Zola: Œuvres complètes, Paris: Cercle du livre précieux 1968, XI, pp. 679-683.

23 "Il y a toujours deux parties très distinctes dans une oeuvre de cet auteur dramatique, ce que j'appellerai le cadre et ce que j'appellerai l'action. M. Sardou cherche le cadre dans l'actualité;" Zola: Œuvres complètes, XI, p. 670.

24 "comme dans les précédentes comédies, nous avons eu deux actes d'exposition, longuement détaillés, suivis de deux actes d'action, très ingénieusement charpentés, et terminés par un acte de dénouement, baclé d'une façon quelconque, mais de manière à laisser partir le public sous une impression gaie." Zola: Œuvres complètes, XI, p. 675.

25 "[Sardou] erfindet neue Hintergründe und gibt dem Ganzen wie dem Einzelnen eine neue Fassung. Das aber, was in diese Fassung hineingestellt wird, ist immer dasselbe." Fontane: Causerien über Theater, NFA, XXII/3, 171.

It rather goes against German taste to see a figure who lets herself be seduced into infidelity by anger or offended vanity being treated as the centre of dramatic interest: we know that things like that happen in real life but we are better able to accept it in reality than in art.[26]

A last example of this encounter from a distance between Fontane and Zola is provided by *L'Étrangère*. The play by Dumas *fils* was first produced at the Comédie Française in January 1876. Zola devoted a long exposition to it in his compilation *Nos auteurs dramatiques* (Our dramatic authors) published in 1881 (but the analysis of this play was certainly written shortly after the first performance), and Fontane saw the play in Berlin in March 1879. Both critics agreed on more than one point concerning the spectacular aspects and the scenes which strive for effect, such as the explanation scene in the fourth act between the Duchess of Septmonts and her husband, whom she treats with great scorn. Both also found the scene in the third act very feeble and unbelievable, where Mrs Clarkson, "L'Étrangère", in a long monologue describes her past as a "vierge du mal" (evil virgin) to the Duchess of Septmonts. When she reaches the end of this explanation, Fontane cites (in German) the response of the Duchess, "There is no point in asking what I gain from the honour of being told all this", and comments: "And here the beautiful duchess spoke just as I felt. I don't know either what I'm supposed to make of confessions of this kind."[27] For Zola Mrs Clarkson was simply "a vixen in a long red cloth dress which gives the impression in the play of being a mannequin stuck on a pole".[28]

But Zola and Fontane diverged at least about one point, namely about the outcome of the play. The death of the duke killed in a duel by the husband of "l'Étrangère" brings no regrets, even for those close to him. Zola declared this to be "original and true [...] No one up to this date had dared to set in the theatre this situation of such a particular philosophical sense, [...] Laughter greeting death, that is what seduced me in the outcome of *L'Étrangère*.[29] Fontane on the contrary could only be shocked and declared:

The duke was not popular, but all the same "blood is a very special kind of juice", and I cannot remember ever having seen a whole congregation of people most closely affected receiving the

---

26 "Dem deutschen Geschmack ist es einigermaßen widerstrebend, eine Gestalt, die sich aus Zorn oder gekränkter Eitelkeit zur Untreue hinreissen läßt, als Mittelpunkt des dramatischen Interesses behandelt zu sehn; wir wissen, daß dergleichen im Leben vorkommt, können uns aber in der Wirklichkeit eher damit versöhnen als in der Kunst." Fontane: Causerien über Theater, NFA, XXII/3, 143-144.

27 "Es erübrigt nur noch zu hören, was mir die Ehre dieser Mitteilungen verschafft"; "Und hier hat mir die schöne Herzogin ganz aus der Seele gesprochen. Ich weiß auch nicht, was ich mit derartigen Bekenntnissen anfangen soll." Fontane: Causerien über Theater, NFA, XXII/3, 210.

28 "une grande diablesse à la longue robe de drap rouge, qui fait dans la pièce juste l'effet d'un mannequin planté au bout d'une perche" Zola: Œuvres complètes, XI, p. 647f.

29 "déclare cela original et vrai [...] Personne jusqu'à présent n'avait osé mettre au théâtre cette situation d'un sens philosophique si curieux [...] Le rire saluant la mort, voilà ce qui m'a séduit dans le dénouement de *l'Étrangère* ". Zola: Œuvres complètes, XI, p. 646.

news of a death with such *sangfroid*. Even in unhappy marriages it is usual to be rather shaken at such moments. [30]

In the end, Zola who said from the start that he "did not appreciate the talent of Mr Alexandre Dumas" condemned the play:

> The work, hybrid and out of place, ends up thanks to its author's technique working more or less, and pleases the coarse public which is not very choosy about the question of its literary delights. But the work remains a monster which irritates all those minds looking for what is true beyond the superficial qualities.[31]

while Fontane, with greater subtlety but as much scepticism made of this play a typical example of modern French drama "no question of composition or artistic direction" and stated that it would not survive beyond its present glory: "All this won't live for a generation, and least of all if we sink further and further into *décadent* sensationalism and that over-exaggerated realism which isn't even what it pretends to be."[32]

This journey among the thirty-eight critical reviews that Fontane devoted to French plays includes no surprises in the end. As a theatre lover, Fontane remained marked by the tradition inherited from Molière, whom he considered to be the greatest French comic dramatist, and whose work was staged at the Königliches Schauspielhaus. Thus he may have been all the more sensitive to the artificial manners of the modern French dramatists, for whom Sardou was a model, and he thought that their success was only temporary, and due to their dramatic technique and their sense of the theatrical. Although, curiously, he assigned to Alexandre Dumas *père*, at least to one of his plays, now totally forgotten, *Mademoiselle de Belle-Isle*, premièred in 1839 in Paris, an importance that is surprising:

> How much higher Dumas the father stands than his son! The younger man may be superior in artistry and intentions to the older one, but the charmingly inspired nature of the latter does not

---

30 "Der Herzog war nicht beliebt; mais enfin 'Blut ist ein ganz besonderer Saft', und ich kann mich nicht entsinnen, eine ganze Versammlung nächstbeteiligter Menschen bei dem Eintreffen einer Todesnachricht in solchem Sangfroid gesehen zu haben. Auch in unglücklichen Ehen ist es herkömmlich in solchen Momenten einigermaßen erschüttert zu sein." Fontane: Causerien über Theater, NFA, XXII/3, 212.

31 "n'aime guère le talent de M. Alexandre Dumas"; "L'oeuvre, bâtarde et mal venue, finit, grâce à la science acquise de l'auteur, par marcher à peu près droit et contente le gros public, peu délicat sur la question de ses jouissances littéraires. Seulement l'oeuvre reste un monstre et irrite tous les esprits qui cherchent le vrai au-delà des qualités de surface." Zola: Œuvres complètes, XI, p. 649.

32 "Von Komposition oder künstlericher Tendenz keine Rede"; "All das lebt kein Menschenalter, und am wenigsten dann, wenn wir immer tiefer in die *Décadence* des Sensationellen und jenes dreimal betonten Realismus hineingeraten, der zuletzt nicht das einmal ist, wofür er sich selber ausgibt." Fontane: Causerien über Theater, NFA, XXII/3, 209.

only cancel out his failings, but produces a surplus that could enrich another dozen people as well.[33]

Further on Fontane sketched a confrontation between the old dramatic school, that of Dumas *père* and of Scribe, and the new:

> In the former [= in the old school], in spite of a wealth of impossibilities, everything is true, in the latter [= in the new school], in spite of a wealth of the sharpest observations, everything is false. Dumas the elder and Scribe, even in their weaker works still enlivening, Dumas the younger and Sardou, even in their best things still deadening.[34]

But this brutal and basic opposition is based on an admission that reminds us that Fontane, even in the theatre, kept a sense of nostalgia for a France which had ceased to exist, namely the one in place prior to the Revolution, the France of the *Ancien Régime*:

> The thing that still gives the elder Dumas's plays their particular charm in my eyes is the specifically old French stamp that they bear. My soul for God, my arm for the king, my heart for women. Everywhere his chivalrous attitude, which is never denied even in the most tricky situations and makes morality fall silent in embarrassment because it begins to see itself as mere prudishness.[35]

During one of his short trips to France, Fontane went to pay his respects at the tomb of Dumas *père* …

Fontane realised that the renewal of the theatre did not reside in the works on which he had to comment; but was he convinced that the French theatre was susceptible to self-renewal? In the novel *Graf Petöfy* (Count Petöfy), published in 1884, he put the following sentence into the mouth of the count: the French people is an "imaginative people that accepts the appearance of things entirely as their essence, a people that

---

33 "Wie hoch steht doch Dumas der Vater über Dumas dem Sohn! An Kunst, an Wissen, an Intentionen mag der junge dem alten überlegen sein, aber die liebenswürdig-geniale Natur des letztern gleicht seine Mängel nicht nur aus, sondern ergibt noch einen Überschuß, der nicht nur den Sohn sondern auch noch ein halbes Dutzend andre reich machen könnte." Fontane: Causerien über Theater, NFA, XXII/3, 206.

34 "In jener [= in der alten Schule], trotz einer Fülle von Unmöglichkeiten, alles wahr, in dieser [= in der neuen Schule], trotz einer Fülle der schärfsten Beobachtungen, alles unwahr. Der ältere Dumas und Scribe auch in ihren schwachen Sachen immer noch erquicklich, der jüngere Dumas und Sardou auch in ihren besten Sachen immer noch unerquicklich." Fontane: Causerien über Theater, NFA, XXII/3, 208.

35 "Was diesen Stücken des älteren Dumas in meinen Augen einen noch ganz besonderen Reiz leiht, ist der spezifisch-altfranzösische Stempel, den sie tragen. Meine Seele Gott, meinen Arm dem König, mein Herz den Frauen! Überall seine chevalereske Gesinnung, die sich auch in den verfänglichsten Situationen nicht verleugnet und die Sittlichkeit verlegen schweigen macht, weil sie sich selbst für bloße Prüderie zu halten beginnt." Fontane: Causerien über Theater, NFA, XXII/3, 207.

performs and puts on display, in a word: a theatrical people";[36] a little later, he refuted all comparison with the Viennese who were known to distinguish reality from fiction, while for a French audience:

> "just as its plays determine its life, so life determines its plays. Each is a continuation and consequence of the other and the final result is that we naturally have a life saturated with theatre and a theatre saturated with life. Hence Realism!" [37]

This term "Realism", encountered before, may be one among those contributing to the difficulties of comprehension between Fontane and France. It sends us back to a larger debate about those "deutsche Sonderwege" ("special German paths") of the nine-teenth century which for a long period led German literature, if not on "Holzwege" ("the wrong tracks"), at least on paths slightly different from the ones followed by other European literatures and in particular by the French. Fontane, as of 1853, in a famous essay insisted on the fact that "the thing that characterises our time on every side is its realism".[38] Later, in an article about the Max Kretzer's novel *Drei Weiber*, (Three Women) he condemned "the latest effort by this dreadful person who seems to have been employed to discredit Flaubert, Zola and true realism."[39] Should we then conclude that the two French authors – who were quoted by Count Petöfy as examples of what could become, in the novel, a realistic literature pushed to extremes – represented authentic realism as conceived by Fontane? It is rather unfortunate that Fontane, whose one character, l'Hermite, in *Quitt*, seems to classify *Madame Bovary* among licentious reading that cannot be seriously offered to young ladies (the same thing goes for *Nana*, by the way), did not have the opportunity to really know the works of Flaubert.

Fontane perceived that the truly modern French literature, the literature that was breaking away from, or at least showing an evolution compared to the preceding period, was expressed in novels and not in the theatre. Zola stated in March 1873, that *Andréa* (by Sardou) was "a Parisian item, far too illuminated to be exported".[40] Fontane could have accepted this judgement. He was also seduced by Zola's novels

---

36 "'ist ein Phantasievolk, dem der Schein der Dinge vollständig das Wesen der Dinge bedeutet, ein Vorstellungs- und Schaustellungsvolk, mit einem Wort: ein Theatervolk.'" Fontane: Graf Petöfy, NFA, II, 50.

37 "wie die Stücke sein Leben bestimmen, so bestimmt das Leben seine Stücke. Jedes ist Fortsetzung und Konsequenz des andern, und als letztes Resultat haben wir dann auch selbstverständlich ein mit Theater gesättiges Leben und ein mit Leben gesättiges Theater. Also Realismus!" Fontane: Graf Petöfy, NFA, II, 50.

38 "Was unsere Zeit nach allen Seiten hin charakterisirt, das ist ihr Realismus." Fontane: Unsere lyrische und epische Poesie, Literarische Essays und Studien, NFA, XXI/1, 7.

39 "die neueste Leistung dieses furchtbaren Menschen, der angestellt scheint, um Flaubert, Zola und den echten Realismus zu diskreditieren." Fontane: Max Kretzer: Drei Weiber, Literarische Essays und Studien, NFA, XXI/2, 269.

40 "un article de Paris, trop enluminé pour les besoins de l'exportation." Zola: Œuvres complètes, X, p.1088.

whose audacity nevertheless alarmed him; but his reservations about the author of the *Rougon-Macquart* probably derived from a poetic rather than a moralistic stance: the triad *Verklärung–Versöhnung–Humor* (transfiguration–reconciliation–humour*)*, which was the basis of his poetics, seemed to him totally absent from the works of Zola and other contemporary French authors, including those playwrights whom he considered to be show-offs rather than artists.

Fontane, as a novelist was probably less audacious than Flaubert and Zola; Fontane as a drama critic aspired to a theatre which would go beyond well-staged entertainment. Therein may have lain his difficulties in understanding French contemporary literature; there too, perhaps, lie the difficulties encountered by his novels in France. France and Fontane: *Unwiederbringlich* – irretrievable – or simply *Irrungen, Wirrungen* – delusions, confusions?

Hans Ester

Problems of translation, arising from the context of Fontane's works

The late André Lefevere who wrote a great number of wonderfully clear studies on
questions arising from the problems of translation, states in his book *Translating
Poetry* (1975) that translations can only be judged by people who have no need for
them:

> The unilingual reader, who does not have the ability to judge, has to be "satisfied" with whatever
> is available, whether it is up to standard or not. Rather than indulge in relativism, the writer of
> studies on translation should therefore be at great pains to establish what a good translation is,
> and, in so doing, give guidance to the unilingual reader.[1]

I, too, regard "guidance" as a keyword. Before a translator starts his or her work, some
very important decisions have to be taken. One of the most elementary decisions
concerns the question: should a translation read as if contemporary with the original?
Or, should a translation read as if contemporary with the translator? Studies on
translation tend to concentrate on the linguistic aspects of literature and therefore on
the linguistic aspects of the translation process. If that happens, the influence of
context on both source and target text will be neglected. This fact became very clear to
me recently, when I studied the translation of Paul Celan's *Von Schwelle zu Schwelle*
(From Threshold to Threshold) into Dutch. It was quite distressing to observe that this
most impressive poetry, balancing on the edge of silence, had lost much of its meaning
in Dutch. In fact, I came to the conclusion that Celan's poetry should not be translated.
Let the Dutch rather learn German properly.

We can conclude that a translator should carefully study the style of language of the
source text in order to represent its elementary characteristics in the target text. The
other aspect is no less important. I therefore return to the idea of the influence of the
context on both the source and target text. Of course, attention should be devoted to
the linguistic problems, but not exclusively. If language expresses that which is
essential for a specific civilisation, then the person who reads the source text is
informed about the history of that civilisation and the reader of the target text should
be put in a position to share that experience.

Speaking about the context of a work of literature, a context that should be
transferred from one language to another, I must define this more clearly. Or, in other
words, I must concentrate on certain aspects, such as time, place and the cultural
traditions. Lefevere mentions the problems that have to do with context and the effort
of contextualisation or the choice of ignoring the context:

> Translators adopt a number of attitudes towards elements of the source text which are very

---

1 André Lefevere: Translating Poetry. Seven Strategies and a Blueprint. Amsterdam: Assen, 1975,
   p. 3.

closely linked to the time, place and tradition in which that source text was written, and have, therefore, become difficult, if not impossible, to understand and appreciate fully in a different time, place and tradition.[2]

In his book *Translating literature: the German tradition. From Luther to Rosenzweig* André Lefevere deals with translation theories in German, starting with Luther and ending with Franz Rosenzweig.[3] Luther belongs to those who established the tradition, whereas Rosenzweig is one of the critics of tradition. To the first category belongs Friedrich Schleiermacher, who is still known as one of the founders of the "science of translation", of *Übersetzungswissenschaft*. The crucial text written by Schleiermacher is "On the different methods of translating". Schleiermacher begins his article with a fundamental observation on the nature of comprehension in general:

> The fact that speech is translated from one language into another confronts us everywhere, under a wide variety of guises. On the one hand this allows people to establish contact who were originally as far apart from each other as the length of the earth's diameter; products of another language that has been dead for many centuries may be incorporated into a language. On the other hand we do not even have to go outside the domain of one language to encounter the same phenomenon. For not only are the dialects spoken by different tribes belonging to the same nation, and the different stages of the same language or dialect in different centuries, different languages in the strict sense of the word, not infrequently requiring a complete translation between them; moreover even contemporaries who are not separated by dialects, but merely belong to different classes which are not often linked through social intercourse and are far apart in education, often can understand each other only by means of a similar mediation.[4]

The choices the translator must make are well described by Schleiermacher. These choices are brought back to one main choice: should a translator bring together the author (this word is part of the discourse Schleiermacher uses) of a product of art and the reader of that product, the one who speaks his own language and not the language of the author, should the translator bring these two together in such way that there is an immediate contact, comparable to that of the author and the original reader? Or, to quote Schleiermacher:

> [...] does he [the translator] merely want to lay open for his readers the same understanding and the same pleasure he himself enjoys, with the traces of hardship it carries and the feeling of the strange which remains mixed into it.[5]

We now come to that fundamental choice Schleiermacher is still known for, if we talk about the basics of proper translation. The genuine translator wants to bring the author and the reader truly together and has two roads open to him: the first road is that the translator leaves the author in peace – as far as possible – and moves the reader

---

2 Lefevere: Translating Poetry, p. 84.

3 André Lefevere: Translating literature: the German tradition. From Luther to Rosenzweig. Amsterdam: Assen, 1977, (Approaches to translation studies, no. 4).

4 Quoted in André Lefevere: Translating literature, p. 68.

5 Quoted in André Lefevere: Translating literature, p. 72.

towards him. The second road is that he leaves the reader in peace and moves the author towards him.

If we can agree as to the first road – that is in fact the method Schleiermacher thinks we should follow – , we have to admit that the most difficult task of the translator is to represent what is foreign in one's mother tongue. How is this going to be done in an acceptable way? Here I would like to mention a remarkable translation where the context of the reader of the target text is introduced to make the meaning of the source text understandable. Psalm 42 in the *Book of Common Prayer* begins with: "Like as the hart desireth the water-brooks: so longeth my soul after thee, O God". In the Dutch translation the hart (the Dutch word is "hert") is attacked by hunters with their dogs. This change was necessary in a country where there is rather too much than too little water. The whole context of a dry country (Palestine) has disappeared.

Let us now try to identify some of the most important elements in Fontane's works that hamper the effort of translating them into another language. If an analysis of the style of a literary work must precede the translation of that work, the translator of Fontane's work can make good use of the stylistic studies that have been undertaken to date. It is well known that Fontane often uses the spoken word to present his characters. He lets them speak in their own way, whether it be Bernd von Vitzewitz, Major-General von Bamme or Aunt Schorlemmer in *Vor dem Sturm* (*Before the Storm*). If we measure the translation according to the basic elements of Fontane's style, we have to experience the individual way of speaking of each person. A great deal is demanded of the translator to establish that impression of individual speech which makes reading Fontane such a wonderful experience. This insight requires the translator to have a good memory for recurrent phrases and reactions. Here the computer might do an excellent job in serving as the memory of the translator. To take an example from *Der Stechlin* (*The Stechlin*): one of Dubslav von Stechlin's regular visitors is the mill-owner Gundermann. He uses the phrase "also Wasser auf die Mühlen der Sozialdemokratie". In William Zwiebel's English translation this has become: "Water on the mills of the social democrats".[6] We may wonder if the force of "social democrats" corresponds to the force of "Sozialdemokratie". What Gundermann rejects may well be socialism as much as democracy. The Dutch translation "Water op de molens van de sociaal-democratie" puts the accent on "social".[7] This is just one example of an expression that must be adequately translated in order to be effective in the same way as the original.

If we look at the cultural context, we immediately find that Fontane's novels are full of details about historical persons or historical events and institutions in a social and political sense that have to be carefully transmitted to the context of the translation, which is a text in a language different from that of the original version. The same problem applies to the use of geographical facts. We cannot expect a reader from

6 Theodor Fontane: The Stechlin. Translated with an introduction and notes by William L. Zwiebel. Columbia, SC: Camden House, 1995, p. 28.

7 Theodor Fontane: Stechlin. Roman over het oude en nieuwe Pruisen. Transl. by Wilfred Oranje, with an afterword by Hans Ester. Amsterdam: Bert Bakker, 1997, p. 32.

another country and from another century to be able to identify those things in a literary text that were part of daily life and daily conversation during the nineteenth century. This, of course, is also the case with the present German-speaking reader in his confrontation with a novel from 1895. None of Fontane's novels is published nowadays without notes to explain the context of time and place and to tell the reader a hundred or more years later which quotations were current in the nineteenth century or that quotations even had the function of flattering the cultural knowledge of those who could identify them, Shakespeare-quotations for example, or verses from Goethe's *Faust* or Heine's *Buch der Lieder* (*Book of Songs*). This is all part of the situation of communication in Fontane's time.

My experience with translations (not only of the novels by Fontane) has taught me that it is absolutely vital for a translator to have enough cultural knowledge to be able to understand the implications or references to the general knowledge of the time in question. To take one example from a translation of Dürrenmatt's *Der Richter und sein Henker* (*The Judge and his Hangman*): somebody who does not know that Berne is built on several levels which are connected by streets will not understand that the word "Haspelstufen" [literally: "Haspel Steps" ed.] refers to a broad pedestrian street leading up from the river Nydegg and that it should not be translated by "staircase" or "winding stairs". To follow Chief Constable Bärlach on his walk through Berne the translator should properly study the features of this city and note on the map that "Marzili" is a park with a swimmingpool and nothing else. Identifying such avoidable mistakes is a task for the expert editor. Before the Dutch translation of *Irrungen, Wirrungen* (*Delusions, Confusions*) was published I was asked to check the text. I discovered for example that the "Görlitzer Bahnhof" was translated by "station of Görlitz" which of course was incorrect. The Görlitzer Bahnhof is the station in Berlin from which the trains to Görlitz depart. After the Dutch translation of *Effi Briest* was published in 1977, I found out too late that the noun "Raps" had been rendered as a family-name and not as the "rapeseed" which is intended.

We cannot deny the enormous gap between us and the nineteenth century. This gap is clearly symbolised by the Potsdamer Platz in Berlin, very close to the Potsdamer Strasse 134C where Fontane lived. Entering the old Fontane Archive in the Dortustrasse in Potsdam the visitor saw two pictures of the Potsdamer Platz, once the busiest square in Europe – in the one horse-trams and coaches, in the other electric trams and motorcars. The Potsdamer Platz has been a genuine witness of history. It was an empty place during the forty years of the German Democratic Republic, but is gradually becoming once more an important centre of the new capital. History has returned to a former situation, but on totally different terms. The capital lies far to the east now and no longer in the middle of the German Empire as it used to be. Therefore the irony of history is not a way back to Fontane's times.

We have to accept that reading Fontane without comment and instruction denies the reader access to underlying layers of meaning. We have – as far as possible – to reconstruct the context in which Fontane's novels were situated and from where they were understood. Otherwise the effect of his novels is only "pläsierlich" (pleasurable).

They are no longer attuned to the questions about society and the individual that Fontane raised in his work.

The method generally chosen to enable the present reader of Fontane's novels to reconstruct the social, political, cultural and geographical implications of his work is to add information in the form of foot- or endnotes. It is worth noting that this method is applied more frequently in relation to Fontane's works than to any other writer of the nineteenth century. Fontane without explanatory notes is unthinkable, but this certainly is not the case with Wilhelm Raabe, Gottfried Keller or Theodor Storm. It is a phenomenon worth thinking about. One would, for example, expect that a complex novel like Thomas Mann's *Doktor Faustus*, a novel about the history of the German mind, about the meaning of the Reformation, about the demonic nature of music, that such a novel would not be able to live, to be significant without expounding the theology of Luther, the Faust motif and the philosophy of Nietzsche, to mention but a few of the novel's essential implications. The same question arises in connection with the literary works written in the German Democratic Republic, which have become obsolete because of the pace of historical development and which will be sealed documents to all those born after 1989. Without help and comment to contextualize we do not understand *Der geteilte Himmel* (*Divided Heaven*) by Christa Wolf. The novel is incomprehensible to readers for whom the GDR is *terra incognita*. We need help to understand the totally different premises of that other German society.

More important than objects of a geographical, physical nature like castles, streets, squares, stations, trains, seem to be the social relationships and institutions which are represented in Fontane's novels. They are a continuous element that influences the way of conversing, in accordance with a supposed hierarchy. These institutions form the subsoil of the social world Fontane presents. His work is reduced to meaningless chatter (a premodern chat-room) if the reader has no appropriate access to these social stratifications. A large part of Fontane research is dedicated to keeping the knowledge of the underlying social conditions alive.

Let me give examples of the two levels on which the present reader must be informed, that is to say, by becoming acquainted with the physical and the institutional *realia*. (These fields, by the way, cannot always be separated from each other.) An initial example of the first level: in *Der Stechlin* industry plays a marginal role, but the industry and the labourers are at least present, embodied in the glass-workers of Globsow. Dubslav von Stechlin sees them as a threat to the social order. A practical question with regard to the workers of Globsow is: how do they produce their carboys for the chemical industry, which Dubslav sees as the beginning of a world-wide revolution. The original text says: "[...] und Stechlin heißt ebenso das langgestreckte Dorf, das sich, den Windungen des Sees folgend, um seine Südspitze herumzieht. Etwa hundert Häuser und Hütten bilden hier eine lange, schmale Gasse [...]".[8] In his *Wanderungen durch die Mark Brandenburg* (Rambles in Brandenburg) Fontane describes Globsow and speaks about the "*Glashütten*, die wie Squatteransiedlungen am Waldsaume lagen. Hütte neben Hütte; sonst nichts sichtbar als der Rauch, der über die

---

8 Fontane: Der Stechlin, NFA, VIII, 5f.

Dächer zog".[9] Fontane speaks about "Wohn- und Arbeitshütten", so that we have a problem for the translator: is the situation correctly translated by "a hundred houses and cottages" as William Zwiebel renders the description in his translation of the novel?[10] At least this is something to consider in the light of the historical conditions under which the workers of Globsow produced their glass.

A second example of the first level already leads to the second level. It concerns the titles used in the novel as representations or portrayals of social hierarchy. William Zwiebel, in the introduction to the novel explains the choices he made in this respect:

> German is a language rich in titles. [...] I have retained many German titles throughout the text unless I felt it unwieldy or impossible. Thus words such as *Herr, Hauptmann, Frau* and other forms of address are used wherever persons bearing such rank are addressed, while their English equivalents are used to refer to the persons objectively in the narrative.[11]

Further on, Zwiebel explains: "Certain commercial titles, which do not exist in English, I have paraphrased in English form".[12] The first example of Zwiebel shows how the reader is brought to the text (author – Schleiermacher), the second example shows how the translator paves the way for the reader and brings the text to him or her. We cannot deny that this method is very problematic. We can understand that the translator wants to inform the reader about the Prussian system of values and rank. But the result of this choice is – at least for European readers – that the "foreign bodies" in the translation themselves require close attention and produce meanings, based on other historical associations, partly based on experience derived from other works of art where German terminology is used for a particular purpose, as for example in films about the Second World War, such as *The longest Day*. Perhaps one might think of Spielberg's film *Saving Private Ryan* in this respect too.

Fontane's representation of his physical world results in the need to supply present-day readers with the information they lack because of changes that have taken place. That makes Fontane's writings comparable to *Eckermann's Conversations with Goethe* or to the diaries of Friedrich Hebbel. Maybe the fact that so many conversations take place in Fontane's novels, and that so many letters are written inside and outside his work, is partly responsible for the amount of world we are confronted with.

In the introduction to his translation of *Der Stechlin* Zwiebel states the following, after having mentioned the finer qualities of the Prussian aristocratic heritage and its provincialism and morbidity in the novel:

---

9 "Glass huts which stood at the edge of the wood like squatters' settlements. One hut next to the other, otherwise nothing visible but the smoke rising over the roof-tops." Fontane: Wanderungen durch die Mark Brandenburg. Die Grafschaft Ruppin, NFA, IX, 317.

10 "Huts for living in and huts for work." Fontane: Wanderungen durch die Mark Brandenburg. Die Grafschaft Ruppin, NFA, IX, 317. Zwiebel: The Stechlin, p. 1.

11 Zwiebel: The Stechlin, p. xv.

12 Zwiebel: The Stechlin, p. xv.

Der Stechlin is thus an essentially Prussian book. Non-German readers will learn a great deal about the values and way of life of the Junker class, the landed gentry of Brandenburg-Prussia during the salad days of the Second German Reich.[13]

This leads us to the second level, that of the social and political institutions of that Second German Empire. To illustrate this, I will focus my attention on *Vor dem Sturm*. The problem the novel discusses, is the question whether violence and revolt are legitimate or not in the situation in which Prussia finds itself in the years 1812 and 1813, the years of the unwelcome friendship of Prussia with Napoleon Bonaparte. I do not know how widespread the general historical knowledge of the events in Prussia is in the countries outside Germany. Therefore I cannot answer the question why this magnificent novel – the German counterpart of Tolstoy – has not attracted any interest outside Germany. Perhaps this interest may still arise. In that case one condition must be fulfilled, the condition of knowing and feeling the tension between the various actors in the novel that Fontane depicts. The private war of Bernd von Vitzewitz is justified with a religious claim. The war is in his view an obligation of the Prussian people towards God who wants to re-establish the national freedom of Prussia. But Fontane is not in favour of such a risky adventure. We see his distance from the attack on Frankfurt an der Oder in the way he varies the original sermon held by the famous Schleiermacher – we have heard about him already – and creates a new sermon for Vitzewitz's vicar Seidentopf. Without knowledge of the strong ties between the Prussian nobility and the unified Protestant church in Prussia we do not understand the underlying roles, the pre-supposed, accepted language in this historical novel. The way Major-General von Bamme treats *his* vicar after a sermon by this servant on Bamme's necrophilia is less than amusing. It has about it the brutal character of the abuse of social power. In the description of the clergyman we are dealing with a literary convention on the one hand – indicating the enormous influence of Oliver Goldsmith's *The Vicar of Wakefield* on German literature of the eighteenth and nineteenth centuries – and a social institution on the other hand. This social institution – the dependency of the village vicar on the patron of his church – is implied in all their conversations and should be taken into account when Fontane's political ideas are discussed. If knowledge about this institution – which exists up to the present day – is lacking, it must be supplied to the reader of a later age and especially to the reader of another mother-tongue and cultural environment by effective indications in the text or by way of comment in notes. Such annotation however tends to give a translation of a novel a scholarly flavour and may well discourage the reader looking for distraction rather than for knowledge or education.

William Zwiebel must have considered all this before he decided to preface his translation with a foreword. A threshold, pointing out the historical implications and meanings of Fontane's *Der Stechlin* is necessary – if only because of the strange title – to direct the reception of this translation. This threshold functions as a bridge between the language that sounds familiar, seeming to open meaning easily on the one hand and

---

13 Zwiebel: The Stechlin, p. viii.

the work of art that is strange and that needs to be recognised in its strangeness on the other hand. A translation is aimed at promoting the accessibility of a work of art of such importance that somebody speaking another language should be able to understand it. On the other hand, the value of that work of art lies in problems and questions that can only be understood if identification is not realised without the acknowledgement of strangeness. It therefore requires a good deal of effort to read Fontane in translation. I am not sure that Fontane will be read in the new century as he was read in the twentieth century. But we will have to see; I hope my fear is unjustified.

Barbara Everett

Night Air: Effi Briest and other Novels by Fontane

I'll begin with a quotation:

> That summer of 1929 they read together *Effi Briest*, by Theodor Fontane, a German classic about
> a young woman who is betrayed by her beauty and her desires into adultery and becomes the
> victim of malice and gossip.[1]

We're further told in this biography (for such it is) that one of the two readers in
question retained "a soft spot for the book ever afterwards – to such an extent that he
urged its reissue in English translation on his publishers many years later".[2] And this
reader, himself a distinguished writer, made his protagonist in *Krapp's Last Tape*
remember "Effie" with tears.

This anecdote about Samuel Beckett is related by Anthony Cronin in his 1996
biography of the writer, *Samuel Beckett. The Last Modernist*. It isn't perhaps necessary
to assume that Beckett himself read and recalled with his character Krapp's lecherous
tears: "Could have been happy with her up there, on the Baltic, and the pines, and the
dunes. (*Pause*) Could I? (*Pause*) And she? (*Pause*) Pah!"[3] Krapp's self-questioning
usefully communicates Fontane's permanent ambiguities. In just the same way,
Cronin's own paraphrase in its simplicity ("betrayed by her beauty and her desires")
manages to remind the reader of the fact that Fontane's novel really isn't like this.

Fontane is at once the simplest and the subtlest of novel writers. Though it may be
regrettable, it is hardly surprising that he has had to wait a century for appreciation
more than random, even when intense: for a reputation international enough for a
scholarly gathering of this kind to wish to salute and celebrate his quality. Non-
Germanists (such as I have to admit to being) are wholly dependent on translations
which have perhaps only recently begun to be able to rise to giving a sense of
Fontane's own verbal and imaginative style: its intelligence, its wit, its reticence, its
luminous modesty. Theodor Fontane is really not at all like the great artists of the
English nineteenth-century novel – perhaps not much like, either, the French or
Russian masters to whom it might seem sensible to compare him. Cronin's "betrayed
by her beauty and her desires into adultery" might do for Emma Bovary or Anna
Karenina. It doesn't do for Effi Briest. Tony Tanner's very absorbing critical classic on
the subject, *Adultery in the Novel*, mentions Effi Briest only in a footnote.[4]

---

1 Anthony Cronin: Samuel Beckett: The Last Modernist. London: Harper Collins 1996, p. 105.
2 Cronin: Samuel Beckett: The Last Modernist, p. 105.
3 Samuel Beckett: Krapp's Last Tape; and Embers. London: Faber and Faber 1959, p. 18.
4 See: Tony Tanner: Adultery in the Novel: contract and transgression. Baltimore: Johns Hopkins
   University Press 1979, p. 137.

All Fontane's best fiction, or work that seems best to a reader appreciative but linguistically limited, is late work. These are the novels of an old man, writing best in the last decades of the nineteenth century: the wonderfully holding if elusive *Irrungen, Wirrungen.* (*Delusions, Confusions*) appearing in 1887, when the writer was in his sixties, and *Effi Briest* and *Die Poggenpuhls* (*The Poggenpuhl Family*) eight years later, in 1895. Fontane, though a writer of long experience, of course did not turn to the novel until he was nearly sixty. The lack of affiliation with the novels of Dickens and George Eliot, the second born in the same year as Fontane himself (1819) and the first only a few years earlier (1812), is as striking as it could be. And the difference cannot, I think, be explained in merely nationalistic terms: though it is a fact that Fontane's essentially more poetic, even more philosophical stories are a world away from the huge Victorian energy and ambition, the outgoing audience-pleasing moralistic splendours of the two English writers.

High Victorian culture begins to change, even to die, in the 1860s and 1870s. The new age begins to begin when a young American writer reviews *Our Mutual Friend,* Dickens's last very great and completed work, in 1865, in terms of mockery and astringent criticism. The critic, who was Henry James, hoped to displace what he was later to call the "loose and baggy monsters" of the English and Russian novel with something simply more aesthetic, more intellectually fine. If we are driven to make comparisons between Fontane and English fiction, then the closest we can come, or so it seems to me, is in those refined, ironic and morally compassionate novels and stories, often about women, and often drawn from the aristocratic and social life of his time, that James himself was writing for the English market through the 1880's and 1890's and on into the twentieth century. James was in fact writing English and writing about England with an American accent, and with a technique intensely aware of French, or more largely European styles of experience.

Late in his life, Henry James's friend and novelistic disciple, Edith Wharton, shocked him by asking why his characters had never lived – never seemed to belong within the physical, natural, social world where we all exist. He was shocked because he hadn't known that it might be true, and he was deeply pained to think that he might have to know it. Probably Wharton failed to understand that James had begun to invent a mode that would supersede, to all intents and purposes, that kind of social realism which she thought still survived, and which her enjoyable though to my mind lesser novels still function in terms of. From the relatively early *The Portrait of a Lady* (1881) to the later masterpieces like *The Awkward Age* (1898) and *The Wings of the Dove* (1901) (which all tell of the destruction of women as young and innocent as Effi, if more virginal and more deeply self-aware), James is producing work recognisable as post-Victorian, if pre-Modernistic. Among the bifurcating if sometimes interconnecting literary streams of the 1890s, a remarkably rich and animated period of English writing, with its New Socialists, its Imperialists, its Aesthetes, James is pursuing a more and more individual path in fiction writing. He is infusing his brilliant images of English society with an American, even Puritan intensity of moral awareness. As a result, these novels grow to be more and more personal legends. James is in fact helping to create the world of modern English fiction, not necessarily either Modernistic or post-Modernistic, but a world to which E. M. Forster's well-known remark is relevant: his weary, ironical and detached concession, "Oh dear, yes, the novel tells a story" – uttered several decades after *Effi Briest* was published, but Fontane might well have found it thoroughly sympathetic.[5]

I began this approach to the work of Theodor Fontane with quotations from and about Samuel Beckett – as little, of course, an English writer in any simple sense as Henry James –, an exiled Irishman who lived in Paris and often wrote first in French: but like James, important and influential in helping to create modern British literature. I am hoping to define the way in which Fontane can be described as decidedly modern in his originality, "modern" without his having to be called "Modernist". His modernity lies in the aesthetic invention with which, like those other two writers, James and Beckett, he learned to create an effect of the peculiarly real without being a naturalist or literalist. He is like James in what he leaves out. We might even go so far as to say that he is sometimes like Beckett in the implicit darkness and emptiness which enclose his stories. Peter Hall's two strong productions of Beckett's best known work, *Waiting for Godot*, were different and were more than forty years apart, but, in both, Vladimir and Estragon were interpreted as some kind of tramp. What sociological class Pozzo and Lucky belong to is a more open question; and behind all four, and the Boy, there extends a night in which one may wait for Godot, but he probably will not come. With *Endgame* and *Happy Days* things get worse, in their blackly comic way, but appear to be similarly without terminus. In the *Last Tape* Krapp even formalises his feelings about both fictional plot and the drama of characters when he reflects to himself: "With all this darkness round me I feel less alone".[6]

I imagine that it was in part an exquisite prose and secular poetry which is (so to speak) above plotting and even above characters that so deeply held Beckett in *Effi Briest*. The same secular poetry touches *Irrungen, Wirrungen* and *Die Poggenpuhls,* both of which have in one sense a magnificently novelistic urban truth. In the first of these, the inhabitants of the working-class Berlin vegetable garden have at least as much solidity, warmth and roundness in their rendering as have the at once touchy and humorously "placed" military clubmen in the book. And the opening conversations of the Poggenpuhls – funny, random, revealing and documentary – are quite remarkable in their new creation of some shabby genteel, metropolitan yet aristocratic world that we see slowly, unstoppably sinking downwards.

One of the best-known and most-often quoted remarks by Fontane himself is his testy response to the fairly poor reception which met *Die Poggenpuhls*: "The book is not a novel and has no content, the 'how' has to do the work of the 'what'."[7] We might

---

5 E. M. Forster: Aspects of the Novel and related writings. London: Edward Arnold 1927, p. 17.

6 Beckett: Krapp's Last Tape, p. 12.

7 Theodor Fontane, Delusions, Confusions and The Poggenpuhl Family. ed. by Peter Demetz; Foreword by J. P. Stern; transl. and with an introduction by William L. Zwiebel, The German Library, vol. 47. New York: Continuum 1989, Introduction, p. xxvii; all translations are from this edition and further references are given in the text. "Das Buch ist kein Roman und hat

set beside this his irritation earlier at a public shocked by what they saw as the immorality of *Irrungen, Wirrungen*: writing tiredly to his son that the book had "nothing to do with the question of morality" (p. viii).

What I want to do here is briefly to try to balance these two facts, the degree to which Fontane's wonderfully accomplished late work is, and is not, novelistic. I shall put no stress at all on the writer's realism, a subject which my very limited experience of German life and literature would not do justice to, and which has in any case been already very well treated, especially in the last two or three decades, by good critics. I have myself particularly admired the work of Henry Garland, and there is much insight too in the lucid Introduction to the Penguin Classics *Effi Briest* by Helen Chambers, as there is in the excellent Foreword and Introduction to the "German Library" edition of the other two novels by J. P. Stern and William L. Zwiebel. Such fine analysis of Fontane's realism I can't begin to offer. I would venture a suggestion, rather, that the very nature of this novelist's realism is a special and original factor in his work. Let me quote a short passage from J. P. Stern's Foreword to the "German Library" *Irrungen, Wirrungen*, which argues that Fontane, a true realist:

> trusts the world [...] to be unblemished by ontological cracks. About the philosophical questions of Being, of Appearance and Reality, he remains incurious [...] Unlike the fictional tradition of *Don Quixote*, his novels and novellas never play with epistemological dubieties (p. viii).

All this is true. These three novels accept the social appearances of their world with a fidelity sometimes farcical and sometimes heart-breaking. Characteristically the two mix into the tragi-comic: as when the almost terminally impoverished aristocrats, the Poggenpuhls, gather together their birthday presents for the mother, who is loving, exhausted, heroic, middle-class by origin and undervalued: offerings consisting of two pairs of cotton gloves, a pair of felt slippers, a pot of heather, a primula, and a bag of ginger biscuits. Into his primula Leo – the wild, hugely charming army officer younger son – has tucked a note inscribed, "A primula from your..." (p.202), in his haste leaving the message incomplete.[8] An elegiac yet laughing truth to fact could hardly go further.

But there is a quality, too, of the carefully unfinished throughout the art of this perfect miniaturist of the novel. A reader may agree with Stern's thesis and yet find "cracks" in Fontane's world. There is the silence concerning conventional morality in *Irrungen, Wirrungen*. There is even a silence here in terms of ordinary plotting, the lack not of a "what" so much as of a "why". At no point does the story stop to debate just why one person has to betray and abandon another. A part of the curiously disturbing truth of the fiction is the absolutely equal weight given to both the loving Lene and to Botho, to the highly intelligent working-class girl (whose birth just might be as distinguished as her character) and the affectionate and decent if more conventional army officer (whose noble family desperately need money to survive).

---

keinen Inhalt, das 'Wie' muß für das 'Was' eintreten." Fontane to Siegmund Schott, 14 February 1897, HFA, IV, 4, 635.

8   "Eine Primel, von deinem ..."; Fontane: Die Poggenpuhls, NFA, IV, 313.

Beginning as it does at a point in time evidently too late for anything to be considered possible but the officer's worldly marriage to a rich popsy, the book resolutely shields the lovers from nonsenses about fault or blame: this is the way things are. Absolutely loving, they marry other people.

These formal originalities are matched in *Die Poggenpuhls*. The book begins by securing the reader with extraordinary precision right inside this group of chattering, socially and financially declining Berlin aristocrats. Represented by Fontane's most brilliant accomplishment, that of subtly characterised if casual conversation, this is a social world that surrounds, holds, buries us without external direction or explanation, a world of recognisable and sympathetic people hanging on to gentility, even to existence, by their finger-nails. And then the silent belonging equally silently breaks apart as this strange short novel itself splits open – the family separates, letters suddenly replace narrative. With the death of the amiable aristocratic uncle, with whom the nicest and cleverest of the daughters is staying, the family's worst money-problems are a little resolved, his middle-class widow showing great generosity. But her gift brings *éclaircissement* about the true nature of their poverty and their lack of romantic hopes for the future; and with her gift, as in some worldly diaspora, family and story finish together. They were alike dependent, always, on hopes, dreams and illusions, both pure and impure: "Finding something where nothing was really to be found was preferable to anything else, and [...] there was something imaginative about it too" (p. 200).[9]

I am not merely suggesting that largely fortuitous thing for Fontane, originality in time. It is a fact that the way this novel opens with exquisitely airy yet nailing conversations foreshadows the forty-years-later English master (minor, but a master, and an influential one) Ronald Firbank. Perhaps the disintegration of Fontane's Poggenpuhl family and the story together make Virginia Woolf's later treatment of death and the passing of time in *To the Lighthouse* seem by comparison more willed, less moving in its accomplishment. A reader might even go so far as to compare the silences about form, plot and meaning in *Irrungen, Wirrungen* to an essentially poetic fabric such as *The Waste Land* possesses.

But Fontane's fictions don't seem to own to the resonant and real self-consciousness of these twentieth-century artefacts. It is his very unpretentiousness, his resolute placing of himself within a nineteenth-century culture, which makes him such a difficult case critically – a nineteenth-century culture which still takes for granted civilised securities and stabilities. Like the good General in *Die Poggenpuhls*, Fontane himself is all "for the small things in life". Despite the clear suggestiveness of, for instance, that opening description in *Effi Briest*, with the bright sunshine falling on Hohen-Cremmen and "the midday silence in the village street" – a sunshine and a silence which give a kind of luminosity to the churchyard next to the house, the "large roundel of flowers with a sundial at its centre" the pond and the "jetty with a moored

---

9   "wenn man noch was fände, wo eigentlich nichts mehr zu finden sei, das sei jedesmal das Beste, und darin läge auch was Sinniges". Fontane: Die Poggenpuhls, NFA, IV, 312.

boat", "and close by a swing" with "posts that were slightly out of true":[10] – despite all this, it may be that Fontane avoids quite the symbolism which several critics have pointed out. A comparison with Eliot's opening description of his finely symbolistic village in East Coker underlines the impression that there may be hardly a symbol to be found in Fontane.

Symbols grant weight; Fontane is in love with the weightless. One of the strangest and most impressive moments in *Effi Briest* involves Effi herself, at this point a young married woman whom it would be somehow farcically coarse to call "fallen" or "adulterous", and concerning whom, indeed, we may feel some real uncertainty about the circumstances of the fall and the adultery. Effi looks out into the night of Hohen-Cremmen, a night that answers the bright morning of the book's opening, and hears the haunting, romantic noise of a train approaching and then passing in the night:

> Then the sound faded and finally died away, and there was only the moonlight falling on the lawn, and all that was to be heard was the plane trees rustling as before, as if light rain were falling. But it was only the movement of the night air. (p. 161)[11]

A section closes at this point, the next beginning "The next evening Effi was back in Berlin" – a pause that gives the image of the night air a curious lingering immanence. I have chosen it for my title for this reason: the "night air" seems to me one of the moments at which it is not quite true that Fontane "trusts the world [...] to be unblemished by ontological cracks". It is possible, almost as in Beckett's painfully desolate worlds, to look through the novelist's true appearances and see "night air" beyond them, a laughably or frighteningly or poetically weightless hint that nothing is there: that human life is more troublingly tenuous or mysterious than nineteenth-century decencies can communicate. When, before the Poggenpuhl birthday, the delightful if hopeless son Leo asks the loyal family servant about his mother's present, "What does she need?" Friederike answers briskly, "Everything!" And the boy responds, "That's too much, that's above my means" (p. 199).[12] The perfect balance of sad humour in these stories contains "nothing" and "everything" inside itself. Their characters, "finding something where nothing was really to be found", live by a triumphant poise, an art of wire-walking, which one of the Poggenpuhls states

---

10 Theodor Fontane: Effi Briest, transl. by Hugh Rorrison and Helen Chambers. London: Penguin Books 2000, p. 5; all translations are from this edition and further references are given in the text; "ein großes in seiner Mitte mit einer Sonnenuhr und an seinem Rande mit Canna indica und Rhabarberstauden besetztes Rondell". Fontane: Effi Briest, NFA, VII, 171.

11 "Dann wurde der Lärm wieder schwächer, endlich erstarb er ganz, und nur der Mondschein lag noch auf dem Grasplatz, und nur auf die Platanen rauschte es nach wie vor wie leiser Regen nieder. Aber es war nur Nachtluft, die ging." Fontane: Effi Briest, NFA, VII, 359.

12 "was braucht sie?" "Gott, junger Herr, die gnädige Frau braucht ja eigentlich alles." "Das ist mir zu viel." Fontane: Die Poggenpuhls, NFA, IV, 311.

financially: "Turn up! How can anything turn up, where is it to come from? It's really a miracle that we've managed to scrape along so far" (p. 192).[13]

The circumstances can, in fact, be financial, political, emotional, even moral. It is worth remembering that Fontane pleaded for an aristocracy – and all these books are about the decaying aristocracy – on the ground that in its existence there resided all that could be found of the poetry of life. The writer was perhaps a realist for whom the social became a datum in a very private poetry. But he knew, always, how fragile, how insecure this individual and inner world of meaning was. Thus, his characters carry and embody, even reflect like a mirror, states of really quite inexplicable or unparaphrasable uncertainty which make sense, however, to the writer and the reader. In this Fontane's people are, we might say, in a line of Philip Larkin's, "out on the end of an event"; or reflective of that terrible light epitaph or doom which closes a poem by Sylvia Plath, "Somebody's done for".

Certainly *Effi Briest* is a social novel. We can say that it indicts a group of human beings locked into the last phase of an aristocracy, losing its way, wasting its energies: depending on social conventions and strategies which rapidly harden into the bars of the cage. Anxiety, fear, ambition and selfishness – all in people self-evidently decent and sympathetic in many ways – between them make up the often tenderly comic story; Effi's father is neglectful, her mother morbidly un-self-knowing, her husband mean and cold, her love trivial and uncommitted. Even Effi herself we can endow with the slightly mindless and commonplace irresponsibility of the young which some readers find even in a Romeo or Juliet: a wildness dangerous because baseless and dislocated, and expressed in the series of up-in-the-air swinging images which surround Effi in the beginning.

The young girl is first met doing gymnastic turns, her mother exclaiming "Effi, maybe you should have been a bareback rider after all. Always on the trapeze, a daughter of the air" (p. 6).[14] Then, already engaged, helplessly contemptuous of Innstetten's prosy prudences ("Yes, the right balance, that's him." (p. 24),[15] Effi opts for an imbalance that is generous in its rejection of mere bourgeois materialism:

> He hasn't the slightest inkling that I don't care about jewellery. I prefer to climb or swing, especially when I'm afraid something's going to snap or collapse and I might fall. (p. 24) [16]

When, already a mother though still half a child herself, Effi returns home for six weeks suggestively unvisited by her new but busy husband, her appetite is for a freedom and solitariness, an adventurous openness to risk, given her only by that small and circumscribed domestic swing:

---

13 "Was finden! Wie soll sich denn was finden, wo soll es denn herkommen? Es ist ja doch eigentlich ein Wunder, daß es noch immer so gegangen ist." Fontane: Die Poggenpuhls, NFA, IV, 304.

14 "Effi, eigentlich hättest du doch wohl Kunstreiterin werden müssen. Immer am Trapez. Immer Tochter der Luft." Fontane, Effi Briest, NFA, VII, 172.

15 "Ja, das rechte Maß, das hält er." Fontane, Effi Briest, NFA, VII, 194.

16 "Er hat keine Ahnung davon, daß ich mir aus Schmuck nichts mache." Fontane, Effi Briest, NFA, VII, 194.

[…] best of all she had enjoyed standing on the swing as it flew through the air, just as in the old days, and the feeling 'now I'm going to fall' had given her a strange tingling sensation, a shudder of sweet danger. (p. 86) [17]

The truly innocent Effi's freedom is darkening towards danger, and when she rides in the sleigh away from the tedious small socialities of Kessin, the remote Baltic town where Innstetten needs to locate his useful wife, and says to herself "The idea of being thrown out appeals to me", this is not quite a child's boldness. The book always makes it possible for us to psychologise and to moralise; more, to indict socially. When Effi phrases her "idea of being thrown out" (p.115), [18] or defines "The house that we live in is … a haunted house; […] It's nice and comfortable, but uncanny at the same time" (p. 72f.), [19] or with a sadly increased knowingness remarks of women, "We have to be seductive, otherwise we are nothing" (p. 90), [20] we remember that this is the decade when Ibsen is having his most potent effect in Europe.

Similarly, it is impossible now to read the novel without deploring the weakness of the men who make up Effi's only life. Nothing gives husband and lover backbone but a code of honour ridiculous even where it is not disastrous. The expert lover, Crampas – who is later quoted in one of his three love-letters as saying "Frivolity is the best thing we have" – is a kind of ironic pastiche of the General's (and Fontane's) love of "small things". (p. 171) [21] The perfection of the novelist's own melancholy comedy comes back at us from Crampas's gentlemanly social poise:

To help a friend one minute and deceive him five minutes later were things his concept of honour had no trouble in accommodating. He did both the one and the other with astounding bonhomie. (p. 99) [22]

An equally "astounding" case of behaviour which seems at least partly right to the actor in terms of the social code, while actually lacking sense and wisdom and human compassion, not to say conjugal love, is the arid and bothered Innstetten's conscientious and, in the event, efficient challenge of a brother officer six years after there may have seemed any nominal occasion for the action. The killing of Crampas is hardly more unforgivable than the social destruction of Innstetten's young wife and his separation of her from her child.

---

17 "Am liebsten […] hatte sie wie früher auf dem durch die Luft fliegenden Schaukelbrett gestanden, und in dem Gefühle jetzt stürz ich etwas eigentümlich prickelndes, einen Schauer süßer Gefahr empfunden." Fontane: Effi Briest, NFA, VII, 269.

18 "wenn ich hinausflöge, mir wär es recht." Fontane: Effi Briest, NFA, VII, 304.

19 "Das Haus, das wir bewohnen ist ein Spukhaus. […] es ist sonderbarerweise gemütlich und unheimlich zugleich." Fontane, Effi Briest: NFA, VII, 253f.

20 "Wir müssen verführerisch sein, sonst sind wir gar nichts." Fontane: Effi Briest, NFA, VII, 273.

21 "Leichtsinn ist das beste, was wir haben." Fontane: Effi Briest, NFA, VII, 371.

22 "Einem Freunde helfen, und fünf Minuten später ihn betrügen, waren Dinge, die sich mit seinem Ehrbegriffe sehr wohl vertrugen. Er tat das eine und das andere mit unglaublicher Bonhomie." Fontane: Effi Briest, NFA, VII, 284.

Yet these people are not monsters. Their pathos and the irony with which their story is rendered depend on their human ordinariness: an ordinariness equipped with grace, humour and charm. The irony and pathos depend on something else. I have mentioned earlier the vital "silences" which tend to distinguish Fontane's stories from their nominal narrative substance. Their lack of ordinary motivation, of explanatory discourse, brings the "night air" into their structure and into their characters' beings. In a very well-known utterance, the novelist said of *Effi Briest* (with that curious pellucidity which has no grain of vanity in it): "Perhaps I have been so successful with it because I wrote the whole novel in a dream-like state, almost as if with a psychograph" – a psychograph being the pen-like implement used in spiritualistic ghost-writing.[23] The novel itself of course has its own ghost: a figure peculiarly unbelievable *qua* ghost, so much so as to make Effi's wistful missing of the ghost once she gets to Berlin, her desperate feeling that even a horrible exotic Chinese spook would be better than the nothingness which grips her there, significant to the action. The young girl's spook is not unlike Roswitha's Roman Catholic profession and confession: as she says, "Never told them nothin' serious though" (p. 164).[24] Effi's marriage has something "serious" missing in it, her whole life and her entire world have something missing in them. As Effi herself says, indicting herself with a blank lack of love and conscience, "I don't have the right feelings" (p. 160);[25] and "That's what's crushing me, the fact that I don't feel it" (p. 160).[26] The simplest explanation of what is wrong in *Effi Briest* is the servant Roswitha's "I just want to die because I can't live" (p. 82).[27]

These utterances are attuned to whatever Fontane meant by his dream-like state. In terms of style and structure, that dream-state expresses itself most remarkably through the most obvious of the silences which obtains here. No novel of adultery says less about the sexual, surely, than *Effi Briest*. This is really why any précis (however reasonable) detailing "a young woman who is betrayed by her beauty and her desires" seems so oddly surprising, for all of what must be its accuracy. The novel comes at the end of a century, indeed of a great sweep of centuries, which had not (as we presumably still have not) lost some dream denoted by the words "Romantic Love". But Effi ruins herself by giving herself to a husband and a lover, neither of whom she loves; neither of whom, perhaps, she even desires. She is destroyed by a handful of letters which she keeps for years (it is necessary to guess) only because they are better than nothing.

Fontane is rightly praised as a novelist for his delicate and thorough realism, for his advanced insight as an urban commentator, even for his distinction as a social satirist. But there is something essential in his art that undermines all this, or at least counter-

---

23 "Vielleicht ist es mir so gelungen, weil ich das Ganze träumerisch und fast wie mit einem Psychographen geschrieben habe." Fontane to Hans Hertz, 2 March 1895, HFA, IV, 4, 430.

24 "Aber das richtige hab ich doch nicht gesagt." Fontane: Effi Briest, NFA, VII, 363.

25 "dann fehlt mir das richtige Gefühl." Fontane: Effi Briest, NFA, VII, 359.

26 "das bringt mich um, da ich sie [Scham] nicht habe." Fontane: Effi Briest, NFA, VII, 359.

27 "Ich will bloß sterben, weil ich nicht leben kann." Fontane: Effi Briest, NFA, VII, 264.

balances it. He is a writer who, in the phrase Robert Frost was to choose, lived "acquainted with the night"; his most loved heroine, Effi, is given the wholly unnerving feeling that she is "being pursued by a shadow". In *Effi Briest*, a very unusual story of adultery, that shadow, that invading breath of "night air", asks to be interpreted as the simple lack of human love, even of human desire, which one might have looked for in this story of social life. The social itself has become meaningless.

When the young married couple move into the metropolis, and upward into success, they advance towards catastrophe. Effi, not even present when that crisis gets under way, but seeking treatment for childlessness, is herself reduced to a kind of shadow, a non-existence. When she goes home to die, goes to her childhood home as if her adult life had never begun, she is accompanied by a simple and loyal servant, and by her dog. The dog Rollo's best moments are like Fontane's an art of silence. Dying on Effi's grave, he fills the book's last sentence, shaking "his head slowly from side to side", following her into the night air (p. 217).[28]

---

28 "schüttelte den Kopf langsam hin und her"; Fontane: Effi Briest, NFA, II, 427.

Inga-Stina Ewbank

Hedda Gabler, Effi Briest and "The Ibsen-effect."

A couple of years ago I went to see a production of *Hedda Gabler* at the Norwegian National Theatre in Oslo. The play was performed on one of that theatre's small stages, the Amfiscene, where the action takes place, not behind a proscenium arch, but at floor level, closely surrounded by the audience on three sides. I had a seat in the front row, and at one point "Hedda" took the manuscript of Ejlert Lövberg's new book – the manuscript she is soon to burn, with such fatal consequences – and put it down on a piece of stage furniture not more than thirty centimetres from my hand. I was seized by an almost uncontrollable urge to grab the manuscript, save it from burning, break into the fiction of the play and tell Lövberg that it was in safe keeping and there was no need for anyone to kill themselves. *Almost*, but of course I did control the urge, and the play rolled on to its tragic ending.

From this experience I wish to draw out two points and make not so much an argument as a path of exploration – setting aside the obvious, but in this context irrelevant, discovery in myself of a hunger for the once-in-a-lifetime bid for notoriety: to go down in theatre history as an equivalent of Herostratos who set fire to the temple of Artemis in Ephesus. "People don't do things like that."[1]

The first point is the quality of involvement that Ibsen creates: the "Ibsen-effect" which Fontane identifies in his review of *The Lady from the Sea* (the Ibsen play which immediately preceded *Hedda Gabler*) as "this effect of working directly on one's nerves and senses".[2] If it is an urge to stop a disastrous action – one that we may well feel in the temptation scene in *Othello* (where individuals in an audience have been known to call out "Can't you see, you fool"), or in King Lear's division of the kingdom (where Kent says it for us: "See better, Lear...") – it arises, as in the Shakespearean scenes, from sympathy with characters but also, and more keenly in the case of Ibsen, from an ineluctable sense of a pattern closing in, of what the playwright's people *have to do*. I experience a similar urge – to "stop it" happening – when I read the scene in *Effi Briest* where the bundle of letters which reveal Effi's affair with Crampas comes to light because Annie has struck her forehead on the boot-scraper and Roswitha, in the panic to find a bandage, breaks open the lock of Effi's sewing-table and scatters the contents. "What happened was what was bound to happen, what always happens."[3]

---

1 The closing line of *Hedda Gabler*.

2 "[Die] Ibsen-Wirkung [...] [diese] unmittelbar die Nerven und Sinne packende Wirkung"; Fontane: Henrik Ibsen. Die Frau vom Meere, Causerien über Theater, II, NFA, XXII/2, 598. Unless otherwise indicated, translations from the German, as from the Norwegian, are my own.

3 "Nun, es kam, wie es kommen mußte, wie's immer kommt." Fontane: Effi Briest, NFA, VII, 175. Cited here from Theodor Fontane: Effi Briest, transl. by Hugh Rorrison and Helen Chambers. London: Penguin Books, 2000, p. 9. In her "Introduction" (p. xviii) Chambers points to the significance of this sentence for the novel as a whole.

The second point follows from the first and has to do with textuality: with the contrary pull which both these fictive scenes exert through reminding us of the text as text, of the art as art. In *Hedda Gabler* the burning of the manuscript is the first decisive action in a play consisting up to this point entirely of dialogue. The moment is a fulcrum for both the verbal and the visual language of the play: the manuscript embodies the future of Ejlert Lövborg (and it is about the future of mankind), and when Hedda burns it, she makes it explicit that she is burning his "child" and Thea's. As Hedda shoots herself, her husband and Thea are beginning the task of re-constituting the text of the manuscript. In *Effi Briest* the letters embody the main event of the novel – the affair six or more years ago which went unnoticed then (*and* unstated by the text) and has been almost forgotten now, existing only as a bundle of letters and notes, forgotten or not – but the text *is* there, and once Innstetten has told it to Geheimrat Wüllersdorf, it prescribes the future, even as it also becomes a text both in the *Fremdenblatt* and the *Kleines Journal*. We are made aware that these are not just the convenient letters of a Scribean intrigue but are a figure of the meaning of the text as a whole, much as is Lövborg's manuscript. "What", as Frau Zwicker writes in her letter, enclosing the newspaper account of the affair and its consequences, "are fires and stoves for? That sort of thing should never be allowed to happen" (p. 190).[4] In Ibsen's and Fontane's arts that sort of thing, the text insists, does happen.

In both these works, although they belong to different genres, the effect of intense involvement co-existing with self-conscious textuality is produced by an art passing through and beyond naturalism. The play and the novel are alike in combining the use of the aesthetics of naturalism with a transcendence of its ideology.[5]

I wish to stress at once that, in setting *Hedda Gabler* (1890) and *Effi Briest* (1895) side by side, I am not pursuing a question of "influence" between two writers. Their life spans and publishing careers run a parallel course: Ibsen was born in 1828 and died in 1906, having completed his last play in 1899; Fontane was born in 1819 and died in 1898, writing to the very end, but his first novel appeared only in 1878, the year between *Pillars of Society* (1877) and *A Doll's House* (1879), the works inaugurating the row of "contemporary" plays which made Ibsen a – or rather *the* – leading European dramatist. Like Fluellen on Henry V and Alexander the Great,[6] one could find other similarities, not least that both writers trained as apothecaries, and that Ibsen lived in Germany (Dresden and Munich) for most of his twenty-seven years of voluntary exile.[7] There is, however no evidence that Ibsen read any of Fontane's

---

4 "Wozu gibt es Öfen und Kamine? [...] dergleichen [darf] nicht vorkommen." Fontane: Effi Briest, NFA, VII, 394.

5 Cf. the discussion of naturalism as a literary mode in David Baguley: Naturalistic Fiction: The Entropic Vision. Cambridge: Cambridge University Press 1990.

6 See William Shakespeare: Henry V, IV, vii, l.14 ff.

7 Fontane himself repeatedly alludes to this coincidence: see, for example, the letter to his daughter, 4 April 1889, in Theodor Fontane: Briefe, ed. by Gotthard Erler, 3. vols.. Berlin and Weimar, 1980, II, 155f.; and the letter to Friedrich Stephany, 17 May 1898, where he excuses the fact that many of Ibsen's characters come "aus der Retorte": "Dafür war er Apotheker." HA, IV, 4, 720. That he attached real significance to the "Apotheker" similarity is suggested by the letter to Martha Fontane

works. He was notoriously unwilling to admit that he read, let alone was influenced by, anything; but the library he left on his death contained a number of works of German fiction – no Fontane, though.[8] Fontane, on the other hand, was clearly familiar with many Ibsen works: he refers to them in his letters,[9] he reviewed a number of productions for the *Vossische Zeitung*, and he even left an unpublished manuscript of an *Entwurf einer Characteristik* (Draft of a Characterisation) of Ibsen.

Nor do I propose to compare the two works from a feminist perspective. It is a truth generally acknowledged that Ibsen's plays, and in particular *A Doll's House* and *Ghosts*, profoundly affected European literature about and by women. Yet, Fontane is an outspoken critic of what he sees as Ibsen's "doctrinaire" presentation of the woman and marriage question and at the end of his life still thought "the much-admired Nora is the greatest talker of rubbish that has ever spoken from the stage to an audience".[10] On the other hand, a comparative case could be made out for Hedda and Effi (at least in her last few years) as representatives of the "nervous" woman of the 1890s – "diese nervösen Frauen" Fontane calls them in his review of *The Lady from the Sea*.[11] Both protagonists are constrained, both consciously and unconsciously, and in the end fatally, by the codes of the nineteenth-century societies they respectively inhabit: and both have fears and longings – Hedda's "vine-leaves" and Effi's Chinaman – of mythic proportions. Seeing Ibsen through his female characters was an accepted approach in Fontane's Germany.[12] But for the purposes of this paper, I am concerned with such

---

of 14 September 1889, where he reports, verbatim and at some length, Emil Ritterhaus's derogatory description of how "Ibsen ganz wie ein Apotheker wirkt; [...] Er ist immer ein kleiner Apotheker, der abwartet und dribbelt und auf der Lauer liegt", and then adds his own – disturbed – comment: "Es ist vollkommen richtig und ich mußte laut lachen, schon um hinter der großen Lache meine eigene Angst zu verbergen". HA, IV, 3, 726.

8 See Ibsenårbok 1985/86, pp. 11-88, for a record of Ibsen's private library, and pp. 89-185, for a list prepared by Gunhild Ramm Reistad, of "Books which Ibsen has read, and books which scholars have argued that he has read".

9 See Theodor Fontane, Briefe, ed. by Gotthard Erler, I, 227; II, 117, 155f., 270; III, 181.

10 "[D]ie bewunderte Nora ist die größte Quatschlise, die je von der Bühne herab zu einem Publikum gesprochen hat", Fontane to Friedrich Stephany, 22 March 1898, HFA, IV, 4, 704. Cf. also the fragment of a commentary on *A Doll's House*, in Fontane: Literarische Essays und Studien, NFA, XXI/2, 355-358; and the letter to Friedrich Spielhagen, 16 February, 1897: "ich wende mich von diesen Liebesformen degoutiert ab und habe für die Trägerinnen derselben (obenan steht Nora) nur die Bezeichnung: Schafslise", HFA, IV, 4, 636. *A Doll's House* had its first performance in German in Flensburg in February 1880. This version, in which the ending was altered to allow Nora to stay with her husband and children, was then played in Hamburg, Dresden, Hanover and Berlin; whereas the first production using the authentic ending opened at the Residenztheater in Munich in March 1880, with Ibsen in attendance. There is no evidence that Fontane saw either version; his incomplete and unpublished essay on the play seems to refer to a reading, possibly in connection with reviewing the performance of *Ghosts* in 1887. (See: NFA, XXI/ 2, 946).

11 "diese nervösen Frauen"; Fontane: Henrik Ibsen. Die Frau vom Meere, Causerien über Theater, NFA, XXII/ 2, 610.

12 See, for example, Lou Andreas-Salomé: Henrik Ibsen's Frauengestalten nach seinen sechs Familien-Dramen, [*A Doll's House, Ghosts, The Wild Duck, Rosmersholm, The Lady from the Sea, Hedda Gabler*]. Berlin 1892, a copy of which, with the author's dedication, was in Ibsen's library.

similarities as part of a more general response, in the art of either author, to impulses of the 1890s which were to take literature from naturalism towards modernism. I can best attempt to define this by exploring Fontane's response to Ibsen.

Hedda Gabler had its world première, in the presence of the author, at the Munich *Hoftheater* on 31 January 1891, and soon thereafter – and again with Ibsen present – it was staged at the *Lessingtheater* in Berlin (10 February 1891). By that time Fontane had – just – given up reviewing for the *Vossische Zeitung*, and I have not been able to find any direct references by him to this play, although it is likely to have been part of that sense of, and attitude to, the Ibsen corpus which he summarised only a few months before his death, by saying that, while he remained "unconverted" (of what that means, more later), his main reaction was "Admiration and gratitude [...] He has created new characters and above all a new language".[13] This is a very different kind of critical discourse from that of the brief *Entwurf* of 1889,[14] where – in what reads like a *jeu d'esprit* – he used the voice of Polonius and defined Ibsen as someone whose madness lacks method, who cannot logically and consistently stick to what is real and true ("eigentlich").[15] The difference between the two Ibsens he constructs, it seems to me, is not only one of occasion; it also measures an evolving sense of what Ibsen does, and why and how he does it – evolving not so much because Fontane changes his mind as because Ibsen writes new and different plays, one of them *Hedda Gabler*, his first play of the 1890s.

In the late 1880s Fontane reviewed four Ibsen productions for the *Vossische Zeitung*: *Ghosts* (*Gespenster*) at the Residenztheater in January 1887, and the same play performed as the *Freie Bühne*'s opening production, at the *Lessingtheater* in September 1889; *The Wild Duck* (*Die Wildente*) at the *Residenztheater* in October 1888; and *The Lady from the Sea* (*Die Frau vom Meere*) at the *Königliches Schauspielhaus* in March 1889. Each time he makes his view of the play as such very clear; on *The Lady from the Sea* this takes so much space that he expands into a second article and still needs a second visit to the theatre and a third article in order to say something about the performance and acting.

The 1887 review of *Ghosts* is, for a Fontane-novice like myself, tantalisingly perverse – which I take to signal ambivalence. It seems at first sight to place Fontane as firmly anti-Ibsen. Ibsen, he says by way of an analysis of the play, nails two theses to "his new version of the Wittenberg Schloßkirche":[16] 1. Marry for love, not for money; and 2. But if you do marry for money and discover you have married a libertine, then leave him at once, or the marriage will be unhappy and immoral, and the

---

13 "Bewunderung und Dank [...] Er hat neue Gestalten und vor allem eine neue Sprache geschaffen", Fontane to Friedrich Stephany, 17 May 1898, HFA, IV, 4, 720.

14 I follow the dating of this manuscript given in NFA, XXI/2, 946.

15 Fontane: Henrik Ibsen. Entwurf einer Charakteristik, Literarische Essays und Studien, NFA, XXI/2, 359.

16 "[S]eine neue Wittenberger Schloßkirche"; Fontane: Henrik Ibsen. Gespenster, Causerien über Theater, NFA, XXII, 2, 691. For the image of Ibsen as a new Luther, see the quotation in note 20 below from Leo Berg: Henrik Ibsen und das Germanenthum in der modernen Literatur. Berlin 1887, p. 5.

children will be cretins. These theses, Fontane says, are wrong ("falsch"): 1. Because, since time immemorial, people have married for convenience ("nach den 'Verhältnissen'") and not for love; and he quotes examples, ranging from Jacob in the Old Testament – with his many healthy sons – via the Spartans and the Moravian Brothers to Disraeli (and this in the year in which he published *Irrungen,Wirrungen* (*Confusions, Delusions*); and 2. Because German divorce laws make Mrs Alving's dilemma quite irrelevant. And, as for the play's suggestion that humankind is on the way to "degeneration" ("Entartung"), this is so far from the truth that he can assert: "to be a modern man or woman is to be a man or woman full of energy and nerve (certainly more full of nerve than of nerves)".[17] So everything about *Ghosts* that might cause anxiety in a reader or an audience is outdated ("uralten Datums"). To anyone who knows how poignantly *Ghosts* did speak to, and help to articulate, anxieties in England, it must seem that Fontane knows how "falsch" are his anti-theses.[18]

Nor do we have to deconstruct this piece of writing very far to find irony in the simplistic reading and blunt dismissal of the play's meaning and in the bold assurance that all is well with modern, and especially German, man and woman. Read in its immediate context, Fontane's text is a self-proclaimed mediator in the conflict of opinions in the same paper three days earlier, when "P.S.", – i.e. Paul Schlenther, an ardent Ibsenite – had published an enthusiastic review to which the editor of the paper had felt bound to add a disclaimer. One, according to Fontane, had done justice to the playwright's talent, the other to public opinion – and Fontane's intervention appears to be conceived as a tongue-in-cheek rebuttal of both. He is not being anti-Ibsen but anti the Ibsen constructed by either of the two sides. The review has to be read against a Berlin reaction to Ibsen much like that extraordinary mixture of execration and adulation of him in England after the first performance of *Ghosts* in March 1891, when most of the press was outraged by what they saw as the play's naturalistic treatment of the unspeakable (congenital syphilis) – "An open drain: a loathsome sore unbandaged; a dirty act done publicly", etc.[19] – while an intellectual élite (William Archer, Edmund Gosse, Bernard Shaw and others) seized on what they saw as Ibsen's ideology (encapsulated in Shaw's *Quintessence of Ibsenism*, 1891) and praised it to the skies. In Germany, in 1887, perhaps the most articulate of such adulators was Leo Berg, whose first study of Ibsen was published that same year, with a title which bespeaks its political agenda: *Henrik Ibsen und das Germanenthum in der modernen Literatur*. When Fontane has Ibsen nail his theses to the door of his new Wittenberg church, he is

---

17 "[E]in moderner Mensch sein heißt ein Mensch sein voll Spannkraft und Nerv (jedenfalls mehr noch voll Nerv als Nerven)", Fontane: Henrik Ibsen. Gespenster, Causerien über Theater, NFA, XXII/2, 694.

18 Ghosts released a spate of fiction dealing with marriages of convenience, venereal disease, and women's right to independence, of which Sarah Grand's The Heavenly Twins (1893) is a notable example.

19 See William Archer's collection of terms of Ibsen abuse in "Ghosts and Gibberings", Pall Mall Gazette, 8 April, 1891, reprinted in Michael Egan, (ed.): Ibsen: The Critical Heritage. London: Routledge 1972; paperback edition 1985, pp. 209-214; the quotation is on p. 209.

surely mocking the ethos of the Bergian appropriation of Ibsen as another Luther and altogether a supreme model of German culture:

> German is his great and single-minded love of the truth and the courage [...] to proclaim it, German is his manfulness and genuinely German his belligerence [...] that belligerence which we find in a Hutten, a Luther, a Lessing.[20]

It is worth noting that the issue of the *Vossische Zeitung* in which Fontane's article appeared (13 January 1887) also carried an account of the banquet ("Festmahl") given in Ibsen's honour two days earlier. Fontane is being something of an iconoclast. At the same time, the review's exaggerated reassurance that all is well in German society surely mocks the public outrage which was itself a sign that deep anxieties had been stirred. Fontane is holding a double mirror up to a complacent society. And to do so he leaves out at least half of his own fundamental attitude to Ibsen: that which he had expressed in a private letter to Schlenther before either of their reviews had appeared when, after objecting to Ibsen's *Weltanschauung*, he concluded "My admiration for the poetic work remains".[21]

The point here is that both sides, whether for or against Ibsen, were seeing the playwright primarily as a social critic, and that this is what Fontane deplores – just as Ibsen himself was increasingly to distance himself from that approach to his plays, and indeed, from the late 1880s, to write plays which were increasingly inaccessible to that approach. In a well-known, but even today not always heeded, speech to the Norwegian Women's Rights League in 1898 he was to say: "I have been more of a poet and less of a social philosopher than people generally seem inclined to believe". This is in fact the essence of what Fontane is saying about him in his second review of *Ghosts*. Writing about the Freie Bühne production in 1889, he can begin with the actors' ability to realise the complexity of Ibsen's characters. This Mrs Alving, for example, unlike the statuesque "Matrone" of the 1887 production, showed "the nervously volatile" temperament of a "modern woman".[22] Writing "straight" this time, he can brush aside "a whole Ibsen literature" on the play's social and moral "message", and assure his readers that the audience was gripped, and *not* by the truth of the content as a social and moral message but by "the artistic seriousness of [Ibsen's]

---

20 It is difficult to do justice to the rhetoric of the original: "Deutsch ist seine große und einzige Wahrheitsliebe und der Muth [...] sie zu bekennen, deutsch ist seine Mannhaftigkeit und echt deutsch seine unbändige Kampfeslust [...] jene Kampfeslust, die wir bei einem Hutten, einem Luther, einem Lessing finden", in Leo Berg: Henrik Ibsen und das Germanenthum in der modernen Literatur, p. 5, quoted from David E. R. George: Henrik Ibsen in Deutschland: Rezeption und Revision, transl. by Heinz Ludwig Arnold und Bernd Glasenapp. Göttingen: Vandenhoeck and Ruprecht 1968, Palaestra. vol. 251, p. 31f.

21 "Die Bewunderung für die dichterische Arbeit bleibt", Fontane to Paul Schlenther, 9 January 1887, HFA, IV, 3, 512.

22 "[D]as nervös Bewegliche [...] Eine moderne Frau ...", Fontane: Henrik Ibsen. Gespenster, Causerien über Theater NFA, XXII/2, 707.

creation".[23] What is "truth" in literature, anyway, he asks. What matters is not *what* Ibsen thinks but the passion of his conviction and its transmutation into art. To an English reader it is not Bernard Shaw but Walter Pater who springs to mind when Fontane insists that the important effect of Ibsen's play is the intensity of its art.[24] He goes on to provide a defence of realism as the modern mode of representation: a secular age, he says, knows that it cannot have Paradise, so it wants "ein Gusten des Lebens" (note, a taste, not a slice, of life). This has led to an emphasis on things which perhaps should have been left out (implying the syphilis in *Ghosts*). But, with an optimism which is as much metaphysical as stylistic, he asserts that in the end even this mode will find "the beautiful" ("das Schöne") – *and* give it a keener presentation because the eye has, meanwhile, learned to see more keenly. He is, it seems to me, very much enquiring into his own art here. Ibsen seems to be having on him the catalytic effect that Henry James defined in his review article on *Hedda Gabler*:[25] if the play doesn't enable us to say that we know Ibsen better, "we may at least say that we know more about ourselves", and about our critical assumptions. This would seem to be confirmed by Fontane's reflections, in a letter to Georg Friedlaender, on his own review of *The Wild Duck*:

> Such reviews do not, perhaps, enlighten anyone else, but they certainly enlighten him who writes them, because they give him the opportunity to tackle the most difficult questions, not in order to solve them but to pose them.[26]

The review of *The Wild Duck* in March 1888 shows this play to be, as one might expect, altogether more congenial to him than *Ghosts*. He admires the everyday "realism" of the play: "It is the most difficult thing there is, and perhaps the highest, to represent the everyday in such a light that that which just now was indifferent and prosaic suddenly moves us with the irresistible magic of poetry".[27] And the example he gives, of Gina adding up her household expenses ("Brot 15, Speck 3, Käse 10, ja, – 's geht auf") puts one in mind of the "magic of poetry" given to "half an Edam cheese,

---

23 "[D]urch den künstlerischen Ernst seines Schaffens", Fontane: Henrik Ibsen. Gespenster, Causerien über Theater NFA, XXII/2, 707.

24 Cf. "To burn always with this hard, gemlike flame, to maintain this ecstasy, is success in life. [...] For art comes to you, proposing frankly to give nothing but the highest quality to your moments as they pass, and simply for those moments' sake": Walter Pater: The Renaissance: Studies in Art and Poetry (1873). London: Macmillan 1912, "Conclusion", pp. 250, 252.

25 "On the occasion of *Hedda Gabler*", New Review, June 1891; reprinted in Egan (ed.): Ibsen: The Critical Heritage, pp. 234-244; p. 235.

26 "Solche Kritiken erquicken vielleicht keinen andern, aber sicherlich *den*, der sie schreibt, weil er in ihnen Gelegenheit findet, sich an die schwierigsten Fragen heran zu machen, nicht um sie zu lösen, aber doch um sie zu *stellen*", Fontane to Georg Friedlaender, 24 October 1888, HFA, IV, 3, 650.

27 "Es ist das Schwierigste, was es gibt (und vielleicht auch das Höchste), das Alltagsdasein in eine Beleuchtung zu rücken, daß das, was eben noch Gleichgültigkeit und Prosa war, uns plötzlich mit dem bestrickendsten Zauber der Poesie berührt", Fontane: Henrik Ibsen. Die Wildente, Causerien über Theater NFA, XXII/2, 696.

which was not really much more than a red rind" in *The Poggenpuhl Family,*[28] a novel which, self-reflectively, has the would-be aristocratic Therese disapprove of "this predilection for the natural that modern art thinks it has a right to. I, on the other hand, believe that art should throw a veil".[29]

In *The Lady from the Sea* Fontane again sees Ibsen's greatness as being in his art and his weakness in what he regards as the "doctrinaire" element, the "marriage problem" which enters into the last two acts and, he feels, turns the dénouement into another Ibsen "thesis", where the magic word ("die Zauberformel") "freedom" transforms the marriage of Ellida and Dr. Wangel into a genuine one. Both he and the *Vossische Zeitung* are for freedom, he writes, but they don't expect *that* much from it. Elsewhere he summed up the play and his criticism of it in an epigram:

> Ellida suffers from longing, from longing for sea and sailor.
> Freedom cures her. It happens. But it happens [here], I think, too quickly.[30]

Ibsen was present and lionised at the performance which the first two instalments of Fontane's review record; and in many ways his criticisms are a reaction against the general, uncritical adulation. It seems that Fontane shared with Ibsen a fondness for saying "On the contrary". The third instalment records a performance two weeks later, and by this time the play itself has come under criticism from critics who did not find enough social morality in it.[31] In contradistinction Fontane now emphasises that the important Ibsen in this play is the poet – a poet betrayed by the "social" critics. The magic of Ibsen's poetic-dramatic art lies in the creation of a woman with mysterious fears and longings – the obsession with the strange sailor, the child with the fish-eyes of this Stranger, the fear of having more children, the homesickness and longing for the sea.

I said I would not speak of influence, and I will not, except to point out that there *could* be a moment of cross-fertilisation here: one could imagine the figure of Ellida, married to a much older man and with sexual hang-ups and indefinite longings centred on the "Meerman", going into the matrix that was to produce Effi Briest. One could also say that Ibsen's move from *The Lady from the Sea* to *Hedda Gabler* could well have been a response to Fontane's criticism. Whether it was or (most likely) not,

---

28 "[D]en halben Edamer, der eigentlich nur noch eine rote Schale war", Fontane: Die Poggenpuhls, NFA, IV, 312. Cited from Delusions, Confusions and The Poggenpuhl Family, ed. by Peter Demetz, transl. by William L. Zwiebel, The German Library, vol. 47. New York: Continuum 1984, p. 200.

29 "Es ist das eben die Vorliebe für das Natürliche, das die moderne Kunst als ihr gutes Recht ansieht; ich glaube aber umgekehrt, daß die Kunst verhüllen soll", Fontane: Die Poggenpuhls, NFA, IV, 343. Zwiebel: The Poggenpuhl Family, p. 257.

30 "Ellida leidet an Sehnsucht, an Sehnsucht nach Meer und nach Meermann.
   Freiheit heilt sie. Es geht. Aber es geht mir zu flink."
   Fontane: Nach der Aufführung von Ibsens "Frau vom Meere", Balladen und Gedichte, NFA, XX, 627.

31 Fontane: Henrik Ibsen. Die Frau vom Meere, Causerien über Theater, NFA, XXII/2, 605-611.

Hedda Gabler is no more "doctrinaire" than *Effi Briest*. It cannot be seen to suggest a social solution, or even a simple social motivation. And in the Ibsen plays which followed in the 1890s – his last four plays: *The Master Builder, Little Eyolf, John Gabriel Borkman* and *When We Dead Awaken* – society is no longer a major antagonist. Their worlds are made up of fraught human relationships, intimate, internalised spheres with their own private demons. Their mode of presentation is still realism (in *Little Eyolf*, a bereaved father can still find himself wondering what's for dinner), and there are psychological explanations for characters' words and deeds, but we have to dig deep into the subconscious to find them, and then they are often multiple and self-contradictory. "Sign is set against sign", as one characters sums up the attempt to fathom Ellida, the Lady from the Sea. The irrational merges into the uncanny – in Master Builder Solness's mind; in the Ratwife of *Little Eyolf*; in Borkman's vision of the spirits of infinite wealth in the mountains; in the death-in-life of Irene, the sculptor's ex-model. As in *Effi Briest*, the apparently spare language sustains a network of echoes and allusions; and revisions in the preserved drafts show that every word has been weighed. The art is as much of the unsaid as of the said – and as readers or members of an audience we are forced to work at what lies beneath the tip of the iceberg. There are no simple cathartic endings. As with Fontane's novels, the immediate effect of details – scenes or moments – is challenged by the after-effect of each work as a whole. The plays are self-reflective, draw attention to their art as art; they also have protagonists who are creators in one form or other and who put before us questions of the relation of art to life.

In the end, we remember, Fontane's attitude to Ibsen came to rest on admiration of his creation of "new characters and *above all* a new language".[32] Though Fontane was dead when Ibsen completed *When We Dead Awaken* (1899), the "new language" in the opening scene of that play may (in a very literal translation) serve to indicate that its author was treading a path similar to that of the author of *Effi Briest*. The burned-out sculptor Rubek and Maja, ageing husband and young wife in a marriage of sterile convenience, are making apparently ordinary, bored, small talk. Rubek is saying how, as they were coming up north on the train in the night, he could tell that they were approaching their own country:

> RUBEK: ... I notice how silent (literally "sound-less") it was at all the little stations [*pause*]. I heard the silence [soundlessness], [*pause*] like you, Maja [*pause*].
> MAJA: Hm, [*pause*] like me. Yes.
> RUBEK: [*pause*] and then I understood that we had crossed the border. That we were really at home. Because at all the little stations the train stopped, [*pause*] though nothing was happening.
> MAJA: Why did it stop then? When there was nothing?
> RUBEK: Don't know. No traveller got off, and no one got on. And the train, it still stood there for a long, endless, time. And at each station I could hear two railway men walking along the platform, [*pause*] one had a lantern in his hand, [*pause*] and they were talking to each other, quietly, and tonelessly and meaninglessly, in the night.

---

32 "[...] neue Gestalten und *vor allem* eine neue Sprache"; Fontane to Friedrich Stephany, 17 May 1898, HFA, IV, 4, 720. The italics are mine.

MAJA: Yes. You are right. There are always a couple of men talking [*pause*]
RUBEK: [*pause*] about nothing.

The dialogue is certainly realistic, an image of a particular relationship; but because of the way the prosaic material has been handled, it also grows into an image of a whole world of individuals wrapped up in silence, walking aimlessly and talking soundlessly of nothing, a world where trains stop for no reason at each isolated station. Ibsen joins Fontane among the forerunners of Samuel Beckett.

Yet, even if we agree that the two writers shared a journey through naturalism towards modernism, it would be wrong to end on a note of desolation. If they shared a mood of pessimism, they also shared a creative joy in modes of expressing it. The Freie Bühne's production of *Ghosts*, we saw, prompted Fontane to envisage how a kind of secular, disillusioned beauty might be achieved through naturalism: "After the desert came the good land".[33] Within a few months he was putting this into practice, in writing the first draft of *Effi Briest*. In his Anglo-Saxon manner Henry James, the subtlest Ibsen critic of the 1890s, made much the same point when *Hedda Gabler* prompted him to write that, in Ibsen's studies of contemporary life, "the impression that is strongest with us is that the picture is infinitely noted, that all the patience of the constructive pessimist is in his love of the detail of character and conduct."[34] Would Fontane. I wonder, have recognised this as the source of the "Ibsen-effect"?

---

33 "Nach der Wüste kam gutes Land." Fontane: Henrik Ibsen. Gespenster, Causerien über Theater, NFA, XXII/2, 708.

34 Henry James: On the Occasion of *Hedda Gabler*. In Egan (ed.): Ibsen: The Critical Heritage, p. 238.

Hans Vilmar Geppert

Prussian Decadence: *Schach von Wuthenow* in an international context

When Edward Waverley goes stag-hunting in the Highlands one of the most sophisticated, most meaningful chapters of the European historical novel is about to begin.[1] And several of its structural features will be a model for Fontane's *Schach von Wuthenow* (*A Man of Honor*). The stags suddenly turn around and race directly towards the hunters. "Throw yourself on the ground" is the general outcry. But Edward does not understand Gaelic. While his convalescence is happily progressing – his skilful leech now in return speaks not one word of English – the clans gather, the Standard is raised, the historical events of the Jacobite Rebellion of 1745 begin their course. Edward suddenly has to defend himself against incriminations of absence without leave, even cowardice; when he tries to regain his troop of Dragoons he is mistaken for a Jacobite spy, imprisoned, freed by a rebel special command, falls ill; meanwhile Bonnie Prince Charlie takes Edinburgh, and Edward has more or less no other option than to join the Prince's cause, reunited with his new-found friends, near the fascinating Flora again, and so on.

Of the roughly three months in which Fabrice del Dongo journeys into history and back again[2] – the first part of Stendhal's *La chartreuse de Parme* (1839) is clearly a little historical novel – he spends exactly thirty-three days in prison and is ill for about four weeks. Between those stretches of inertia he somehow takes part in the Battle of Waterloo (18/19 June, 1815). But of these forty-three hours of fighting he is most of the time carried along, or is asleep, does not understand a thing ("rien à rien") of what is going on. He does not know the famous Field Marshal Ney, and when his idol, Napoleon himself, is riding past, and everybody is shouting "vive l'empereur", Fabrice, after no breakfast and a few gulps of *eau-de-vie*, misses even this highlight of historical experience. Weeks later on his way home he has to ask himself whether what he had seen was a battle and whether that battle had been Waterloo?[3]

"Dinner took a long time and was delicious."[4] It is almost enough to quote this sentence to evoke the whole pattern. It is the night of 23 February 1848. On the streets of Paris the revolution is flaring up. The next day, also the beginning of the first part, the historical one, of Gustave Flaubert's *L'Éducation sentimentale* (1869), the "hero" Frédéric Moreau will see in the morning the storm on the Palais Royal and hear late in

---

1   Sir Walter Scott: Waverley (1814), ed. by Andrew Hook. London: Penguin Classics 1985, pp. 186-195 (Chapter 24).

2   Stendhal: La chartreuse de Parme, ed. by Michel Crouzet, Garnier Flammarion 26. Paris: Flammarion 1964, pp. 37-107.

3   "Ce qu'il avait vu, était-ce une bataile, et en second lieu, cette bataille était-elle Waterloo?" Stendhal: La chartreuse de Parme, p. 105.

4   "Le repas fut long, délicat ", Gustave Flaubert: L'Éducation sentimentale, ed. by Édouard Maynial, Classiques Garnier. Paris: Garnier 1964, p. 284. All translations into English are my own.

the evening that the provisional government has been proclaimed. But tonight he is taking the easy-going Rosanette to dinner and then into the little flat he had lovingly prepared for "somebody else".[5] The love he confesses to her, while weeping for the "other one", hearing as a distant rolling sound the preparations for the next day, is a lie. So is, according to Flaubert, the revolution. In this context, the little sentence "le repas fut long, délicat" is not only like a slap in the face of the enthusiastic people around, especially of Frédéric's friends. The distance and completeness of the past historic has an effect of instant disillusion. The double predication adds a meaning of insipidness to the predicate "delicious" and of emptiness to the predicate "long". Lifetime and the time of history are for one significant moment completely out of joint. Still, their narrated synchronisation creates between private and public life a meaningful trope of synecdoche (*"partem pro toto"*).[6] Yet their common semantic content, the generalisation between them, is a lie. While the possibility, the form of understanding history springs up, its sense is negated.

Is there not also in Fontane's consciously constructed synecdoche of Schach's personal and Prussia's general fate in the summer of 1806 a distinctly negative semantic history to be heard?[7] And is Schach, hiding in Wuthenow from the ridicule caused by his relations to two women, mother and daughter, the daughter having, from smallpox, "a few dimples too many",[8] while war between Prussia and France is becoming more and more inevitable – is Schach here so very different from Frédéric having a long and sophisticated meal on the eve of the Revolution? As Frédéric hears in the morning the grumbling of agitated masses on the march, so Schach, reporting back to barracks after his holiday which began on about 3 August, should have heard the tidings that on 8 August the King of Prussia had mobilised the greatest part of his army.[9] Or consider the situation that Schach on the Sunday before the Friday of his wedding, as the narrator tells us, "with an imaginative inventiveness otherwise completely unlike him, was carried away by all kinds of images and plans for possible

---

5 "Le logement préparé pour l'autre", Flaubert: L'Éducation sentimentale, p. 285.

6 The "metahistorical" readings of historical novels in this paper are inspired above all by the work of Hayden White, namely Metahistory: The Historical Imagination in Nineteenth-Century Europe. Baltimore and London: Johns Hopkins University Press 1973; The Content of Form: Narrative Discourse and Historical Representation. Baltimore and London: Johns Hopkins University Press 1987; Auch Klio dichtet oder Die Fiktionen des Faktischen: Studien zur Tropologie des historischen Diskurses, transl. by Brigitte Brinkmann-Siepmann and Thomas Siepmann. Stuttgart: Klett 1986. For further discussions of tropology see also Jacques Dubois, F. Edeline and others: Allgemeine Rhetorik, transl. and ed. by Armin Schütz. Munich: Fink 1974, pp. 152-201.

7 Fontane: Schach von Wuthenow. Eine Erzählung aus der Zeit des Regiments Gensdarmes (Schach von Wuthenow. A Tale from the Times of the Gensdarmes Regiment) (1882), NFA, II, 271-388. Further references are made to the commentary in HFA, I, 1, 951-991.

8 "ein paar Grübchen zu viel", Fontane: Schach von Wuthenow, NFA, II, 383.

9 For the exact chronology in *Schach von Wuthenow* see below, footnote 14; details of the historical context can be found in any history of nineteenth-century Germany, for instance Gebhardt: Handbuch der Deutschen Geschichte, 9th edition, ed. by Herbert Grundmann, vol. 3: Von der Französischen Revolution bis zum Ersten Weltkrieg, ed. by Karl Erich Born et al.. Stuttgart: Union 1970, pp. 41-50.

voyages".[10] Travel plans of an ambitious career officer in a crack regiment, practically on the eve of war: does not the whole situation have not only an aura of tragedy (Schach has already made his firm resolution) but like Frédéric's behaviour, something absurd about it, too?[11]

However, Fontane does not inform the reader about this albeit important historical background. His art is one of changing arguments. Let us start with a look back at the tradition. What gives *Schach von Wuthenow* a place in the avant-garde of Walter Scott reception in the nineteenth century is the skilful use of that experimental fictional-historical synecdoche which Walter Scott invented. Only small incidents of history are presented, glimpses of historical people are given, but they imply long and important traditions. Especially in the French reception of Walter Scott,[12] Alfred de Vigny's *Cinq Mars* (1826), Stendhal, Flaubert, this synecdoche took a negative turn: the part negating the whole in favour of the life of the soul, memory, art, style – we shall investigate aestheticism in *Schach von Wuthenow* later on. Fontane, like no other German writer before him, indeed plays with the negative semantics of history. But his negations are only functional, not an end in themselves. The force of synecdoche here once more takes a different turn.

It is deliberately constructed and at the beginning of the novel very explicit. We know that Fontane found in the Berlin "chronique scandaleuse" the anecdote involving the spirited but ugly Fräulein von Crayen and the debt-ridden man about town, one Major von Schack, and that he moved this anecdote from 1815 back to 1806 in order to gain the specific negative historical significance it now has.[13] In the first part of the novel the talk in the salons and coffee-houses is packed with historical allusions, beginning with the treaty between France and Prussia of 15 February 1806 concluded by Graf Haugwitz and so on.[14] But after the sleigh-ride (which is itself historical and

---

10 "Schach hing mit einer ihm sonst völlig fremden Phantastik allen erdenklichen Reiseplänen und Reisebildern nach", Fontane: Schach von Wuthenow, NFA, II, 377.

11 Manfred Dutschke: Geselliger Spießrutenlauf. Die Tragödie des lächerlichen Junkers Schach von Wuthenow. In: Theodor Fontane: Text und Kritik, ed. by Heinz Ludwig Arnold. Munich: text u. kritik 1989, pp. 103-116, stresses the "Welt des Scheins" (p.106) and the element of a "funktionslos gewordener [...] Repräsentant der Repräsentation [...], lächerlich in dem Augenblick, in dem die Aura der Unantastbarkeit seiner Kavaliersmaske durch das Bekanntwerden einer banalen Intimität zerstoben ist"; "representative of official prestige [...] who has lost his function [becoming] ridiculous when the untouchable aura of his mask as a gentleman is instantly dispersed on the revelation of his banal intimacy." (p. 113f.). But does Schach not gain beyond the ridicule a new absurdly tragic dimension?

12 Cf. my article, Ein Feld von Differenzierungen. Zur kritisch-produktiven Scott-Rezeption von Arnim bis Fontane. In: Beiträge zur Rezeption der britischen und irischen Literatur des neunzehnten Jahrhunderts im deutschsprachigen Raum, ed. by Norbert Bachleitner. Amsterdam and Atlanta: Rodopi 2000, pp. 479-500.

13 For the details see the commentary in HFA, I, 1, 951-991, especially pp. 952-958, or Walther P. Guenther: Preußischer Gehorsam: Theodor Fontanes Novelle Schach von Wuthenow, Text und Deutung. Nördlingen: Greno 1981, pp. 181-186 and 197-199.

14 "Hannover", as it is mentioned in this passage, does not refer to the treaty of Schönbrunn (15 December 1805) named in the commentary in HFA, I, 1, 971 but to the later treaty. The action of the

happened on 23 July), that is, after Victoire's confiding in her mother and the plot entering its peripetic stage, these allusions stop completely. Fontane does not mention for instance the declarations of mutual support between Prussia and the Tsar, the latter given on 24 July, the same day that Frau von Carayon insists on "legalising what has happened".[15] Fontane does not mention the "Säbelwetzen" ("sabre-sharpening") of Schach's regimental comrades on the steps of the French embassy (a typical subject for a traditional historical novel, presented for instance as an excusable prank by Willibald Alexis in his *Vaterländischer Roman: Ruhe ist die erste Bürgerpflicht* (1852), and which replaced the sleigh-ride in the film-version of *Schach von Wuthenow*). The end of the German Empire and the mobilisation of the Prussian army soon afterwards – on 8 August, therefore during the time Schach spends at Wuthenow am See – are not mentioned either. We can see how deliberately Fontane constructed his "case of Schach" and then the limbo in which he lets Schach and the Carayon family move. Right at the end of the novel, as we know, Fontane consciously returns to his technique of historical allusions. He makes Bülow write: "War has been declared".[16] But even here, Fontane plays a little with the difference between fiction and history.[17] Bülow, as always in the novel, knows everything better than anybody else. On 14 September, the date of his letter, he can only allude to the Prussian ultimatum, the rest is his perfectly competent personal interpretation, of course verified later on. (The war was declared on 9 October, Prince Louis fell in a skirmish on 10 October, the devastating defeat at Jena and Auerstadt followed on 14 October.) Yet Fontane deliberately stops at the anticipation of history. He constructs a trope that may be called ana-synecdoche: *pars pro toto futuro*, the historical event just over the horizon interpreting the fictional case and vice versa. This is in itself an innovation, deliberately used later on, for instance, by Louis Aragon in *La semaine sainte* (*Holy Week*) (1958) or by Jurek Becker in *Jakob der Lügner* (*Jacob the Liar*) (1969) or, as I will show, several times by Uwe Johnson.

And there is more. The aposiopese, the meaningful silencing of historical allusions during the Schach-Carayon crisis has changed the direction of the inference the readers are to draw, from implication to replication (in replication we can indeed infer from the result to the premise). As this is the fundamental structure of narration ("la logique à rebours")[18] it is not only the narrated mediations, in the two concluding letters, but the argument itself which makes the discourse of the novel self referential. It says for

---

novel begins in April 1806 and ends on about 20 August 1806 (cf. Guenther: Preußischer Gehorsam, p. 259).

15 "Legitimisierung des Geschehenen", Fontane: Schach von Wuthenow, NFA, II, 341.

16 "Der Krieg ist erklärt ", Fontane: Schach von Wuthenow, NFA, II, 384.

17 The "productive difference between fiction and history" seems to me a better definition of the constructive/deconstructive principle of the historical novel than the "Hiatus". Cf. Hans Vilmar Geppert: Der 'andere' historische Roman. Theorie und Strukturen einer diskontinuierlichen Gattung. Tübingen: Niemeyer 1976; a revised edition, Der historische Roman, Traditionen – Strukturen – Vergleiche. Tübingen and Basel: Francke, is forthcoming.

18 Algirdas Julien Greimas and Joseph Courtés: Sémiotique. Dictionnaire raisonné de la théorie du langage. Paris: Hachette 1979, p. 245.

instance: all this is a construct, a staged, narrated theatre, with a deliberate distance between foreground and background. Then it says: delve into this case of Schach, read again, analyse his character, his motives, circumstances and so on. Read Schach in the knowledge of Prussian decadence and defeat! And as a third impulse for the "implied reader" of *Schach von Wuthenow* this ana-synecdoche and replication let the argument stop at the single, limited *totum* of defeat.[19] The "case of Schach" is not to be blended into historical evolution and progress – as was always the case in Walter Scott's novels, and even more so in Fontane's own *Vor dem Sturm (Before the Storm)* (1878). There is indeed nothing in the novel that points to Prussian reforms, the war of 1813 or the rise of Prussia in the nineteenth century. This is even more remarkable compared with the massive forward-looking perspectives that Alexis provided in his corresponding novels, where he makes it abundantly clear that "Katzbach" and "Leipzig" are to come after "Jena".[20] On the contrary the historical Gensdarmes Regiment will be shamefully dissolved, the historical Bülow will die one year later in a Russian prison, Victoire is to go into a kind of exile.[21] Fontane concentrates on aporia, presents a consciously staged foreground and background and between the two sets very clear markings of aposiopese, even of the absurd.

Let us look from here at two more international examples of avant-garde Scott reception and their possible heuristic relevance for *Schach von Wuthenow*. At the end of the first fifth of William Faulkner's *Absalom, Absalom!* (1936), the family history told in many different voices and on extremely different levels of time and memory, this family history of a self-made man from the North fiercely identifying himself with the southern aristocracy, comes to a decisive turning-point. But Miss Rosa, a never young old maid, living herself in a sort of limbo of almost total isolation, imagines a romance, love and a wedding between her niece and a handsome, decadent young man from New Orleans. So she sets herself the task of "sewing tediously and without skill on the garments which she was making for her niece's trousseau [...] while news came of Lincoln's election and of the fall of Sumpter".[22] This not only reminds one of Walter Scott's laconism regarding history ("here he heard the tidings of the decisive battle of Culloden");[23] it is quite a "historical romance" Miss Rosa has in mind, similar to Aunt Marguerite who knew all the time what a tender web Victoire and Schach were weaving; and it is certainly the fictional-historical synecdoche Scott invented that is

---

19 Cf. Dubois: Allgemeine Rhetorik, pp. 162-170: An "exocentric referential" function (part of a "thing" as "totum") is relevant in this historical synecdoche. That Fontane prefers arguments of singularity is well known; yet this is a very deliberate case: the narrator "igelt sich ein" ("rolls up like a hedgehog"), Hugo Aust: Theodor Fontane: Ein Studienbuch. Tübingen and Basel: Francke 1998, p. 89.

20 Willibald Alexis (W. Häring): Ruhe ist die erste Bürgerpflicht. Vaterländischer Roman, ed. by H. Marshall. Halle: Hendel undated, p. 823f. Victorious Prussian battles took place at Katzbach and Leipzig in 1813.

21 Cf. Commentary to Schach von Wuthenow, HFA, I, 1, 951-991. (p. 954f. and p. 971).

22 William Faulkner: Absalom, Absalom! London: Penguin 1971, p. 64.

23 Walter Scott, Waverley, p. 429.

here, in the tradition of Stendhal and Thackeray[24] and Fontane taking another experimental turn. We recognise in the motive of voluntary prison and voluntary exile from life, both repeatedly emphasised in *Absalom, Absalom!*, that theme of time aporia, which briefly came up in Edward Waverley's illness and imprisonment, grew stronger in the total disillusionment in *La chartreuse de Parme*, is dominant already with Flaubert (the famous end of the fifth and the beginning of the sixth chapter of the third book) and which of course makes the end of *Schach von Wuthenow* so thrilling.

The influence of William Faulkner on Uwe Johnson, as on many German post-war novelists, is well known.[25] Faulkner translated, so to speak, the Walter Scott tradition insofar as he turned its *pars pro toto* into a two-fold traumatic history. A personal trauma gives access to a historically general traumatic past. Thus Quentin Compson in his cold student dormitory in Harvard, far away and sixty years later, tells this story of incest and murder, because one half-brother had "a little spot of negro blood", all this in the context of the civil war and its still haunting memory.[26] Subconsciously, but his mind is open for the reader, he remembers his own traumatic relationship to his sister, which the reader can know from *The Sound and the Fury* (1929). Trauma and time aporia here enhance each other: Quentin, after being the last voice in *Absalom, Absalom!*, as again one can tell from the earlier novel, has less than half a year to live until his suicide.

The end of Uwe Johnson's *Jahrestage* (1970-1983) is not as dense, certainly not as full of pathos. Yet, for Gesine Cresspahl her time in New York had been a kind of voluntary exile ("Unknown. Nobody, disguised. Not recognisable."). It was in this exile that she – and Johnson himself even more so – could tell their so typically German traumatic history of the Nazi period, cold war, oppression in the GDR, restoration in the West. The end of the novel especially lets several stories of personal-political aporia and of the death of the men in Gesine's life overlap, so to speak, on several levels of time: for instance her lover Jakob's suicide (or accident, or murder?) on the day and on the railroads Russian troops rode on towards Hungary at the end of October 1956. Gesine's short stay in Denmark at the end of *Jahrestage* is, without her knowing it, an exile from exile. Her crossing of borders will lead nowhere. She is on her way to Prague, she intends to help build up a new democracy there: "History is a project". But it is now 20 August 1968, at about four in the afternoon. Gesine takes a stroll by the sea, remembering her life, her finished manuscript, her people, seeing

---

24 Historical events "need not be described", "need scarce be told", "of this action there is little need to speak" and so on are typical remarks in William M. Thackeray's novel The History of Henry Esmond (1852), ed. by John Sutherland and Michael Greenfield. London: Penguin 1985, p. 274 and p. 314.

25 Uwe Johnson: Mutmaßungen über Jakob (Speculations about Jacob) (1959), Günter Grass: Katz und Maus (Cat and Mouse) (1961), Johannes Bobrowski: Levins Mühle (Levin's Mill) (1964), Alfred Andersch: Efraim (Efraim's Book) (1967), Christa Wolf: Nachdenken über Christa T. (The Quest for Christa T.) (1968) and Kindheitsmuster (Patterns of Childhood) (1973), Uwe Johnson: Jahrestage (Anniversaries) (1970-1983) among others.

26 Faulkner, Absalom, Absalom!, p. 254.

herself "on her way to the place where the dead are".[27] Back at night, untold by Johnson but inevitably, she must hear that the Warsaw Pact troops on this same day have invaded Czechoslovakia and struck out her future. Is this so very different from Victoire whispering confidentially to Schach: "Till tomorrow. Do you hear? ...Where will we be tomorrow?"[28] minutes before Schach's suicide, while all around Prussian-French tensions are mounting? And is there not an interesting analogy between this scene and that of Judith Sutpen in Faulkner's *Absalom, Absalom!* waiting in the big house, waiting for her lover who for her brother is "the nigger that's going to sleep with [his] sister", all this in the midst of the Confederate troops streaming back?[29]

"We shall read *Schach von Wuthenow*. [From this book] we had learned to read German."[30] This not only frames one of the most explicit quotations and meta-critical literary reflexions in *Jahrestage*; it introduces, I am convinced, a model of reading that Uwe Johnson recommends for his own book. I cannot explain here the allusions and cross-references he uses. Of greater interest is the close link Johnson seems to see between the traditions of modernism, Faulkner for instance, traditions Johnson has adopted, and Fontane's novel. I will try to show two things. First, how Fontane indeed anticipated the time stratifications we find later on in Faulkner, or in Uwe Johnson, or, for instance, in a novel like Graham Swift's *Waterland* (1993), so clearly influenced by Faulkner, too. And secondly, the theme of time aporia in *Schach von Wuthenow*.

When Bülow maintains: "We shall perish through the same world of seeming through which Schach perished", and that this "case" of Schach could only have happened there and then, he is right and wrong at the same time.[31] In any case he says more than he could ever know. By limiting and concentrating his story, by crossing out simple historical continuity, Fontane generalises in a way completely beyond Bülow's grasp. In other words, in the second reading, so clearly recommended, the ana-synecdoche, characteristic of Fontane and which we just now recognised in Johnson, this trope *pars pro singulo toto futuro* turns into two new discontinuous tropes (*per immutationem* and *per transmutationem*):[32] a metaphor of general decadence, in which Bülow himself becomes part of the case, and a discontinuous metonymy of the Prussia of 1806 and that of Fontane's own time.

---

27 Uwe Johnson: Jahrestage: Aus dem Leben von Gesine Cresspahl, 4 vols., Frankfurt a. M.: Suhrkamp 1970-1983, p. 1037 "Unbekannt. Niemand, getarnt. Nicht kenntlich."; p. 1891 "Geschichte ist ein Entwurf", "unterwegs an den Ort, wo die Toten sind".

28 "'Bis auf morgen. Hörst du? ... Wo sind wir morgen?'" Fontane: Schach von Wuthenow, NFA, II, 381.

29 Faulkner: Absalom, Absalom!, p. 295.

30 "Wir lesen *Schach von Wuthenow*. [Hier hatte wir] das Deutsche lesen gelernt", Uwe Johnson, Jahrestage, p. 1694 and p. 1707.

31 "Wir werden an derselben Welt des Scheins zugrunde gehen, an der Schach zugrunde gegangen ist." Fontane: Schach von Wuthenow, NFA, II, 384.

32 Dubois: Allgemeine Rhetorik, p. 78f. One could also use the terms "paralepsis" and "analepsis", according to Gérard Genette: Discours du récit, Figures III. Paris: Éditions du Seuil 1972, pp. 77-121; the fundamental concept is that of the *ordo artificialis*.

In one sense *Schach von Wuthenow* is packed with metaphors of decadence, blending the romanticism of around 1806 with the symbolism of the second half and the end of the nineteenth century: the morbid Don Juan attitudes of Prince Louis, taken up later by Schach, the symbolism of the swan flotilla,[33] that of the dark avenue of cypresses people repeatedly look into, of course the dark moths that surround Schach at Wuthenow, and especially his falling asleep in a small boat, drifting on dark waters. If we could combine this water-picture with the cypresses we might come quite close to one of Arnold Böcklin's favourite subjects. And does not Victoire on the evening of the seduction take on features of the *femme fragile*?

More interesting of course is Schach himself. The way Fontane presents him ("pretending to have all sorts of official tasks") he seems to have nothing to do with military duties, drudgery and drill. His idleness, anti-bourgeois attitude, the sought after status of "der Aparte", ("someone out of the ordinary") the almost too easy role of being ill, his distance, during the crisis in his life, from anything public or political, the *ennui* he anticipates for his foreseeable future, "I have been here now for twelve hours and it seems to me like twelve years [...] for ever and ever and ever", his confessed escapism – is it not a *voyage à l'inconnu* he plans, not just to the borders of Europe and Africa but to "mirrorings of a mysterious distant land", even into a world of imagination: "pictures in the air", "scenes and people [from a] laterna magica", "enchantment [of] colours"? Each of these would, if isolated, seem insignificant, but taken together they make a telling picture. That Schach is so handsome is mentioned almost too often. In the context of nineteenth-century literature one could see something "feminine" in the fate that he is forced to marry after one *faux pas* and that, even more, he pays with his life for his amoral adventures. Schach's aestheticism, his need "to reduce everything to the question of beauty", his *délicatesse* at Tempelhof, not willing even to be seen publicly with Victoire, his refined taste, having a little doll-like English groom, his marked interest in "engravings and racehorses", even such a detail as his "saffron-yellow nightgloves", all this seems to take up topics often retold in the last decades of the nineteenth century.[34]

---

33 The symbolism of the "swan flotilla" (the swans greet Prince Louis, Fontane: Schach von Wuthenow, NFA, II, 321) is indeed interpreted in a replicative way by the soon to follow (historical) death of the prince. And the whole discursive connexe turns into a metaphor of décadence. Guenther, Preußischer Gehorsam, points out repeatedly the theme of the *décadence* of the "ancien régime", centred around Prince Louis, the "Vertreter einer raffinierten Dekadenz, die zum Untergang verurteilt ist" (p. 234). Ronald Speirs: Fontane und die Dekadenz. In: Theodor Fontane im literarischen Leben seiner Zeit: Beiträge zur Fontane-Konferenz vom 17. bis 20. Juni 1986 in Potsdam, ed. by Friedhilde Krause. Berlin: Deutsche Staatsbibliothek 1987, pp. 134-149, shows many "decadent" motifs in Fontane's work, stresses the overall critical aspect under which Fontane sees *décadence* and points especially to the scene of the "swan flotilla" in the context of "poplars, sunset, the dark outline of the cupola of the castle" and so on (p. 142f.).

34 "Allerhand Dienstliches vorschützend", "jetzt bin ich zwölf Stunden hier, und mir ist, als wären es zwölf Jahre [...] immer und ewig und ewig und immer", "der geheimnisvolle [...] Weltteil in Luftbildern und Spiegelungen", "Szenen und Gestalten [einer] laterna magica", "Zauber [der Farben]", "Kupferstiche und Rennpferde", "safranfarbene Nachthandschuhe", Fontane: Schach von Wuthenow, NFA, II, 283, 358, 377, 287, 307, 289. Schach's aestheticism has been repeatedly

On the one hand Schach looks like the Prussian cousin of the *fin-de-siècle* dandies in Paris, London or Vienna. On the other hand he seems to stand himself at the beginning of a tradition, specific, as far as I know, to German and above all to Austrian literature. These decadent officers reappear in Fontane's own novels: on the periphery of *Graf Petöfy* (Count Petöfy) (1884), more centrally in *Cécile* (1887) and *Irrungen, Wirrungen* (*Confusions, Delusions*) (1888), or in the character of Crampas in *Effi Briest*, in a mild and friendly light in *Der Stechlin* (1898). But far more similar to Schach for instance is Arthur Schnitzler's *Leutnant Gustl* (1901) with his completely empty sense of etiquette and his condition of being totally at the mercy of time.[35] In Heinrich Mann's undeservedly little known novel *Eugénie oder die Bürgerzeit* (Eugénie or the Bourgeois Age) (1928), a novel on the crisis of values set in 1873, the two officers literally play their life ("not much has ever taken any hold of me"), but luckily escape into its trivial pursuits.[36] It has often been remarked that the character of Pasenow and his world in the first volume of Hermann Broch's *Schlafwandler* trilogy (*The Sleepwalkers*) (1931) is reminiscent of Fontane. Pasenow believes in the "idea" of the "uniform", it takes the place of his ego or at least allows no clear border between "himself and his uniform".[37] This would have been far too explicit for Fontane, but Schach has indeed, like Pasenow, lost his personality, his independent character and free judgement by identifying completely with the forms in the society and the profession he belongs to. What Bülow calls "empty drill and empty play" has for Schach become his life. "The appearances" (for instance in Schach's criticism of Prince Louis) are paramount and the ridicule is a death-warrant. What began as aestheticism turns under pressure into a lie he is unable to give up: he could "not conquer himself", the nothingness his self had become, as Victoire puts it at the end.[38]

---

generalised. Gerhard Kaiser: Schach von Wuthenow oder die Weihe der Kraft: Variationen über ein Thema von Walther Müller-Seidel zu seinem 60. Geburtstag. In: Jahrbuch der deutschen Schiller-gesellschaft 22 (1978), pp. 474-496, stresses that Schach "nur eine äthetische Form erfüllt und daß solche äthetische Form menschlich sensibler, zugleich aber brutaler ist als jede andere"; "merely fulfils an aesthetic form and that such aesthetic form makes for a more sensitive human being but also a more brutal one than any other" (p. 486). Peter C. Pfeiffer: Tod, Entstellung, Hässlichkeit: Fontanes Schach von Wuthenow. In: Zeitschrift für Deutsche Philologie 113 (1994), pp. 264-276, sees the abstract, proto-critical side of Schach's behaviour: "Schach interagiert unter ästhetischen Prämissen [...] Er bewahrt die Konvention weder als bloße Konvention, noch als gesellschaftlich moralische, sondern als ästhetische" (p. 268f.). But what seems to me important is the significance of this aestheticism for Fontane's own time.

35 Cf. The many interesting observations in Hubert Ohl: Zeitgenossenschaft: Arthur Schnitzler und Fontane. In: Jahrbuch des Freien Deutschen Hochstifts (1991), pp. 267-307, especially p. 293.

36 "An mir hat nie viel gehaftet", Heinrich Mann: Eugénie oder Die Bürgerzeit. Hamburg: Claasen 1961, p. 136.

37 Hermann Broch: Pasenow oder die Romantik. Frankfurt a. M.: Suhrkamp 1969, pp. 22-27.

38 "Dressur und Spielerei", "[er konnte] nicht siegreich sein gegen sich selbst", Fontane: Schach von Wuthenow, NFA, II, 310, 386.

If the decadence of Schach and his society, which is a world of seeming, of "surrogates", "symbolic actions", "vanities" instead of convictions[39] – the sleigh-ride for instance is a pseudo-protest against a pseudo-questioning of pseudo-values –, if this general metaphor of decadence ("*totum pro toto*") is at the same time metonymically linked with Fontane's own time ("*pars pro parte*"), then the two tropes of history enhance each other. Fontane not only confronts the militarism of Prussia after 1871, which saw itself as superbly victorious, with its defeat in 1806: he generalises and concentrates this decadence and possible defeat into an actual significance. So Fontane indeed implied those different traumatic time levels the novel of the twentieth century has worked out. He did not see aestheticism and decadence as symptoms of a productive crisis,[40] in the way, for instance, impressionist and symbolist art aimed through themes of decadence at a transformation of aesthetic possibilities and a new awareness of reality. The discontinuity of the argument – this is specific to *Schach von Wuthenow*, not to Fontane's *oeuvre* in general, rather the opposite – says all the time: do not look for the positive continuities in these Prussian traditions, their crisis of then and today offers in itself no future perspective.[41] Look rather for an alternative, old or new, inside or outside of Prussia!

There is a repeated theme of exile at the end of *Schach von Wuthenow*. It was already audible subconsciously and only as a negative urge in Schach's medieval or Hyperborean or African escapism. The historical Adam von Bülow will die in a Russian prison. Victoire has more or less fled to Italy and into a markedly different culture. Her child certainly is a general symbol of hope, but the way Fontane presents it, this hope springs up completely outside the Prussian world of the novel.[42] Is there not now a more than superficial analogy again to the distinctly American Marie in Uwe Johnson's *Jahrestage*, no better but different, for whom, as far as intratextual communication is concerned, these stories are told? And the different culture at the end of the novels, the new child, are constant themes in Faulkner: only the "black"

---

39 "Surrogate", "symbolische Handlungen", "Eitelkeiten", Fontane: Schach von Wuthenow, NFA, II, 318, 286, 280.

40 I cannot agree here with Kaiser: "Der Fall Schach ist aber auch der Fall Fontane. Der Autor ist die ins Produktive gewendete ästhetische Existenz"; ("However Schach's case is also Fontane's case. The author is aesthetic existence made productive.") Gerhard Kaiser: Schach von Wuthenow oder die Weihe der Kraft, p. 493, and would support rather Pfeiffer: "Die realistische Ästhetik siegt über den Ästhetizismus des Titelhelden", der "realistische Roman" über den "l'art pour l'art-Ästhetizismus" ("The realistic aesthetic is victorious over the aestheticism of the eponymous hero, the "realist novel" over the art for art's sake aestheticism"), Pfeiffer: Tod, Entstellung, Hässlichkeit: Fontanes Schach von Wuthenow, p. 276.

41 The view of Pierre-Paul Sagave (quoted in Guenther: Preußischer Gehorsam, p. 209), that these "Traditions périmées [sont] incapables d'accepter un renouveau social" seems to me more convincing than Guenther's own conclusion: "Fontane stößt weit über den Rahmen des Realismus hinaus ins Verklärende"; "Fontane penetrates well beyond the framework of realism, right through to transfiguration", Guenther: Preußischer Gehorsam, p. 223.

42 "Ein Hoffnungsschimmer nach der Katastrophe"; ("A glimpse of hope after the catastrophe"), but also a clear warning for the Wilhelmine era not to believe in "blue-eyed" historical continuity or "fulfilment" (Aust: Theodor Fontane: Ein Studienbuch, p. 92).

offspring of the family surviving in *Absalom, Absalom!*, the completely different child being adopted in *Light in August* (1932), the family traditions wearing out in the new-born infant, born after his father's death, in *Sartoris* (1929) and so on.

What makes the Fontane-Faulkner comparison especially telling is the theme of "time aporia" already mentioned. Wherever Schach goes and returns, when he enters and leaves the scene, every time he becomes a little more questionable, meaner, more vulnerable, less free in his judgement and actions. The "chronotopos" of the novel (the spatio-temporal form-content-pattern, the dynamic plot model)[43] is clearly that of visiting and meeting: visiting and meeting places and people. Those chronotopoi and spatial semantics wear Schach down. The way the story is told, Schach moves for instance directly from Wuthenow to Charlottenburg: the fairy-tale motif has made any return impossible, the massive symbolism has transformed Wuthenow into a place of death, when Schach comes back from Charlottenburg he moves as in an invisible shrinking room. Already then his lifetime is looking like "a question of minutes, a difference between today and tomorrow".[44] His plans for a voyage, absurd in the staging of the fictional scene against the historic prospect, are quite rightly compared by Victoire to the hallucination of someone lost in a desert: "fata morgana". His last ride, closed in the box-like coach, moving without his control, no way out while alive, speaks for itself. I have already shown how the rhythms of Schach's lifetime and of historical time (the difference of two discourses) are out of joint. It has often been observed how the abstract chronological time, the striking of clocks when Schach leaves Victoire or when he spends the night at Wuthenow, the surprisingly exact counting of days during the crisis are carefully marked in the text – this enhances the time aporia Schach is getting into more and more deeply. All this is again multiplied by the clashing of different personal times: the plans of mother and daughter Carayon for engagement and wedding differ painfully from the time rhythm in which the caricatures appear, Schach tries in vain to create against both these time pressures an independent pattern, and so on.

If we consider again for one moment the interplay of fictional-historical tropes, we can now talk of irony or of catachresis of time-patterns: a negative metaphor, that is, a transfer of meaning by negations implying each other. The argument for an alternative, which was already prepared as a gap in "ana-synecdoche", as a change of inferential function in replica, a double-negation in the self-consuming metaphor of decadence and as an opening actualisation in the metonymy of past and present, is again drastically enforced. This alternative is essentially open and void. The negative semantics of history dominate *Schach von Wuthenow*, but not completely. Again Fontane seems to anticipate authors like Faulkner or Uwe Johnson, Alfred Andersch or Graham Swift. It would take more time than I have now to show this "metahistorical alternative", as I shall tentatively call it, the act of writing and telling as opposed to its

---

43 Cf. Michail M. Bakhtin: Formen der Zeit im Roman: Untersuchungen zur historischen Poetik, transl. by Michael Dewey, ed. by Edward Kowalski and Michael Wegner. Frankfurt a.M.: Fischer 1989.

44 "Eine Frage von Minuten, eine Differenz von heut' auf morgen", Fontane: Schach von Wuthenow, NFA, II, 373.

content. So I shall just suggest two applications of the idea, one brief and the other very brief.

It has often been remarked that Victoire is at the centre of a sub-text in *Schach von Wuthenow*.[45] Schach's aporia makes her surviving even more meaningful. His decadence contains as many allusions to the *fin de siècle* as Victoire's proto-emancipation ("I am myself", "I can do anything"),[46] her independent judgement, breaking away from moral, national and religious traditions. All this is dimly sketched but forms a clear pattern. She is the one who writes, and her discourse, as has been remarked, in its conciliatory empathetic tendencies resembles Fontane's own more than anybody else's in this novel.[47] We reach the same conclusion by way of a different interpretation. Paul Ricoeur has shown how the experience of time aporia, the friction between lifetime and world-time, is a *condition humaine*, and that this aporia can only be answered by narration: refiguration, configuration and prefiguration of time.[48] I myself have maintained at length, and still maintain, that literary realism sets the continuity of discourse, of the narrated experiment in its ordered reflectivity against the discontinuity of the stories and especially against the "reality crisis" that springs up again and again.[49] I would suggest a nexus between Victoire surviving and Fontane writing on, writing, exploring, experimenting with, not least, Prussian history and society. That Schach, whose name means "chess", is a "chessman in a game of destruction"[50] seems too simple an interpretation. Is not his role in Fontane's larger game of narrative strategies far more interesting, a game played with and against Prussian history? And I see a certain analogy again to the suppressed traditions surviving in Faulkner's *Absalom, Absalom!*, the female and the "black", and to his and far more so to Johnson's metahistorical argument that the narrative configurations contain the most valid perspectives on the future.

My final remark concerns *Schach von Wuthenow* and *Der Stechlin (The Stechlin)*. There is no end of telling contrasts and therefore correspondences. It would be extremely interesting to investigate all this anew in an international context. In any case, the correspondence between Walter Scott's *Waverley* and *Der Stechlin* that has

---

45 Fontane himself speaks of his novel several times as a "Fräulein v. Crayn Novelle", cf. Dichter über ihre Dichtungen: Theodor Fontane, ed. by Richard Brinkmann and Waltraud Wiethölter. Munich: Heimeran 1973, II, pp. 294-297.

46 "Ich bin ich", "ich darf alles", Fontane: Schach von Wuthenow, NFA, II, 326 and 292.

47 "Fontanes Erzählen ist Victoires Perspektive sehr viel näher als dem Bülowschen Entlarvungs-gestus", Kaiser: Schach von Wuthenow oder die Weihe der Kraft, p. 494.

48 Paul Ricoeur: Zeit und Erzählung, transl. by Andreas Knop, 3 vols.. Munich: Fink 1988-1991.

49 Hans Vilmar Geppert: Der realistische Weg. Formen pragmatischen Erzählens bei Balzac, Dickens, Hardy, Keller, Raabe und anderen Autoren des 19. Jahrhunderts, Communicatio 5. Tübingen: Niemeyer 1994.

50 "Schachfigur im Untergangsspiel", Aust: Theodor Fontane, p. 91; similarly the name "Mirabelle" alludes not only to Victoire's "gefährliches Spiel" ("dangerous game") (Guenther: Preußischer Gehorsam, p. 220) between the King and the republic (i.e. the social democrats) but to Fontane in his own time and situation.

been suggested, not only in many details, but in the type of novel itself,[51] is a conscious retelling of *Schach von Wuthenow*: a counter-experiment, a construction of semantics of a sought after harmony, a hypothesis of balance, progress and consensus, always challenged and enhanced by the risk that history might take the turn *Schach von Wuthenow* played out.

---

51 "[Ein] Romantyp, der, indem er menschliche Schicksale darstellt, den Ausgleich der Extreme sucht. Er tritt für Besonnenheit und Toleranz ein und wirbt für einen Wandel zum Besseren auf der Basis moralischen, verantwortlichen Verhaltens und Maßhaltens"; "[A] type of novel, which, by representing human fates, searches for the reconciliation of extremes. It pleads for circumspection and tolerance and seeks to propagate a change for the better based on moral, responsible conduct and moderation." Stefan Neuhaus: Freiheit, Ungleichheit, Selbstsucht? Fontane und Großbritannien. Frankfurt a. M.: Lang 1996, p. 252.

Barbara Hardy

Tellers and Listeners in *Effi Briest*

The story within a story is as old as narrative art. From Homer to Beckett narrative artists have used inset narratives for various ends, conscious and unconscious: mimesis, thematic shaping, social, psychological and ethical analysis and evaluation, and self-reflection. Fontane uses many conspicuously formal, defined, and interwoven acts of telling, in which listeners as well as narrators are important.

Several narrative forms are conspicuous in *Effi Briest*. There is the use of one dominating inset story, the love-story – if it is one – or the ghost-story – if it is one – of the Sea Captain, the Chinese servant, and the bride who danced then disappeared on her wedding day. There is the conspicuous gap and uncertainty in the key narrative and other inset stories, which draws attention to gaps and uncertainties in the novel itself. There is Fontane's striking variation and multiplicity of internal narrative forms. There is his interest in newspapers and reporting, perhaps especially marked in a novel originating in actual gossip. But the novel weaves a web of telling and listening characteristic of nineteenth-century novels, as its key story and cluster of narrative variations take their place in a dense network of psychic, social, and artistic narrations. There is a wide range in style and genre. Fontane is a virtuoso of narrative, and each of his many inset stories is given an individual shape and style, like the individual metric of each poem by a brilliant lyricist – say George Herbert – who never repeats a verse-form. In *Effi Briest* the main inset story is told piecemeal, by several tellers, in different ways, to several listeners. Many of the other internal narratives are fully and formally spelt out, with strongly marked introductions, beginnings, middles and ends, as illustrated by Effi's story of her mother's love, her parents' marriage, and Innstetten's heartbreak; and also by the last of Crampas's literary synopses. Crampas's tales from Heine are elegantly shaped, linked and varied as an *ensemble*. Some stories are curtly compressed and foreshortened, like the place-inspired retrospects of Effi and Innstetten, the servants' gossip, Roswitha's storytelling to Effi and Annie (mentioned but never dramatised) and much allusion to literary narrative, while some are left untold, like the history of Frau Kruse, the coachman's disturbed wife who stays in her overheated room cradling a black hen, her version of the ghost-story, hinted in nods and about to be told, to Roswitha, in two minutes, and the secret of her hen, said by Effi to know "everything" and to tell "all it knows".[1] One of the interesting narrative omissions is that of Wüllersdorf's personal story, just mentioned to Innstetten, who unlike the reader already knows it, in the natural way of phatic communion. The psychological range of course includes memory and anticipation, emphasising Effi's romantic fantasies and conservative expectations of marriage, – the stories of her culture – and a full social range, rumour, oral and written gossip, letters, newspaper report, literature, drama, song, and jokes.

---

1 "'[…]das weiß alles und plaudert alles aus'", Fontane: Effi Briest, NFA, VII, 321. Theodor Fontane: Effi Briest, transl. by Hugh Rorrison and Helen Chambers. London: Penguin Books, 2000, p. 128. All translated quotations are from this edition and further references are given in the text.

These blended psychological and sociological narratives are mimetic in the most rudimentary way: because human beings are story-telling animals and you cannot write a novel without showing them telling stories to each other and to themselves, as they remember and anticipate, in realistic and stylised modes, gossip, tell truths and lies, and sometimes tell stories as formally and selfconsciously as Othello or Falstaff; and as they make, and are made by, the stories of their society. The psychic and social narratives function within the novel, as characterisations, promotions of plot, analogues and microcosms which thematise and generalise, creating a complex taxonomy of resemblance and contrast. They are reflexive, signalling alertness to their novel, emphasising, generalising, and deconstructing its forms and figures. They are analyses and evaluations of the cultural and psychic narrative modes they represent, a larger reflexivity, generic and extra-literary. They also have a common conspicuousness as inset story: the characters often say they're going to tell a story or ask for a story, and as in *Macbeth* and *The Winter's Tale*, the word "story" recurs.[2] There are innumerable examples, like Innstetten's introduction of Kessin and its inhabitants to Effi, who says it sounds like six novels, or his postponed full narrative of the ghost-story which he begins by saying beginnings are difficult, or Marietta Tripelli's distinction between ghosts in fiction and ghosts in real life, amusingly unstable because articulated by a character in fiction.

Emphasis and source vary. The ghost-story continues for most of the novel, the Roswitha story is referred to several times and told fully once, long after she has entered the Innstetten household, but because it is her key story and a terrible story, and she is said to harp on it, it looms large. It attaches itself. Explicitly as well as implicitly – " 'Oh my lady, may Mary Mother of God preserve you from misery like that' " (p. 129) – to the stories of women's suffering, through sex, love, marriage, maternity, which cluster to generalise Effi's story, and include Frau Briest's love-story, Frau Kruse's dark history, Marietta Trippelli's adventures, which skirt the real-life story of the celebrated "Viardot", the fate of Effi's childhood friends, and the cult of Hertha.[3]

Details of social narratives are not just realistic details but self-analysing. For instance, three sensitive nodes in the narrative network are newspaper reports.Their brutal form of external and synoptic report is tacitly contrasted with the novel's sympathetic and complex telling, and with the fastidious nervous secrecy of the main characters, as a newspaper report and the inner story of an alcoholic suicide are juxtaposed in James Joyce's *A Painful Case*. (The novel's wide web also includes newspapers and journals underlined and circulated by the good Gieshübler.) Johanna and Roswitha, the people immediately responsible for revealing Effi's past, have to learn some things from the papers. After Innstetten tells her Effi is not coming back Johanna rushes to inform Roswitha but is upstaged by the concierge who has already

---

2   Helen Chambers observes this in the "Introduction" to the Penguin Classics edition of Effi Briest, p. xviii.

3   "'Ach, gnädigste Frau, die heilige Mutter Gottes bewahre Sie vor solchem Elend.'" Fontane: Effi Briest, NFA, VII, 322.

shown Roswitha the paper, "'It's only the *Fremdenblatt*: but Lene has gone out to get the *Kleines Journal*. There will be more in that; they always know everything'"(p. 180) (like the black hen).[4] Johanna confirms, "'There's next to nothing in this one'" (p. 182) after reading it aloud, displeased that her news had been overtaken, "'The things these papers print'" (p. 181); Roswitha imagines people calling her "'poor, dear mistress all sorts of things'" (p. 181).[5] The story grows, and we follow the growth as Fontane tells his story through the stories his characters tell, interested in those stories as complex means and ends.

Frau Zwicker's letter to her bosom friend and fellow man-hater about the discovery is written ten hours after Effi gets her letter from Hohen-Cremmen, and the easy gossipy speculation about "the real story" (bringing out the contrast between the news and deeper reading-knowledge) is complemented by details hot from the press in a cutting from an unnamed paper, brought by a servant from the landlady who marked the report in blue: "'You'll see from it that I was *not* wrong. [...] first she writes notes and letters and then she goes and keeps his letters! What are fires and stoves for?'" (p. 190)[6] There is a little narrative mystery here, about a subject necessarily often kept dark, the editor's source of information. Frau Zwicker reads the full newspaper report on the day Effi gets her letter, in a slightly delayed mail delivery by a named postman, Böselager, "'from Siegen way, no gumption'"(p. 183), five days after she last heard from Innstetten.[7] It informs her of the discovery, the duel, Crampas's death, her impending divorce, and plans for her future. This is written after the Briests receive Innstetten's letter, which Johanna posts (noting the address) in between reading two newspapers. Since then someone has passed on the story of the cache of Crampas's letters, at great speed. We never know who, and the implied or quoted details in the three newspapers leave us to observe, compare, and speculate.

Fontane may have been careless and his narrative circulation not intended for critical scrutiny, but this is unlikely. An experienced journalist, a foreign correspondent, and a novelist who prided himself on *finesse*, he is fascinated in asking who could have told whom and when, indulging in a grim in-joke about the speed with which bad news travels, the *paparazzi* of his day, and varying modes of transmission, perhaps with a covert back-reference to the ambiguous Johanna, already seen at her gossip's work chatting about the Innstettens with the "nosy" Frau Paaschen, the clerk's wife. When Innstetten tells her Effi is not coming back, he refers her to the paper, but she and Roswitha have seen the telltale letters "right at the bottom" (p. 169) when Roswitha breaks open Effi's sewing-table, and she has seen Innstetten with the little

---

4 "'Es ist bloß das Fremdenblatt; aber Lene ist schon hin und holt das kleine Journal. Da wird wohl schon mehr drin stehen; die wissen immer alles.'" Fontane: Effi Briest, NFA, VII, 382.

5 "'[...] das hier ist so gut wie gar nichts.'" Fontane: Effi Briest, NFA, VII, 385; "'Was solche Blätter nicht alles schreiben '", Fontane: Effi Briest, NFA, VII, 383; "'Und das lesen nun die Menschen und verschimpfieren mir meine liebe, arme Frau.'" Fontane: Effi Briest, NFA, VII, 383.

6 "'Du siehst daraus, daß ich mich *nicht* geirrt habe [...] erst selber Zettel und Briefe schreiben und dann auch noch die des anderen aufbewahren. Wozu gibt es Öfen und Kamine?'" Fontane: Effi Briest, NFA, VII, 394.

7 "'Er ist aus dem Siegenschen und hat keinen Schneid.'" Fontane: Effi Briest, NFA, VII, 386.

bundle.[8] What Roland Barthes calls the *lisible* story, which the reader must try, by close reading, re-reading, trial and error, (and often fail) to assemble, here particularises, in almost parodic detail, the specificities of correspondence and communication, clock, calendar, newspapers and letters, postings, deliveries, letters about letters, papers about letters and letters about papers. But it also puts together the jigsaw of uncertainties, undercurrents, externalities, treacheries, shocks, judgements and tolerances which compose gossip and rumour, and the imitation may seem to compound, but, drawing our attention to narrative unreliabilities and multiplicities, undermines realism.

Many minor acts of telling and listening are the building-blocks of cultural mimesis and reflexive analysis. Surface and symbolism converge or diverge. The men are the joke-tellers, but there is more than social realism in their joking, usually some resonance of character or theme. At the eve-of-wedding dinner, we improve our knowledge of the Briest marriage as Effi's father, apparently – as elsewhere in the novel a narrative is made conspicuous by cutting – tells conventional slightly improper jokes about marriage, to be resignedly rebuked by his wife. Dagobert, Effi's Berlin cousin amuses his aunt and cousin with a silly joke. Like another tragic heroine of the nineties, Tess Durbeyfield, Effi is undereducated but not ignorant or unintelligent, and when Dagobert asks one of the fashionable (and untranslatable) *Bibelwitze*, about the first coachman, her suggestion "Apollo" is praised by her cousin (though she is slow to grasp the correct punning answer) and is mythological. In Chapter 19, at Ring's party, Güldenklee makes a speech on behalf of the guests and as is usual on such occasions, tells a story, adapted from Lessing's *Nathan der Weise*. In another example of the circulation of narrative which Fontane likes to use, he cheapens it and wrenches it from context to make it his own, using it for a pun on Ring and a conservative reference to an inner circle, rejecting and so emphasising, the symbolism in which three rings represent three races, and reinforcing the novel's critique of provincial prejudice and xenophobia:

> there is even a story which we all know, which is called the story of the three rings, a Jewish story, which like all that liberal fiddle-faddle, has caused and continues to cause nothing but confusion and disaster [...]. I'm for *one* ring [...] a ring who sees all that is good in this old Pomeranian circle of ours, all who stand with God for King and Fatherland. (p. 113)[9]

Once more the response to a story is marked: when the party replies with the Prussian anthem, Innstetten drily criticises the facile conventional patriotic enthusiasm, "they

---

8 "Ganz zu unterst." Fontane: Effi Briest, NFA, VII, 370.

9 "' [...] es gibt sogar eine Geschichte, die wir alle kennen, die die Geschichte von den drei Ringen heißt, eine Judengeschichte, die, wie der ganze liberale Krimskrams, nichts wie Verwirrung und Unheil gestiftet hat und noch stiftet [...] ich bin vielmehr für *einen* Ring [...] ein Ring, der alles Gute, was wir in unsrem altpommerschen Kessiner Kreise haben, alles, was noch mit Gott und König für Vaterland einsteht." Fontane: Effi Briest, NFA, VII, 302.

don't have anything like that in other countries'", with one of his several sympathetic touches, "'in other countries they have other things'"(p. 113).[10]

Then there is the woman's story. An important single act of narrative is Roswitha's story, the old story, the story of the woman's seduction and pregnancy, the woman's fall and punishment by the patriarchy. Roswitha's terrible story of pregnancy, being threatened by her blacksmith father with a hot iron, then having her child taken away, is dismissed as boring obsession by the unsympathetic Johanna, but only once narrated in full in the novel. When she mentions it for the last time she reverts to what she feels as worse and better memories, of her desolation and rescue by Effi. The bad memory is displaced by the grateful memory, a benign recall in a novel where most memories are bitter. The rescue by Effi is promoted by her brief story, after she is stranded by her mistress's death. (One of the many gaps in the novel is the absence of any information about her baby's fate.) Of course her sexual fall, her isolation, her child and her rescue find parallels in Effi's history. Effi's compensations are secular, and when Roswitha the Catholic scathingly dismisses the Catholic story of confession she endorses the novel's quiet firm secularisation. Finally, and reticently, by implication only, she tells the story of her Effi's isolation and need, when she writes to Innstetten to send Rollo, naïvely articulating Effi's truth that animals make no moral judgments, and invoking the men's admiration.

All the stories converge on Effi, who is the theme or listener when she is not the teller. The more conspicuous stories are told by her, and to her by Innstetten and Crampas. With the exception of Innstetten's, they are highly formal stories, conspicuous but naturalistically made part of Fontane's subtly finessed narrative web. Crampas's stories are literary, and so too are Effi's two most important stories in her adult life. Innstetten, one of the most interesting cuckolds in fiction, more complex than Charles Bovary or Karenin and almost as sympathetic as Leopold Bloom, has no formal story to tell. He starts off telling or partly telling the ghost-story, though in a way it is initiated by Effi, as well as being re-enacted by her. Her actual, or imagined, experience, or imagining of the ghost, is provoked by a literary source, the story of the White Lady of the Hohenzollerns she comes across in a guidebook chosen as calm bedtime reading. Fontane knows that we do not construct stories in isolation, and that they have multiple sources, but puts Effi in the position of Alice imagining a passage through the looking-glass, or Kafka's K deciding his role in the Castle. She is allowed to make the creative fiat, as the centre of Fontane's imagining of imagination. When told about the "people from all corners of the globe" who turn up in Kessin, she says casually – but casual words are resonant in a good novel – "'perhaps a Negro or a Turk, or even a Chinaman'" and Innstetten replies, "'A Chinaman too. What a good guess.'"(p. 33)[11] Only then does he begin his telling.

---

10 "' […] so was hat man in anderen Ländern nicht.'" "'In anderen Ländern hat man was anderes.'" Fontane: Effi Briest, NFA, VII, 302.

11 "Menschen aus aller Welt Ecken und Enden.." Fontane: Effi Briest, NFA, VII, 204.

"' […] vielleicht einen Neger oder einen Türken, oder vielleicht sogar einen Chinesen.' 'Auch einen Chinesen. Wie gut du raten kannst.'" Fontane: Effi Briest, NFA, VII, 205.

Innstetten's later story about his wife's adultery is reluctantly told to his friend and second, Wüllersdorf, in one of the novel's skilfully evaded, judged and analysed social and personal narratives. When Wüllersdorf says, "'let's hear what it's all about'" Innstetten gives the gist, a curt outline: "'It is about a lover of my wife's, a man who was my friend, more or less'"(p. 171).[12] Reticently and fastidiously, he tells the full story through the letters which told it to him: "'Read these'"(p. 171).[13] The telling of the secret is socially crucial and important to the plot, because once it is told it determines action. Innstetten's military honour-culture, almost though not quite internalised, makes it impossible for him not to tell his chosen second, and once told it determines the rest – divorce, custody of the child, and his duel to the death with Crampas. He himself understands the paradox of secrets and confidences, telling his friend there is no such thing as a kept secret or a safe confidence. Wüllersdorf swears he would not betray his confidence, but Innstetten perfectly imagines what it would be like for them both if he did not behave as honour dictates. The act of confidence is harshly illumined, in clear illustration of the genre and the culture.

Effi tells three important stories. Here too, each act of telling is strikingly different, each equally effective. The first story is direct, naïve and simply revealing, showing a young girl's ignorance and innocence. It is the conventional, romantic, ignorant story of her own mother, her husband-to-be and her father, taking for granted the sacrifice of feeling to marriage-convention, introduced by her facile comment that no story that ends in renunciation is entirely bad. In some ways her own story of renunciation – life-renunciation – is entirely bad for her, but as tragedy with meaning, not entirely bad. At the beginning she tells – who better? – the woman's story, the story of the marriage, the family, the time, and the culture. Her telling shows how assimilated and formative it is, so conservatively, and powerfully influential and appealing. The telling is fatal and proleptic, and Fontane gives it full play, first drawing it out in a rambling, digressive, self-conscious suspension of beginning, which makes it as perfect an example of Goethe's retarding principle as Aeneas's reluctant telling of the tale of Troy to Dido, or Othello's story of his storytelling and Desdemona's spellbound listening.

Effi begins in the first chapter, with the natural mention of her mother's visitor, an old friend, "'I'm going to tell you about that later'" and describes it as a love-story (p. 7). It may be the only true love-story in the novel. She goes on to say that it is "'complete with hero and heroine, and ending in renunciation. You'll be amazed, you won't believe your ears [...]'"(p. 7)[14] and a little later, the listeners – sometimes specified, sometimes cleverly made choric – urge, "'Well then Effi, it's time now, let's have this tale of love and renunciation. Or is it really that bad?'", which elicits the

---

12 "' [...] Aber nun sagen Sie, was es ist.' 'Es handelt sich um einen Galan meiner Frau, der zugleich mein Freund war oder doch beinah.'" Fontane: Effi Briest, NFA, VII, 372.

13 "'Lesen Sie.'" Fontane: Effi Briest, NFA, VII, 372.

14 "' [...] von dem ich euch nachher erzählen muß, eine Liebesgeschichte mit Held und Heldin, und zuletzt mit Entsagung. Ihr werdet Augen machen und euch wundern.'" Fontane: Effi Briest, NFA, VII, 173.

famous naïve irony, "'A tale of renunciation is never bad [...]'" (p. 7).[15] Later she asks, "'But how did I get on to all this? I'm forgetting the story'", to which they reply, "'Yes, you do keep going off at a tangent; maybe you don't want to tell us after all'", and she says, "'Oh I want to all right, but it's true of course, I do keep getting off the subject, because it's all rather strange, in fact, it's almost romantic'" (p. 8).[16] After a longer gap, Hertha resumes, "'let's get on with the story'", and she replies, "'All right, be patient, I'm just going to start ... So, Baron Innstetten. He wasn't quite twenty [...]'" (p. 9).[17] Significant details include the generalisation which is wiser than she knows, "'What happened was what was bound to happen, what always happens'" (p. 9).[18] Throughout there is reflection on narrative method, casual but apt, as in "'To cut a long story short'" (p. 9).[19]

The pathetically young story is told during one of Effi's last childhood games, out of doors, before the friends drown the bag of gooseberry skins with a joke about the drowning of unfaithful wives ..."'oh and that reminds me, this is how they used to drown poor unfortunate women, from boats like this, for infidelity of course'" (p. 10).[20] Effi replies to the Ibsenlike objection "'But not here.'" again more significantly than she knows, "'But in Constantinople,'" and looking back to geography lessons, "'I remember that kind of thing'" (p. 10).[21]

Like many other details this is a resonant detail for George Eliot readers: in *The Mill on the Floss* Maggie's sacrificial death is early foretold by the picture of the old woman suffering witch-trial by drowning. Like George Eliot, Fontane also generalises the theme of sacrifice, as he does in his later allusion to the cult of Hertha and the sacrificial stones with blood-grooves. Effi's early reference to remembering stories about women drowned for infidelity, like the detail of mythology being her favourite subject, when she discusses school with Annie, is a sign of her mythological awareness as well as a pre-echo. The references explain and emphasise her own mythopoeia, most impressive in her imaginative promotion of literary anecdote to myth, her

---

15 "'Nun aber Effi, nun ist es Zeit, nun die Liebesgeschichte mit Entsagung. Oder ist es nicht so schlimm?'
'Eine Geschichte mit Entsagung ist nie schlimm.'" Fontane: Effi Briest, NFA, VII, 174.
16 "'Aber ich komme vom Hundertsten aufs Tausendste und vergesse die Geschichte.'
'Ja, du brichts immer wieder ab; am Ende willst du nicht.'
'Oh, ich will schon, aber freilich, ich breche immer wieder ab, weil es alles ein bißchen sonderbar ist, ja, beinahe romantisch.'" Fontane: Effi Briest, NFA, VII, 174f.
17 "'Aber nun endlich die Geschichte.'
'Nun, gib dich zufrieden, ich fange schon an... Also Baron Innstetten! Als er noch keine zwanzig war [...]'" Fontane: Effi Briest, NFA,VII, 175.
18 "'Es kam, wie es kommen mußte, wie es immer kommt.'" Fontane: Effi Briest, NFA, VII, 176.
19 "'Kurz und gut [...]'" Fontane: Effi Briest, NFA, VII, 176.
20 "'Wobei mir übrigens einfällt, so vom Boot aus sollen früher auch arme unglückliche Frauen versenkt worden sein, natürlich wegen Untreue.'" Fontane: Effi Briest, NFA, VII, 177.
21 "'Aber doch nicht hier.'
'Aber in Konstantinopel. [...]'
'Ich behalte so was.'" Fontane: Effi Briest, NFA, VII, 177.

honourable and ironic post-metaphysical narrative of death, and her authoritative self-re-naming which gives the novel its title.

Before she makes myths, she has to recognise them. The rambling, relaxed, uncontrolled and naïve story, told just before she becomes betrothed to the story's hero and her mother's old lover, marks childhood and the end of childhood, and Effi's telling develops with her experience. (If *Effi Briest* is not a *Bildungsroman*, no novel is.) Her later stories are curt, tense, oblique, understated and allegorical. Their brevity, control, and sophistication are signs of her intellectual growth, the obliquity and under-statement of secrecy and depth, and all promote the powerful generalisation of her own story.

The story she tells Crampas also contrasts strongly with the stories he tells her, which are about love and death, like the ghost-story her husband tells her. Crampas expatiates on Innstetten's motive for telling his story, so draws attention to his own more obvious motives. His are seducers' stories, conventionally romantic with their mix of love and death, morbid, military, indulgent, obviously erotic, literary, second-hand, and compounded by repetition. In Chapter 16 he tells the story of Innstetten's storytelling in the regiment, saying he affected "'mystical leanings'"(p. 95) and told ghost-stories to make himself interesting, and we never know if it is true or not.[22] He expands his story into an indictment of Innstetten as the manipulative jealous narrator, guarding his wife's honour by fear, "'a ghost is like a cherub with a sword'" (p. 97), and we never know if that is true either, though Effi thinks so and both Innstetten and Johanna seem at times to frighten her deliberately.[23]

These histories and interpretation are followed in the next chapter by Crampas's own manipulative story-telling from Heine. His first story is "The Sea Spectre", about the buried city, which he follows with a slightly adapted quotaton which is a cue to touch his rapt listener, mention his own writing, and bring up the subject of love. He goes on to mention the many executions in Heine, "'often, it's true, as a consequence of love'"(p. 101), and the second story he paraphrases dwells on the god Vitzliputzli and bloody sacrifices of prisoners.[24] He ends with the long story of Don Pedro and the Knight of Calatrava, again stressing the morbidities. He tells the stories self-aggrandisingly, flirtatiously, and charmingly, though savouring cruelties. The telling becomes increasingly personal, though there are analogues and anticipations not yet clear to him or the listener or the reader.

As always in this novel, the listening is as marked as the telling. Effi realises he is unreliable before he tells the stories. She is fascinated, occasionally shocked, finds the last tale is beautiful but asks him to stop and to tell a different kind of story. He does not but she eventually does, though not in this scene. His fantastic stories reflect their novel, in fatalities, secrecy, love, jealousy, even the faithful dog who accuses a murderer, whom Crampas jokingly and flirtatiously calls Rollo – and it works, because Effi susceptibly tells the dog she cannot look at him without thinking of the "'Knight of

---

22 "'seine mystische Richtung.'" Fontane: Effi Briest, NFA, VII, 280.

23 "'Aber solch Spuk ist wie ein Cherub mit dem Schwert.'" Fontane: Effi Briest, NFA, VII, 283.

24 "'[…] allerdings vielfach aus Liebe.'" Fontane: Effi Briest, NFA, VII, 286f.

Calatrava whom the Queen secretly loved'" (p. 103).[25] The dialogue of telling and listening is intimate, the stories loaded with innuendo. To some extent Effi is charmed and complicit but she shows resistance, irony, and good sense, and sees through him, especially when he moves from literature to literary behaviour. She drily interprets his sentimental appropriation of the drinking-glass as a sign that he sees himself as the King of Thule before his time. She knows he is putting on the style but of course it is more interesting than Innstetten's lack of style.

Before she succumbs to Crampas she resists again, by telling a story. Her first allegory, like her last, is a secular abridgement of a long pious tale from Brentano, in every way unlike Crampas's rambling tales from Heine. She answers literature with literature, and her self-awareness is clear and amused. When there is talk about being snowed up Effi says the idea makes her feel safe, and when she hopefully introduces the protection of allegory, she draws attention to literary origins and influence. The story itself is told in two sentences, brilliantly curt:

> "ideas are a funny thing, they don't just come from one's personal experience, but also from things one has heard somewhere or just happens to know. You're well-read Major but in the case of one poem – not quite Heine's 'Sea Spectre' or 'Vitzlipultzli' I admit – I do seem to be one up on you. The poem is called 'God's Wall', and I learnt it by heart from our pastor at Hohen-Cremmen many, many years ago, when I was still quite small."
>
> "'God's Wall'", Crampas repeated. "A nice title, and what's it about?"
>
> "A little story. Quite short. There was a war somewhere, a winter campaign, and an old widow who lived in great fear of the enemy prayed for God to 'build a wall around her' to protect her from her country's enemies. And God had the house buried in snow, and the enemy passed it by." (p. 110) [26]

Crampas is "visibly disconcerted"(p. 110),[27] and changes the subject, recognising her counter-move. But it is only temporarily successful, and in the next chapter (Chapter 19), when she is driving alone with him, she recalls it, thinks of Brentano's "little mother", and internalises the prayer in his story, "so did she pray now".[28] But the prayer and the retelling fail. Like Claudius in *Hamlet* Effi feels her words are dead. She tells without the sense of someone listening.

---

25 "'den Kalatrava-Ritter [...], den die Königin heimlich liebte.'" Fontane: Effi Briest, NFA, VII, 289f.

26 "'mit den Vorstellungen ist es ein eigen Ding, man macht sie sich nicht bloß nach dem, was man persönlich erfahren hat, auch nach dem, was man irgendwo gehört oder ganz zufällig weiß. Sie sind so belesen, Major, aber mit einem Gedichte – freilich keinem Heineschen, keinem 'Seegespenst' und keinem 'Vitzliputzli' – bin ich Ihnen, wie mir scheint, doch voraus. Dies Gedicht heißt die 'Gottesmauer', und ich hab es bei unserm Hohen-Cremmner Pastor vor vielen, vielen Jahren, als ich noch ganz klein war, auswendig gelernt.'
'Gottesmauer', wiederholte Crampas, 'Ein hübscher Titel, und wie verhält es sich damit?'
'Eine kleine Geschichte, nur ganz kurz. Da war irgendwo Krieg, ein Winterfeldzug, und eine Witwe, die sich vor dem Feinde mächtig fürchtete, betete zu Gott, er möge doch eine Mauer um sie bauen, um sie vor dem Feinde zu schützen. Und da ließ Gott das Haus einschneien, und der Feind zog daran vorüber.'" Fontane: Effi Briest, NFA, VII, 298f.

27 "sichtlich betroffen." Fontane: Effi Briest, NFA, VII, 299.

28 " [...] wie das Mütterchen, so betete auch sie jetzt." Fontane: Effi Briest, NFA, VII, 308.

The preliminaries of seduction and the attempted resistance are conducted through the clandestine exchange of literary narrative. Crampas uses sly suggestiveness to which Effi cannot reply directly, so resorts to explaining herself in pious fable. But the religious story cannot be repeated for her. She is not a simple old believer. He is not a simple military enemy. This is not a simple story. This is a narrative combat, a dialectic, a surreptitious dialogue in which everything is a cryptic metaphor, metonymy, or sub-text, nothing straight or simple.

Effi's last story is another allegory and another literary anecdote of great power. It is secular and minimal, and stands her in good stead. Its small-scale moralising recalls Wüllersdorf's stoical philosophy of minor pleasures, the master-builder's props and stays (*Hilfskonstruktionen*), and his examples of story-telling. The story is particularised for – and by – a woman capable of abstraction though not given to abstract language. She depersonalises her story in another story, on another occasion when it is easier to be oblique than direct. But this metaphor or metonymy is crystal-clear. It is an amused, ironic, and bravely understated explanation of her attitude to her own death, told on her deathbed to her mother. It is in Effi's curt style:

> "I think," said Frau Briest, "you were going to tell me something."
> "Yes, I was. It was because you said I was still so young. And of course I am still young. But it doesn't matter. In the good old days Innstetten used to read to me in the evenings; he had very good books, and one of them had a story about someone who had been called away from a festive dinner, and the next day asked what had happened after he left. And the answer was, 'Oh, all sorts of things, but really you didn't miss anything.' You see, Mamma, these words stuck in my mind – it doesn't matter much if you are called away from the table a little early." Frau von Briest was silent. (p. 215f.) [29]

It is another two-sentence story. Once again Effi uses narrative with rhetorical sophistication, ironically, almost playfully, revising literature, generously showing that she has assimilated the education her husband patronisingly provided. She is more advanced here than in "God's Wall", making her own symbolism in a modest stoical story which modestly shows what Fontane thinks we may write and read in literature.

The much discussed central story of the Chinese servant's death, the disappearing bride, and the Sea Captain, is structurally emphatic and analogic, like the story of The Odyssey in Joyce's *Ulysses* or the Grail legend in *The Waste Land*. It is reflexively enigmatic, uncertain, and incomplete with many unreliable narrators. Innstetten, Effi, Johanna, Kruse and his wife, Marietta Trippelli, Roswitha, who all tell it, or bits of it,

---

29 "'Aber ich glaube', nahm Frau Briest das Wort, 'du wolltest mir was erzählen.'
'Ja, das wollte ich, weil du davon sprachst, ich sei noch so jung. Freilich bin ich noch jung. Aber das schadet nichts. Es war noch in glücklichen Tagen, da las mir Innstetten abends vor; er hatte sehr gute Bücher, und in einem hieß es: Es sei wer von einer fröhlichen Tafel abgerufen worden, und am andern Tage habe der Abgerufene gefragt, wie's denn nachher gewesen sei. Da habe man ihm geantwortet: 'Ach, es war noch allerlei; aber eigentlich haben Sie nichts versäumt.' Sieh, Mama, diese Worte haben sich mir eingeprägt – es hat nicht viel zu bedeuten, wenn man von der Tafel etwas früher abgerufen wird.'
Frau von Briest schwieg." Fontane: Effi Briest, NFA, VII, 424f.

to each other. Everyone tells or contributes to the local legend, which is about love, death, marriage, class, gender, race, and religion. It is a recent history, embedded in gossip, rumour, and superstition, expressive of its culture, and like Othello it collocates problems of race and gender. It is told by several people to Effi (and to others) and retold by her, to Johanna, Roswitha, and her husband, in a letter to her mother, and to Crampas, in a plausible circulation of narrative, with functional speculation, overlap and variation.

The story is a reflector of theme and genre in ways both direct and oblique. It is fantastic, but its fantasy is realistically placed and acknowledged, making a generic analogue which is in some ways directly and simply thematic but also categorically subversive, uncertain, vague and incomplete. In the small and the larger story, there are lacunae. The inset story keeps its secrets, and its end remains completely unknown. The novel keeps some secrets, and its end raises questions and doubts. The inset story is an outline, telling nothing about feelings and motives, and encouraging us to see that some of the most interesting gaps in the novel's full trajectory are in motivation. We know a fair amount about the characters' feelings, but the characters often do not know why they do things – their motives are feeble or instinctive or conventional or vague or unknown – not flattering human dignity. Why they marry, do not marry, commit adultery, keep incriminating letters, fight duels, and get divorced, is usually not clear. Some conventional motives are rejected: *Effi Briest* is not a love-story, though some of its characters imagine the possibility of love. Effi admits candidly that she did not love her lover, and though she forgives her husband she accuses him of not being capable of love, with detachment and assurance, summing and itemising their story in her last words – the last words she speaks in the novel.

> "Everything he did was right. The business with poor Crampas – what else could he possibly have done? And then – that was what hurt me most – bringing up my own child to ward me off [...] that was right too. [...] There was a lot of good in his nature, and he was as noble as anybody could be who lacks the real capacity for love." (p. 216) [30]

After the two main clauses of praise, accusation is surprisingly tucked into those last seven stinging words, smoothly subordinated in syntax, calmly taken for granted. Quietly Effi assumes authority. Her telling is unimpassioned, unintense, and highly original.

The key story, about whose action, characters, and causality we know next to nothing, answers to, and for, the novel. The haunting enlarges the political implications, linking Effi's woman's death not only with the vanished bride but also with the foreign servant's death, that of a male, so that the social restriction and construction is not only that of gender. Effi is a victim of Prussian social codes, and

---

30 "' [...] daß er in allem recht gehandelt. In der Geschichte mit dem armen Crampas – ja, was sollt er am Ende anders tun? Und dann – womit er mich am tiefsten verletzte, daß er mein eigen Kind in einer Art Abwehr gegen mich erzogen hat, [...] er hat auch darin recht gehabt. [...] Denn er hatte viel Gutes in seiner Natur und war so edel, wie jemand sein kann, der ohne rechte Liebe ist."' Fontane: Effi Briest, NFA, VII, 425.

more broadly, of history, but so are Innstetten and Crampas. The key story's muted problems of class, gender, foreignness and regional culture broadly reveal what the whole novel subtly proposes. Effi's blood sacrifice, brought out by the sinister cult of Hertha, which the Innstettens come across on holiday, links her with the heroines Dorothea Brooke, in *Middlemarch*, and Tess of the D'Urbevilles, both associated with images of sacrifice and sacrificial stones, and both complex victims of history. Like George Eliot and Thomas Hardy, Fontane is a historically conscious novelist who constructs stories in order to ask questions about the individual in history.

The ghost-story is a structural anticipation or prolepsis, in the form of a warning to Effi: the ghost comes or seems to come, out of narrative into her life when her husband has left her alone for the first time. It is also suggested by a superstitious play of the women, the picture from a child's book stuck on the chair by Johanna and Christel, which seems to surprise Innstetten when he and Effi see it, and later, for no stated reason, taken to the new house in Berlin. Its bride, like Effi, leaves her husband, perhaps because of another love; the Chinese servant, like Effi, comes as a foreigner to Kessin, and like Effi is memorialised in a stone set among flowers, near but outside a churchyard. It is uncanny (*unheimlich*), and the word is used by Effi in an early conversation with Innstetten, "'And then there's the crocodile: it's all so uncanny here'" (p. 57), and later in a letter to her mother, "it's nice and comfortable, but uncanny at the same time, very odd" (p. 73), is wonderfully apt since the ghost makes the marital home unhomelike, disturbing sleep, impeding hospitality, and in the end uncoupling the married pair.[31] The house itself, with its odd disposal of rooms, lack of an obvious dining-room and guest-rooms, and its grotesque objects, is "not a proper house at all" (p. 72).[32] It is uncomfortable to live in, quite apart from its ghost, and the social and supernatural are nicely tangled.

Unheimlichkeit also raises questions of home and place. In German, there is an ironic reinforcement too since one of the meanings of *heimlich* is "clandestine", and if Effi suffers from an unhomely home, in Kessin, the home that seems homely also turns out to be unhomely. Novels about the badness of bad marriages sometimes carry a significant subtext about the badness of good marriages, because what they are really about, whether they know it or not, is the badness of marriage.

Certainly there is no satisfactory place for Effi: one house is haunted and inhospitable, the other – apparently *heimlich* – is dangerous. (Something similar happens to Jane Eyre, also searching for home, who moves from one bad place to another, from Lowood to Thornfield.) Kessin has no society, but domestic and social life in Berlin does not last and is unhealthy, the new marital home in Berlin, suspiciously damp at the start and only briefly habitable, turns out to be haunted after all, the boardinghouse will not do, even the flat with Roswitha's company is satisfactory only for a while, and Effi's last happy days in Hohen-Cremmen are only made tolerable by the company and protection of the pet dog – a realistic and

---

31 "'Und dann das Krokodil; es ist alles so unheimlich hier.'" Fontane: Effi Briest, NFA, VII, 235; "'es ist sonderbarerweise gemütlich und unheimlich zugleich.'" Fontane: Effi Briest, NFA, VII, 254.
32 "kein richtiges Haus." Fontane: Effi Briest, NFA, VII, 253.

unsentimental point about the vulnerability of a woman's life, the problems of human relationships, and the relative historical freedom of a non-human animal.

Hohen-Cremmen is the place for childhood and dying, when human beings are arguably most free, and both periods are associated with a sense of holiday, health, play, protected solitude, and liberty, and so perhaps carry the vision of an escape from contingency and history, that glimpse of the unconditional, provided by Thomas Hardy in the brief holidays and respite he imagined for Tess, Jude, and Sue. Effi's actual grave, at home, perhaps in unconsecrated ground, may add a gratuitous sense of insecurity, an ironic secularisation, and a sense of individuality, rather like those "unvisited" tombs at the end of *Middlemarch*. Like Effi's, the Chinese servant's white stone tomb, though free, flowering, and pastoral, is an outsider's, near but outside the churchyard. His is unsuccessfully proposed for consecrated ground but though Fontane brings up the question of his burial-place very explicitly, he seems to do the exact opposite when he comes to bury Effi. Whatever point he is making about her grave seems unclear, as far as I can discover, to modern readers. (Perhaps some research on contemporary German funeral customs is needed.)

I have called the key story "the ghost story" for convenience, but neither characters nor readers know whether the story is about haunted houses, or not. According to Freud, in his classic essay of 1919,[33] *Unheimlichkeit*, generic and symbolic, is enhanced by the element of doubt. Freud read Fontane, and it is almost as if reading *Effi Briest* influenced the definitions, it fits them so perfectly. In any case, the generic uncertainty of the key story, which may or may not be a ghost-story, makes a more intelligently unnerving tale of the supernatural, like *Hamlet* or Henry James's *The Turn of the Screw* and *The Jolly Corner*, because it is more realistic, leaving scope for natural and rational explanations, and because it is more metaphysically and physically unsettling. Uncertainty compounds or qualifies narrative motive, like the novel's troubling components of incompleteness, mystery, missing pieces, and opacity, which say or suggest that we cannot tell or know the whole story, of our motives, feelings, destinies, and history.

Perhaps most teasingly, for the nineteenth-century historically conscious novelist and to the post-Freudian, post-Marxist, postmodern reader, it says that we do not know how much we are constructed by nature, how much by nurture. It is typical of the novel's imaginative uncertainty that like its key story, and also like several earlier English novels – Charlotte Brontë's *Villette*, Thackeray's *The Newcomes*, and *Middlemarch*, it ends with uncertainty. Like *Middlemarch* it asks questions as it concludes.

George Eliot's narrator insists that although Dorothea's life was not ideally beautiful, and though many thought her life was wasted in its domestic assimilation, no one could say what else she was able to do, given her circumstances. (In some ways like Effi's words about Innstetten.) Less certainly, and more tragically, than Dorothea's, Effi Briest's story ends as parents ask the key question about parenting. (Parenting here

---

33 Sigmund Freud: The Uncanny. In: Collected Papers, transl. by Joan Rivière. New York: Basic Books, Inc. 1959, pp. 368-407.

is literal and synecdochic.) Like Effi, looking back over the narrative with narrative awareness, recognising the end of the story, as fictional characters often do, Effi's parents come to the end of their chorus, in which there has quietly run the subtext of their own story. Now the mother says questions keep coming into her head, and asks "'Whether perhaps it was *our* fault, after all?'" and "'I wonder if perhaps she wasn't too young?'" and the father replies, "'that's *too* vast a subject'" (p. 221).[34]

"Ach [...] das ist ein zu weites Feld": the field is broad indeed, broader than its times and places. Briest's comic language tag, like the key story, reveals itself as totally resonant, exquisitely responsive – to adapt what Coleridge said about *The Winter's Tale* – to its character and its novel in not only refusing to give an answer but in knowing that we do not know even how to ask the question.

The ghost-story raises to high relief the question of narrative causality, displacing, deconstructing, destorying, but not destroying the concept or expectation of realism in what has been, and apparently still is, in German studies, seen as the classic realist novel. It provides a self-analysis, both explicit and implicit, which says we do not tell stories in order to tell the truth, but to educate, frighten, subdue, amuse, entertain and seduce. What is true of Innstetten the bourgeois authoritarian husband and Crampas the small-town seducer, both military men, is true of the larger culture. And yet its uncertainty and multiplicity and openings look like attempts at truthfulness, especially in this last refusal to create conclusion, after Effi's death. But the parents' dialogue is like a postscript, and there is a displacement in the death itself. As with the bride in the ghost-story, we do not know when we have seen the last of Effi.

The habit of displacement works in more ways than one. The novel, in spite of its fullness, sometimes assumes an air of résumé. The occasional strong sense of an excerpted and synoptic, rather than a complete story, is confirmed by Fontane's innovative habit of retrospective gap-filling, in allusions to past episodes not previously related, like the source of the newspaper reports, Innstetten's evening readings to Effi, the episodes of adultery, or Effi's youthful relations with Dagobert. It creates what film-makers call back-story. It flaunts selectivity and partiality, as well as delivering surprises to the reader. It undermines narrative sequentiality and encourages the reader's recall and rereading. Sometimes it invites us to imagine the possible elucidation or completion of an episode as back-story.

On my last reading of the novel I was struck by one more uncertainty and implication, its presence also emphasised by the habit of back-story and the uncertainties and incompleteness of what may or may not be a ghost-story. There are several occasions – perhaps more that I have not noticed – in which a crucial event or response, each time bringing some suggestion of desire and death, is accompanied by an unexplained sound, which Effi thinks she hears, and one or two similar occasions when the sound is explained. It is important and unusual in also being muted. Almost, it escapes notice. It is the strongest gap in the story of quotidian experience, and especially interesting in such a rational and secular novelist, though in the end, as I

---

34 "'Ob *wir* nicht doch vielleicht schuld sind [...] ob sie nicht doch vielleicht *zu* jung war?'" Fontane, Effi Briest, NFA, VII, 427; "'[...] das ist ein zu weites Feld.'" Fontane: Effi Briest, NFA, VII, 427.

shall suggest, it confirms his rationality and secularity, his examination of creatures of history.

Driving home with Sidonie on what is to be a crucial ride, before Effi is joined and then left with Crampas, and just before they reach the dangerous Schloon, at once solid and symbolic, Effi thinks she can hear a mysterious sound. She makes a remark, like her childish words of delight in falling, about fancying the idea of being "thrown out [...] straight into the breakers", then asks:[35]

"Can you hear anything by the way?"
"No."
"You don't hear something like music?"
"An organ?"
"No, not an organ. That would make me think it was just the sea. No it's something else, an infinitely delicate sound, almost like a human voice."
"It's an hallucination... You're hearing voices. Pray God that you may hear the right voice too."
"I hear ... well, of course it's too silly, I know, otherwise I'd imagine I'd heard the mermaids singing ..." (p. 115) [36]

This ambiguous, beautiful and dangerous image of singing mermaids, even more remote than J. Alfred Prufrock's (and not unlike it), and placed within Effi's imagination, may refer back to a significant occasion (in Chapter 16) when a seal appears, Crampas thinks of a hunt, Innstetten invokes the law, and Effi, with Rollo, waits for the "mermaid" (this time "die Seejungfrau") to reappear: the word mermaid is used abruptly, without explanation, to refer to the seal. If the forest music is Effi's siren song, it is modulated and changed.

On holiday at Hohen-Cremmen, after Innstetten has gone back to Berlin, Effi recovers from a fit of remorse – for not feeling proper remorse – and hears a comforting sound as she sits at the open window, like several women in Jane Austen's and George Eliot's novels. "Everything was so still, and a quiet, gentle sound from the plane-trees, as if it was raining, struck her ear" (p. 161).[37] A little later, after the rattling of a train, it returns: "all that was to be heard was the sound of the plane trees

35 "'[...] wenn ich hinausflöge, am liebsten gleich in die Brandung.'" Fontane: Effi Briest, NFA, VII, 304.
36 "'...Übrigens hören Sie nichts? '
'Nein.'
'Hören Sie nicht etwas wie Musik? '
'Orgel?'
'Nein. Nicht Orgel. Da würd ich denken, es sei das Meer. Aber es ist etwas anderes, ein unendlich feiner Ton, fast wie menschliche Stimme...'
'Das sind Sinnestäuschungen [...] Sie hören Stimmen. Gebe Gott, daß Sie auch die richtige Stimme hören.'
'Ich höre ... nun gewiß, es ist Torheit, ich weiß, sonst würd ich mir einbilden, ich hätte die Meerfrauen singen.'" Fontane: Effi Briest, NFA, VII, 304.
37 "Alles war so still, und ein leiser, feiner Ton, wie wenn es regnete, traf von den Platanen her ihr Ohr." Fontane: Effi Briest, NFA, VII, 359.

rustling as before, as if light rain were falling" (p. 161).[38] Then isolated in a new paragraph, "But it was only the movement of the night air" (p. 161).[39] This may remind us of an earlier scene after the first bad night in Kessin, when the relief of air is simply mentioned as Effi asks Johanna to "'open the window a little so that I can have some air and light'" (p. 55).[40]

Neither passage would be noticeable if it were not for the recurrence of a similar mood of rest, associated with more mysterious sounds, heard more mutedly, towards the end. Effi is taking pleasure in one of her country walks, and as she breathes and looks, "a faint ringing noise drifted over to her. And at that she felt as if she must close her eyes and lapse into sweet oblivion" (p. 214).[41] This sound is unidentified, but when something like it recurs in the last episode of her life, another window scene, it is identified, (reinforced as we recall the earlier occurrence) as the night air on the plane trees. (The night air has a benign resonance, but it is also accelerates her death, from tuberculosis.)

In the last image of listening, Effi's consciousness expands, in what with characteristic narrative originality, Fontane does not clearly place as a death-scene, only as the heroine's last appearance in the novel. Afterwards a month elapses and we find her buried. He avoids the popular and climactic death-narrative, making suggestions rather than statements of freedom and rest, using but not pressing the "once more", anticipating and separating that suggestive sweet oblivion. The last scene could be re-read or retold as a back-story, of death, but never is. Its last two words are remarkably unattached, in spite of their speech-marks, and it is impossible to locate them either inside or outside the character's imagination:

> … Effi rose too and sat by the open window to draw in the cool night air once more. The stars shimmered, not a leaf stirred in the park. But the longer she listened, the more clearly she could again hear something falling like a fine drizzle on the planes. A feeling of liberation came over her. "Peace, peace." (p. 216) [42]

The last example is linked with the listening scene two pages earlier, but if we read "like a fine drizzle on the planes" without recalling its antecedent twelve chapters before, where the planes are rustling, it seems more mysterious and less natural. It may seem too fine a nuance to emphasise, but I think Fontane may have wanted to do two

---

38 "[…] nur auf die Platanen rauschte es nach wie vor wie leiser Regen nieder." Fontane: Effi Briest, NFA, VII, 359.

39 "Aber es war nur die Nachtluft, die ging. " Fontane: Effi Briest, NFA, VII, 359.

40 "'…und dann machen Sie das Fenster ein wenig auf, daß ich Luft und Licht habe.'" Fontane: Effi Briest, NFA, VII, 232.

41 "Dabei klang ein leises Läuten zu ihr herüber. Und dann war ihr zu Sinn, als müsse sie die Augen schließen und in einem süßen Vergessen hinübergehen." Fontane: Effi Briest, NFA, VII, 422.

42 "[…] Effi [erhob sich] auch und setzte sich an das offene Fenster, um noch einmal die kühle Nachtluft einzusaugen. Die Sterne flimmerten, und im Parke regte sich kein Blatt. Aber je länger sie hinaushorchte, je deutlicher hörte sie wieder, daß es wie ein feines Rieseln auf die Platanen niederfiel. Ein Gefühl der Befreiung überkam sie. 'Ruhe, Ruhe.'" Fontane: Effi Briest, NFA, VII, 426.

things at the end of his finely nuanced novel:[43] to isolate its romantic climax and strangeness, but also to provide a rational explanation, unemphasised, tucked away in the back-story, to be forgotten, or remembered, or tracked down.

The sounds are all associated with nature, sometimes with freedom and rest, also with desire and death. I do not press interpretation of these poetic images of attractive and sometimes unidentified sound, only remark their lyrical intensification of emotion and their strangeness, their inside-outside oscillation, their unemphatic repetition, their irregular relationship – once we notice them as a series we have to read back, because the form and content of the repeated motifs is neither prominent nor clear. Only when they are grouped can we start making speculations about meaning, but their relation to each other makes inference problematic.

Perhaps they are inner voices or visions of Effi's imagination and isolation. Perhaps they are solicitations of desire, liberation and death. They open delicate cracks in the solid phenomenal world and the authored text of Fontane's secular and historical narrative, through which uncertainty and mystery may seem to insinuate themselves. But in the end the images are recognisable as natural and rational, the insinuations are unromantic and tactful, if teasing. They are suggestive and specious invitations, created by a rational, secular, and flexible imagination, to imagine a noumenal or metaphysical experience of freedom. They are solicitations which take us to an apparent threshold, but not across it, so they should not be accepted. We reach not a threshold but a limit. History and nature are all we have.

---

43 'Wanted' is used loosely, and does not insist that the repetitions and variations are wholly conscious, though I think they probably were.

Patricia Howe

"A visibly-appointed stopping-place":
Narrative Endings at the End of the Century

In Henry James's critical prefaces, published between 1907 and 1909, he looks back to his first novel, *Roderick Hudson*, published in 1875, and recalls the terror of the young novelist trying to balance narrative energy and continuity with form and the appearance of finality. He asks:

> Where, for the complete expression of one's subject, does a particular relation stop – giving way to some other not concerned in that expression? Really, universally, relations stop nowhere, and the exquisite problem of the artist is eternally but to draw, by a geometry of his own, the circle within which they shall happily appear to do so.[1]

Switching metaphors, he goes on to describe "a young embroiderer of the canvas of life" covering a larger and larger surface in his effort to define the shape of his work, but always being tempted forward:

> in the presumability somewhere of a convenient, of a visibly-appointed stopping place. Art would be easy indeed, if [...] such conveniences, such simplifications, had been provided. We have, as the case stands, to invent and establish them, to arrive at them by a difficult, dire process of selection and comparison, of surrender and sacrifice.[2]

James seems to suggest here that endings appear appropriate because they are projected and constructed according to the internal logic of the narrative. This sense of an ending and of how it is determined fits his conception of the work as organic, growing from what he calls the "germ" of a beginning – a conception that may also be inferred from Trollope's and Fontane's references to a "kernel of story", perhaps with a common origin in Romantic philosophy and criticism.[3] But James's changing metaphors, – of growing, drawing, embroidering and discovering, of surrender and sacrifice – signal the theoretical slipperiness of endings, their complex determinants and functions. Indeed, he also describes endings, with some scorn, as "a distribution at the last of prizes, pensions, husbands, wives, babies, millions, appended paragraphs,

---

1 Henry James: The Art of the Novel. Critical Prefaces. New York: Charles Scribner's Sons 1934, p. 5.
2 James: The Art of the Novel, p. 6.
3 Fontane speaks of "der Keim der Geschichte", which corresponds to Trollope's reference to a "kernel of story"; Hans Blumenberg suggests that the idea of the germ is one that Coleridge shares with Romantic philosophers and critics in Germany after Herder. See Hans Blumenberg: The Concept of Reality and the Possibility of the Novel. In: Richard E. Amacher and Victor Lange (eds.): New Perspectives in German Literary Criticism. A Collection of Essays. Princeton: Princeton University Press 1979, p. 38.

and cheerful remarks".[4] This view differs in sentiment but not in sense from Friedrich Schlegel's comment, "Novels like to end where the Lord's Prayer begins, with the kingdom of God on earth" or Trollope's cheerful suggestion that "The end of a novel, like the end of a children's dinner party, must be made up of sweetmeats and sugar-plums."[5] Remarks like these, and there are many more, imply that endings are determined not only by the internal logic of the text, but also by its interaction with other discourses, and that they represent the final stage of a process in which cultural values are absorbed into the text and projected back on to the world from it. Serious novelists, like James, may scorn endings that proceed from extrinsic judgements or from pragmatic issues like serialisation, for serious novels are transgressive, they are oppositional discourse with other things to do apart from confirming traditional moral schemes.[6] And, yet, of course, the endings of their novels are still doubly determined, for even in their opposition they reflect traditional schemes, which they overcome in new strategies.

As well as being doubly determined, endings fulfil a double function of closing and framing. We read towards "the satisfaction of closure", a complex manoeuvre by which we construct a coherent narrative retrospectively. This means, above all, reading towards the completion of a paradigm, such as desire and fulfilment, sin and redemption.[7] Although such paradigms may themselves be cultural constructs, it is completing them that gives the impression – perhaps I should say the illusion – that an organism has grown to its proper shape. But a narrative ending is also part of a frame, a line of demarcation, that shows, as Lotman says, that "What is on the outside does not enter into the structure of the given work; it is either not a work or another work."[8] As demarcation it marks the end of fictionality and returns the reader's attention to actuality with the sense of having recovered a coherent fictional world from a text. The

---

4 Quoted by Frank Kermode: The Sense of an Ending. Oxford, New York: Oxford University Press 1967, p. 22.

5 "Die Romane endigen gern, wie das Vaterunser anfängt: mit dem Reich Gottes auf Erden", Friedrich Schlegel: Kritische Fragmente, Nr.18, Kritische-Friedrich-Schlegel-Ausgabe, Abteilung I, Bd.2: Charakteristiken und Kritiken I (1796-1801, ed. and introduced by H. Euchner. Munich Paderborn, Vienna 1967, p. 148; Anthony Trollope: Barchester Towers (1857). London and New York: Dent and Dutton Everyman edition 1906, p. 459. All translations into English are my own.

6 See: Edith Wharton: The Writing of Fiction. New York: Charles Scribner's Sons 1925, p. 108, "About no part of the novel should there be a clearer sense of inevitability than about its end; any hesitation, any failure to gather up all the threads, shows that the author has not let his subject mature in his mind. A novelist who does not know when his story is finished, but goes on stringing episode to episode after it is over, not only weakens the effect of the conclusion, but robs of significance all that has gone before."

7 Peter J. Rabinowitz: Before Reading. Narrative Conventions and the Politics of Interpretation. Columbus, Ohio: Ohio University Press 1987, p. 201: "there is a general tendency in most reading to apply rules of coherence in such a way that disjunctures are smoothed over so that texts are turned into unified wholes – that is, in a way that allows us to read so that we get the satisfaction of closure. This interpretive technique [...] may be connected to an innate psychological drive for closure."

8 Jurij Lotman: The structure of the artistic text, transl. by Ronald Vroon. Ann Arbor: University of Michigan 1977, Slavic Contributions no.7, p. 209.

two functions of closing and of framing combine to promote an optimal understanding of this fictional world.

When James speaks of "appended paragraphs and cheerful remarks", he may be acknowledging that the paradigm and the narrative text are not always co-extensive. Although Fontane rarely ends his novels with "a distribution of prizes", we are often aware of the gap between the moment when the paradigm is complete and the text ends. But it would be misleading to describe the space between them as an 'appended paragraph'; it is not just a formulaic signing off or tidying up, but an integral part of the narrative. In his early novels it is like the simple framing device of the ballad, which foreshortens the distance between the past time of events and the present time of reading, but in the course of his writing it grows until it is not just a frame or a comment, but has become a site of interrogation, interpretation and resistance. And from registering a sense of sameness it comes, eventually, to register difference. I shall consider how this happens and some of its implications for the narrative.

When Fontane speaks about the endings of his own novels, he is often ironic, casual, or self-deprecatory, and describes them in terms of the most banal narrative conventions, namely marriages and deaths. The last chapter of his first completed novel, *Vor dem Sturm* (*Before the Storm*), begins with the words: "Stories end with betrothals or weddings", but it passes rapidly through events of this kind to end with an inscription on a gravestone.[9] And he would have us believe that the same events, in reverse order, make up the whole of the action in his last completed novel, *Der Stechlin, (The Stechlin)*: "At the end an old man dies and two young people marry – that's more or less all that happens in 500 pages."[10] In practice he re-examines many variations on these conventional endings. Some are already present in the conclusion of *Vor dem Sturm*, which combines the endings of a family history, a historical chronicle, a ballad, and a fairy-tale. Most of these only recur in conjunction in *Effi Briest* – and then as fragments or empty hints – but they are distributed and re-examined singly in other narratives.

As a group the endings of his "crime stories" might be placed alongside the drastic endings of Storm's chronicle novellas, with which they are more or less con-temporaneous. The "authorising idea" of each is an event, prompted by greed, fear, passion or anger – the burning of Tangermünde, a poacher's death, and so on –, and the paradigmatic structure is complete when the narrative reaches this event.[11] To the drastic event Fontane adds a framing line, a paragraph or even a chapter that closes the text and registers a balladesque sense of continuity beyond the individual life.[12] In

---

9 "Erzählungen schließen mit Verlobung oder Hochzeit." Fontane: Vor dem Sturm, NFA, I, 636.
10 "Zum Schluß stirbt ein Alter, und zwei Junge heiraten sich; – das ist so ziemlich alles, was auf 500 Seiten geschieht." Fontane to Adolf Hoffmann, (draft) May/June 1897, HA, IV, 4, 650.
11 Edward Said: Beginning. Intention and Method. New York: Columbia University Press 1985, describes the core of a narrative as its authorising idea.
12 The most obviously balladesque ending is probably that of *Ellernklipp* which unites the narrative with its title and embeds the fates of individuals in the permanence of the landscape:
   "Ihr Begräbnis war ein großes Ereignis, wie's einst ihre Hochzeit gewesen war, und am selben Tage noch trug der Geistliche die Daten ihres Lebens und Sterbens in das Kirchenbuch ein.

Grete Minde continuity is expressed as sameness; after her death in the fire the text says "everything was as usual", and when the puppet play is performed without her "Nobody noticed the change".[13] The narrative thus has the kind of ending that confirms the shape and meaning of a life, and this may explain why, despite its dramatic events, Fontane describes *Grete Minde* as "a picture of a character".[14] The static quality is maintained by a Calvinistic sense of destiny, emphasised by sayings like "The law is eternal and unchanging" with which Fontane's crime stories echo.[15] Yet it is undermined by the narrator's sympathetic insight into the life of the criminal/hero. This makes it difficult to reconcile destiny with a sense of moral justice, and means that the reader who has followed the narrative of *Grete Minde* from its idyllic opening to its violent close can hardly assent to the claim to sameness. The gap between closure and frame is thus already provocative, because it seems to deny the experience both of the central character, and of the reader. In the closing chapter of *Quitt*, which was written and published later than the other crime stories, the discrepancy between destiny and justice, between morality and legality is explicitly discussed when Herr Espe, a character on the fringe of events, questions whether the law is satisfied by the self-sacrificing death of the former poacher, Lehnert Menz. The irrelevance of Espe's objection to self-sacrifice as a moral equivalent of the processes of law in the final pages of the novel, and his wife's sense of their futility, points forward to *Effi Briest*, where it is matched by the irrelevance of Luise Briest's belated questions and Briest's sense of their futility.

The reader's perception that something has changed but that nothing is resolved, stems, I think, from the fact that the narrative itself fails to recognise that the closing of the paradigm makes a difference. But with *L'Adultera* (*The Woman taken in Adultery*) this kind of recognition appears when aspects of interpretation left entirely to the reader of the crime stories are thematised and articulated by the characters. The moment of recognition comes precisely between closing and framing. As Melanie, having overcome shame, ostracism and poverty, prepares to celebrate Christmas she receives a miniature of the Tintoretto painting of the adulteress, bought by Van der Straaten at the beginning of the novel. The painting became an omen for her first marriage, and now reappears, in miniature, packed into the two halves of an apple and made to replace its core. The symbolism is inescapable; Rubehn tries to banish the

---

Da stehen sie, mahnend wie der Spruch auf ihrem Grabe.
Aber beides überdauernd, ragt über Dingels Mühle die weiße Felswand auf und auf ihrer Höhe die weit vorgebeugte Tanne von *Ellernklipp*".
("Her funeral was a great event, just as her wedding had been, and on the very same day the pastor entered the dates of her birth and death in the parish chronicle.. There they stand, a warning like the motto on her grave. But outlasting both and towering above Dingel's mill is the white rock face, and on its summit the fir tree leaning out over the edge of *Ellernklipp*.") Fontane: Ellernklipp, NFA, II, 269.

13 "[...] alles war wie sonst." Fontane: Grete Minde, NFA, III, 90; "Niemand achtete des Wechsels" Fontane: *Grete Minde*, NFA, III, 91.

14 "Es ist ein Charakterbild." Fontane to Paul Lindau, 23 October 1878, HFA, IV, 2, 625.

15 "Ewig und unwandelbar ist das Gesetz." Fontane: Ellernklipp, NFA, II, 269.

omen by naming and discussing their story, telling Melanie: "[...] don't take it more tragically than necessary and don't brood too much on the tedious old topic of guilt and expiation".[16] Naming the issue apparently lays it to rest and the novel ends in a sudden access of harmony. The ending brings together the miniature and the heroine, uniting the narrative with its title in – to use Fontane's words – "a rounder roundness".[17]

From *L'Adultera* onwards the ending is part of a more self-reflexive text. The final paragraphs, or, more often, final chapter, provide a commentary on and a corrective to earlier acts of reading and interpretation in the text itself. In the structure *of Schach von Wuthenow (A Man of Honor), Cécile* and *Unwiederbringlich (Beyond Recall),* the process of interpreting behaviour from and in letters is present throughout the narrative and is formalised in the letters with which the novels end. In *Schach von Wuthenow* the two concluding letters extend the debates about Schach's character, his political and private behaviour, that inform the conversations between his political friends and enemies on the one hand, and of Victoire and her mother on the other, and give different explanations of Schach's suicide. Bülow's reflections on Schach's false concept of honour as an historical symptom stand next to Victoire's realisation that he would never have been, so to speak, husband material. However, they are not mutually exclusive but suggest a political, moral and psychological continuum. This is not made explicit, for there is no commentary. The narrator reduces his control over interpretation to the ordering of the letters. The reader outside the text automatically privileges the second letter, – readers inside the text don't see both letters – not because Victoire's explanation is better, or more conciliatory, or even because she is more sympathetic, but just because she has the last word.

The final chapter of *Cécile* offers a more startling disjunction. The tension between old and new that informs Fontane's writing is evident here in an ending that deals with the long shadow of the past in a form close to montage. It consists of four texts, held together by a minimal commentary: a newspaper announcement of Gordon's death in a duel with St Arnaud; St Arnaud's letter of explanation and request for Cécile to join him in the South of France, and a letter from a pastor, telling St Arnaud that Cécile is dead, with, finally, her will. Even more than in *Schach von Wuthenow* the reading of behaviour, the construction of meaning is a conscious theme and process in this novel. Together these four last documents – I am tempted to say "four last things", since they do deal with deaths and judgements, if not with heaven and hell – draw together the strands of what has gone before and offer a critique of earlier readings of Cécile's life. Again the narrator renounces the authority of the emphatic closure, delegating judgement and interpretation first to characters and then to readers. The sense of

---

16 "nimm es nicht tragischer als nötig und grüble nicht zuviel über das alte leidige Thema von Schuld und Sühne." Fontane: L'Adultera, NFA, IV, 124.

17 "eine rundere Rundung." Fontane to Salo Schottländer, 11 September 1881, HFA, IV, 3, 161. Wolfgang Hädecke: Fontane. Biographie. Munich: Hanser 1997, p. 285 points out that the ending is conciliatory but that the child Anninettchen who might represent the harmony of their life together is absent, and asks whether this is an artistic failure on the part of the narrator or a hint that the lovers are egoists who are only interested in themselves. It may be, however, that Fontane is consciously avoiding a sentimental cliché.

disjunction between form and reference occurs because the four texts speak of outdated conventions and of a woman overwhelmed by but also retreating into her past, while the form points forward. It looks forward to *Buddenbrooks*, where the last chapter expands this pattern into four sections, from the clinical-cum-mystical account of Hanno's death to the final act of faith from Sesemi Weichbrodt. And if one looks further, one finds not an ending, but a beginning – namely the opening of Ulrich Plenzdorf's *Die neuen Leiden des jungen W.*, which documents the death of an individual in four announcements in a newspaper, and thus thematises the process of reading towards the coherence that is recovered from endings.

In these works interpretation is thematised and formalised as the area between completing the paradigm and framing the narrative expands. But what does this do to conventional patterns of closure? The short answer seems to be that the events that mark them are ironised, or suppressed and recuperated from their effects. The traditional "nuptial chapters" or death-bed scenes of nineteenth-century literature become gaps, clichés or jokes. Indeed, John R. Reed makes the point that, by the time Meredith names the "nuptial chapter" in *Diana of the Crossways* (1885), it is already a self-conscious convention, used by writers to expose the loveless marriage of convenience as an uneasy, even desperate accommodation.[18] Fontane's "nuptial chapters" in *Irrungen, Wirrungen* (*Confusions, Delusions*) and *Frau Jenny Treibel* (*Jenny Treibel*) are meditations on and ironisations of this convention which just fall short of the self-conscious manner of Meredith and, more pertinently, of Thackeray. Fontane's nuptial chapters begin to resemble the conclusion of his beloved *Vanity Fair*, where marriage is treated somewhat perfunctorily as "the beginning of formal disenchantment."[19]

Irrungen, Wirrungen and *Frau Jenny Treibel* re-examine the nuptial chapter, doing away with sentimentality and the uniqueness of romantic love, and replacing them with sober rationalism, even disillusion, and satire. The ending *of Irrungen, Wirrungen* strips the nuptial chapter of what Meredith calls "decorative illusions" and provides an unromantic testimony to the distorting power of gossip. The ending offers hypocritical and snobbish readings of the events of the narrative and their conclusion; malicious bystanders comment on Lene's wedding to Gideon, noting the absence of the "Kranz", the bridal wreath symbolising virginity; and Käthe's comment on the newspaper announcement unwittingly provides a commentary on her own marriage. Botho's question and assertion: "What have you got against Gideon, Käthe? Gideon is better than Botho."[20] seems to offer a corrective, which makes sense only to the reader of the whole text, but does not necessarily command that reader's assent. Following

---

18 The expression is used by John R Reed: Victorian Conventions. Ohio: Ohio University Press 1975, p. 123, but taken from George Meredith: Diana of the Crossways (1885) where the last chapter is entitled "Nuptial Chapter; And Of How A Barely Willing Woman Was Led to Bloom With the Nuptial Sentiment". Reed says of Meredith that his highly self-conscious attitude to the convention is representative of feeling in the latter part of the century.

19 John R Reed: Victorian Conventions, p. 121.

20 "Was hast du nur gegen Gideon, Käthe? Gideon ist besser als Botho." Fontane: Irrungen, Wirrungen, NFA, III, 232.

immediately after the comments of the bystanders at Lene's wedding it invokes the socially unthinkable marriage between Botho and Lene, so that the text ends with an absence or a negation.

The ending of *Frau Jenny Treibel* subverts the nuptial chapter by combining disillusion with satire. Marcell's perpetual willingness to marry Corinna recalls Dobbin's eighteen-year pursuit of Amelia in *Vanity Fair*. A satirical element reminiscent of Keller is also present, not only in the obvious intertextual references to *Das Fähnlein der sieben Aufrechten* (The little flag of the seven upright men), but in the comic techniques of multiplication and trivialisation, also evident at the end of *Vanity Fair*. As Corinna and Marcell become engaged and marry, engagements spread like a rash: the arrival of the announcement in Frau Jenny Treibel's house is a signal for the engagement of Leopold and Hildegard: "This day brought two betrothals".[21] The perfunctory description of the wedding:

> On the twenty-seventh there was a small party in the Schmidts' apartment, on the following day the wedding in the English House. Pastor Thomas officiated. At three the carriages pulled up in front of St. Nicholas's Church, six maids of honour, among them the two Kuh fillies and the two Felgentreus.[22]

is followed by the multiplication of folly that recalls Keller and, again, the last chapter of *Vanity Fair*. The passage continues:

> The last-named, as may be revealed here, betrothed themselves during the interval in the dancing to the two students from the quartet, the same young gentlemen who had gone with them on the excursion to Lake Halen. The yodler, who had naturally also been invited, was besieged by the Kuhs but resisted, because as the son of a corner house, he was accustomed to such violent assault. The Kuh daughters accepted this failure easily "he wasn't the first and he won't be the last", said Schmidt – and only the mother behaved with persistent bad grace.[23]

The random choice of bridegrooms anticipates Effi's chillingly insouciant remark that "Anyone is the right one", and, like Corinna's honeymoon journey to Verona, confirms the demise of romance and of the nuptial chapter.[24] The final framing of the text in a

---

21 "Dieser Tag bedeutete zwei Verlobungen." Fontane: Frau Jenny Treibel, NFA, VII, 162.

22 "Am siebenundzwanzigsten war kleiner Polterabend in der Schmidtschen Wohnung, den Tag darauf Hochzeit im 'Englischen Hause'. Prediger Thomas traute. Drei Uhr fuhren die Wagen vor der Nikolaikirche vor, sechs Brautjungfern, unter denen die beiden Kuhschen Kälbe und die zwei Felgentreus waren." Fontane: Frau Jenny Treibel, NFA, VII, 163.

23 "Letztere, wie schon hier verraten werden mag, verlobten sich in einer Tanzpause mit den zwei Referendaren vom Quartett, denselben jungen Herren, die die Halenseepartie mitgemacht hatten. Der natürlich auch geladene Jodler wurde von den Kuhs heftig in Angriff genommen, widerstand aber, weil er, als Eckhaussohn, an solche Sturmangriffe gewöhnt war. Die Kuhschen Töchter selbst fanden sich ziemlich leicht in diesen Echec – "er war der erste nicht, er wird der letzte nicht sein", sagte Schmidt – und nur die Mutter zeigte bis zuletzt eine starke Verstimmung." Fontane: Frau Jenny Treibel, NFA, VII, 163.

24 "Jeder ist der Richtige." Fontane: Effi Briest, NFA, VII, 182.

comic celebration held by "the seven orphans" underlines the artificiality, perhaps the emptiness of what it represents:

> "... And poor Corinna she's at Trebbin, on the first stage to Juliet's grave.
> ... Juliet Capulet, the very sound of it! By the way, it's supposed to be an Egyptian sarcophagus, which is really much more interesting... And then, all in all, I don't know that it's right to travel all night like that; it didn't used to be the custom, people used to be more natural, I mean more moral. A pity my friend Jenny's gone, she ought to decide. Personally I'm convinced nature is morality, and the most important thing of all."[25]

Juliet's grave and the death of romance – also invoked in *Effi Briest* – appear in novels about marriage as deaths and death-bed scenes disappear or are minimised. Deaths are alluded to, or happen, so to speak between the lines. They become gaps in the text and in consciousness; those contemplating death see it not as a monstrous boundary, but as instantaneous release. When Schach von Wuthenow grasps that a single moment can arrest the flux of time, he feels free, "'Life,' he said to himself. 'What is life? A matter of minutes, a difference between one day and the next.'" And for the first time after days that had weighed on him heavily, he felt light and free."[26] Petöfy too speeds mentally past his own death to a future he will create for his wife and nephew, "And then, what is the individual? Nothing. And especially the individual who has already lived and has his life behind him. It can be a joy, the last and greatest joy, to smooth the path of happiness for others." [27] It is not only potential suicides who see death this way. In *Unwiederbringlich* Holk's thoughts rush past his wife's unhappiness to her death, strangely telescoping argument and event: "'The light of our lives is happiness, and if it goes out, night falls and if this night is death, it's the best thing.'"[28] The verse his wife leaves behind as the explanation of her death: "Peace may be the best part/ Of all joy in the world" echoes his precipitate conclusion.[29] These extreme moments are felt to be insights in need of acknowledgement, but the characters are barely capable of articulating this, and so their language sets into shallow aphoristic formality, suggesting that, death, as an ending, has become a cliché or a contrivance. In *Graf*

---

25 "'...Und die arme Corinna! Jetzt ist sie bei Trebbin, erste Etappe zu Julias Grab ... Julia Capulet, wie das klingt. Es soll übrigens eine ägyptische Sargkiste sein, was eigentlich noch interessanter ist ...Und dann alles in allem, ich weiß nicht, ob es recht ist, die Nacht so durchzufahren; früher war das nicht Brauch, früher war man natürlicher, ich möchte sagen, sittlicher. Schade, daß meine Freundin Jenny fort ist, die sollte darüber entscheiden. Für mich persönlich steht es fest, Natur ist Sittlichkeit und überhaupt die Hauptsache.'" Fontane: Frau Jenny Treibel, NFA, VII, 166f.

26 "'Leben, sprach er vor sich hin. Was ist leben? Ein Frage von Minuten, eine Differenz von heut auf morgen.' Und er fühlte sich, nach Tagen schweren Druckes, zum ersten Male wieder leicht und frei." Fontane: Schach von Wuthenow, NFA, II, 373f.

27 "'Und zudem, was ist der einzelne? Nichts. Und nun gar der einzelne, wenn er gelebt hat und seine Tage hinter ihm liegen. Es kann ein Glück sein, ein letztes und höchstes, dem Glück anderer die Wege zu bereiten. '" Fontane: Graf Petöfy, NFA, II, 159.

28 "'Das Licht unseres Lebens heißt die Freude, und lischt es aus, so ist die Nacht da, und wenn diese Nacht der Tod ist, ist es noch am besten.'" Fontane: Unwiederbringlich, NFA, V, 218.

29 "Die Ruh ist wohl das beste/ Von allem Glück der Welt." Fontane: Unwiederbringlich, NFA, V, 42, 223.

Petöfy (Count Petöfy) this goes together with living as an aesthetic act, with playing parts and constructing a life and a death according to literary models. Just before he commits suicide Petöfy remembers warning Franziska that life is not to be treated as a fairy-tale, but realises that this is exactly what he did. This insight does not stop him from constructing his death as the conclusion to a chivalrous romance, "'Yes, the thing I wanted, it was just a chivalrous whim, and in the end I have to accept that it wasn't the key to all doors. But for what I'm going to do now, for the only thing left to do, for that it fits.'"[30]

The developments sketched here come together in the ending of *Effi Briest*, and make it both a highpoint and a pivot. While it offers formally and referentially an interrogation of the old, the novels that come after it are more open to the new and more porous in texture. *Effi Briest* anticipates their wider view in a number of ways: it registers difference; it thematises interpretation; it subsumes the endings of other possible literary models in its own, and so clears a space for a different kind of ending.

The last chapter begins with the prospect of change, with Rollo's return, the hope of Effi's recovery and convalescence in the South of France. Differences are registered immediately; Rollo has grown old, but, if possible, his loyalty is even greater; Effi believes that she has changed her parents' lives and made them old, "'And really I've changed your lives and made you old before your time.'"[31] Difference is not only explicitly articulated, but can also be measured in spatial structures. Effi's life is circumscribed, as it was at the beginning, by the garden, but the way out of the garden is not, as it was then, by the garden gate to the church and marriage, or across the pond, anticipating her adultery in the reference to drowning adulterous women. Effi explores different spatial arrangements: she turns inwards to search her heart, mind, memory, in reflection and self-examination; and outwards to measure her life in the landscape around her home. But her way out of the garden involves vertical movements, upwards and downwards. The beginning of the end of the novel is located in a sentence, whose peculiar syntax and abrupt change of tone alert us to its pivotal function, "Poor Effi, you had looked up too long at the wonders of heaven and thought about them, and in the end the night air and the mist rising from the pond cast her down on her sick-bed again".[32] The sentence shifts from "you" – Fontane uses the intimate "Du" – to "she", from looking upwards to being cast down, from sentimental address "Poor Effi", to the abrupt comment of Dr Wieseke to Briest "'Nothing to be done; be prepared for a quick end.' "[33]

---

30 "'Ja, was ich wollte, war eine Kavalierslaune, von der ich schließlich einsehen muß, daß sie nicht der Schlüssel war, der überallhin schließt. Aber für das was ich vorhabe, für das, was noch zu tun übrigbleibt, dafür paßt sie. '" Fontane: Graf Petöfy, NFA, II, 162.

31 "'Und eigentlich hab' ich doch euer Leben geändert und euch vor der Zeit zu alten Leuten ge-macht.'" Fontane: Effi Briest, NFA, VII, 423.

32 "Arme Effi, du hattest zu den Himmelswundern zu lange hinaufgesehen und darüber nachgedacht, und das Ende war, daß die Nachtluft und der Nebel, die vom Teich her aufstiegen, sie wieder aufs Krankenbett warfen." Fontane: Effi Briest, NFA, VII, 424.

33 "'Wird nichts mehr; machen Sie sich auf ein baldiges Ende gefaßt.'" Fontane: Effi Briest, NFA, VII, 424.

This peculiar manoeuvre turns the narrative towards closure, and, more immediately, towards the final, apparently conciliatory but ultimately unsatisfying discussion between Effi and her mother. This discussion, like the final conversation between Briest and Luise makes interpretation into a theme. As with the last words of *Irrungen, Wirrungen*, what is said does not necessarily command the reader's assent, because the points of view put forward are subjective, prompted by the speaker's own version of the story and miss the point. In the dialogue between Luise and Effi the reader can detect gaps; it does not read as one might expect the final words between a mother and her dying daughter to do, but, as Renate Böschenstein says in her contribution to this volume, like a judgement informed by a stern kind of maternal love. The reader can choose to interpret Effi's message to Innstetten and her apparent acceptance of her guilt as inspired by genuine insight into her own behaviour and his; or, he or she can read it as a final conciliatory message from a dying woman, for whom all this is now irrelevant, to the living – to Innstetten and to Luise, the stern mother but also the woman who once loved and renounced Innstetten. Death becomes not so much an event as a context, in which, contrary to any notions of finality or absolute value we might entertain, the meaning of words is relativised.

Difference and its interpretation come together in the final scene between Briest and Luise. The marble gravestone brings "a slight change" to the garden, the final framing of Effi and her life.[34] But before the final conversation between Briest and his wife, he sends for a carriage, saying: "'I want to drive across country with Frau von Briest'";[35] his intention recalls his earlier reference to living off the land when Luise says that society will cut them dead for taking Effi back, and in both cases it signals resistance. *Effi Briest* begins with the commanding authority of the house at Hohen-Cremmen, but at its end Briest, the owner of this house, dismisses this authority and the suffocating enclosure it has come to mean. This departure suggests a sense of irrelevance close to Effi's, a sense that grows as he dismisses his wife's questions and her search for scapegoats, which scarcely begin to explain Effi's fate, and which even the dog rejects. Briest's final "'Leave it alone, Luise, it's too big a question'" may be read not as an expression of resignation or defeat, but as deferring a cogent explanation.[36]

Yet the narrative as a whole encourages readings of Effi's life according to various conventional patterns and contemporary discourses. Some provide a complete paradigm for her life. Michael Minden sees in it parallel narratives consisting of a prosaic anecdote about a society lady who commits adultery, is divorced and, poetically, dies young, and of a brutal tale of waste and injustice towards a *Naturkind*.[37] Her death, which is not part of the anecdote on which Fontane based his novel, is common to both. Schuster constructs Effi's life from the dual figure of Eve/Mary in the garden, first as the story of fall and redemption and then as a

---

34 "[…] eine kleine Veränderung." Fontane: Effi Briest, NFA, VII, 426.

35 "'Ich will mit der Frau über Land fahren. '" Fontane: Effi Briest, NFA, VII, 295.

36 "'Ach,, Luise, laß … das ist ein zu weites Feld.'" Fontane: Effi Briest, NFA, VII, 427.

37 M. R. Minden: Effi Briest und "die historische Stunde des Takts". Modern Language Review 76 (1981), 871-879.

Marienleben ("Life of the Virgin"). He sees the ending and her return to the garden as a return to paradise where "[…] Effi can pick an apple from the tree – Fontane does not disclose this until the very last page –, and bite bravely into it, in order to say immediately after this in the text: 'I was always a bad Christian'".[38] He notes the symbolism of her death in the same month as Mary, the cross on her grave, "the sign of redemption for a life pleasing to God" and the heliotrope, "that symbol of a life constantly moving towards God and thus a life led in imitation of Christ".[39] He suggests that with this ending Fontane treated the Christian ideals of his society ironically and, at the same time, seriously.

While the struggle with Christian ideals may provide a paradigm for the entire narrative, other narrative patterns, and the endings they entail, appear as phases and as interrogative discourses. Near the beginning the novel briefly takes up the possibility of fairy-tale invoked by Count Petöfy, but cuts it off with Effi's marriage. During her trip to Berlin she sees Bendix's *Cinderella*, at the party on the eve of her wedding her friends perform a scene from Kleist's *Das Käthchen von Heilbronn*, another Cinderella story, but Briest indignantly dismisses the notion that she is Cinderella. There are possible parallels with another fairy-tale in *Effi Briest*, but the potential for fairy-tale is thwarted here by Effi's mother. As a girl who is married, with the encouragement if not coercion of her mother, to a man who might have been her father, Effi resembles the eponymous heroine of *Allerleirauh* (*Donkey-Skin*). In *Allerleirauh* the dying mother insists that her husband should re-marry only if he can find a woman as beautiful as she is, and he eventually decides to marry his daughter. The daughter demands a trousseau of beautiful dresses and a coat made from hair and fur from all the animals in her father's kingdom; from this she gets her name. The fur coat protects her, while she works, like Cinderella, in the kitchen of another king, until she is mature enough to avoid her widowed father's desire for her and to choose her own husband. Effi's fairy-tale reverses these motifs; when Effi asks for a fur coat as part of her trousseau, Luise refuses it because it will make her seem older than her years; she inherits a husband who is not, but might have been her father, but, reversing the progress of Cinderella or Allerleirauh, is first elevated and then degraded. The singling out of the hero or heroine that takes place at the beginning of a fairy-tale is balanced by the hidden interconnectedness that makes help available when needed and ensures a just outcome.[40] In *Effi Briest* isolation comes later, and the pervasive "Gesellschaftsetwas" ("social something") is not this benign interconnectedness, but a malign force involving mutual fear, rivalry or hostility, while Effi's helpers are marginal figures with

---

38 "Dort darf Effi - Fontane teilt es erst auf den allerletzten Seiten mit - einen Apfel vom Baum pflücken und 'tapfer' hineinbeißen, um gleich anschließend im Text zu sagen: 'Ich war immer eine schlechte Christin'." Peter Klaus Schuster: Ein Leben nach christlichen Bildern. Studien zur deutschen Literatur, vol. 55. Tübingen: Niemeyer 1978, p. 130.

39 "Zeichen der Erlösung für ein gottgefälliges Leben"; "jenes Sinnbild eines ständig auf Gott hin gerichteten und damit […] eines in der imitatio Christi geführten Lebens." Peter Klaus Schuster: Ein Leben nach christlichen Bildern, p. 130.

40 See: Max Lüthi: The European Folktale, Form and Nature, transl. John D. Niles. Philadelphia Institute for the Study of Human Issues 1982.

limited powers. In this network of motifs fairy-tales, and the endings they entail, are invoked, and thwarted or negated.

The pattern of chivalrous romance also proves to be invalid, as it did for Count Petöfy. Innstetten's early history makes him into something like a would-be Parzival – Innstetten likes Wagner – , who believes that, if he matures, he will be able to return, ask the right question and receive his reward. But the world of the novel is not that of chivalrous epic or courtly romance, above all it is not a timeless world in which passive heroines wait to be claimed. The attempt to recover the past founders on the difference between Luise and her daughter, which is not just a matter of temperament but of generation.

But the narrative also offers glimpses of a more relevant, contemporary discourse, namely the discourse of orientalism. When the fairy-tale has been thwarted, Effi's marriage appears as the mixture of eroticism, conquest and trade implied by this discourse, and represented by her reference to Constantinople, which German travellers saw as the beginning of the Orient; by her request for a Japanese screen; by the exotic dead creatures hanging in the hall at Kessin; and above all, by the image of the Chinaman, a stranger brought to this place by commerce, as, in a difference sense, is Effi.[41] The connection with commerce is confirmed when Innstetten tells Effi that Johanna has removed the image of the Chinaman from the back of the chair in the house in Kessin and keeps it in her purse.

The careful patterning of the conclusion of *Effi Briest*, its references to the opening chapter, its rhythm of hope and resignation, show the narrator's command and control of material. But the inadequate explanations, the pointless questions and resigned gestures also make the ending into a site of resistance: resistance to explanation in the discourses available to the society that produced Effi Briest and her story, to the moral design of Victorian fiction, or to patterns of fairy-tale or romance.[42] It may not be entirely resistant, in its openness, to the patterns of Judaeo-Christian thought, which suggest that, really, the endings of novels can only ever be allusions to deferred completion. It also prepares the way for the relatively *uneventful Die Poggenpuhls* (*The Poggenpuhl Family*) and *Der Stechlin* and for their more contemporary discourses. Although the endings of both these novels are precipitated by deaths, these are the deaths that belong to a long span of life, and they give way to different, if unpredictable lives. This makes for undramatic, tentatively speculative, unremarkable endings. Indeed when Fontane sends the proofs of *Die Poggenpuhls* to his son, he crosses out the word "Ende":

> I crossed it out because, if nothing else follows, everyone can see, "Yes, now it's over". But this word "end", presumably added by our friend Dobert, amused me because it is quite properly

---

41 I have used the term "Orientalism" in the broad sense although in German the term "Orient" is often restricted to the Middle East.

42 The term is used by John R Reed: Victorian Conventions, p. 4ff.

critical. Nobody can suppose that that's an ending, and so the reader had to be assured, "yes, my friend, now it's over; for good or ill".[43]

In *Der Stechlin* the assimilation of interpretation and explanation into the narrative and the projection of the fictional world beyond the text in the closing words "Long live Stechlin", opens up the ending.[44] It minimises the barrier between text and world, or text and context, and goes together with a narrative texture whose boundaries, throughout the novel, are fuzzier and less firmly fixed. The wide-ranging conversations give the impression that much if not everything is admissible. Fontane's plans and sketches for *Der Stechlin* show that he polishes this ending until it conveys continuity: "The only thing that interests me is that there are people who know what's going on in the world. In other words the Stechlins don't interest me, only Stechlin does".[45] In treating the last days of Dubslav von Stechlin, of the class and culture he represents, and his problematic relations to the future and its developments, Fontane has reached something like the point made by Henry James in his preface *to The Wings of the Dove*, when he says about writing of the novel that

> the way grew straight from the moment one recognised that the poet essentially can't be concerned with the act of dying. Let him deal with the sickest of the sick, it is still by the act of living that they appeal to him, and appeal the more as the conditions plot against them and prescribe the battle.[46]

The sense of interconnectedness that Lake Stechlin has with the world, counteracts the malign force of the "Gesellschaftsetwas" in *Effi Briest*, so that the last words sound like a benediction.

This brings me, finally to a brief comparison with the way endings work in Henry James's *The Wings of the Dove* (1901) and Edith Wharton's *The Custom of the Country* (1913) novels by American writers that examine the European context. The interrogation of the old by the new is extended and expanded by both of them into an interrogation of the Old World by the New, and vice versa. Their central characters also extend acts of reading, writing and interpreting their own lives. Undine Spragg, the heroine of *The Custom of the Country*, is, like Effi Briest, the only daughter of devoted parents, beautiful, spirited, socially ambitious and fond of distractions. Her name, Undine, signals her capacity for charming a succession of husbands while

---

43 "Das habe ich gestrichen, weil, wenn weiter nichts kommt, jeder sieht: 'ja, nun ist es aus'. Es amüsierte mich aber das mutmaßlich von Freund Dobert hinzugefügte Wort 'Ende' doch sehr, weil sich darin eine ganz richtige Kritik ausspricht. Kein Mensch kann annehmen, daß *das* ein Schluß ist, und so war es nöthig, dem Blatt-Leser zu versichern: 'ja, Freund, nun ist es aus; wohl oder übel.'" Fontane to Friedrich Fontane, 13 June 1896, HFA, IV, 4, 565.

44 "Es lebe der Stechlin." Fontane: Der Stechlin, NFA, VIII, 361.

45 "Mich interessiert nur, daß Leute da sind, die wissen, was in der Welt los ist. Mit andern Worten mich interessieren nicht die Stechline, mich interessiert blos – der Stechlin." The quotation is taken from the commentary on the plans and preparations for writing the novel in HFA, I, 5, 452.

46 James: The Art of the Novel, p. 289f.

remaining emotionally unmoved. Her successive marriages bring disillusion, divorce, suicide and ruin to her husbands and their families, while she mutates from the small town girl, Undine Spragg first – and more or less clandestinely – into Undine Moffatt, wife of a stranger with a dubious reputation, secondly into Undine Marvell, member of old New York society, thirdly, into the aristocratic Marquise de Chelles, and finally back into Undine Moffatt, wife of the "railway king". Despite her emotional indifference to her husbands, marriage changes her, for she unwittingly develops a sense of older cultures and more refined practices that spoil her pleasure in mere money. When, in the final chapter, she stands in Elmer Moffatt's magnificent ballroom, wearing the rubies given by Ralph Marvell and since re-set, and surveying the tapestries sold under duress by the Marquis de Chelles to her present husband, she realises that these trophies do not compensate for his abiding vulgarity. And when he tells her that, as a divorcée, she can never be the wife of an ambassador, she learns that there is something that cannot be achieved by another change of husband.

The *Custom of the Country* reaches an end because the past catches up with Undine, as it does with Effi, in written texts. The past proves to have been not a series of stepping stones to a bright future, but a growing shadow. Undine is caught out by her reluctance to read – to read texts, people or situations – as anything but reflections of herself. Wharton's ending, – as in *Effi Briest* a dialogue between husband and wife–, in which the husband tells her about an announcement in the newspaper that her rival is now the wife of an ambassador, closes off further developments and mocks her social progress through a series of advantageous marriages. Yet the past remains and is recorded in texts available to better readers, most obviously to her neglected child, Paul Marvell, who has learnt from a newspaper cutting that his mother lied to obtain her divorce. At the end of the novel the reader knows that Paul's reading is a time bomb ticking away in Undine's house, and this means that the ending projects beyond the text in a more ominously predictive way than it does in Fontane's novels.

Reading, writing, and mis-reading also go further in *The Wings of the Dove*; they are present in its metaphorical language and in the strategies of its central characters. Kate Croy, who is described as dazzling and is therefore much more dangerous than the radiant Effi, and Morten Densher try to write their future as the legacy of Millie Theale's death. They dissimulate in order to manipulate; but Morten Densher gets caught up in this, he sees that there is something that transcends the construction of reality that he and Kate are working on. It is Millie's construction of her own life and death. It is not, in the end, Millie's money and her will that make a difference to his life and Kate's, but the fact of having known her, of having witnessed her illness and of being moved by her, even of having fallen for his own story of loving her. At the end Kate accuses him of being in love with Millie's memory, so that his romance with her is insufficient. The ending is again a dialogue, which nods at the conventional ending of marriage, while probably destroying the possibility of it, but we can never be sure. Densher replies to Kate's accusation with:

"I'll marry you, mind you, in an hour."
"As we were?"

"As we were."
But she turned to the door, and her headshake was now the end. "We shall never be again as we were." [47]

Ending is not tying up, not quite closing but measuring distance, showing how far the narrative has come and how it projects beyond the text, and so returning the reader to his or her own world in the knowledge of the difference it has made. In contrast to the mid-nineteenth-century novel from whose rounded endings we may infer that "the world's the same as it used to be",[48] these endings seem, as Barbara Hardy suggests, to model "a world where there is no end to change and crisis".[49] Yet, what is really tantalising about *The Wings of the Dove*, is the fact that, despite its subtlety, its absorption of morality into individual consciousness and the strenuous fictionalising of its protagonists, James's "peculiar geometry" still goes some way to fulfilling the naive definition supplied by Oscar Wilde's Miss Prism, "The good ended happily, and the bad unhappily. That is what Fiction means".[50]

It is not, however, what Fontane's fiction means; and while we can see that he is not as modern as James or Wharton, we cannot see him as a novelist who maintains the conventions of mid-nineteenth-century fiction uncritically or uncreatively. He moves away from simple schemes towards ambivalence and complexity. The "appended paragraphs" that make up the frame grow longer and more complex. There is a development from endings that confirm a story but make it static, a portrait, fixed and finished, receding and making no difference; through ambiguous, polyphonic endings; to those that combine gestures of closure with statements about difference. He alludes to but also interrogates simple interpretations and traditional cultural and literary models, thereby bringing together the internal geometry of the text with the society it reflects and examines, and begins to create the kind of ending that Trilling identifies as modern, "the ending which is satisfying but not final", and in which "the recognition of ambiguity or uncertainty of experience is institutionalised as form".[51]

---

47 Henry James: The Wings of the Dove. New York: Charles Scribner's Sons 1937, p. 405.
48 George Eliot: Silas Marner. London: Penguin Books, 1967, p. 242.
49 Barbara Hardy: The Appropriate Form. An Essay on the Novel. London: The Athlone Press 1964, 1971, p. 50.
50 Oscar Wilde: The Importance of Being Earnest (1895). London, Vermont: Everyman Paperbacks 1996, p. 443.
51 Lionel Trilling: Sincerity and Authenticity. Cambridge, Massachusetts: Harvard University Press 1973, p.154.

Helmut Kuzmics

Aristocracy and Bourgeoisie in Late Nineteenth-Century Prussia and England: Comparing Processes of Individualisation in Fontane and Trollope

1. Chances and Limits of Female Individualisation in Fontane's *Effi Briest*

When Effi Briest gives birth to her first and only child, the doctor, patting her hand, welcomes the new earthly being with the following words:

> Today is Königgrätz Day; a pity it's a girl. But there's enough time for the other, and the Prussians have plenty of victory anniversaries.[1] (p. 84)

This concise statement is likely to attract the anger both of women and of Austrians, even today.[2] Both may have their problems with triumphant, male Prussia, but the doctor's comment introduces two leitmotifs that form the subject of this paper: what can we learn from a comparison of novels by Fontane and Trollope about the freedom of action women enjoyed in two rapidly changing European societies in the nineteenth century? What importance was given in both of them to the male, warrior-like principle of honour? How can we explain relevant differences between them in terms of their histories? And, finally, how far can these differences be grasped as differences in the degree and kind of bourgeois individualisation processes between the English (or British) and Prusso-German societies?

This paper, therefore, aims at a sociological description via fiction and not at a deeper understanding of the novels themselves. As Helen Chambers's thorough study of the reception of Fontane shows, there have always been realist interpretations of the Prussian aristocratic way of life, the duel-culture and Effi's tragic fate as typical of the clash between individual aspirations and societal norms.[3] The closer the year of

---

1 "Wir haben heute den Tag von Königgrätz; schade, daß es ein Mädchen ist. Aber das andere kann ja nachkommen, und die Preußen haben viele Siegestage." Fontane: Effi Briest, NFA, VII, 267; translated quotations are from Theodor Fontane: Effi Briest, transl. by Hugh Rorrison and Helen Chambers. London: Penguin Books 2000. All translated quotations are from this edition and further references are given in the text.

2 The battle of "Königgrätz" (or "Sadowa", as it is otherwise known to Western Europeans) decided the struggle for hegemony between Austria and Prussia in favour of the latter.

3 Cf. Helen Chambers: The Changing Image of Theodor Fontane. Columbia: Camden House 1997. She mentions, among others, Ernest K. Bramsted: Aristocracy and the Middle Classes in Germany. Social Types in German Literature 1830-1890. Chicago, London: University of Chicago Press 1964, revised edition; the materialist interpretation of Lukács: Der alte Fontane. In: Georg Lukács: Deutsche Realisten des 19. Jahrhunderts. Berlin: 2nd edition 1952; consideration of German state-formation and the role of women in Walter Müller-Seidel: Theodor Fontane, Soziale Romankunst in

interpretation is to the 70s, 80s or to the post-modernist and relativist 90s, the more the reality-content of fiction is disputed.[4] Although the sociologist has to accept that genres, formulas, plots, narrative structures, symbols and metaphors must be understood as such, and should not be naively interpreted as properties of an easily observable reality, he or she cannot be forbidden to detect those modes of experiencing society as "real" which can scarcely be described with the help of conventional sociological wisdom alone. Fiction, then, very often allows us to paint a detailed picture of the emotions and interactions of human beings precisely when it is read against the intentions of the novelist.

"Individualisation", as a process occurring in the Western world since the Renaissance and Reformation but gaining considerable momentum during the last century, has led to many flights of fancy. It consists of several sociologically comprehensible properties.[5] In so far as it has to do with separation and turning away from human groups – as a farewell to the village, the family, the tribe, the state – individualisation is accompanied by feelings of loss, but also by hopes for the new. Separation from others very often may mean feeling distant also towards the individual's own body: social alienation can turn into self-estrangement. Individualisation also means an increase in the number of options. It allows for a closer accord between social needs and opportunities. The more powerful a person is, the greater will be her freedom of action. But, at the same time, more autonomy

---

Deutschland. Stuttgart: Metzler 1975; the analysis of paternalist hierarchy and modern middle-class society in Susanne Konrad: Die Unerreichbarkeit von Erfüllung in Theodor Fontanes "Irrungen, Wirrungen" und "L'Adultera". Strukturwandel in der Darstellung und Deutung intersubjektiver Muster. Frankfurt a. M.: Lang 1991; the work on Fontane's Prussia in Gerhard Friedrich: Fontanes preußische Welt. Armee – Dynastie – Staat. Herford: Mittler 1988; the reconstruction of Innstetten's duel as exemplification of the Prussian code of honour, in: Leslie L. Miller: Fontane's *Effi Briest*. Innstetten's decision: in defence of the gentleman. In: German Studies Review, 4, (1981), pp. 383-402; and work on the social history of Berlin in Katherine Roper: German Encounters with Modernity: Novels of Imperial Berlin. New Jersey, London: Humanities Press International 1991.

4 Helen Chambers refers to the study of metaphors and symbols as in Mary E. Gilbert: Fontane's Effi Briest. In: Der Deutschunterricht, 11, (1959), pp. 63-75, dealing with the train as symbol for life; Eugène Faucher, Farbsymbolik in Fontanes *Irrungen, Wirrungen*. In: Zeitschrift für deutsche Philologie 92, (1973) (Sonderheft), pp. 59-73, and Riechel's (1979) works on the symbolism of colours and numbers. Another interesting idea is the treatment of Effi as an inverted Cinderella (Anna Marie Gilbert: A New Look at *Effi Briest*: Genesis and Interpretation. In: Deutsche Vierteljahrsschrift 53, (1979) pp. 96-114; or as a mermaid, Karla Bindokat: *Effi Briest:* Erzählstoff und Erzählinhalt. Frankfurt a. M., Berne: Lang 1984. Finally, there is the large family of literary critics who are in search of quotations, allusions and all other kinds of recurring patterns, like Bettina Plett: Die Kunst der Allusion: Formen literarischer Anspielungen in den Romanen Theodor Fontanes. Cologne, Vienna: Böhlau 1986, Andrea MhicFhionnbhairr:, Anekdoten aus allen fünf Weltteilen: The Anecdote in Fontane's Fiction and Autobiography. Berne, Frankfurt a. M., New York: Lang 1985, or Norbert Mecklenburg: Figurensprache und Bewußtseinskritik in Fontanes Romanen. In: Deutsche Vierteljahrsschrift 65, (1991), pp. 674-694; (all quoted in Chambers, passim).

5 Cf. Norbert Elias: Die Gesellschaft der Individuen. Frankfurt a. M.: Suhrkamp 1987, pp. 48-54; 79-95; 209-219.

condemns people to the torments of selection. As a result, the "self" also becomes more and more complex, colourful and different from the selves of others. This is all accompanied by a process of increasing reflexive self-monitoring: people no longer act according to programmes, to fixed patterns which are more or less enforced from "outside" or "above". Instead, severe constraints by others, through group-opinion or paternal authority, give way to a close-meshed, tightly woven and indestructible web of mild but relentless considerations and self-restraints which can be either of an automatic or a more or less reflexively negotiated nature.[6]

The ancient European society of warriors, priests and peasants does not belong to a past so remote that we have to see ourselves as categorically and totally different human beings. Here, the belatedly unified Prussia-Germany, with her caste of "Junker", seems to be much closer to this past than early industrialised and (eventually) parliamentarised England.

It was, apparently, a past which generated massive social fears resulting from subordination in a quite strictly hierarchical society, compared with the more bourgeois, softer modes of behaviour we associate with a more commercialised, middle-class type of society. There is, furthermore, a lot of evidence that the type of affect-regulation we tend to call "conscience"[7] is much more severe and anxiety-ridden in the former than in the latter. It is this special kind of self-steering behaviour according to a rather rigid super-ego that I would like to bring to the focus of attention. Can novels help us to decide which forces determine the outcome of these processes in both Prussia and England?

Let us start with Effi and Prussia. Effi was born into a minor aristocratic kinship group that still tended to arrange marriages. Her parents have an enormous share in the decision to choose Innstetten, who is more than a generation older than Effi, as a future husband. Although she could refuse to consent (scarcely having seen him), she does not, because she sets the principles of pride of place and of making a good match above those of romantic love and affection. Her first reference-group is the family, and Effi does not rebel against it. Her later *separation* from her family is a totally unwanted one and a punishment for her misbehaviour. Her second reference-group is the local Brandenburg and Pomeranian aristocracy. Here as well, she readily accepts the postulates, concepts of honour and moral standards of this somewhat narrow world, accusing herself in a resigned, quiet manner. It is only in the big city of Berlin and after the rupture in her marriage that Effi can evade the closely-knit control of this social formation; "City air makes one free." ("Stadtluft macht frei.") A system of reciprocal, ritualised, largely rather boring visits and festivities helps to secure the

---

6 Cf. Norbert Elias: The Civilizing Process. vol. I: The History of Manners. Oxford: Blackwell 1978; vol. II: State Formation and Civilization. Oxford: Blackwell 1982.

7 Literature on the "authoritarian" side of the Prusso-German "habitus" abounds. From Heinrich Mann's Der Untertan (The Man of Straw) through the work of several theorists of the Frankfurt School to Nipperdey's brilliant analysis of the German "Macht- und Obrigkeitsstaat" there can be found a continuous flow of negative judgements. Cf. Thomas Nipperdey: Deutsche Geschichte 1866-1918, vol. II: Machtstaat vor der Demokratie. Munich: Beck 1998, pp. 202-226.

coherence of this local "good society" and to preserve the ethics of duty and self-discipline which is less directed against good food and drinking than against sexual laxity and non-conformity of any kind (particularly of the lower classes). It is against "insolence and lack of discipline" that an old spinster rages during the meal after the christening ceremony. The "flag of discipline" flutters high above Major Crampas, and the whole network of this local aristocratic society is kept together by rank and "honour", which leads to the fear of "disgrace" as the most important and threatening constraint of all. The awareness of rank and formality of behaviour also dominates the manners and codes of social intercourse between members of this group; but these are harsh and crude and lack most of the finesse of courtly gallantry – Potsdam was never Schönbrunn, nor even Versailles.

But what about Effi's options, her *opportunities for choice*? Fontane paints a picture of a marked contrast between the complex and broad range of shades in Effi's private behaviour, in her domestic circle, in the restriction of her role in public, and in the sphere of basic decisions within the family household and the wider society. A profession is something that is totally alien to her. In any case, her rank corresponds to that of her husband. Innstetten has the final say in all matters during their honeymoon trip, during which Effi is obliged to visit numerous museums. It is he who determines which room will be given to her mother during her visit. He does not allow her to share his professional world, and most of the time Effi is treated like a child. The mocking, playful "daughter of the air" (Tochter der Luft), with all her claims to tenderness and love, is turning into a young woman who suffers from loneliness and all kinds of fear and who learns to curb her desires from early on. Effi's control of the world around her just extends over the servants, and over one fatal summer, over the courting Major Crampas.

In another sense, namely that of *difference*, Effi is of course highly individualised – and develops a complex personality as well. Fontane characterises her as taking pleasure in cultivated acts of consumption, like dressing, furnishing according to the standards of luxury, grand bourgeois comfort, enjoying the theatre, novels and music. Although her degree of sexual fulfilment leaves some room for guess work which may raise rather unsavoury suspicions (she is afraid of Innstetten,[8] respects him, but scarcely more), she develops a cultivated liking for meeting ingenious, sensitive and artistic people, like Gieshübler, and for the peculiarities of a loose milieu of artists. It is different in the public-professional sphere. Here, she entirely remains a little child in face of her much older husband, who is both highly principled and bold[9] (Innstetten had also been an officer before he became a magistrate).

Thus, we turn to the fourth and last dimension of individualisation. It necessitates novel forms of the self-regulation of affects and emotions, *new forms of self-control*

---

8 Cf. Fontane: Effi Briest, NFA, VII, 195. The large difference of age between a well-established official or professor and his very young, inexperienced wife is a common feature of the institution of the bourgeois family in the nineteenth century. See: Reinhard Sieder: Sozialgeschichte der Familie. Frankfurt a. M.: Suhrkamp 1987, p. 135.

9 Fontane: Effi Briest, NFA, VII, 180, 195.

and conscience regarding what is right or wrong. While we need not waste many words on Effi's indubitable talent for making a favourable impression through her rank and appearance on the social world around her, for appearing as desirable and attractive, as skilful in all questions of rank and etiquette, two decisive problems become visible in another respect. These are problems of monitoring her emotions, of self-control. They relate to Effi's way of dealing with temptation and seduction, particularly in the management of the emotions of being carried away, of fascination, but also her way of dealing with her fear of looming danger. Also problematic is the way she tries to cope with her moral failure before and after the event – in what we would call her "conscience". In contrast to the puritan, hoydenish Alice Vavasor (in Trollope's *Can You Forgive Her?*), Effi is no erotic neutrum. She develops strong feelings for Crampas, even if she knows that it will never be more than an affair. But to what extent is she master of her own emotions? One quotation may be typical of her frame of mind. Knowing already that the affair with Crampas might become dangerous, she tells him a little story:

> "' God's Wall'", Crampas repeated, "A nice title, and what's it about? "
> "A little story, quite short. There was a war somewhere, a winter campaign, and an old widow who lived in great fear of the enemy prayed for God to 'build a wall round her' to protect her from her country's enemies. And God had the house buried in snow, and the enemy passed it by."
> Crampas was visibly disconcerted and changed the subject.[10] (p. 110)

The author manages wonderfully well to render visible the strange logic of the complex situation in which Effi finds herself. Temptation and seducer appear as enemies that can no longer be fought against. Deeply mistrusting her own conduct, she no longer seems able to turn things in a given direction. Nevertheless, it seems possible that higher forces will step in. And while she is communicating this, she appeals to the "enemy" to restrain himself to a certain degree while at the same time signalling that the fortress is ready to be taken by assault. Effi's feelings are at least still foreseeable for her, but not her reactions to some of what will happen. If one is able to locate all affect-controls on a continuum between a maximum degree of spontaneity and a long-term calculability and controllability (as Norbert Elias's civilisation theory has it), Effi is somewhere in the middle. Fontane uses a highly poetic metaphor in order to illustrate the dilemma of Effi's situation. It is, indeed, rather unlikely that he could have witnessed a dialogue like this. If we interpret such a construction as "realist", as an authentic observation of social reality, we have to be careful. This sentence has, probably, never been said. But the novelist has a kind of theory about female behaviour. The metaphor helps him to express this theory in aesthetically satisfying

---

10 "'Gottesmauer'", wiederholte Crampas. 'Ein hübscher Titel, und wie verhält es sich damit?'
  'Eine kleine Geschichte, nur ganz kurz. Da war irgendwo Krieg, ein Winterfeldzug, und eine alte Witwe, die sich vor dem Feinde mächtig fürchtete, betete zu Gott, er möge doch 'eine Mauer um sie bauen', um sie vor dem Landesfeinde zu schützen. Und da ließ Gott das Haus einschneien, und der Feind zog daran vorüber.'
  Crampas war sichtlich betroffen und wechselte das Gespräch." Fontane: Effi Briest, NFA, VII, 299.

terms. In any case, this quotation denotes that the archaic power of fate can become stronger than the human ability to have command over the emotions. But Effi's moral principles are not strong enough, nor is she a female strategist in eroticism like the courtly master stage-manager conceived by Choderlos de Laclos.

The second subject is guilt. If one compares the easy-going, pleasant way of coping with adultery that has been described by Updike in the early 1970s (in *Couples*), then fear, peril, fate and guilt hit home here with full force. Effi's super-ego does not cease to condemn her for her misdeed. This becomes clearly visible in her farewell letter:[11]

> "… *your* behaviour may be excusable, not mine. My guilt weighs very heavy on me. But I may yet escape from it.That we have been transferred from here I take as a sign that I may yet be accorded mercy." (p. 138)

Even before that, Effi is frightened when she notices some casual remarks made at the ball on New Year's Eve and she becomes ashamed and blushes when Crampas addresses her with kind words.[12] A dark cloud looms large over her, in striking contrast to the Catholic maid-servant Roswitha, whose conscience is of a much more elastic, flexible kind. But nevertheless, time might also have healed this wound.

2. Female individualisation in Trollope: the example of Alice Vavasor

Let us now cast an eye at the England of Trollope, more than one generation earlier. *Can You Forgive Her?* is but one of forty-seven novels from the pen of John Major's favourite author, and one could have easily picked out a different one. The novel contains a lively picture of the state of women's liberation in the upper classes, while at the same time it is also part of an established discourse in which Trollope deliberately took part.[13] The book shows how the economic freedom of women of property could co-exist with paternalism in aristocratic families (mostly belonging to the gentry). It also shows the progress of what Lawrence Stone has aptly called "affective individualism",[14] based on an egalitarian partnership of the sexes in marriage, and including deep feelings of loyalty between man and wife and between parents and their children and vice versa. In contrast to Prussia, a much more individualised and individualising world is mirrored here. Alice, the main character, follows in the footsteps of several English heroines of the eighteenth and nineteenth centuries (Moll Flanders, Pamela, Jane Eyre, to name but a few) who emancipate themselves from their families and husbands. She asserts herself successfully and goes her own way of

---

11 "*Ihr* Tun mag entschuldbar sein, nicht das meine. Meine Schuld ist sehr schwer. Aber vielleicht kann ich noch heraus. Daß wir hier abberufen wurden, ist mir wie ein Zeichen, daß ich noch zu Gnaden angenommen werden kann." Fontane: Effi Briest, NFA, VII, 333.

12 Cf. Fontane: Effi Briest, NFA, VII, 313, Rorrison and Chambers, Effi Briest, p. 121.

13 Anthony Trollope: Can You Forgive Her? Oxford, New York: Oxford University Press 1982. Cf. Victoria Glendinning: Trollope. London: Hutchinson 1992, p. 326.

14 Cf. Lawrence Stone: The Family, Sex and Marriage, 1500-1800. London: Weidenfeld and Nicolson 1977.

independence (although she ends up meeting the interests of her family and England better than before, in a kind of harmony of a higher order). There are numerous situations in which she takes decisions on her own and against tradition – she dispenses with her good match to a "worthy man" (at first, but in the end she gets him nevertheless), in order to follow her supposed "true needs". The novel shows the importance kinship still has here, but also the revolt against it. In this respect, a stage in the century-long process of western individualisation (against family ties) is described here.

But *Can You Forgive Her?* is also a novel that describes changes in the traditional image of "the gentleman" and its transmission and diffusion to the rising middle-classes. If we are to follow David Cannadine[15] and Lawrence and Jeanne C. Fawtier Stone[16] who stress the stability and undamaged position of the English land-owning class until around 1880 (after this date, a tumultuous change occurs), we can already see in this novel that modification of the gentleman-ideal which, according to Stone and Stone, should lead to an aristocratic bourgeoisie and not to a bourgeois aristocracy.

What are the most important changes here? New virtues complement the old ones of chivalry, magnanimity, of keeping proud distance from those below and of good manners towards peers of equal rank. Affective control is intensified in the service of the ideal of constancy and perseverance, referring to the necessity of foresight and prudence. The relation between public and private life shifts in favour of privacy. Passions have to be controlled, both sexual and other bodily desires, and also anger and grief. As the Duke de Sully once remarked, "The English take their pleasure sadly".

Alice is also not able to think of an independent professional career. She is content to exercise some political, public influence through the new fiancé she has chosen for herself, who is striving hard and by illicit means to become a Member of Parliament. However, on her journeys across half of Europe Alice enjoys a far greater freedom of action than the very young Effi. Grey and her cousin Kate, who serves as a kind of chaperone, scarcely confine her. They only make the journey safer in two respects, namely by preventing sexual and other molestations that may still threaten (female) travellers. We thus experience the peculiarity of a male code of chivalry which eventually turns men into slaves of high-ranking women, but which also rejects their elementary rights in the public sphere. In contrast to Effi, Alice also takes full responsibility for her misbehaviour – in dissolving her engagement with John – but also in contrast to Effi, no adultery is involved. Alice keeps her cards close to her chest – no one, not even her best friend, learns of her problems with the rascal George. She stubbornly rejects help and counsel at the price of her looming financial self-destruction, of which she accepts all the consequences. This is the most individualised

---

15 Cf. David Cannadine: The Decline and Fall of the British Aristocracy. New Haven, London: Yale University Press 1990.

16 Cf. Lawrence Stone, Jeanne C. Fawtier Stone: An Open Elite? England 1540-1880. Oxford: Clarendon Press 1984.

and lonely way of dealing with the result of a wrong decision: she suffers immensely and does not utter a single word of complaint.

According to Trollope, her creator, Alice is certainly not a *femme fatale* or a person inclined to romantic love, rather, she is more like a bookkeeper of the soul. She was apparently modelled after Trollope's young American friend Kate Field (for whom he had developed a strong affection) and "the ladies of Langham Place", the early English feminists.[17] Trollope's familiarity with the milieu and characters of this circle can be taken for granted. Numerous travels led him also to the continent; there can be no doubt that he knew the social world he portrayed in his books. He also knew how rare the social conditions for arousing strong sexual desire were, if one tried to find them in the upper middle classes of Victorian England. Passion only occurs in Lady Glencora's affair with the desperate and hapless Burgo Fitzgerald. Therefore, it is difficult to imagine Alice being hunted to death by the demons of fate. Her super-ego is less oppressive than Effi's, her self-control much more elaborated.

3. Duel and male honour in Prussia and England

The Prussia that Fontane describes so intensely, with great patriotic fervour and wholly un-Teutonic ease and grace, was a country that owed its rise to power from the seventeenth century largely to its warrior caste and to an efficient, centralised bureaucratic state. After the Prussian-dominated German unification of 1871, these ancient warriors were not visibly reduced. On the contrary, their values and ways of behaving became a model for the rest of Germany. Nearly all the male characters in the novel are thoroughly militarised or are officials in high positions. Their forms of addressing people mirror the world of the military: "Yes, sir, at your service, sir" (p. 31)[18] answers Innstetten's coachman on his master's request. It is no wonder that the archaic warrior code of the duel remained intact for much longer in Prussia than in Western Europe. Damaged honour could not be restored by the all-embracing state, which still did not extend its monopoly of violence over the privileged members of this warrior caste.

The central institution of the newly Prussianised Germany was the army. As Nipperdey remarks in a balancing statement, the German army remained Prussian, and Germany became more Prussian too, as a consequence.[19] And the military's top positions were still filled primarily with men from the nobility, much more so in Prussia than in Bavaria or Saxony.[20] Therefore, the warrior ethos and the related norms

---

17 Cf. Glendinning: Trollope, p. 326.

18 "Zu Befehl, Herr Landrat." Fontane: Effi Briest, NFA, VII, 203.

19 Cf. Nipperdey: Deutsche Geschichte 1866-1918, vol. II, p. 202.

20 In 1913, 48% of all Prussian colonels and generals had a bourgeois background, against 1860 with only 14%. The general staff consisted, in 1906, of 60% aristocratic officers (in contrast to Bavaria and Württemberg, where the share of the nobility was considerably lower – between 13 and 25%, according to Nipperdey: Deutsche Geschichte 1866-1918, vol.II, p. 220f.

and values were passed on in manifold ways to the rising bourgeoisie, although the old nobility already came to fear the decline of its role as a consequence of the mounting power of money and of people chasing after it.[21]

The key episode of the novel is probably Innstetten's discovery of the letters that reveal Effi's infidelity, and his decision – despite his reference to the statute of limitation – to challenge Crampas to the fatal duel, to repudiate and cast off his wife. (Dramatically effective, this decision causes Effi's protracted grief and later death – but we now know that the real Effi lived much longer.)[22]

Innstetten reveals his motivation to his friend Wüllersdorf. He confesses that he still loves his wife, that he certainly feels unhappy and hurt, but without feelings of hatred or the thirst for revenge.[23] Although Wüllersdorf agrees that Innstetten's situation is indeed terrible and his whole future happiness destroyed, he asks him, why all this, "why bother with this whole business?" if Innstetten is able to forgive his wife? Fontane has Innstetten provide a deeply sociological answer by explaining the principles that underlie his understanding of "honour":

> "Because there's no way round it. I've turned it all over in my mind. We're not just individuals, we're part of a larger whole and we must constantly have regard for that larger whole, we're dependent on it, beyond a doubt. [...] But wherever men live together, something has been established that's just there, and it's a code we've become accustomed to judging ourselves by, ourselves as well as others. And going against it is unacceptable; society despises you for it, and in the end you despise yourself, you can't bear it any longer and put a gun to your head. Forgive me for lecturing you like this, when all I'm saying is what we've all told ourselves a hundred times." [24] (p. 173)

This passage is also quoted by Gordon Craig,[25] who places it in the context of Fontane's deep-seated convictions that the Prussian aristocracy was, fatefully, caught in its tribal conventions, causing terrible harm for Prussia and, by way of influencing

---

21 Both "Junker" and money-oriented bourgeoisie were massively criticised by Fontane; cf. Gordon A. Craig: Über Fontane. Munich: Beck 1998, p. 234.

22 The "real" Effi's name was Elisabeth von Ardenne, and the duel between her husband Armand and her former lover Emil Hartwich took place in 1886. There was a divorce after that, but Elisabeth von Ardenne survived it comparatively well. Cf. Ute Frevert: Ehrenmänner. Das Duell in der bürgerlichen Gesellschaft. Munich: Deutscher Taschenbuch Verlag 1995, p. 280.

23 Cf. Fontane: Effi Briest, NFA, VII, 373, Rorrison and Chambers, Effi Briest, p. 172.

24 "wozu die ganze Geschichte?" "Weil es trotzdem sein muß. Ich habe mir's hin und her überlegt. Man ist nicht bloß ein einzelner Mensch, man gehört einem Ganzen an, und auf das Ganze haben wir beständig Rücksicht zu nehmen. [...] Aber im Zusammenleben mit den Menschen hat sich ein Etwas ausgebildet, das nun mal da ist und nach dessen Paragraphen wir uns gewöhnt haben, alles zu beurteilen, die andern und uns selbst. Und dagegen zu verstoßen geht nicht; die Gesellschaft verachtet uns, und zuletzt tun wir es selbst und können es nicht aushalten und jagen uns die Kugel durch den Kopf. Verzeihen Sie, daß ich Ihnen solche Vorlesung halte, die schließlich doch nur sagt, was sich jeder selber hundertmal gesagt hat." Fontane: Effi Briest, NFA, VII, 373f.

25 Cf. Craig: Über Fontane, p. 239.

the middle-classes, for Germany as a whole. Fontane here was influenced by what Elias called the moral ideals of humanist middle-class elites.[26]

Joseph Roth's Jewish regimental doctor Demant argues similarly in *Radetzkymarsch* (*The Radetzsky March*), but in a more tired and fatalistic way. In any case, Innstetten is no longer able to return to forgetfulness, especially since Wüllersdorf is in on the secret; the stain on his shield of honour can only be removed by the duel. Perhaps, if he had had more command of himself, and not told his friend, but, as it is, his fear of shame is only too justified and wholly rational:

> "And supposing I were to take a conciliatory line in some quite ordinary matter of honour because it's 'without malice aforethought' or something along those lines, the shadow of a smile will cross your face, or it will at least register a twitch, and you'll be thinking deep down, 'Good old Innstetten [...] He's never choked on anything yet,' ... am I right or wrong, Wüllersdorf? "[27] (p. 174)

The fear of shame is simply too great for him. Although this "cult of honour is idolatry", as Wüllersdorf thinks, there is no longer any choice.

As Ute Frevert reports in her book on the history of duelling, a substantial proportion of all duels were fought between men because there was a woman involved.[28] But the number, she thinks, would rise if we were to take into account that duels very often occurred in a social environment characterised by a massive presence of women. This could mean that men sought to present themselves as courageous heroes; or to protect the honour of their ladies; or, as in the case of Innstetten, to preserve their own male honour against a sexually successful rival. This matter of fact relates the bloody ritual of duelling to the degree of female individualisation: after the fateful occasion, the role of women was that of more or less passive bystanders.

A totally different outcome results from a basically quite similar constellation in Trollope. Here, the gentleman appears in several guises: there is a trend-setting main type and there are some deviations. First the ideal, as represented by "John Grey, the worthy man". As in former times, a gentleman is portrayed as gallant and attentive, but he no longer shoots tigers, nor does he fight persecutors. The ideal has already become very peaceful: a gallant attitude of self-sacrifice in a highly structured world. A key scene involves John Grey quarrelling openly with his "wild" rival who challenges Grey

---

26 Cf. Norbert Elias: The Germans. Power Struggles and the Development of Habitus in the Nineteenth and Twentieth Centuries, ed. by Michael Schröter, transl. from the German and with a Preface by Eric Dunning and Stephen Mennell. Cambridge: Polity Press 1996, pp. 134-154.

27 "Und ereignet sich's gar, daß ich in irgendeiner ganz alltäglichen Beleidigungssache zum guten rede, 'weil ja der Dolus fehle' oder so was ähnliches, so geht ein Lächeln über Ihr Gesicht, oder es zuckt wenigstens darin, und in Ihrer Seele klingt es: 'der gute Innstetten [...] Er ist noch nie an einer Sache erstickt' [...] Habe ich recht, Wüllersdorf, oder nicht?" Fontane: Effi Briest, NFA, VII, 375.

28 Cf. Frevert: Ehrenmänner. Das Duell in der bürgerlichen Gesellschaft, p. 281. 14 out of 53 Prussian officers who had been sentenced because of duelling between 1897 and 1913 were involved in duels because of illicit social intercourse with women, against 32 cases of a physical insult and 7 cases of verbal insult.

to a duel, insults and nearly kills him. Grey's honour is preserved. He is quiet and superior and refuses to accept the duel.

> "I have come here to see if you are man enough to resent any insult that I can offer you; but I doubt whether you are."
> "Nothing that you can say to me, Mr. Vavasor, will have any effect upon me; – except that you can, of course, annoy me."
> "And I mean to annoy you, too, before I have done with you. Will you fight me? "
> "Fight a duel with you, – with pistols? Certainly not."
> "Then you are a coward, as I supposed."
> "I should be a fool if I were to do such a thing as that."[29]

Perseverance and constancy until he finally achieves success are Grey's virtues. Their lack marks the contrast in two other characters of the novel: the untempered and criminal George, and the thoughtless, not too clever, though charming young Burgo Fitzgerald, whom all his aristocratic relations support because he lacks calculation and is unaware of his advantages. Even more clearly visible is the low value an English author like Samuel Butler attributes to honour (or "reputation", as he belittles it) in his novel, *The Way of All Flesh*.[30] Here, Butler places money and health far above reputation. Without money, one is not able to exist, without reputation one may exist perfectly well, not least because money is even capable of restoring health or reputation to a human being who escapes into the anonymity of a commercialised, urbanised society. With respect to all these aspects, Prussian society at the time of Fontane's writing was different: the sword was still more important than money, the state official more important than the merchant or industrial entrepreneur, the narrow face-to-face-world of the petty aristocracy more relevant than the abstract principles of business and trade, principles which Fontane also regarded with distaste.

4. Fate, honour and the Prussian-German "habitus"

What do both social phenomena – the freedom of action women enjoyed in the English and Prussian-German upper classes and the male code of honour in England and Prussia – have in common? How can the substantial differences between the two societies be explained?

A common element is a certain degree of bourgeois individualisation in relation to powerful kinship groups and the social formations based upon them. The difference is that between an older warrior-peasant society in Prussia and a much more monetarised market type of society in England, where the gentry of the sixteenth century had already undergone a process of commercialisation ("peasants" turned into farmers, lords of the manor turned into agrarian businessmen). And a second, equally important difference lies in the respective processes of state-formation. England was centralised, and thus pacified, at least since the Norman Conquest. Her leading position in the

---

29 Trollope: Can You Forgive Her?, vol. 2, p. 330.
30 Cf. Samuel Butler: The Way of All Flesh. Ware, Hertfordshire: Wordsworth 1994, p. 239.

struggles of state competition stemmed – from the seventeenth century onwards – largely from her command over a powerful navy. It did not need a standing army of the size Austria and Prussia had to develop. Prussia's fate was to be located on the eastern border of a deeply split and heterogeneous political unit – the Holy Roman Empire. It was Norbert Elias who recently contributed to our understanding of the formation process of the German state in a volume of collected essays considering the various stages of this particularly troublesome process.[31] He shed light on the important role a new institution played in the formation of a new, Germany-wide "establishment", a good society: the student fraternities, the famous *Burschenschaften* and their contribution to personality formation in a new elite. In his model, attention is focussed on the particular conditions that led to the reproduction of an ancient warrior-code under changing circumstances – the circumstances that consisted of the process of development towards an essentially bourgeois nation-state.

Elias's analysis has not been undisputed. In a comparison of the German and English histories of duelling, Ute Frevert turns against the notion of the duel as a remnant of feudal times.[32] She stresses the bourgeois character of much of nineteenth-century duelling and sees it rather as an extension of than as a contradiction to the practices of the classically oriented *Bildungsbürgertum* (educated middle classes). Frevert also concentrates on the ritualistic elements of the duel, its value as a means of distinction from the lower classes, and supports her argument with statistics: 70% of all convicted Prussian duellists from 1800-1914 were of bourgeois origin, according to court archives.[33] (These archives, however, most certainly tend to underrate the proportion of aristocrats; the latter's privilege was their special relationship with the monarchy and the state.) Frevert also plays down the differences to England – until the middle of the nineteenth century, she sees only a few, mainly resulting from the differing status of universities and the military in both societies, and the different role of officials and their relationship with the state. England – *pace* Frevert – did not develop the strict boundaries between the various estates each with their own particular honour. She refutes Elias's interpretation by wrongly ascribing to him a mere "compensation-theory",[34] to the effect that the "good society" of the newly united Reich would have tried to overcompensate for its lack of tradition and power. This reconstruction is wrong and misrepresents a tiny element of Elias's explanation for the much more complex whole. Acknowledging the unobjectionable difference between England and Germany in the second half of the nineteenth century, she can only refer to the sudden shift of English public opinion, which led to the foundation in 1843 of an "association for the discouragement of duelling", against the belated establishment in

---

31 Norbert Elias: The Germans. Power Struggles and the Development of Habitus in the Nineteenth and Twentieth Centuries.

32 Cf. Ute Frevert: Bürgerlichkeit und Ehre. Zur Geschichte des Duells in England und Deutschland. In: Jürgen Kocka (ed.): Bürgertum im 19. Jahrhundert. Deutschland im europäischen Vergleich, 3 vols.. Munich: Deutscher Taschenbuch Verlag 1988, vol. 3, pp. 101-140.

33 Frevert: Ehrenmänner. Das Duell in der bürgerlichen Gesellschaft, p. 332.

34 Cf. Frevert: Ehrenmänner. Das Duell in der bürgerlichen Gesellschaft, p. 361, n. 91.

Germany of the "Anti-Duell-Liga" in 1902.[35] She relates this early development to the rise of the public school and the reduced role of the English military in public life.

But Elias's argument is more complex and theoretical.[36] First, there was the so-called *Bestimmungsmensur*, the ritual fencing match of the male student youths. It diverged from the ancient "duel" – whose aims were the defence of honour by means of a sword, dagger or pistol without appealing to state courts – in more than one respect. The *Bestimmungsmensuren* were organised by the fraternities. They were thus not spontaneous activities and had the function of a "means of education". Together with drinking rituals, they formed part of a deliberate reanimation of student customs in the spirit of the common ancient European warrior code. Elias points out that these duels can be seen as rites of passage, being neither bloodier nor more cruel than similar tests of courage in many simpler societies of the world. The corresponding code obtains its special meaning in the context of the formation of a German nation state. The peaceful German *Bildungsbürgertum* of the eighteenth century, far from politics and the sphere of power, became "militarised" under the aegis of the Prussian Junkers who unified the Reich by means of force. A new personality structure was modelled and reproduced itself through several generations.

The fraternities here had the function of a linking structure between the micro-sphere of everyday-life in the interior of a pacified state society and the macrosphere of the state, the class structure and the web of European competition between nation states. Elias's analysis stresses the weight and emotional meaning of membership in a student fraternity. It shows the degree of severity with which frustrations and premiums that steered behaviour were felt, and indeed in a special way, distinct from that in other nations. We come to perceive the importance of character training that stresses rigour and ruthlessness as elements of an ancient, untamed warrior ethos that has been given new life under the aegis of partly bourgeois groups. For Elias, this is an attitude that is not restricted to the narrow sphere of its origin, but – and this is crucial – it is an attitude that spreads out to other domains and social relations where people do not fight with rapier in hand. The tendency of members of the new German leading strata to hit hard and without mercy if someone shows weakness can also be seen elsewhere. Identification with others and compassion give way to *Schadenfreude*, the delight in seeing others lose. Furthermore, Elias regards as one element of this kind of character training the capacity to gain (dubious) meaning from suffering severe frustrations. The blindness of unintentional social constraints sees a personal reinterpretation as "meaningful". To become "hard" and "smooth" turns into a personal goal. Yet it is the (almost accidentally) victorious war that encourages the encroaching of a warrior code: aristocratic groups owe their hegemonic position to the wars against Austria and France. The attitude of "gritting our teeth in order to become men"[37] causes stigmatisation and exclusion that endanger the whole of a later career. The "modelling of affects" towards a bourgeois version of the warrior ideal is only possible

---

35 Cf. Frevert: Bürgerlichkeit und Ehre, p. 101.
36 Cf. Elias: The Germans, pp. 44-120.
37 Cf. Elias: The Germans, pp. 110-112.

since it is enforced on pain of expulsion from the highest-ranking stratum. The literary example helps to make clear how much this hurts: with such experiences, the sense of meaning and self-esteem are threatened. An almost "Hobbesian" image of man in a struggle of all against all is the unplanned result. Hardness and honour become important traits in the German national character, moral questions lose weight. Elias shows how this unplanned process is mirrored further in Nietzsche's ethos of hardness and mercilessness, whereby the latter indeed is quite unlikely to have reflected the origins of his world view.

The core of this "habitus" was the generation of a personality structure in which "constraints from others" of a hierarchical group received a comparatively larger share in controlling and directing short-term needs and desires than "self-restraints" according to the imperatives of a humanistic, middle-class moral code, involving the idea of individual self-regulation by an autonomous "conscience". Virtues like physical strength and skill achieved central importance, as did those of courage in a bloody duel, slavish obedience to closely woven rules established by the older generation, as well as survival in very tough competition under constant danger of exclusion from a powerful social formation.

The warrior code regards negotiation and compromise as weakness, in striking contrast to the code of the highly commercialised landowners and industrial classes of England. Trollope's characters, therefore, are able to steer their independent course between the certainly very demanding postulates of society. Is it an accident that most English novels of the nineteenth century have happy endings, while the forces of fate always crush the Germans?

Jacques Legrand

Fontane and Stendhal: Mediators of a European Idea of Intellectual Nobility

1

When one has reached a certain age and has read many books, aggregations, combinations, constellations of figures form in the imagination and in the memory – groups of real or fictional characters – who belong together because of a certain *je ne sais quoi*, sometimes in a quite mysterious way, and such configurations can be quite different from each other depending on the temperament and cultural background of the individual involved. Thus in my mind, for example, Byron and d'Annunzio come together, Walter Savage Landor and Paul-Jean Toulet, Giuseppe Ungaretti and René Char. In a similar way in Alejo Carpentier's delightful novel *Baroque Concerto* Vivaldi, Scarlatti and Handel come together at Stravinsky's graveside. If I mention Fontane and Stendhal in the same breath, then this conjunction derives *a priori* not from any reality but from *my* reality. The problem that now presents itself for investigation is whether there are any points of correspondence between my particular sense of reality and reality as it is more generally perceived.

If we first consider the lives of the two men, then we find that they have hardly anything in common. When Stendhal died, Fontane was twenty-three years old. He does not appear to have known the Frenchman. He mentions Balzac, Hugo, Scribe and Zola, but never Stendhal. Stendhal's life is at first sight that of an "adventurer", Fontane's is that of a "bourgeois". It is unthinkable that Stendhal should ever have married, and it is even more unthinkable that, had he married, he would have presented his wife with a Hymn Book and a Household Accounts Book inscribed with the following verse:

> If the accounts do not work out
> And credit over debit climbs
> Then Luther's well-loved ancient hymns
> Bring comfort now and peace of mind.[1]

Conversely, it is unthinkable that Fontane could have answered the following question of Stendhal's in the affirmative:

> The wife of the Marshal de Rochefort said to the famous Duclos, "As for you, I have no concerns about your paradise: some bread, some cheese and the first girl who comes along, and you'll be

---

1 "Wenn das Wirtschaftsbuch nicht stimmt/ Und das Debet das Credit überklimmt,/ Geben die alten Luther-Lieder/ Trost und Contenance wieder." Fontane: Balladen und Gedichte, NFA, XX, 537. Translations of Fontane quotations in the text are by Helen Chambers.

perfectly happy." Would the reader care for such happiness? Would he not prefer the passionate and unreasonable unhappiness of Rousseau or Lord Byron?[2]

These two quotations encapsulate central aspects of the lifestyle and approach to life of the two men.

In the beginning there was the father. Both had a particularly strong and peculiar relationship with their fathers. Stendhal's mother died prematurely, so that he hardly knew her, but none the less worshipped her, but he could not stand his father. He needed him because he needed money, but constantly complained about him. While Fontane held his father – a weak man, a gambler and a show off – in great affection, an affection which he denied his mother. She features in her son's life as a judge. A negative fluid emanates from her, as it does later to an extent from his wife, and this grey-black aura colours Fontane's life.

Here we touch on a further difference. A key word in Stendhal is *le bonheur*, happiness; one of his main concerns is *la chasse au bonheur*, the pursuit of happiness. Fontane often speaks of happiness too, and strangely enough he, who never cites Stendhal, frequently uses this same expression. The editors of the Hanser edition speculate that it is an allusion to a painting by the same name, by the historical painter Rudolf Henneberg, or to Paul Heyse's Novelle *Die Reise ins Glück* (The Journey to Happiness). [3] When Fontane uses this formulation, it is in order to reject it. The big city, he writes in a letter to Friedlaender on 21 December 1884, has "no time for happiness. What it creates a hundred thousand times over is only 'the pursuit of happiness', which is the same as unhappiness".[4] And again eight years later he complains in a letter to Karl Zöllner on 13 August 1892 about the "noise, all the chaotic hustle and bustle, the pursuit of happiness and the bridge that collapses".[5] Perhaps the word "pursuit" (*Jagd*) disturbed him, for he certainly rejects the "chaotic hustle and bustle", the hustle to acquire something that seems to be happiness, but is not.

In fact this word has a different resonance for Fontane than for Stendhal for whom the notion of "chaotic hustle and bustle" does not arise. Fontane has in mind an idea of happiness that was current in the *Gründerjahre*, the period of industrial expansion in post-1870 Germany. His own idea of it has a more melancholy ring:

---

2 "La maréchale de Rochefort disait au célèbre Duclos: 'Pour vous, je ne suis pas en peine de votre paradis: du pain, du fromage et la première venue, et vous voilà heureux.' Le lecteur voudrait-il d'un tel bonheur? N'aime-t-il pas mieux le malheur passioné et déraisonnable de Rousseau ou de lord Byron?" Stendhal: Voyages en Italie. Paris: Gallimard (la Pléiade) 1973, p. 495.

3 See: HFA, IV, 5/2, 733.

4 "sie hat [...] nicht Zeit zum Glück. Was sie hunderttausendfältig schafft, ist nur 'die Jagd nach dem Glück', die gleichbedeutend ist mit dem Unglück." HFA, IV, 3, 369.

5 "Der Lärm, all das wüste Treiben, die Jagd nach dem Glück und die Brücke, die bricht." HFA, IV, 4, 205.

It is really a source of happiness to suck all one's life on a feeling of longing; some even say that the whole of life exists for the sole purpose of desiring what is remote and ill defined.[6]

And with this we have an anti-Stendhal. He would never have agreed with Fontane's verse, which is an almost literal translation – certainly an unwitting one – of Lucian's *Sed satis est jam posse mori*:

The best thing that life sends
Is the knowledge that it ends.[7]

For the French writer "the great art of being happy" is the main thing.[8] He makes an ironic entry in his diary on 1 May 1810, "I admire *all the pains that people take for not being happy*".[9] He does not need "to take pains" to be happy, he has what Eichendorff calls "a talent for happiness", his disposition is such that everything becomes a source of happiness to him, not least, "[...] *nosce te ipsum*, know thyself, is a source of happiness".[10] Fontane would have been glad to subscribe to this, and would probably also have agreed with the wonderful formulation about which Nietzsche was so enthusiastic, namely that beauty is "nothing other than a promise of happiness".[11] But he would scarcely have recognized the love of Italy, of sensuality and of melancholy as its source. Of the last of these Stendhal said, "This melancholy character [of the Italians] is the soil in which the passions most readily germinate".[12]

Here we have a new key word, "passion". In *Le rouge et le noir* someone remarks, "There are no real passions left in the nineteenth century: that's is why one becomes so bored in France".[13] Passion, however, explains Stendhal's love of music which for Fontane, by his own confession, was of no great importance. The Frenchman was much more enthusiastic about painting too than the German, who showed interest in art rather than enthusiasm. Stendhal viewed himself as a talented "specialist" in artistic matters, writing a *Vie de Rossini* (Life of Rossini) and an *Histoire de la Peinture en Italie* (History of Painting in Italy). In fact rapturous enthusiasm – *Schwärmerei* – is a watchword for Stendhal. Strangely this does not apply in the case of nature, which

---

6 "Eigentlich ist es ein Glück, ein Lebenlang an einer Sehnsucht zu lutschen; einige sagen ja sogar, das ganze Leben sei nur dazu da, sich das Ferne, das Unbestimmte zu wünschen." Letter to Friedlaender, 6 January 1886: HFA, IV, 3, 445.

7 "Das Beste, was das Leben sendet/Ist das wissen, daß es endet." Fontane: 'Leben', Balladen und Gedichte, NFA, XX, 407.

8 "le grand art d'être heureux". Stendhal: Voyage en Italie, p. 377.

9 Stendhal: Journal. In: Oeuvres intimes. Paris: Gallimard (la Pléiade) 1955, p. 924.

10 "[...] *nosce te ipsum*, connais-toi toi-même, est une source de bonheur". Stendhal: Journal. In: Oeuvres intimes, p. 726 and p. 1053.

11 "La beauté n'est jamais, ce me semble, qu'une *promesse de bonheur*." Stendhal: Voyages en Italie, p. 311.

12 "Ce caractère mélancolique est le terrain dans lequel les passions germent le plus facilement." Stendhal: Journal, p. 1113.

13 "Il n'y a plus de passions véritables au XIXè siècle: c'est pour cela que l'on s'ennuie en France." Stendhal: Le rouge et le noir. Paris: Garnier 1964, p. 302.

could be expected to belong among his passions. In Fontane's works nature is more sharply focused in a broader Romantic context than in the Frenchman's work, although Stendhal too liked landscapes, often with cultural associations. For example, he sees in the countryside around Dresden "an enchanting landscape, worthy of Claude Lorrain".[14] He admires nature as a work of art, whereas Fontane experiences it – as do the protagonists in his novels. Therein lies his particular kind of Romanticism.

2

However despite these differences, the similarities between Fontane and Stendhal should not be overlooked. Firstly their love of the theatre. Stendhal tried all his life to write plays. Fontane made the attempt too – at least at one play, but abandoned the genre. He then functioned for years as theatre critic, while Stendhal was for years a keen fan of stage and opera (and of the ladies of the theatre). Then their love of travel, of movement in whatever form. In both there is a dynamic of being elsewhere. Their old comrade Laurence Sterne invented a system for classifying travellers according to the reasons for their journeys. Without doubt our two friends belong among the "curious" and "sentimental" travellers.[15] Sentimental, because for them (particularly for Stendhal) the journey is a source of happiness. Curious, because they act quite literally out of a desire for the new. They are not "tourists" (both of them use the term, which came from England at the beginning of the nineteenth century, and although Stendhal did not bring it, he gave it common currency with his *Mémoires d'un touriste*). They "feel", one might say, too much, they are very interested in people, and exploit the opportunity for self discovery, the opportunity to gain deeper knowledge of the self. "I like to observe myself and others" notes Stendhal in Italy.[16] For Fontane, on the other hand, foreign travel is a way of discovering one's native land: "Not until we go abroad are we taught the value of our homeland."[17]

This taste for travel was fed not just by short journeys but by longer periods spent abroad. Like Valéry Larbaud, also a kindred spirit, who for his part said that he always put off going on "proper" journeys – but who actually went to live in Spain, in Italy and in England, as Fontane and Stendhal did in England and Italy – they travelled a great deal in their own country and wrote about it. In addition to this they each sought out a preferred country, a kind of substitute native land or *Ersatzheimat*. In Stendhal's case it was Italy, in Fontane's it was England. He really only admired Italy, while Stendhal was positively enthusiastic about England too. An earlier companion of our two friends, Lichtenberg also breathed in fresh air in this country. Indeed they all found a spiritual home in the land of Shakespeare and Sir Walter Scott (two of Stendhal's and Fontane's favourite writers), and that is a third common factor. On the

14 "[...] un paysage enchanteur, digne de Claude Lorrain." Stendhal: Journal, p. 1225.
15 Laurence Sterne: A Sentimental Journey, ed. by Ian Jack. London, New York, Toronto: Oxford University Press 1968, p. 10f.
16 "J'aime à observer moi et les autres." Stendhal: Voyages en Italie, p. 252.
17 "Erst die Fremde lehrt uns, was wir an der Heimat besitzen." Fontane: Die Grafschaft Ruppin, Wanderungen, NFA, IX, 5.

one hand, like Lichtenberg and Voltaire before them and Larbaud after them, they sharply criticised religious practices or malpractice in England, the hypocrisy in English society of the period. On the other hand they felt a deep affection for this land which bestowed a priceless gift on them, something they had felt the lack of in their respective homelands: a liberal atmosphere, a breath of freedom – though not of course in our contemporary sense of the word – and this love of freedom stayed with them to the end of their lives.

Albeit in moderation. Their liberal tendencies are fairly limited. The main thing is that they are against authoritarianism and tyranny. But they distrust democracy, for example as it is exercised in America, with what Gottfried Benn referred to as "the mill of the majority vote". "I despair of the arts since we have started marching towards government by *opinion*," writes Stendhal.[18] Monarchy humiliates, democracy reduces everyone to the same level – such would be the view of both of them. Fontane dismissed the formulation "Liberty, equality, fraternity" as a "boring old saying".[19] When he writes this, perhaps he has forgotten the daring words he had put some years earlier into the mouth of the eccentric General Bamme in his novel *Vor dem Sturm* (*Before the Storm*): "Not much will come of the Frenchmen's fraternity or of their liberty; but there is something in what they've stuck in between the two."[20]

For Fontane, none the less, freedom was a thing of great value, just as it was the breath of life to Stendhal. So that if I speak of distrust, that does not mean that they were against democracy as such. Their attitude to it is positive on the whole. Fontane longs – perhaps for aesthetic reasons – for the bourgeois republics of the towns of Lombardy and Flanders[21] and Stendhal writes, "I hate the canaille [...] at the same time as under the name of *the people* I passionately desire their happiness."[22] But things take a very bad turn when Stendhal like Fontane decides that this people, in order to be happy, should not have access to education. In 1838 Stendhal says: "In ten years time common soldiers will be able to read, and they will no longer be prepared blindly to obey those officers from the *leisured* classes."[23] Exactly forty years later, on 3 June 1878, Fontane draws the following conclusion in a letter to his wife: "[...] compulsory schooling has taught everyone to read and with the arrogance of the semi-educated has

---

18 "Je désespère des arts depuis que nous marchons vers le gouvernement de l'*opinion* [...]" Stendhal: Voyages en Italie, p. 581.

19 "einen alten, langweiligen Spruch" Fontane: Abteikirche von St Denis. Kriegsgefangen. Aus den Tagen der Okkupation, NFA, XVI, 247.

20 "Mit [der Franzosen] Brüderlichkeit wird es nicht viel werden, und mit der Freiheit auch nicht: aber mit dem, was sie dazwischengestellt haben, hat es was auf sich." HFA, I, 3, 706.

21 Letter to Emilie, 17 April 1852, HFA, IV, 1, 223.

22 "J'abhorre la canaille [...], en même temps que sous le nom de *peuple* je désire passionément son bonheur [...]" Stendhal: Vie de Henry Brulard. In: Oeuvres intimes, p. 132.

23 "[...] d'ici à dix ans les simples soldats sauront lire, et ils ne voudront plus obéir aveuglément à ces officiers tirés de la classe des *gens de loisir*." Stendhal: Voyages en France. Paris: Gallimard (la Pléiade) 1992, p. 425.

buried the last remnants of authority."[24] And with this we have arrived at a new and unnervingly negative piece of common ground.

If one takes into account this bi-polar attitude, then one can understand both men's admiration for Napoleon, indeed for men of action. Hearing Stendhal expatiating on the Roman robbers is like listening to Fontane celebrating Scottish or Prussian commanders – or the notorious Prince Heinrich, Frederick the Great's brother, the epitome of the *frondeur*, the rebel, whose romantic shadow lurks in the background of *Vor dem Sturm*, *Der Stechlin* (*The Stechlin*) and the *Wanderungen* (Rambles in Brandenburg).

3

This predilection for exceptional individuals takes us into a deeper layer of affinity between the two writers. Ludwig Harig, whom I would like to include in this constellation, on account of the sovereign freedom of his thinking, called two volumes of his great trilogy *Weh dem, der aus der Reihe tanzt* (Woe to him, who breaks with conformity) and *Wer mit den Wölfen heult, wird Wolf* (He who howls with the wolves, will become one of them). At first glance one might think that Fontane did howl with the wolves, but Stendhal didn't, that Fontane never broke with conformity and Stendhal constantly did. In fact, if one looks more closely, one finds that the Frenchman is not such a non-conformist, and that Fontane on the other hand does not conform so completely, and that even if he sometimes howled with the wolves, he never became one of them.

Stendhal's diaries often show him to be quite well behaved, a fairly nervous conformist with regard to social convention: that's not done, that's not said. To take just one telling example: in Brunswick, 23 July 1807 (he is only 24 years old), he reproaches the Germans for not observing the correct social tone, they are too familiar, "The direct manner in which M. de Heert courts Minette would be the height of indecency, absurdity and immorality in France."[25] This respect for the norms of society is superficial, a mere convention. In his works and particularly in his diaries and letters, as in his private life, Stendhal does not hesitate to eroticise, often to the point of pornography. But there is one noticeable tendency, which interestingly coincides with a similar tendency in Fontane: a great capacity for compassion, for suffering with (*Mit-Leiden*), a great love of "fallen" women, of beautiful sinners. Stendhal despises "respectable women" for whom he felt "a mortal disgust",[26] he can only find happiness "far away from what goes by the name of *virtue* in women."[27]

Fontane's position corresponds to this. More often than Stendhal he chose "fallen women" for his novels, and he treated them with great affection. Effi, Melanie, Lene,

---

24 "[...] der Schulzwang hat alle Welt lesen gelehrt und mit dem Halbbildungsdünkel den letzten Rest von Autorität begraben." HFA, IV, 2, 576.

25 "La manière ouverte dont M. de Heert fait la cour à Minette serait le comble de l'indécence, du ridicule et de la malhonnêteté en France." Stendhal: Journal, p. 836.

26 "J'avais déjà alors un dégoût mortel pour les femmes honnêtes [...]." Stendhal: Henry Brulard, p.10.

27 "[...] que loin de ce qu'on appelle *vertu* chez les femmes". Stendhal: Journal, p. 1081.

Cécile, are light, bright characters in European literature, in contrast to Madame Bovary or to Stendhal's Lamiel, who do not radiate any light. In this matter of radiance, Fontane's heroines are closer to Goethe's Philine or Balzac's wonderful courtesan Esther Gobseck. Fontane might have said of the latter, what he wrote to Colmar Grünhagen – with unparalleled boldness – on 10 October 1895, "Honesty too means a great deal to me, and it is more common in the Magadalens of life than in the Genovefas."[28]

In this context there emerges from the seventeenth century the figure of a brave companion for our two heroes, a woman who was not just "de bonne encre" but also open-minded and stretched out a helping hand to the ladies just mentioned: Madame de Sévigné, whose letters are full of cheerful or less cheerful "Magdalens", and who on one occasion – indeed on several occasions – voices a thought, which Stendhal and Fontane would have and did agree with:

> We have once more seen confirmation of a truth which we had experienced in this country, with you, with regard to good and bad company. We found that bad company was incomparably more desirable; it lets you breath more freely, and leaves you feeling happy.[29]

One of the lightest female figures in Fontane's work is Countess Melusine in *Der Stechlin*, not as it happens a "fallen woman", but a divorcee, which came to much the same thing at the time. And she speaks freely. Her encounter with Dubslav von Stechlin's sister Adelheid, the prioress at Kloster Wutz, is not only a delightful bravura piece but a key passage for our understanding of Fontane's stance with regard to bourgeois morality.

This morality has its origins in religion, or more precisely in the Church. And in this our two friends once more display a shared attitude, namely a negative one. Both the Catholic Stendhal and the Protestant Fontane detest the *Pfaffen* (the "Holy Joes", Fontane), the *vermine* (the "vermin", Stendhal).[30] Lichtenberg earlier saw in the "Clerisey" a "scourge of the earth".[31] It is also worth noting that they both frequently mention priests in the same breath as the aristocracy, whom they also on occasion view in a negative light, especially the provincial aristocracy.[32] Stendhal observes:

---

28 "Sehr viel gilt mir auch die Ehrlichkeit, der man bei den Magdalenen mehr begegnet als bei den Genoveven." HFA, IV, 4, 488.

29 "Nous avons renouvelé la vérité que nous sentîmes en ce pays, avec vous, sur la bonne et la mauvaise compagnie. Nous trouvâmes que la mauvaise était incomparablement plus souhaitable; elle fait respirer agréablement, elle rend heureux ceux qu'elle laisse." Mme de Sévigné: Correspondance, III. Paris: Gallimard La Pléiade 1978, p. 717.

30 Stendhal, following in the footsteps of Schiller's "Greek Gods" and Heine's "Exiled Gods", laments the passing of the Gods of antiquity.

31 Wilhelm Grenzmann: Georg Christoph Lichtenberg. Salzburg, Leipzig: Pustet 1939, p. 280.

32 "Stuffy and rancid" was Valéry Larbaud's opinion. See Béatrice Mousli: Valéry Larbaud. Paris: Flammarion 1998, p. 142: "Ce qu'il y a de plus rance et de plus moisi", in an unpublished letter to his mother, 27 March 1909.

> Since by 1870 we will be more greatly disabused about *Kings*, aristocrats and priests than we are today, I feel tempted to exaggerate certain characteristics in my attack on these vermin of the human race.[33]

and Fontane comments in similar vein,

> I am turning away more and more from my beloved aristocracy, sad figures, offensively unpleasant self-seekers, narrow-minded to a degree beyond my comprehension, only surpassed in wickedness by those Holy Joes of clergymen, pleased as Punch with themselves, those Devil's kinsmen, who try to make us swallow as "God's ordinances" their concoction of unreason and brutal egotism.[34]

For this reason the prioress Adelheid in *Der Stechlin* is condemned by Fontane gently but mercilessly.

"Gently", I said. Fontane, despite his sharp criticism of everything that displeases him, is for all that tolerance itself – he criticises ideas and tendencies more sharply than their proponents – "more gently" than Stendhal whose irony can be more biting, than Fontane's often tender mockery. Fontane loves his characters, even when they embody what he hates: Adelheid, Frau Jenny Treibel, the weakling Briest, the conventional Innstetten. In both cases however it is a strongly anti-bourgeois attitude. Stendhal writes, "I have always, and as if by instinct [...] deeply despised the bourgeois."[35] Fontane observes in a letter to his daughter Martha, 25 August 1891, "I hate all that is bourgeois as passionately as if I were a fully signed up Social Democrat."[36] One can imagine the tenor of the marginalia with which he glossed his copy of *Vanity Fair*.

They lived in a bourgeois society, but they were artists. And art mattered more than anything. Naturally more than bourgeois morality. Stendhal asserts that, "any moral purpose [...] is inevitably fatal to a work of art",[37] and Fontane writes to Paul Schlenther on 28 June 1888, "For like Mortimer I would swear on the host that the old so-called moral standpoint is quite foolish, quite outmoded and above all quite

---

33 "De même qu'on sera bien plus détrompé des *Kings*, des nobles et des prêtres vers 1870 qu'aujourd'hui, il me vient la tentation d'outrer certains traits contre cette vermine de l'espèce humaine." Stendhal: Souvenirs d'égotisme. Oeuvres intimes. p. 1476.

34 "Von meinem vielgeliebten Adel falle ich immer mehr und mehr ganz ab, traurige Figuren, beleidigend unangenehme Selbstsüchtler von einer mir ganz unverständlichen Bornirtheit, an Schlechtigkeit nur noch von den schweifwedelnden Pfaffen (die immer an der Spitze sind) übertroffen, von diesen Teufelskandidaten, die uns eine Mischung von Unverstand und brutalem Egoismus als 'Ordnungen Gottes' aufreden wollen." Letter to Friedlaender 12 April 1894: HFA, IV, 4, 343.

35 "J'ai toujours et comme par instinct [...] profondément méprisé les bourgeois." Stendhal: Henry Brulard, p. 18.

36 "Ich hasse das Bourgeoishafte mit einer Leidenschaft, als ob ich ein eingeschworener Sozialdemokrat wäre." HFA, IV, 4, 148.

37 "Je sentais bien confusément mais bien vivement et avec un feu que je n'ai plus que tout but moral [...] tue tout ouvrage d'art." Stendhal: Henry Brulard, p. 226.

hypocritical."[38] And it is greatly to his credit that he labelled Oscar Panizza, who was given a year's prison sentence for his *Das Liebeskonzil* (Council of Love), a "martyr to unbelief" and declared his support for him with words that are astonishingly reminiscent of Diderot, although Diderot operates even more incisively:

> Whoever expects of me that I believe the story of Christ's conception, whoever demands that I should imagine heaven in a manner consonant with the view of the pre-Raphaelite painters: God in the middle, Mary on the left, Christ on the right, Holy Ghost in the background as a radiant sun, a garland of Apostles at his feet and a garland of prophets above and then a swag of saints – whoever expects that of me, forces me onto Panizza's side, or at the very least moves me to say, "what you put in, is what you get out." [39]

Should we then be surprised that Fontane and Stendhal (just like Lichtenberg, Diderot, Jean Paul) took such pleasure in their acquaintance with Laurence Sterne, who for Nietzsche was the "great master of *ambiguity*"? [40]

4

We have now assembled a collection of facts, of ideas, which all point towards intellectual freedom – a collection too of instances of delectable impertinence, which introduce Fontane and Stendhal into a secret society, to which not all have access, a society which none the less counts among its members people like Montaigne and Swift, Madame de Sévigné and Sterne, Boccaccio and Cervantes, Diderot and Lichtenberg, Jean Paul and Heine, Voltaire and Nietzsche ... some of the most noble names in the world of European culture.

It is not without reason that I use the adjective "noble" (*vornehm*) here. We find it well placed in Fontane's writings, that is in the second volume of the *Wanderungen*, *Das Oderland* (The Oderland). Fontane tells of the visit Alexander von der Marwitz paid Goethe in 1806 and quotes his judgement on the great man of Weimar:

> He was a big, handsome man who always presented himself as the complete minister of state and he represented the dignity of his rank admirably in embroidered court apparel, powdered, with his hair in a net and wearing a ceremonial sword, *even if the naturally free manners of a person of nobility were lacking.*

The final clause is underlined by Fontane, who goes on to comment:

---

38 "Denn daß der alte sogenannte Sittlichkeitsstandpunkt ganz dämlich, ganz antiquiert und vor allem ganz lügnerisch ist, *das* will ich wie Mortimer auf die Hostie beschwören." HFA, IV, 3, 618.

39 "Wer mir zumuthet, daß ich die Zeugungsgeschichte Christi glauben soll, wer von mir verlangt, daß ich mir den Himmel in Übereinstimmung mit den präraphaelitischen Malern ausgestalten soll; Gott in der Mitte, links Maria, rechts Christus, heiliger Geist im Hintergrund als Strahlensonne, zu Füßen ein Apostelkranz, oben ein Kranz von Propheten und dann eine Guirlande von Heiligen – wer mir das zumuthet, der zwingt mich zu Panizza hinüber, oder läßt mich wenigstens sagen 'wie's in den Wald hineinschallt, so schallt es auch wieder heraus.'" Letter to Maximilian Harden, 8 August 1895, HFA, IV, 4, 465.

40 "der große Meister der *Zweideutigkeit*." Friedrich Nietzsche, Menschliches, allzu Menschliches,.Werke in drei Bänden, Munich: Hanser 1966, II, 1, § 113. vol. I, p. 780.

So even Goethe could not raise himself in his bearing and appearance to become his [Marwitz's, J.L.] equal. He was a well-mannered minister and a great poet, a friend to his prince and the shining star of the court, but born the son of a bourgeois in Frankfurt, he still "lacked the free manners of a person of nobility". An inexpressible something was missing, perhaps the training for higher things afforded in the Gensdarmes Regiment.[41]

We can apply this view *mutatis mutandis* to our subject. Goethe, Balzac, Flaubert, Keller are "shining stars" of European literature, but measured against the great figures who embody intellectual freedom, they lack a romantic lustre, that "inexpressible something" which is woven out of nobility, sentiment, intellectual elegance and sovereign humour, that quality which makes our chosen favourites *unsichere Passagiere* ("unreliable types", a favourite motif of Fontane's) and *grands seigneurs* at the same time.

I am tempted to see this affinity encapsulated in one small word which Fontane uses repeatedly, almost to the point of obsession: the adjective *apart* ("out of the ordinary") The writer indisputably feels himself to be *à part*, and Stendhal indisputably is, as are all artists really. But within the company of artists our two are particularly "apart". They belong with their predecessors, contemporaries and successors in that secret society which Stendhal characterised with an expression which has become famous, "the happy few" – "l'heureux petit nombre" – as Valéry Larbaud translates it. *The happy few*, are the *âmes sensibles*, the *gefühlvolle Seelen*, the sensitive souls.[42] We can take this formulation as Stendhal's version of *apart* and in so doing we enter a sphere in which intellectual freedom, independence of spirit are the ultimate value. Flaubert does not belong here, he is too much a slave of an ideology, the ideology of fine style. It is obvious that in this context any ideology is taboo, we stand outside any kind of utilitarianism. So there is no question of "committed" literature, *littérature engagée* – even if our writers are committed *citoyens*. The very broad spectrum of their interests and views, which may appear opposed to each other, shows precisely that they cannot be pigeon holed. They are amateurs; *amateur* is a word Valéry Larbaud uses too. Stendhal's enthusiasm for Napoleon is just that, an enthusiasm and not an agenda. The inclination towards what is new, towards the adjustment of values, *Umwerthung*, in Fontane,[43] even if it is repeated on numerous occasions, has little in common with

---

41 "Er war ein großer, schöner Mann, der stets im gestickten Hofkleide, gepudert, mit einem Haarbeutel und Galanteriedegen, durchaus nur den Minister sehen ließ und die Würde seines Ranges gut repräsentierte, *wenngleich der natürlich freie Anstand des Vornehmen sich vermissen ließ.*" Fontane's emphasis. "Also auch Goethe konnte sich in Haltung und Erscheinung nicht bis zur Ebenbürtigkeit erheben. Er war ein anstandsvoller Minister und ein großer Poet, war der Freund seines Fürsten und der leuchtende Stern des Hofes, aber geboren als ein Bürgerssohn zu Frankfurt, ließ er doch den 'freien Anstand des Vornehmen' vermissen. Es gebrach ein unaussprechliches Etwas, vielleicht die hohe Schule des Regiment Gensdarmes." Fontane: Das Oderland. Wanderungen. NFA, X, 221.

42 Letter to Crozet, 28 September 1816. Stendhal: Correspondance, 1. Paris: Gallimard (la Pléiade) 1962, p. 822.

43 *Der Stechlin* announces the Epiphany of Social Democracy in Germany, and it is positively evaluated by Fontane.

Dickens's engagement in the cause of exploited children or Zola's for the proletariat. He observes the rise of Social Democracy with sympathy, perhaps with hope, but he could not be expected to fight for it: "[...] among my small virtues," he wrote on 15 January 1880 to Mathilde von Rohr, "I count the fact that I do not wish to change the human race."[44] A kind of freedom, then, beyond all ideology, but also beyond all convention. Conventional admiration is avoided. Great figures like Victor Hugo, Chateaubriand, Homer do not impress the Frenchman, who for his part however does admire Goethe's *Die Wahlverwandtschaften* (*Elective Affinities*) more than his German colleague. Fontane does admire it but "finds it deeply boring".[45]

Die Wahlverwandtschaften is an ideal touchstone for measuring the distance between Goethe and Fontane, and/or Stendhal. If (treading in the footsteps of Friedrich Spielhagen and Thomas Mann) we compare it with *Effi Briest*, but also with *Cécile* or *Le rouge et le noir*, a certain weight – not to say ponderousness – strikes us, something pedantic and abstract, which admittedly sounds very modern. As with Adalbert Stifter's novel *Der Nachsommer* (*Indian Summer*) it is almost like reading a *nouveau roman*. "Cold and colourless" complains Fontane in the letter cited: instead of real landscape, an abstract space, nameless places. Apart from a few Christian names and one family name we meet only nameless people who have turned into concepts: the captain, the count, the assistant, the baroness. The "charming" speech in rhyme by a "well turned out" bricklayer at the foundation stone laying ceremony for a house would be unthinkable in Fontane or Stendhal. Ottilie's diary would be unthinkable under the pen of Effi, Cécile or Mathilde de la Mole! In Goethe there is a need for pedagogy, for moralising, to "elevate" (or do I mean reduce?) a novel to the level of useful reading matter. This need can be found too in Keller or Freytag, and to a lesser extent in Raabe. In Freytag's *Verschollene Handschrift* (The Lost Manuscript) a scholar goes on at great length about the advantages of scholarship. In *Cécile* we see an engineer at work. When he talks about his profession he highlights its "exotic" colours. Gordon does not feel the need to give a lecture on the usefulness of laying cables. Let us stay with *Cécile*: even the pedantry of the delightful Eginhard Aus dem Grunde (would Goethe have invented such a name?) is not the product of a pedagogical impulse on Fontane's part, but is (like Homais' philistinism in *Madame Bovary*) an integral aspect of the character in question. Of course Fontane, like Flaubert, mocks his character – Fontane does so with affection – but at the same time he uses him as a mouthpiece for his own views on history, which are never dull.

If Stendhal wrote *Entwicklungsromane* (novels of development), then that is not the case with Fontane. The hero most capable of development in his works, Lewin von Vitzewitz in *Vor dem Sturm* is, like Fabrice del Dongo in *La chartreuse de Parme*, thrown directly into a life of action and develops, himself, without reading, without a theory, without an ideology. And this life in turn is played out in a landscape (whether rural or urban, whether in the Harz or on Lake Como, whether in Berlin or Milan)

---

44 "[...] zu meinen kleinen Tugenden zählt die, die Menschen nicht ändern zu wollen." HFA, IV, 3, 58.
45 "[...] finde es tief-langweilig." Letter to Karl Zöllner, 23 July 1870, HFA, IV, 2, 325.

which is named, with which the readers are perhaps acquainted, or with which at least they could be acquainted.

Just as this landscape arises quite naturally, so too do the heroes of the tale move easily within it, and equally the language in which everything is narrated and which the characters speak flows freely. And this is equally true of the writers in their letters and diaries. Here too a comparison with Goethe is worth making. Both are against the emphatic, against exaggeration and bombast. Stendhal has no great opinion of Chateaubriand and Madame de Staël. The word that occurs to me is *understatement*. It is admittedly more appropriate for Fontane, than for Stendhal. It is a language which, with the greatest precision, combines fluidity, elegance and nonchalance: no dead time, no philosophical digressions, no long descriptions, such as are the norm in Balzac's work for example. The fact that these constitute one of the finest components of Balzac's work is irrelevant here. Historical matter only where the action demands it. In Fontane's case it serves to give rise to wonderful and curious conversations.

I would gladly term this language "natural and unreflected" in contrast to the language which is spoken by some characters not only in Goethe's works but also in Balzac's, Freytag's and Zola's. And here there emerges again a name which epitomises "natural" prose: Madame de Sévigné. This kind of prose is to be found too in the works of the proponents of intellectual freedom already mentioned: Sterne, Swift, Lichtenberg, Diderot, Turgenev, Chekhov, Nietzsche, Larbaud, Savinio ... here we are in the middle of a baroque concert, where Fontane and Stendhal quite naturally take their places. The language they speak is the language of freedom, unaffectedness, humour, the language of noble impertinence.

Just three days before his death on 17 September 1898 Fontane wrote to his daughter Martha:

> The main thing is the free tone, the lack of inhibition, which can at any minute tip over into a joke or something far more risqué, in which case of course you must know exactly where to draw the line.[46]

"Lack of inhibition" – Stendhal borrowed the word *egotism* from the English, which he invested with his own particular meaning. I would like to adopt this coinage for both our authors and some other kindred spirits and use it in the sense of *Edelegoismus*, of noble egotism of that "Egotism of the cultivated individual who holds himself constantly in high regard" and who "is not so bad [...] as the pessimists think".[47] This corresponds – perhaps consciously – to one of Nietzsche's many answers to his repeated question: "What is noble?"[48] "The noble soul has reverence for itself."[49] That

---

46 "Die Hauptsache ist der freie Ton, die Ungeniertheit, die sich jeden Augenblick bis zu Ulk und selbst bis zu Gewagtheiten (bei denen man dann freilich an richtiger Stelle die Grenze ziehen muß) steigern kann." Letter to Martha Fontane, 17 September 1898, HFA, IV, 4, 753f..

47 "Es ist mit dem Egoismus des gebildeten, beständig auf sich achtenden Menschen vielfach nicht so schlimm, als die Pessimisten glauben [...]". Letter to Martha, 22 May 1889, HFA, IV, 3, 693.

48 "Was ist vornehm?"

is not to say that Nietzsche's concept of "Nobility" can be seen as a hundred per cent applicable here! This kind of egotism, then, is a condition for artistic creation: "The maxim: 'Put our pleasure first' is always fruitful: scandalous and fruitful."[50] However there are relatively few of them, of the individuals, in whose hands we feel at ease, *the happy few* who make us *happy*.

Translated from the German by Helen Chambers

---

49 "Die vornehme Seele hat Ehrfurcht vor sich". Friedrich Nietzsche: Jenseits von Gut und Böse. In: Werke in drei Bänden. Munich: Hanser 1966, § 287, vol. 2, p. 750. Translation from Friedrich Nietzsche: Beyond Good and Evil, transl. by R. J. Hollingdale, with an introduction by Michael Tanner. London: Penguin 1990, p. 215.

50 "La maxime: 'Préférer notre plaisir à tout,' est toujours féconde: scandaleuse et féconde." Valéry Larbaud: Journal 1912-1935. Paris: Gallimard 1955, p. 290.

W. J. Mc Cormack

Haunted Realism: Beckett through Fontane

"This is not the end. It is not even the beginning of the end.
But it is, perhaps, the end of the beginning." (Winston Churchill, 10 November 1942)

It was Martin Esslin who observed that the fundamental shape of *All that Fall*, Samuel Beckett's first radio play, was based on the complementary relation of *anabasis* and *katabasis*.[1] His intention was to mitigate the apparently trivial dialogue of Maddy Rooney and her husband, and the parodic stage-Irish setting, by pointing to a classical structure discernible beneath such comic exchanges and ludicrous sound-effects as:

> *Silence. A donkey brays. Silence.* [Mrs. Rooney resumes] That was a true donkey. Its father and mother were donkeys.[2]

Xenophon has more relevance to themes of Beckett's work than might at first appear. And eugenic purity among donkeys cannot be wholly written off as a comic matter. Writing in the mid-1930s, Sigmund Freud revealed a wish to have his controversial work, *Moses and Monotheism*, classified as a historical novel because:

> as the sexual union of horse and donkey produces two different hybrids, the mule and the hinny, so the mixture of historical writing and free invention gives rise to different products which, under the common designation of historical novel, sometimes want to be appreciated as history, sometimes as novel.[3]

Fontane's masterpiece, published in 1895 but set up to twenty years earlier, is a typical historical novel (of the better kind) in its awkward relation to time past. The immediate context of Freud's problem of classification was the crisis in German literature made evident by the consolidation of Nazism after 1933. Thomas Mann's great tetralogy, *Joseph and his Brothers*, commenced publication in that year which, like Freud's work-in-progress, combined biblical study and historical construction. Arnold Zweig, a lesser novelist than Mann, had just published *Bilanz der deutschen Judenheit 1933*

---

1 Martin Esslin: Meditations. Essays on Brecht, Beckett, and the Media. London: Eyre Methuen 1980, p. 132. (The original observation lies much further back in time than 1980.) For some useful comment on Esslin's contribution to the development of interest in Beckett, see Jonathan Kalb: The Mediated Quixote: the Radio and Television Plays, and Film. In: John Pilling (ed.): The Cambridge Companion to Beckett. Cambridge: Cambridge University Press 1994, pp. 124-144, especially p. 126. For a specialist account, see Clas Zilliacus: Beckett and Broadcasting. Abo: Abo Akademi 1976.

2 Samuel Beckett: All that Fall. In: Collected Shorter Plays, London: Faber 1984, p. 30.

3 Quoted by Yosef Hayim Yerushalmi: Freud on the "Historical Novel": from the Manuscript Draft (1934) of Moses and Monotheism. In: The International Journal of Psycho-Analysis, 70 (1989), p. 379. See p. 393f. for the German text of the introduction in full.

(Account of German Jewry 1933), to which Freud was at one level responding. Mann frequently acknowledged the greatness of Theodor Fontane, borrowing a phrase from the author of *Effi Briest* (1895) – "a ghostly presence behind the scenes " – to characterise his awareness of his own medical condition.[4] Oddly enough, Freud was not prolific in his references to Fontane though there is in *Civilization and its Discontents* (1930) the pregnant observation "'We cannot do without auxiliary constructions,' as Theodor Fontane tells us".[5]

These large themes of the 1930s clearly have their general relationship with Xenophon, whose *Anabasis* may be regarded as one of Europe's earliest war-novels (a faction, if ever there was one) provided Freud's insistence on the dual character of historical fiction is allowed. For the *Anabasis* not only recounted the Greeks' invasion of Asia Minor and their eventual safe return, it also celebrated those events by comparing the participants to their ancestors who fought in the Persian Wars.[6] In a sense which is relevant to Fontane's account of late nineteenth-century Germany, Xenophon demonstrated in antiquity how all narrative is historical. And while the differences between these two writers must strike any fair-minded reader as more evident than their resemblances, the Germanic view of the Greeks – also the more urgent Germanic view of the Jews – was pervasively influential in the arts, politics and sciences. Psycho-analysis – naming itself from the Greek word for "soul" – was to be denounced as "the Jewish pseudo-science".

Returning now to *Effi Briest*, what immediately registers upon the reader's mind is its rich lexicon of non-German references. When Effi herself exclaims "We have so many foreign names here", she may be pointing out how the singer Trippelli was really the daughter of Pastor Trippel, and that Italianisation is a feature of her profession, not her origins.[7] Yet the early pages of the novel disclose the "little Ventivegni" (p. 8) as one of Effi's neighbours, while Innstetten's account of his home town establishes the presence of a Scottish engineer and a Portuguese surgeon virtually living next door.[8]

But as one pursues this line of enquiry – there's a Swedish goldsmith, and also Captain Thomsen who Effi speculates may have been a Dane or an Englishman – the

4 "auch wenn dann manches nur, wie Fontane sagte, 'hinter der Szene spukt'". The citation of Fontane occurs in a letter to Frederick Rosenthal, Mann's doctor, 5 November 1946; see Thomas Mann's Briefe, 1937-1947, ed. by Erika Mann. Kempten: Fischer 1963, p. 512. For the English translation see Richard and Clara Winston (eds.): The Letters of Thomas Mann 1889-1955. London: Penguin 1975, p. 372.

5 Sigmund Freud: Civilization, Society and Religion. Penguin Freud Library, vol. 12. London: Penguin 1985, p. 262.

6 See Nicole Laraux: The Invention of Athens: The Funeral Oration in the Classical City. Cambridge, Mass.: Harvard University Press 1986, p. 133.

7 "Wir haben ja so viele fremdländische Namen hier." Fontane: Effi Briest, NFA, VII, 241. The English translation is from Theodor Fontane: Effi Briest, transl. by Hugh Rorrison and Helen Chambers, London: Penguin Books 2000, p. 62. Further references are from this translation and are given in the text.

8 "der kleine Ventivegni", Fontane: Effi Briest, NFA, VII, 174. For Innstetten's reference to the Scottish engineer and the Portuguese surgeon, see Fontane: Effi Briest, NFA, VII, 205f., Rorrison and Chambers: Theodor Fontane: Effi Briest, p. 33f.

mere facticity of these diverse figures subtly changes into something "uncanny". While Thomsen had been at sea "on the so-called China run for many years carrying cargoes of rice between Shanghai and Singapore," (p. 61) the disappearance of his "granddaughter or niece" followed by the death of his Chinese servant reproduces in the town of Kessin, even in the house where Effi and Innstetten will first live together, the absences and silences (the *repressions*) of oriental trading.[9] These events have taken place some time in the past but, through the unexplained noises upstairs and through the picture of a Chinaman pasted to a chair-back, they are re-presented in the present.[10] The house's history is accessible through the *unheimlich* (the uncanny) in a manner which fully justifies Freud's observation that "*heimlich* is a word the meaning of which develops in the direction of ambivalence, until it finally coincides with its opposite, *unheimlich*."[11]

Freud's essay of 1919 is sufficiently well known to require no further buttressing through citation of Fontane's novel with its repeated use of the crucial, ambivalent term. What is of greater urgency is the historical dimension to the socio-psychic repressions of Wilhelmine north Germany as depicted in *Effi Briest*. The time depicted is that following the war of 1870, which had resulted in the defeat of France, the annexation of Alsace-Lorraine into the victor's territory, and the transformation of Prussia into a German Empire. Sedan Day (2 September) is celebrated in the Briest household, because it marked the great German victory and the humiliation of Napoleon III (the Man of Sedan) who was forced to surrender his sword to the Kaiser. Fontane's choice of detail locates the recent military victory in an "uncanny" domestic economy. Seventeen-year-old Effi fantasises about fur coats and married life in Kessin ("half way to Siberia"); her mother is busy at the table "on which the pile of linen and underwear constantly grew, while the newspapers, which just took up space, became fewer and fewer" (p. 20).[12] In this post-war mimic-war, news or information – *intelligence* – dwindles before the combined forces of imaginary furs and virgin knickers. The subdued eroticism of this Sedan Day is complemented by Effi's intended and his military experience in 1870. According to Major Crampas – Effi's seducer – Innstetten had been billeted in the episcopal palace at Beauvais:

> and by the by, this might interest you, it was a Bishop of Beauvais, rejoicing in the name of "Cochon", who condemned the Maid of Orleans to be burnt at the stake – and never a night

---

9 "[...] viele Jahre lang ein sogenannter Chinafahrer, immer mit Reisfracht zwischen Shanghai und Singapore". Fontane: Effi Briest, NFA, VII, 239.

10 See Fontane: Effi Briest, NFA, VII, 232, Rorrison and Chambers: Theodor Fontane: Effi Briest, p. 54.

11 Sigmund Freud: The "Uncanny". In: Art and Literature. Penguin Freud Library, vol. 14. London: Penguin 1985, p. 347. For Fontane's repeated use of "unheimlich" and variants, see Chapters 6, 10, 12, 18 – but not, I think, later chapters.

12 "[...] auf dem die Leinen- und Wäschevorräte beständig wuchsen, während der Zeitungen, die bloß Platz nahmen, immer weniger wurden.." Fontane: Effi Briest, NFA, VII, 189.

passed without Innstetten going through some kind of incredible experience. Or half going through it. (p. 96) [13]

This may be the point at which we can take up the seemingly casual reference to Fontane's novel in Samuel Beckett's radio play of 1957. Blind Mr Rooney is anticipating an evening by the fire with his wife reading aloud. "I think Effie is going to commit adultery with the Major."[14] The intertextual moment might as well be identified with Crampas's recollection of his comrade's nocturnal experience (or half experience) and its vertiginous stumble backwards in history towards the immolation of the defeated French virgin. Innstetten's daylight comment on the times vainly seeks to stabilise these dangerous movements of body and psyche – "Here history is over for the next thirty years" (p. 91).[15]

Though the desire to opt out of history is one which Beckett would have recognised from his southern Irish middle-class protestant birthright, the peculiar condition of North German society as delineated by Fontane deserves further attention. Though *Effi Briest* is sometimes described as being set among Junker families, and thus is read as a critique of German aristocratic behaviour, in practice Fontane presents a less elevated cast. Innstetten's Baltic townsfolk are "good souls for the most part, but they're not exactly refined"(p. 45).[16] Class is closely related to occupation rather than to inherited position. Alonzo Gieshübler, the apothecary, can cite four generations of the family living in the same town. "If there were a chemist's aristocracy…"(p. 46) but his words lapse into silence.[17] Beza the surgeon may in fact really be little more than a barber; given both descriptions, he becomes an anachronism, an eighteenth-century barber-surgeon. Politics is a racket, organised locally by the half-Polish Golchowski.

> But he likes to act the loyal subject, and when the gentry from Varzin go by, he all but prostrates himself in front of their carriages […] We can't offend him because we need him. He has the constituency in his pocket and knows how to run an election like nobody else, and he's supposed to be well off. (p. 32) [18]

Irish politics was not wholly dissimilar, as Beckett recognised.

---

13 "[…] beiläufig, was Sie vielleicht interessieren wird, war es ein Bischof von Beauvais, glücklicherweise 'Cochon' mit Namen, der die Jungfrau von Orleans zum Feuertod verurteilte – und da verging denn kein Tag, das heißt keine Nacht, wo Innstetten nicht Unglaubliches erlebt hatte. Freilich immer nur so halb." Fontane: Effi Briest, NFA, VII, 281.

14 Samuel Beckett: All that Fall, p. 29.

15 "Hier ist die Geschichte, glauben Sie mir, auf dreißig Jahre vorbei." Fontane: Effi Briest, NFA, VII, 275.

16 "[…] aber die meisten davon: gute Menschen und schlechte Musikanten." Fontane: Effi Briest, NFA, VII, 215.

17 "[…] und wenn es einen Apothekeradel gäbe … " Fontane: Effi Briest, NFA, VII, 221.

18 "Er spielt sich auf den Loyalen hin aus, und wenn die Varziner Herrschaften hier vorüberkommen, möcht er sich am liebsten vor den Wagen werfen. […] Wir dürfen es nicht mit ihm verderben, weil wir ihn brauchen. Er hat hier die ganze Gegend in der Tasche und versteht die Wahlmaschine wie kein anderer, gilt auch für wohlhabend." Fontane: Effi Briest, NFA, VII, 203f.

Geert Innstetten holds an important official position in the district, but in his wife's eyes their house "isn't actually a proper house at all, just an apartment for two people and scarcely that for we don't even have a dining room" (p. 72).[19] Though Effi is hardly the most objective of sociologists, there are ways by which her verdict is authenticated; to Crampas, the Landrat's residence is a mere cottage which, if it first impressed Effi with its abundance of light, features primitive lamps of unadorned tin. [20] Yet the contested facticity of these descriptions again slides towards a qualitatively different scale of perception. The house is haunted, even though its lumber rooms have no lumber. It is, as Effi very exactly says, *unheimlich*.

This unhomeliness does not reduce to the legend of the Chinaman nor the swishing noises of a dance long ago. For all the incidental Portuguese and Italian names that populate the margins of *Effi Briest*, – and a servant who may be black – the rapidly focusing racialism of the *Reich* is accurately depicted. Innstetten is said to admire the Ring-master. "Why he was drawn to this composer was uncertain; some said it was his nerves, others put it down to Wagner's stand on the Jewish question."(p. 75)[21] The next sentence acutely translates itself into a sexual idiom, "Probably both were right. By ten fatigue would be setting in and Innstetten would essay one or two tired if well-intended caresses, which Effi permitted without in any real sense reciprocating." (p. 75)[22] The language of Old Güldenklee, discussing Napoleon III's wife, is coarser yet caked in courtesy:

"This Eugénie – and I shall ignore her connection with the Jewish banker, for I loathe people preening themselves on their virtue – had a touch of the café chantant, and if the city she lived in was Babel, then she was the whore of Babylon. I don't wish to be more explicit, for I know," and he bowed to Effi, "what I owe to German womanhood." (p.48) [23]

If Maddy and Dan Rooney in *All that Fall* are about to resume their study of Fontane's novel, then adultery was not all that awaited them. In the end, Effi dies in her parents' home, from – it is pretty clear – tuberculosis. To begin to understand the underlying connections between Beckett's writing and the Rooney's reading we could do worse than have recourse to biography. In the autumn of 1928, the twenty-two year old

---

19 "[…] gar kein richtiges Haus ist, sondern nur eine Wohnung für zwei Menschen, und auch das kaum, denn wir haben nicht einmal ein Eßzimmer." Fontane: Effi Briest, NFA, VII, 253.

20 See Fontane: Effi Briest, NFA, VII, 209 and 282. Rorrison and Chambers: Theodor Fontane: Effi Briest, pp. 36 and 97 for references to the tin lamps.

21 "Was ihn zu diesem hinübergeführt hatte, war ungewiß; einige sagten, seine Nerven, […] andere schoben es auf Wagners Stellung zur Judenfrage." Fontane: Effi Briest, NFA, VII, 256.

22 "Wahrscheinlich hatten beide recht. Um zehn war Innstetten dann abgespannt und erging sich in ein paar wohlgemeinten, aber etwas müden Zärtlichkeiten, die sich Effi gefallen ließ, ohne sie recht zu erwidern." Fontane: Effi Briest, NFA, VII, 256.

23 "'Diese Eugénie – über deren Verhältnis zu dem jüdischen Bankier ich hier gern hingehe, denn ich hasse Tugendhochmuth – hatte was vom Café chantant, und wenn die Stadt, in der sie lebte das Babel war, so war sie das Weib von Babel. Ich mag mich nicht deutlicher ausdrücken, denn ich weiß', und er verneigte sich gegen Effi, 'was ich deutschen Frauen schuldig bin.'" Fontane: Effi Briest, NFA, VII, 224.

Beckett travelled to Germany, primarily to spend time with his cousin, Peggy Sinclair. She was tubercular, the daughter of a Dublin Jewish art-dealer. They passed a holiday on the North German coast where, amidst the incoherence of his youthful love for her, they read Fontane's novel, set in its central chapters on the same Baltic coast. This was echoed in more than one play of Beckett's. In *Krapp's Last Tape*, the now ageing monologist seems gradually to ventriloquise:

> Crawled out once or twice before the summer was cold. Sat shivering in the park, drowned in dreams and burning to be gone. Not a soul. [Pause.] Last fancies. [Vehemently.] Keep 'em under! [Pause.] Scalded the eyes out of me reading *Effie* again, a page a day, with tears again. Effie … [Pause.] Could have been happy with her, up there on the Baltic, and the pines, and the dunes.[24]

Krapp's recollected attention is fixed first on the novel, *Effie*, and then on the character Effie. His mind does not fully distinguish between his own past and that of the fiction, so that Beckett's dramatic fragment for a moment becomes a passage of un-de-composed autobiography.

Crazy though it might seem, the Sinclairs contemplated moving to Hamburg – Hitler was not an invisible presence by then. In any case Peggy died in May 1933. But Sam and Peggy surely read other books together? Why should Fontane's novel feature as the signifier of their brief encounter? To be sure, there is the poignancy of coincidence – the Baltic holiday and the fictional setting. Beyond this, one might remotely discern a common French ancestry in Beckett and Fontane or – less remotely – a shared interest in depictions of protestant society, more particularly protestant clerical society. Effi's adolescent friends memorably include Hulda, daughter of Pastor Niemeyer whose refracted Lutheranism pervades the novel, while Maddy Rooney will hum a hymn tune and comment on the biblical text chosen for the next Sunday's sermon. It is Psalm 145:14 which provides the play with its title.

Amid these suburban ironies, does one need a comparison with Xenophon's *Anabasis*? Such strategies as Esslin's may now seem excessive, when Beckett is regarded as self-evidently a master of the theatre and a highly conscious, even erudite, writer of prose fiction. But in the 1950s and 60s, it was still necessary to rescue him for the Anglophone world from the suspicion that he was just another Paris existentialist or – worse – one of Joyce's least disciplined disciples. The play opts decisively and derisively for a south-Dublin setting, at a time when the Irish capital was recovering from one of its recurrent minor scandals between public morality and actual sexual grief. While Beckett lived in France, he attended to the auxiliary manoeuvres of his kinsfolk.

The Nurse Cadden Affair, as historians have yet to refer to it, was the dominant domestic Irish news story of the year of Suez and the Soviet invasion of Hungary, the

---

24 Samuel Beckett: Krapp's Last Tape. In: Collected Shorter Plays, p. 62. In the published text, matter given in square brackets is also italicised. However, in order to contrast *Effie* with Effie in this passage I have given the bracketed phrases in roman type.

year in which Beckett was invited by the BBC to experiment with radio drama.[25] The court-case, by no means the beginning or end of the affair, revolved on an illegal abortion, fatal to the mother. The defence was supported by sundry members of Dublin's non-Catholic middle class, and intelligentsia, including J. L. Synge (nephew of the celebrated playwright). The confessional-anti-sexual atmosphere in which the trial took place was intensified the following year (the year of *All that Fall*) when a production of Tennessee Williams's *The Rose Tattoo* was forced off the Dublin stage by police action on behalf of the Catholic bishop. This was not simply a legacy of Ireland's self-exemption from reality during the Second World War, it (including Beckett's deliberate choice of a Dublin suburban setting and his reversion to the English language) constituted an exchange of Cold War fire. The authors of *Effi Briest* and *All that Fall* were both working in a post-war atmosphere, albeit different in the German and Irish cases.

The reference to Fontane, however, opens up the question of other literary allusions. Beckett cites, quite blatantly, *The Divine Comedy* – though hardly the most comic part – when he has Mr Rooney compare his progress homewards with Maddy to "Dante's damned, with the faces arsy-versy. Our tears will water our bottoms."[26] A similar blend of pedantry and toilet humour is heard when Dan Rooney applies Grimm's Law (1822) to Boghill Station's bogs. Allusion does not always take such palpable forms. Katherine Worth has descried a resemblance between the parodic animal noises of Beckett's radio play: "The cows – [*Brief moo.*] – and sheep – [*Brief baa.*] ruminate in silence. The dogs – [*Brief bark.*] are hushed and the hens – [*Brief cackle.*] sprawl torpid in the dust" and a scene in Sean O'Casey's war-time play, *Purple Dust* (1943).[27] When, in *All that Fall*, Mrs Rooney predicts rain ("Soon the first great drops will fall splashing in the dust"), her husband feebly replies "And yet the glass was firm."[28] Some may hear, here, an echo of Louis MacNeice's *Bagpipe Music* (1937).[29] Different though they undoubtedly are, what these texts (half-alluded to in Beckett's play) have in common with Fontane's *Effi Briest* (explicitly cited) is a pre-occupation with war and the "auxiliary constructions" by which mankind tries to grapple with its horrors.[30] The novel uncannily anticipates the dreadful conflict to come, partly obeying the

---

25 Beckett insisted *All that Fall* had not been commissioned, which is technically true. However, on 21 June 1956, Celia Reeves informed John Morris (both BBC), "I have written to Beckett asking if he would write a piece for Third [Programme]…". Beckett supplied a manuscript on 27 September. See Esslin: Meditations: Essays on Brecht, Beckett, and the Media, p. 126f.

26 Beckett: All that Fall, p. 31.

27 Beckett: All that Fall, p. 32; Sean O'Casey: The Complete Plays. London: Macmillan 1984, vol.3, p. 56f. etc.; Katherine Worth: The Irish Drama of Europe from Yeats to Beckett. London: Athlone Press 1978, p. 251.

28 Beckett: All that Fall, p. 29.

29 Louis MacNeice: Selected Poems. London: Faber 1988, p. 45 ("The glass is falling hour by hour, the glass will fall for ever,/ But if you break the bloody glass you won't hold up the weather.").

30 Freud expands on the novelist's phrase "There are perhaps three such measures: powerful deflections, which cause us to make light of our misery; substitutive satisfactions, which diminish it; and intoxicating substances, which make us insensitive to it. " Freud: Civilization, Society and Religion, p. 262.

Freudian logic of dreams in which the alternative "either-or" cannot be expressed. What one apprehends in *Effi Briest* is the co-existence of past and present, war and peace, violation and virginity, the *unheimlich* at home. Or, to be precise, Fontane's novel strives to represent the ambivalences which underlie Effi's virginity, Innstetten's peace.

Freud and Fontane converge. "'No' seems not to exist so far as dreams are concerned."[31] "There's one good thing about Berlin: it has no haunted houses" (p. 133).[32] The geography of this psychic terrain turns peculiarly uncanny when, holidaying on one of the Baltic islands, Effi is told that a local village is Crampas.[33] The temporary resort becomes through its name the temporary adulterous lover of a previous time. Pressing this logic of condensing to its extreme conclusion, one reads the holiday from work-a-day civilian duties *as* the Major. "The work of condensation in dreams is seen at its clearest when it handles words and names," Freud continues; "words are frequently treated [...] as though they were things."[34]

If we allow that the ghosts which haunt rooms and houses are analogous to the neuroses which torment individual minds, then it may be permissible to extend this conceit into the social world. The process of condensation which Freud observed in dreams of the late nineteenth century bears an analogous relationship to the concentration of political power in the state, the capital, the bureaucracy. Fontane's novel lays before the reader a seemingly relaxed geography, opening in the Briests' country house at Hohen-Cremmen, looking towards Kessin where Effi moves on to marriage to Innstetten, briefly including (in a sardonic tribute to Goethe's dis-encumbered travels) a honeymoon in Italy, and even allowing for a return to the Baltic coast at Crampas. But the fundamental itinerary of the novel's energy carries it to Berlin, to the new imperial capital ratified and dignified in the aftermath of the 1870 war. Whereas Fontane himself had joked that every third Berliner was a Frenchman, the coming present times were different, that is, increasingly homogeneous. In the novel, the city is to be the site of Innstetten's promotion, but also of Effi's exposure as an adulterous wife. The past is uncovered in a drawer; a file of ageing love-letters dispatches Innstetten to kill Crampas in a duel and also banishes Effi to shameful isolation. The duel has mirrored the tryst.

The engine of this centralised plot, domestic and political at once, is (quite literally) the train. The engagement of Effi and Innstetten initiates various slight, impetuous erosions of an allegedly Old Order – her father declares that "the formal mode of address should be dropped within the family" (p. 13), and mother and daughter depart to Berlin from their country home in search of a trousseau.[35] The mode of transportation is repeatedly specified, thus "Cousin Dagobert was at the station when

---

31 Sigmund Freud: The Interpretation of Dreams. Penguin Freud Library, vol.4. London: Penguin 1976, pp. 427-429.

32 "Ein Gutes hat Berlin gewiß: Spukhäuser gibt es nicht." Fontane: Effi Briest, NFA, VII, 327.

33 Fontane: Effi Briest, NFA, VII, 351. Rorrison and Chambers: Theodor Fontane: Effi Briest, p. 153.

34 Freud: The Interpretation of Dreams, p. 403.

35 "[...] das allgemeine Familien-Du zu proponieren." Fontane: Effi Briest, NFA, VII, 181.

the ladies set out on the return journey to Hohen-Cremmen [...] About midday the two ladies arrived at their Havelland station"(p. 17).[36] Trains, however, do not run solely for the convenience of the principal characters. Visiting Golchowski at his Prince Bismarck Inn, Effi and her husband hear an approaching train:

> "It's the Danzig express; it doesn't stop here. But I always go up and count the coaches, and sometimes there's somebody I know standing at a window. Just beyond my yard there are some steps up the embankment up to lineman 417's hut..."
>
> [...]
>
> And so all three of them went out and took up position, when they got to the top, beside the lineman's hut in a strip of garden which at the moment was under snow, though a space had been shovelled clear. The lineman was there already with his flag in his hand. And now the train raced through the station and in the next instant was passing the strip of garden. Effi was so excited that she saw nothing and was left as if spellbound, looking after the last coach which had a brakeman sitting on top.
>
> "At six-fifty it gets into Berlin," said Innstetten, "and an hour later, if the wind is in the right direction, the folk at Hohen-Cremmen will hear it rattling past in the distance." (p.64) [37]

The overload of details and numbers should not conceal the fact that Effi sees nothing. Nothing justifies such detail in terms of realism, except that Fontane's is a haunted realism in which these forces of modernisation are doubled as anachronisms and archaic vestiges. Effi's seeing nothing is soon "explained" by reference to tears prompted by the thought that the train will be heard also by her parents. But this is an "auxiliary construction", a sentimental and yet anticipatory restatement of a far more searing insight – blindness to trains, to their passengers, freight or cargo, their passengers as freight or cargo.

It is tempting to match this long, doggedly detailed paragraph with a speech of Dan Rooney's in *All that Fall* where a passionate, yet clumsy obsession takes on its own sinister life. In the same speech which anticipates that "Effie is going to commit adultery with the Major" he becomes exasperated by the number of steps at the railway-station:

---

36 "Vetter Dagobert war am Bahnhof, als die Damen ihre Rückreise nach Hohen-Cremmen antraten [...] Gegen Mittag trafen beide Damen an ihrer havelländischen Bahnstation ein." Fontane: Effi Briest, NFA, VII, 186.

37 "Das ist der Danziger Schnellzug: er hält hier nicht, aber ich gehe doch immer hinauf und zähle die Wagen, und mitunter steht auch einer am Fenster, den ich kenne. Hier gleich hinter meinem Hofe führt eine Treppe den Damm hinauf, Wärterhaus 417..."

[...]

Und so machten sich denn alle drei auf den Weg und stellten sich, als sie oben waren, in einem neben dem Wärtehaus gelegenen Gartenstreifen auf, der jetzt freilich unter Schnee lag, aber doch eine freigeschaufelte Stelle hatte. Der Bahnwärter stand schon da, die Fahne in der Hand. Und jetzt jagte der Zug über das Bahnhofsgeleise hin und im nächsten Augenblick an dem Häuschen und an dem Gartenstreifen vorüber. Effi war so erregt, daß sie nichts sah und nur dem letzten Wagen, auf dessen Höhe ein Bremser saß, ganz wie benommen nachblickte.

"Sechs Uhr fünfzig ist er in Berlin", sagte Innstetten, "und noch eine Stunde später, so können ihn die Hohen-Cremmer, wenn der Wind so steht, in der Ferne vorbeiklappern hören." Fontane: Effi Briest, NFA, VII, 243.

When I think there are six there are four or five or seven or eight, and when I remember there are five there are three or four or six or seven and when I finally realize there are seven there are five or six or eight or nine.[38]

Fontane's apprehension of the train as a harbinger of catastrophe is strangely caught in a poem – instantly dashed off – commemorating a Scottish rail disaster of 1879, when two hundred passengers and crew were killed. By one of those coincidences we ignore at our peril, the same event inspired William McGonagal – the world's worst poet – to write *The Tay Bridge Disaster*. If neither Fontane nor McGonagal are celebrated as poets of the first (or even the second) order, the former at least holds his own as a great artist in a different literary genre. It was this secure reputation of Fontane's which sanctioned quotation of the novelist's poem in a Berliner Rundfunk broadcast of February 1932. On that occasion, however, Walter Benjamin's avowed purpose was to portray the disaster as "no more than a minor episode in a great struggle from which human beings have emerged victorious and shall remain victorious unless they themselves destroy the work of their own hands once more."[39]

Now that the much anticipated publication of Benjamin's *Arcades Project* has taken place, this radio-simple announcement can be reassessed in the larger context of his obsession with technology and experience. The broad consensual twentieth-century view of *Effi Briest* as a prophetic work – exploring forces in German society which will seize power in 1914 or 1933 or 1939 – can be confirmed in so exact a detail of the novel as its reiterated emphasis on trains. Trains also "feature" in Beckett's far from simple radio play where the reading of Fontane by/to a blind commuter is indirectly associated with inexplicable death.[40]

Doom, degeneration – these are the unuttered, or scarcely conceived issues of *All that Fall*. "Did you ever want to kill a child," Mr Rooney asks his wife, "Nip some young doom in the bud."[41] Beckett's play opens to the strains of Schubert's *Death and the Maiden*, which prepares the Anglophone listener for the abrupt reference to Effi's coming adultery and consequential death. Closer in time and (to some extent mood)

---

38 Beckett: All that Fall, p. 29.
39 Walter Benjamin: Selected Writings, Volume 2, 1927-1934, transl. by Rodney Livingstone et al.. Cambridge, Mass.: Belknap Press 1999, pp. 563-567. See also Walter Benjamin: The Arcade Project, transl. by Howard Eiland and Kevin McLaughlin. Cambridge, Mass.: Belknap Press 1999. For the Scottish epic, see William McGonagal: Poetic Gems. Dundee: Winter 1934, pp. 42-43.
40 For a measure of Fontane's assured place in the canon, see Erich Heller: In the Age of Prose. Cambridge: Cambridge University Press 1984. Clas Zilliacus notes that, in Beckett's day, "the foremost German radio drama prize [was] judged by a jury of the war blind." In: Zilliacus: Beckett and Broadcasting, p. 61, note 119.
41 Beckett: All that Fall, p. 31; Terence Brown discusses the radio-play in an essay 'Some Young Doom: Beckett and the Child', but sees nothing more dangerous behind its allusiveness than an Irish Protestant "anti-life" attitude. This latter cliché, borrowed from Declan Kiberd, should be reviewed in the historical context of Mary Cadden's prosecution for illegal abortion, and the Pike Theatre's for allegedly displaying a condom (french letter) on the Dublin stage. See: Terence Brown: Some Young Doom: Beckett and the Child. In: Ireland's Literature. Selected Essays. Dublin: Lilliput Press 1988, pp. 117-126.

would have been the music of Gustav Mahler, especially the *Kindertotenlieder* (1901-1905), with the two opening songs of *Des Knaben Wunderhorn* added perhaps for their undertone of military activity. The theme of death in childhood, or of the fatally ill child, is to be heard also in the fiction of Thomas Mann.

For Beckett, a few notes of Schubert are an adequate introduction of the Germanic theme. Mrs Rooney, on her pedestrian way to Boghill station, hears a train which she is not concerned to meet though its whistle or siren underlines the slow progress:

> Heavens, there is that up mail, what will become of me! [*The dragging steps resume.*] Oh I am just a hysterical old hag I know, destroyed by sorrow and pining and gentility and church-going and fat and rheumatism and childlessness.[42]

The "up mail" scarcely suggests erotic excitation until the "childlessness" is more closely examined. A bathetic final term in Maddy's long list of complaints, it is promptly chellenged by Maddy's own enquiry of a neighbour:

> MRS ROONEY: ...What news of your daughter?
> MR TYLER: Fair, fair. They removed everything, you know, the whole...er...bag of tricks. Now I am grandchildless.[43]

Mrs Rooney, it seems, has endured a similarly ambiguous trauma. She is not so much childless in the permanent sense, as childless *now*. Her daughter evidently died, and what endures are calculations of a cancelled future:

> MRS ROONEY: [*Brokenly.*] In her forties now she'd be, I don't know, fifty, girding up her lovely little loins, getting ready for the change.[44]

Here is a dispersed, serialised and – very discreetly – systematised child-loss. From being "childless" Maddy emerges as the mother of dead Minnie; this clarification has been reached through Mr Tyler's announcement of his own daughter's hysterectomy, an operation he declines to name but which has been ghosted in Mrs Rooney's description of herself as hysterical. *All that Fall* keeps in touch with what might be thought a mere incident of casual dialogue through the characters of Jerry, Dolly, the Lynch twins, and the nameless child on the train.

Jerry is a boy grudgingly paid a penny to assist blind Dan Rooney on his journey from the station homewards. Like many in the play he is asked a question about parent or child: in his case, the enquiry is made of his father. Jerry replies, "They took him away, Ma'am."[45] Dolly, who with her mother, stands atop the station steps, is invited to "Oh look, Dolly, look!" in the sightless radio play; she responds accordingly "What, Mamma?" A moment or two later, her mother's voice warns, "Give me your hand and

---

42 Beckett: All that Fall, p. 14.
43 Beckett: All that Fall, p. 14.
44 Beckett: All that Fall, p. 16.
45 Beckett: All that Fall, p. 28.

hold me tight, one can be sucked under."[46] The connection has been made between trains and risk of death. If children have featured so far as victims, a reversal takes place later when cries of the Lynch twins prompt anxious queries from Mr Rooney, "Will they pelt us with mud today, do you suppose?"[47]

It was Donald Davie who first emphasised the local and contemporary quality of humour in *All that Fall*, and its parodic parochialism deserves to be celebrated. Just as the passing of time has altered *Effi Briest* by confirming its prophetic aspect, so *All that Fall* ceases to be read in its immediate Irish context. Dolly's mother's concern that they should "take up our stand before the first class smokers" now excites no second-class amusement. Conversely, the taking away of Jerry's father and the possibility of the Rooney's being pelted with stones or mud have acquired more sinister overtones. Even within the text at its most printerly, the last incident provokes adult fury:

> MR ROONEY: Did you ever wish to kill a child? [*Pause.*] Nip some young doom in the bud. [*Pause.*] Many a time at night, in winter, on the black road home, I nearly attacked the boy. [*Pause.*] Poor Jerry! [*Pause.*] What restrained me then? [*Pause.*] Not fear of man.[48]

This tone of anger and resentment finds a very temporary focus in Dan's account of his own ill health, "The day you married me they came for me with an ambulance" – and he tries to settle into a prosaic narrative of the day's events. This, however, blows suddenly back across the hot ashes of fury:

> MR ROONEY: We drew out on the tick of time…I had the compartment to myself, as usual. At least I hope so, for I made no attempt to restrain myself. My mind…[49]

But Dan's mind wanders in his recitation, and some minutes elapse before he can recall and then resume his "relation". When it comes, it is a matted text of travel prices, calculations about journeys and costs, not to mention "rent, stationery, various subscriptions, tramfares to and fro. Light and heat, permits and licences … and a thousand unspecifiable sundries …"[50] Extended into other speeches of equal length, Dan's detailed accountancy of life is interrupted by paradoxical asides of a painful nature. Mrs Tully's cries are heard. "Her poor husband is in constant pain and beats her unmercifully", followed by thoughts of "the happy little healthy little howling neighbours' brats".[51] His absorption on the train had sheltered him from a realisation that it had come to a standstill, and he now proceeds to explain how, with the delay:

---

46 Beckett: All that Fall, p. 24f.
47 Beckett: All that Fall, p. 31.
48 Beckett: All that Fall, p. 31.
49 Beckett: All that Fall, p. 32. Dan's non- idiomatic "tick of time" is underlined by Mr Tyler's earlier (p. 15) use of the idomatic "nick of time". Is Dan's phrase another signal of his anxiety?
50 Beckett: All that Fall, p. 32.
51 Beckett: All that Fall, p. 33.

gradually a – how shall I say – a growing desire to – er – you know – welled up in me. Nervous probably. In fact now I am sure. You know, the feeling of being confined.[52]

Being blind, Dan could not look out to see what caused the delay. Due to the same disability, once he reached Boghill station he required Jerry to lead him "to the men's, or Fir as they call it now, from Vir Viris I suppose, the V becoming F, in accordance with Grimm's Law."[53]

The radio play moves towards its grim conclusion through seemingly disparate, comic fragments. There is Maddy's scattered recollection of a psychologist's lecture about a girl "who had never really been born". This is followed by questions as to whether hinnies can procreate, and whether Christ's mode of transport into Jerusalem a week before his death was an ass's colt or not. Biblical traces allowed one commentator to regard the play as "Beckett's *To Damascus*, a station drama portraying the passion of Maddy Rooney," a judgement which sounds too much like changing trains in mid-stream.[54] Indubitably, on the ear falls the distant sound of Schubert's music as the couple return homeward, and they discuss the Sunday sermon quoting the Old Testament Hebrew text, "The Lord upholdeth all that fall and raiseth up all those that be bowed down."

The train, it seems, has long departed for its next destination. But the Rooneys are pursued by young Jerry who tries to deliver something Dan Rooney has dropped. "It looks like a kind of ball. And yet it is not a ball." Opposed by her husband, Maddy enquires about the train's delay:

JERRY: It was a little child fell out of the carriage, Ma'am. [*Pause.*] On to the line, Ma'am. [*Pause.*] Under the wheels, Ma'am.[55]

The uncertain conclusion to Beckett's play had led some rash commentators to conclude that Dan Rooney is a murderer. Terence Brown, who does not reject its classification as a *policier*, spends some time deliberating whether "the child-phobic Dan has caused the death of a child, almost unconsciously."[56] This is surely to supply a wrong answer even without waiting for a right question – about, for example, the heightened ambivalence in Dublin of the issue of terminated pregnancy. Not all wisdom is local, of course. The steady association of children, death and trains in *All that Fall* cannot be reduced to character-analysis, albeit of a pathological kind, any more than it can be decoded as a skit on Irish protestant liberalism. Schubert and Fontane have been deliberately placed in the script's unconsciously unfolding communion with the listener as indicators of a far less local concern. Beckett may have been unaware of *The Children of Drancy*, an essay by his fellow Irishman, Hubert

---

52 Beckett: All that Fall, p. 35.
53 Beckett: All that Fall, p. 35.
54 Zilliacus: Beckett and Broadcasting, p. 137.
55 Beckett: All that Fall, p. 38f.
56 Brown: Some Young Doom: Beckett and the Child, p. 121.

Butler, on the transportation by train and mass murder of French Jews in 1942.[57] But as a resident of Paris before and after the war, and as a member of the Resistance during the Nazi Occupation, he was all too well aware of the fatal association of children and trains.

Fontane's *Effi Briest* has been diagnosed as haunted realism and premonitory text. What it foresaw was encoded in the play through the relentless pounding of locomotive engines (what Dan Rooney will call the "lilt of the boogies") across the Great North German Plain. In 1932, Benjamin could still advise his listeners to look up the *Funkstunde* where they would "find a picture of the damaged [Tay] bridge that appeared at the time in the *Leipziger Illustrierte*". Germany, on the eve of the Nazi success, could look back complacently on train fatalities which had been merely accidental. Benjamin's broadcast concluded with a celebration of modern construction sites – "thought reigns over sheer muscle power".[58]

No great step from that motto to "Arbeit macht Frei". Benjamin did not live to review the whirlwind romance of technology and fascism. His friend T. W. Adorno, was more cautious and more fortunate. In American exile during the war, he wrote (with Max Horkheimer) a *Dialectic of Enlightenment* which traced back to the eighteenth century that instrumental reason which made the extermination camps possible. (The book's unauthorised legacy, which currently "finances" the irrationality of postmodernism, cannot be blamed on Adorno.) But its culminating assault on the new "culture industry" prepared the way for a later essay on Beckett, unpublished in Adorno's lifetime. While the essay deals exclusively with *Endgame* (1956) its central thrust applies equally well to the radio play of the following year:

> The violence of the unspeakable is mirrored in the fear of mentioning it. Beckett keeps it nebulous. About what is incommensurable with experience as such one can speak only in euphemisms, the way one speaks in Germany of the murder of the Jews.[59]

What is prophetic (and necessarily veiled) in *Effi Briest* is equally veiled in *All that Fall*, veiled in such euphemisms (or not) as "They took him away."

This is of course to distinguish radically between what one might call the setting of action or foresight and the setting of reception or haunted retrospect. It would be a relatively simple matter to balance this dimension by detailing Fontane's own dislocated realism – his allusion to unseen populations of Kashubins and Slavs, to a sunken town in Heine's poetry, to a novel by Zola, to the legend of a Wendish temple near Kessin, and to apparitions associated with the Belvedere. Indeed, the dead are

---

57 See Hubert Butler: The Children of Drancy. Dublin: Lilliput Press 1988. The title essay (pp. 186-196), unpublished before 1988, is dated 1968/78, but opens with a reference to three earlier accounts of the Paris deportation.

58 Benjamin: Selected Writings, vol. 2, p. 567. These final sentences were unacknowledged quotations (rendered by Benjamin into the past tense) from A. G. Meyer's Eisenbauten (1907); see The Arcades Project, pp. 156-161.

59 Theodor W. Adorno: Trying to Understand Endgame. In: Notes to Literature: vol. 1, New York: Columbia University Press 1991, p. 245f.

invoked as an outer yet intimate circle within which Effi moves while yet alive among the townspeople of Kessin. These implied settings tend towards an ambivalent position of denied setting – non-setting, even (we might say, at the risk of a solecism) up-setting. Fontane catches this in Crampas, a seducer and sanctuary, person and place. Location is denied any kind of ontological fixity.

Beckett's play plays with "the abhorred name" of Boghill, and mentions linguistic change even if only in inscriptions over lavatories. More pervasively, it alludes to dust – a word which occurs eight times (perhaps more) within a very short text. Here is another lack of fixity, comical when a passing van leaves Mrs Rooney "white with dust from head to foot", ponderous when she exclaims "This dust will not settle in our time."[60] Clouds of dust have a certain aptness in a radio play where they dummy in a dialogue for the listeners' frustrated desire to see. The image, and the specific dramatic genre chosen by Beckett, testify to the dissolution fallen upon such concepts as setting, realism and representation since the days of Fontane. One of Theodor Adorno's formulations of the principle "No Poetry After Auschwitz" occurs in the essay on Samuel Beckett; another occurs in a more general context where Adorno surely implies a Beckettian scenario when he writes, "Even the most extreme consciousness of doom threatens to degenerate into idle chatter."[61] In the dusty country-road context of *All that Fall*, his observation that "Beckett's dust-bins are the emblems of the culture rebuilt after Auschwitz" allows us to see the inside and outside of unstable, cliché-ballasted dialogue, the euphemism which denies the train-loads and which serves as the only way they can be signalled. The couple (parents) in dust-bins lost their legs in an accident "on the road to Sedan" (Beckett's phrase) where one army regularly destroys another.[62] Thus, without intending to, Adorno has returned to the celebrations of 2 September 1870 with which *Effi Briest* had opened.

This also constitutes a return to Martin Esslin's remark on the structure of Beckett's radio play. What is central here is the notion of the elliptical movement, whether in time or space. Unlike Saul's fall into Pauline sainthood on the road to Damascus (germane for its background of persecuting certain Jews), there is "going back". There is little else. *Anabasis*, in Greek, is literally a "going up"; its complementary term, *katabasis*, is a "going down". We are more familiar with the former term through Xenophon's account of Cyrus II's calamitous campaign of 401 BC, which was an *anabasis* until the Battle of Cunaxa, and became then a *katabasis* as the survivors made their way back down the coast and "thalassa, thalassa". Esslin saw Mrs Rooney's journey to Boghill Station as an analogue of the first movement, her return homeward with Mr Rooney as an analogue of the second. To be precise, he described the movement within the play as tripartite, with Maddy's wait at the station forming the

---

60 Beckett: All that Fall, p. 15f.

61 Theodor W. Adorno: Cultural Criticism and Society. In: Prisms, transl. by Samuel and Shierry Weber. Cambridge, Mass.: MIT Press, p. 34.

62 Adorno: Trying to Understand *Endgame*, p. 266f. The American translator had used the term "trash-cans" but I have modified for obvious European reasons.

middle section, a non-movement. By implication (conscious or not) its meaning revolves on the undisclosed events of that phrase.

Beyond noting a contextual "aporia" in Dublin opinion, I do not want to attempt to solve the *policier*. Rather I want to draw attention to another aporia, or impassable path. This involves the relation between *Effi Briest* – a single allusion in Beckett's play – and *All that Fall*. One cannot, without lapsing into a ludicrous idealism, propose that Fontane ineffably prophesies the Holocaust which Beckett, then, must most indirectly register. Yet there are tangible critical and philosophical bonuses to be recorded in considering the two authors together – using "bonus" here in its Latin sense. The premonitory aspect of *Effi Briest* – which does not seem to have struck Adorno, Benjamin or Freud, though Thomas Mann was struck – is confirmed in *All that Fall*. But this vindication is only available through a reading of Beckett's radio play as itself a failure, a necessary failure, of representation with regard to what it is/was that the novel anticipates.

In this negated opinion, *Effi Briest* lives on, a tribute unquestionably to its author, but also (in due proportion) in tribute to Beckett as a reader of Fontane, and (finally) to Esslin's Xenophonic reading of Beckett.

Domenico Mugnolo

Theodor Fontane and the Nineteenth-century Italian Novel. A Contrastive Comparison.

While his first novel, *Vor dem Sturm* (*Before the Storm*), was still being serialised in the periodical *Daheim*, prior to book publication, Theodor Fontane wrote to Ludovica Hesekiel on 28 May 1878, in a much quoted letter, that his situation was "critical" for he was making his début as a novelist at an age "at which most authors generally lay down their pens", concluding from this that:

> If it is unsuccessful, then I am lost. I have burned my boats, and – even if I do not have triumphs to celebrate – I must at least avoid complete failure. My work must at least be good enough to permit me on the strength of it to open a small novelist's shop and be able to count on a few loyal, and that means paying, customers.[1]

These words are cited in this context, not because of the precise and disabused diagnosis of Fontane's own situation portrayed in them, but because they give the impression that in the two decades in which Fontane's novels and stories were appearing, it must have been authors of the younger generation who were setting the tone if his contemporaries were really preparing "to lay down their pens". But what is the truth of the matter? What were they doing – Stifter, Fritz Reuter, Gutzkow, Hermann Kurz, Berthold Auerbach, Otto Ludwig, Freytag, Louise von François, Storm, Keller, Conrad Ferdinand Meyer, Spielhagen, Marie von Ebner-Eschenbach, Heyse, Raabe, Ferdinand von Saar? What were these writers doing, whom Hans-Heinrich Reuter names in his biography of Fontane as the ones who were beating the drum for "the triumphal march of the novel, novella and story" in German literature whom he presents as belonging to the same generation as our author?[2] Some of them – such as Stifter, Reuter, Kurz, Otto Ludwig – were already dead. However of those who were still alive, and who certainly had made their débuts much earlier than Fontane in the field of the novel and novella, the most important were not remotely contemplating "putting down their pens". Storm, who was born two years earlier than Fontane, in 1817, was still, after moving to Hademarschen in 1881, working on a significant number of novellas – among them *Ein Doppelgänger* (A Doppelgänger), and *Ein Bekenntnis* (A Confession) –, and indeed his masterpiece *Der Schimmelreiter* (*The Dykemaster*) appeared in the year in which he died, 1888. The first book edition of

---

1 "[…] wo die meisten Schriftsteller die Feder aus der Hand zu legen pflegen"; "Mißglückt es, so bin ich verloren. Ich habe meine Schiffe verbrannt, und darf – wenn ich auch keine Siege feire – wenigstens nicht direkt unterliegen. Meine Arbeit muß zum Mindesten *so* gut sein, daß ich auf sie hin einen kleinen Romanschriftsteller-Laden aufmachen und auf ein paar, treue, namentlich auch zahlungsfähige Käufer rechnen kann." Fontane to Ludovica Hesekiel, 28 May 1878, HFA, IV, 2, 572.

2 Hans-Heinrich Reuter: Fontane, 2 vols.. Munich: Nymphenburg 1968, I, pp. 27-28.

Keller's *Züricher Novellen* (Zurich Novellas), has the same imprint as *Vor dem Sturm*, 1878, while *Das Sinngedicht* (The Epigram) followed in 1881, and the novel of his old age, *Martin Salander*, conceived at the beginning of the eighties, was published in 1886. The following by the somewhat younger Conrad Ferdinand Meyer appeared between 1878 and 1891: *Der Schuß von der Kanzel* (The Shot from the Pulpit), *Der Heilige* (The Saint), *Plautus im Nonnenkloster* (Plautus in the Convent), *Gustav Adolfs Page* (Gustavus Adolphus' Page), *Das Leiden eines Knaben* (A Boy's Suffering), *Die Hochzeit des Mönchs* (The Monk's Wedding), *Die Versuchung des Pescara* (The Temptation of Pescara), *Angela Borgia*. A complete list of the works produced by Wilhelm Raabe, some ten years Fontane's junior, in the last two decades of the nineteenth century can be dispensed with here. Suffice it to note among them *Das Odfeld* (The Odfeld), *Stopfkuchen* (Plum Duff), *Die Akten des Vogelsangs* (The Vogelsang Files) and *Hastenbeck*. Apart from Storm, Keller, Meyer, Raabe und Fontane himself, between the end of the seventies and the end of the nineties Marie von Ebner-Eschenbach, Ferdinand von Saar, Paul Heyse and Friedrich Spielhagen were also publishing actively.

As representatives of younger generations active at the same period, names such as Ludwig Anzengruber, Max Kretzer, Paul Lindau, Karl Bleibtreu, Hermann Conradi and Michael Conrad deserve consideration. All of these were born between 1839 and 1862, but it is not until 1893 that narrative works by truly innovative authors of a younger generation still – among them Arthur Schnitzler, Hugo von Hofmannsthal, Heinrich und Thomas Mann – begin to appear.

Italian literature at the same period presents a completely different picture. Apart from the fact that the generation to which Storm, Keller, Fontane, Meyer and Raabe belonged did not produce a comparable volume of talent in the area of prose narrative, in the final two decades of the nineteenth century the most important representatives of this generation were either dead or had virtually ceased to write. Ippolito Nievo, without doubt the most significant novelist of this generation, had died in 1861 at the age of thirty; his masterpiece *Confessioni di un italiano*, that is, "Confessions of an Italian" was published posthumously in 1867.[3] The older writer Giovanni Ruffini, born in Genoa in 1807, had died too, in 1881. As a supporter of Mazzini he had had to live in exile in London and Paris for years for political reasons, and in consequence had written his strongly autobiographical novels *Lorenzo Benoni* (1853) und *Doctor Antonio* (1855), in English. These works, however, had already been published back in the mid-fifties when *Cento Anni* (A Hundred Years), a substantial historical novel by Giuseppe Rovani, born in Milan in 1818, was also published. Rovani was to produce two further historical novels, in 1868 and 1872, *La Libia d'oro* (Golden Lybia) and *La giovinezza di Giulio Cesare* (Julius Caesar's Youth). He also died, in 1874. Francesco Domenico Guerrazzi, born in 1804, author of numerous historical and socially critical novels had died a year earlier in 1873. Even two younger experimental writers, Iginio Ugo Tarchetti and Emilio Praga, both born in 1839, died prematurely – in 1869 and

---

3 The work is translated into English as *The Castle of Fratta*, transl. by Lovett F. Edwards. London: Oxford University Press 1957.

1875 respectively – while each was working on a major work which was then left uncompleted.[4]

Italian narrative literature in the last two decades of the century is thus represented primarily by Luigi Capuana, Giovanni Verga, Emilio De Marchi, Antonio Fogazzaro and other, less important writers, none of whom was born before the forties and fifties. Indeed Federigo De Roberto and Italo Svevo were born even later, in 1861; the former wrote his first novel as early as the mid-eighties and produced his masterpiece *I Viceré* (*The Viceroys*) in 1894, while Svevo's first novel *Una vita* (*A Life*) appeared in 1892; finally Gabriele d'Annunzio was born in 1863, and between 1889 and 1900 he published *Il piacere* (*Lust*), *Giovanni Episcopo*, *L'innocente* (*The Innocent*), *Il trionfo della morte* (*The Triumph of Death*), *Le vergini delle rocce* (*The Virgins of the Rocks*) and *Il fuoco* (*The Flame*).

The fact that the younger generation of Italian writers of prose narrative determined its direction is worthy of emphasis for a quite particular reason: for whereas the atmosphere in which the older generation grew up was characterised by revolutionary hopes and aspirations, by the great expectations of the *Risorgimento*, that is, the movement for Italian unification, the atmosphere in which authors like Capuana, Verga, De Marchi, Fogazzaro (to say nothing of the younger Svevo, De Roberto and D'Annunzio) grew up, was marked by the deep disappointment, which the results of the process that was now drawing to a close, could not fail to produce. This was a contributory factor in shifting the writers' attention away from history to criticism of the present. A development which had been in evidence as a tendency below the surface since the fifties, was now brought into the open, as writers left their hitherto preferred field of historical subject matter (the analsysis of which had for decades fulfilled the purpose of legitmising the demands for national unity, while also providing an excellent means of circumventing the particularly strict censorship that was applied to subjects with contemporary relevance).[5] They now addressed themselves to depicting the many problems of contemporary life. An anamnetic view of the past, such as that attempted by Fontane in the eighties with *Schach von Wuthenow* (*A Man of Honor*) was, for reasons we cannot go into here, out of the question in Italy.

So the decade from 1861 and 1870 can, just as in public life in general, also be considered as a turning-point in the art of storytelling with the most sweeping consequences. In 1870, when Rome became the capital of the Kingdom of Italy, a process came to an end in which the writer had felt called upon to serve the unification of the fatherland – and as a leader, no less. From now on the role of *praeceptor nationis* which, explicitly or implicitly, they had so happily assumed in the first half of the century, on the one hand loses its function when its aim is achieved, and on the

---

4 Fosca appeared in the year of the author, Tarchetti's death, after his friend Salvatore Farina had completed the novel; Emilio Praga's Le Memorie del Presbiterio (Memories of the Presbytery) appeared in 1881 in a version completed by Renato Sacchetti.

5 Cf. Gino Tellini: Il romanzi italiano dell'Ottocento e Novecento. Milan: Edizioni Bruno Mondadori 1998, pp. 32-45.

other is discredited by the fact that the result of the process is felt to be in no way commensurate with expectations.

The decline of the writer's traditional role is closely connected with the crisis of the omniscient narrator in Italian fiction in the second half of the nineteenth century. From an Italian point of view, the arguments with which Fontane staunchly defends the narrator's right of comment in *Vor dem Sturm* against a reviewer's criticism are totally devoid of validity: "This constant springing back and forth of the puppetmaster in person I find extraordinarily appealing in fact it is the very thing that creates the calm and repose that the epic genre is supposed to induce".[6] In the Italian novel in the years after 1861 such a puppetmaster is scarcely to be found, a circumstance that should not of course be attributed to considerations related to narrative technique. It is not by chance that Fontane himself in the later novels abandons his insistence on such "constant springing back and forth of the puppetmaster". In the case in question his decision in favour of an omniscient author and of authorial commentary derives from several factors. From the fact that the novel is written out of a specific conviction ("Gesinnung"),[7] from his aim of depicting "the introduction of a great idea, a great moment, into simple social circles",[8] from his programme of "exalting love of country above and beyond a somewhat stuffy form of 'loyalty'".[9] No Italian author sets himself aims like this at the end of the seventies.

In 1880, only two years after *Vor dem Sturm*, there appears *Vita dei campi* (*Life in the Fields*) in many ways an epoch-making collection of novellas by the Sicilian writer Giovanni Verga. In a short introduction to the novella *L'amante di Gramigna* (*Gramigna's Mistress*) the author promises his friend, Salvatore Farina, to whom the work is dedicated, to tell a story he heard in the country in approximately the same "simple and picturesque words" so that in the act of reading, one confronts the bald event face to face, without having to seek it in the lines of a book through the lens of the author.[10] Of Fontane's puppetmaster there is naturally no trace in the text. What Verga is aiming for is the total absorption of the narrator into the milieu of the story he tells. The beginning of the novella *Rosso Malpelo* is an exemplary realisation of this programme. "He was called Malpelo because he had red hair, and had red hair because

---

6 "Dies beständige Vorspringen des Puppenspielers in Person hat für mich einen außerordentlichen Reiz und ist recht eigentlich das, was jene Ruhe und Behaglichkeit schafft, die sich beim Epischen einstellen soll." Fontane to Wilhelm Hertz, 14 January 1879. HFA, IV, 3, 8.

7 Fontane to Wilhelm Hertz, 1 December 1878, HFA, IV, 2, 637.

8 "[...] das Eintreten einer großen Idee, eines großen Moments in an und für sich sehr einfache Lebenskreise." Fontane to Wilhelm Hertz, 17 June 1866, HFA, IV, 2, 163.

9 "[...] Vaterlandsliebe über die bloße, mehr oder weniger geschraubte 'Loyalität' hinaus." Fontane to Wilhelm Hertz, 8 January 1879. In: Theodor Fontane: Briefe an Wilhelm und Hans Hertz 1859-1898, ed. by Kurt Schreinert, completed and with an introduction by Gerhard Hay. Stuttgart: Klett 1972, p. 207.

10 "parole semplici e pittoresche". In: Giovanni Verga: Opere, a cura di Gino Tellini, I classici italiani 14, Milan: Mursia 1988, p. 389. The English quotation is taken from Giovanni Verga: Cavalleria rusticana and other stories, translated and with an introduction by G. H. McWilliam. London: Penguin Classics 1999, p. 93.

he was a mischievous rascal who promised to turn out a real knave."[11] In reality, the protagonist, this boy named Rosso Malpelo, becomes not a real knave, but a victim of work and duty, and a hero of love for his parents. One reviewer of the collection claimed to see a crass contradiction between the authorial point of view and the end of the novella, an artistic shortcoming on the part of the writer. Verga, he claimed, creates expectations which are not fulfilled, to which the author replied that it had been in no way his intention to depict Rosso Malpelo as a real knave. On the contrary his purpose had been to "eliminate" the author and to replace observation with representation,[12] hence the unspoken assumption of a popular way of thinking, which connects red hair with congenital wickedness. As far as attempting to eliminate the author is concerned, it might be more appropriate to speak of simulating an author who belonged to the same social milieu as the figures depicted. The causal connections the text pre-supposes, and which the reviewer took to be the expression of an authorial point of view, clearly do not stand up to the normal logic, but as if he were himself proposing them, the author avoids contradicting or even correcting them. The express purpose of this mode of depiction – as one can readily imagine – is to create the illusion of reality, the *fata morgana* of all realists. For the same reason the individual figures in the later novel *I Malavoglia* (*The House by the Medlar Tree*) (1881) are never introduced to the reader. To one critic who found fault with this, Verga responded that he could best create an illusion of reality by getting among his characters and treating them as if they were already known to the reader.[13]

As I have said, the *Vita dei campi* novellas are for a variety of reasons to be considered both epoch-making and seminal. They mark the end of the development of Verga as a novelist who here takes leave of the worldly urban society of his early novels and applies his scrutiny to the archaic society of Sicily. This development corresponds, as I shall now demonstrate, to a mainstream tendency of the time.

The utopian picture of Italy in the decades before the establishment of the unified state is based on the conviction that the country is an organic whole. In this respect the beginning of Ippolito Nievo's novel with the revealing title *Le confessioni di un italiano* (The Confessions of an Italian)[14] can be regarded as exemplary: "I was born on the 18th of October 1775, the name-day of Luke the Evangelist, as a Venetian and I

---

11 "*Malpelo* si chiamava così perché aveva i capelli rossi; ed aveva i capelli rossi perché era un ragazzo malizioso e cattivo, che prometteva di riescire un fior di birbone." Giovanni Verga: Opere, p. 368. The English translation is from Giovanni Verga: Cavalleria rusticana and other stories, translated and with an introduction by G. H. McWilliam. Penguin 1999, p. 78.

12 Pietro Trifone: La coscienza linguistica del Verga. Con due lettere inedite su "Rosso Malpelo" e "Cavalleria rusticana". In: Quaderni di filologia e letteratura siciliana, 4 (1977), pp. 5-29.

13 Letter to Felice Cameroni, 27 February 1881. Giovanni Verga: Opere, p. 1372.

14 The title of the English translation, The Castle of Fratta, and that of the German translation, La Pisana, both fail to do justice to the programmatic dimension of the Italian title. The earliest publisher Le Monnier insisted on the title *Confessioni di un ottuagenario* (Confessions of an Octogenarian) hence the title of the first German translation is: *Erinnerungen eines Achtzigjährigen*, translated by I. Kurz, Leipzig: Grunow 1877. See also note 3.

will die by the grace of God an Italian, if that providence which mysteriously rules the world so wishes."[15]

The social processes of the decades after 1871 bring about the decline of this picture. Benedetto Croce in his *History of Italy from 1871 to 1915* indicates what in his opinion was the irresistible cause of this disenchantment, namely the conviction that the newly founded state had proved incapable of fulfilling its own destiny, a destiny over which furthermore opinion was divided. Some had in mind the liberation of all oppressed peoples, others the liberation of the world from the spiritual yoke of the Catholic church, others still the establishment of a "third Rome" which would adopt and fulfil politically and spiritually cosmopolitan aims. "He who sits in Rome", no less a figure than Theodor Mommsen is supposed to have said, "cannot avoid adopting cosmopolitan aims."[16] The disenchantment documented in contemporary narrative fiction, however, has little to do with cosmopolitan aims or dreams. On the contrary.

The strongly centralist character of the newly founded state provokes reactions in literature that were evidently totally unexpected, and which, not to put too fine a point on it, are mainly connected to the virulence of the social question, the strength of regional cultures and the absence of a unified language. The worry that the problems of individual regions might be neglected or deferred, causes writers – in particular writers of prose fiction – to turn their gaze on their native provinces.[17] All of the factors named here must be taken into consideration, if one wants to understand the peculiar character – also from a national standpoint – of the process of regionalisation in the area of prose fiction. For this has hardly anything to do with, for example, the phenomenon of the *Dorfgeschichte* ("the village tale").

Giovanni Verga is not the sole representative of this process, but he is among the main representatives, perhaps even the main one, because he is the most systematic in its application. The choice of subject matter from Sicilian life is in his case connected, as has been shown, with his adoption of a point of view which can express thought processes which emanate from an archaic culture, which the author in no way advocates or approves. The high literary language which had served to sketch the idealised picture of an organic whole did not come into the frame for this type of writing, and for this reason the writer creates his own language according to the recommendations of the linguistician Isaia Graziadio Ascoli from the year 1872. He concerns himself less with form in the abstract, and more with the concrete, historically conditioned wealth of regional and social variations.[18] The result of this experiment is an astonishing linguistic amalgam characterised by the use of words and expressions from the demotic usage of a Sicilian village. The "Sicilian" linguistic material is not, however, used to characterise individual figures in the novels (as Fontane was wont to do, making servants, coachmen, gardeners or other figures of

---

15 "Io nacqui veneziano ai 18 ottobre del 1775, giorno dell'evangelista san Luca; e morrò per la grazia di Dio italiano quando lo vorrà quella Providenza che governa misteriosamente il mondo." Ippolito Nievo: Opere, a cura di Sergio Romagnoli, La letteratura italiana. Storia e testi 57. Milan, Naples: Riccardo Ricciardi editore 1952, p. 3.

humble social station speak Low German), but was actually integrated into the narrative flow, and this not only by means of appropriate narrative devices such as indirect speech or interior monologue, but more especially through the placement of the narrator in the same social ambience as the characters he describes in the novels.

Both in Verga's novels and in those of other authors who are part of this process of regionalisation (mention could be made of the Sicilians Luigi Capuana and Federigo De Roberto, the Tuscans Mario Pratesi and Mario Fucini, the Genoese Remigio Zena, Edoardo Calandra from Turin, the Milanese Emilio De Marchi, the Neapolitan Matilde Serao), the misalliances and marital problems which are so characteristic of many of Fontane's novels and stories are almost unthinkable as subjects. This has to do not only with the objectively different social realities in the novels of Fontane and Italian writers, but also with the fact that the Italian authors belong to a different generation, and consequently treat different subjects and focus on different social circles, (French Naturalism is received earlier in Italy than in Germany, and adapted to Italian conditions). One seldom meets young officers or civil servants in these novels, but frequently finds fishermen and labourers, who with indefatigable industry make it to large-scale landowners, small farmers, day labourers, female vegetable sellers, employees in general. So in Italian novels the subject is often money, survival; and the exact and detailed descriptions of small businesses, of the mechanisms of social mobility, up and down, show not only that the authors know the subject intimately, but also that such matters were of central importance in the society being described – or at least that the authors consider them to be of central importance.

In the middle of the nineteenth century the individual regions of Italy had been characterised by different cultures and different economic and production structures, and now the completion of the process of unification brought them together. The values that predominated in the economically stronger regions now penetrated the weaker regions too. This is what gives rise to the conflict that for example characterises Giovanni Verga's *I Malavoglia*. Sicilian fishermen allow themselves to be seduced by the wish for rapid betterment of their until now basically satisfactory lives into a dangerous enterprise which ends in their ruin. In the novel we are shown how the simple life of a Sicilian village goes to seed when new, foreign values come into contact with old traditional customs.

Such questions, on the rare occasions when they arise in Fontane's novels, are only of secondary importance. If money matters arise there is always – usually dearly purchased – a solution to hand: Botho von Rienäcker, the protagonist in *Irrungen,Wirrungen* (*Delusions, Confusions*) gets into financial difficulties (which the

---

16 Benedetto Croce: Storia d'Italia dal 1871 al 1915, Opere di Benedetto Croce in edizione economica IX. Bari: editori Laterza 1967, p. 3.

17 Cf. Gino Tellini, passim; on the problem of language in the nineteenth-century Italian novel see Enrico Testa: Lo stile semplice. Discorso e romanzo, Einaudi Paperbacks 264. Turin: Giulio Einaudi editore 1997.

18 Graziadio Isaia Ascoli: Il Proemio all "Archivio glottologico italiano." In: Graziadio Isais Ascoli, Scritti sulla questione della lingua, a cura, con introduzione e nota bibliografica di Corrado Grassi, Piccola Biblioteca Einaudi Testi 7. Turin: Giulio Einaudi editore 1975, pp. 5-45 (pp. 27-35).

reader only hears of in a letter from his mother), but marriage to his rich cousin Käthe von Sellenthin offers salvation, though he has to abandon his beloved Lene Nimptsch to attain it. The decisive factor is that the social norms which he accepts prescribe exactly how he should behave. None of Fontane's figures rejects such social norms or the expectations of society – not even female figures who have often been considered the bearers of an ability "to go beyond the compromises and half-heartedness of their range of social experience".[19] That they are part of this society is not open to question. And precisely therein lies their tragic dimension. They are tortured by the irreconcilable contradiction between accepted social rules and subjective inclinations.

In Verga's novels the tragic conflict arises from incompatible values being forcibly brought together. *I Malavoglia* was intended as the first part of a cycle of novels called *I Vinti* (The Defeated Ones) which was never completed. The protagonists were to be the losers in the conflict, in other words the weaker parties.

The novel *I Viceré* (*The Viceroys*) of 1894 by another Sicilian, Federigo De Roberto, is set in quite another milieu. The narrator introduces his readers to aristocratic circles, and here too material interests are at stake and the weak are the losers, and furthermore the newly unified state, far from promoting the moral improvement of social life, provides a framework in which corruption and cynical vested interests are best fitted to survive. The high Sicilian aristocracy seems to be integrating into the liberal state not out of deep, honest conviction, but quite simply because this promises the best way to cultivate their own material interests. This theme incidentally recurs almost seventy years later in Giuseppe Tomasi di Lampedusa's *Il Gattopardo* (*The Leopard*).

Here too there is a discernible difference between Fontane and the Italian novel of his time. When Fontane writes his "political novel" *Der Stechlin* (*The Stechlin*), what he has in mind is "to show side by side the aristocracy in our country as it *should* be, and as it *is*",[20] and under this banner he overcomes the scheme of indisoluble conflict that characterises his earlier novels. There is nothing of this sort in De Roberto who is fundamentally pessimistic. Political life in the new state seems in his novel to be in the inescapable control of arch-villains. More akin to Fontane's "political novel" is Antonio Fogazzaro's *Daniele Cortis* (1885), in which the main role is played by a Catholic politician who uses Christianity as a basis to overcome social divisions and achieve co-operation among all classes. What Fogazzaro signally lacks, is precisely what makes Fontane's novel seminal, the profound conviction that there are no incontrovertible truths. Like Verga, De Roberto, Capuana and other contemporaries, the Catholic Fogazzaro too portrays social problems, but he also provides satisfactory solutions.

---

19 "[...] über Kompromisse und Halbheiten des gesellschaftlichen Erfahrungsbereichs hinauszu-gelangen." Martin Swales: Epochenbuch Realismus. Romane und Erzählungen. Berlin: Erich Schmidt 1997, p. 156.

20 "Gegenüberstellung von Adel, wie er bei uns sein sollte und wie er ist." Fontane to Carl Robert Lessing, 8 June 1896, HFA, IV, 4, 562.

Fontane and the Nineteenth-century Italian Novel. A Contrastive Comparison

Seen from today *The Viceroys* can be viewed as the peak of a long succession of novels for which political and in particular parliamentary life in the Italian State provides the subject. At the beginning in 1862 stands *I moribondi di Palazzo Carignano* (The Moribund in the Palazzo Carignano) by Ferdinando Petruccelli della Gattina, after which in 1877 Vittorio Bersezio's *Corruttela* (Corruption), in 1885 Matilde Serao's *La conquista di Roma* (The Conquest of Rome), Francesco Domenico Guerrazzi's posthumous *Il secolo che muore* (The Dying Century), and Enrico Onufrio's *L'ultimo borghese* (The Last Citizen), Gerolamo Rovetta's *Le lagrime del prossimo* (The Tears of the Nearest) in 1888 and *La baraonda* (The Tumult) in 1894, and on to Alfredo Oriani's *La disfatta* (The Defeat) in 1896. From differing literary and political positions the authors of these novels express the general dissatisfaction with the results of years of revolutionary struggle, the disappointment with the daily grind which stifles all hope, anger at rampant opportunism and corruption. At that time D'Annunzio's response, in his 1895 *Le vergini delle rocce*, to the unease caused by political conditions in the country seemed a more accurate pointer to the future – in it we find the apotheosis of an omnipotent, anti-bourgeois, anti-democratic hero. Although the young and long unrecognised Italo Svevo was quick to point out the great significance of Verga,[21] it was D'Annunzio's response that was soon to prevail, not only on the literary and aesthetic plane, but also on the political plane.

Only many years later would Verga, De Roberto, Svevo be recognised as the real founders of the contemporary Italian novel. In 1940 Massimo Bontempelli noted, "Twenty years before D'Annunzio closed the gate on the nineteenth century, [Verga] had thrown open the door to the twentieth".[22] In spite of Thomas Mann's early appreciation, Fontane's narrative art was to suffer a similar fate.

Translated from the German by Hugh Rorrison

---

21 See reviews by E. Samigli (nom-de-plume of Italo Svevo) of Mastro-don Gesualdo (in "L'Independente", Trieste, 17 December 1889). Brian Moloney: I. Svevo e "L'Independente": sei articoli sconosciuti. In: Lettere italiane, 25 (1973), 4, pp. 536-554.
22 " [Verga ha spalancato] le porte del Novecento, vent'anni prima che d'Annunzio finisse di chiudere quelle dell'Ottocento." Massimo Bontempelli: Verga (1940). In: Massimo Bontempelli: Introduzioni e discorsi. 5. Edizione (Milan: Arnoldo Mondadori Editore 1964), p. 134.

Teresa Martins de Oliveira

Fontane's *Effi Briest* and Eça de Queirós's *O Primo Bazílio*: Two Novels of Adultery in the Context of European Realism

The two novels which I am going to compare, *O Primo Bazílio* (*Cousin Basilio*)[1] and *Effi Briest*,[2] belong to a series of realist novels on the theme of adultery which appeared in various European countries in the nineteenth century.[3] The first major novel in this series was Flaubert's *Madame Bovary*, published in 1857. Other works in this group are Tolstoy's *Anna Karenina*, 1875-76, *La Regenta* by Clarín, published between 1884-85 and Theodor Fontane's novels of adultery, *L'Adultera* (*The Woman taken in Adultery*) (1880) and *Cécile* (1887). It is important to note that the Portuguese novel, *O Primo Bazílio*, appeared in 1878, almost twenty years before *Effi Briest*, which is a very late example of this type of novel.[4]

The Portuguese writer, José Maria de Eça de Queirós, was born in 1845 in a small village in the north of Portugal and graduated in Law from Coimbra in 1866. His first writings date from the end of this period spent in Coimbra; *feuilletons* in which the influence of Victor Hugo and Michelet can be seen together with that of Baudelaire,

---

1 The edition of the text used is Eça de Queirós: O Primo Bazílio, ed. by Luiz Fagundes Duarte. Lisbon: Publicações D. Quixote 1990. The novel appeared in English as Cousin Basilio, transl. by Roy Campbell. London: Max Reinhardt 1953.

2 The edition used is Theodor Fontane: Effi Briest, transl. by Hugh Rorrison and Helen Chambers, London: Penguin Books 2000.

3 I have compared these two novels in my thesis 'A Mulher e o Adultério nos romances *Effi Briest* de Theodor Fontane e *O Primo Bazílio* de Eça de Queirós', University of Oporto, Ph.D., 1998. The critical bibliography on this theme is very limited. Only the four following articles deal with the comparison of the two novels, and it is interesting to note that all of the articles appeared in the 80s and 90s, which demonstrates the increasing interest in comparative literature in the literature of non-central-european countries: Helmut Hatzfeld: Die religiöse Diskussion in *O Primo Bazílio* (1877) und *Effi Briest*. Aufsätze zur portugiesischen Kulturgeschichte, vol.16 (1980), pp. 66-74; Christoph Rodiek: Probleme der vergleichenden Rangbestimung literarischer Werke (*Effi Briest, La Regenta, O Primo Basílio*). In: Neohelicon. Acta comparationis Literarum Universarum, 15, 1 (1988), pp. 275-300; Heinz L. Kretzenbacher: Das Kulturthema Ehre. Über Ehre, Ironie und kulturelle Interferenz: Ehebruch und Ehrenkonflikt bei Theodor Fontane und Eça de Queirós. In: Jahrbuch Deutsch als Fremdsprache, vol. 16 (1990), pp. 32-75; Teresa Martins de Oliveira: Dienst-mädchengestalten in den Romanen *O Primo Bazílio* von Eça de Queirós und *Effi Briest* von Theodor Fontane. In: Runa - Revista Portuguesa de Estudos Germanísticos, 26, 2 (1996), pp. 553-561. Some approaches on this theme also appear in Orlando Grossegesse: Konversation und Roman. Untersuchungen zum Werk Eça de Queirós. Stuttgart: Franz Steiner 1991.

4 Cf. Alexander Coleman: Eça de Queirós and European Realism. New York: New York University Press 1980. Other articles on the theme of women and adultery in the work of Eça de Queirós in English are: Elizabeth Lowe: Love as liturgy and liturgy as love: The satirical subversion of worship and courtship in Eça de Queiroz. In: Hispania, 61, 4, December (1978), pp. 912-918; and Peggy Sharpe-Valadares: The heavenly and the earthly cities: the female paradigm in the work of Eça de Queirós. In: Luzo-Brazilian Review, 24, 2 (1989), pp. 117-130.

Nerval and Heine. The strange nature of Eça's writings caused surprise among the literary circles of the time. In Coimbra, Eça came into contact with young academics, who were fascinated by the happenings in Europe and by thinkers such as Darwin, Michelet, Hegel, Comte and above all, Proudhon.

After graduating, Eça settled down in his parents' house in Lisbon and began his professional life; after a short period spent working as a lawyer, he took up administrative posts and finally opted for a diplomatic career. As Portuguese consul he lived first in Havana and later in Newcastle-on-Tyne, where he wrote *O Primo Bazílio*, which he finished in 1876. He was later transferred to Bristol, and then to Paris, where he died in 1900. He had a brilliant career as a journalist, social critic and novelist, which is why he is the best known Portuguese writer of the 1800s, and along with Antero de Quental, the most prominent figure of the *Generation of 70*, a group whose aim was to reform Portuguese society and to introduce a new realist type of writing. Their philosophical models were mainly Taine and Proudhon and their literary models were above all Flaubert, but also Baudelaire and Zola. Later, Eça de Queirós went through another stage in his writing, a *fin-de-siècle* style in which he concentrated more on the development of characters and less on their socio-economic background, which had been such a strong trait in his earlier works.[5]

Just as Fontane is considered the chronicler of Berlin society at the end of the last century, so Eça de Queirós can be considered the chronicler of the Lisbon of his time, painting a true and all-encompassing picture of this society. He studies the effect of the clergy on the middle class in *O crime de Padre Amaro*,[6] and adultery committed by a woman in *O Primo Bazílio;* the decadence of the upper-middle-class and the aristocracy is the main theme of *Os Maias,*[7] he also studies other character types, such as the politician, the man of letters, the Don Juan, the pious woman and the woman corrupted by romantic art. While Fontane gives prominence to the aristocracy in his writing, Eça's main focus in his novels is on the bourgeoisie, of which he is highly critical.

O Primo Bazílio, published in Lisbon in 1878, belongs to a school of writing that the author himself describes as realist-naturalist and its trademark is a caustic irony which is typical of Eça's style.[8] As in the other novels on the theme of adultery which appeared in Europe in the second half of the nineteenth century, the analysis of the situation of women allows us clear insight into the society of the time which it chronicles.

In theme and structure, semiotics and narrative, the work is very similar to *Effi Briest*. Luíza de Brito is a twenty-five-year-old middle-class woman from Lisbon.

---

5 About the different stages on Eça de Queirós' writing, cf., among others, Óscar Lopes e Arnaldo Saraiva: História da Literatura Portuguesa. Oporto: Porto Editora 1996, p. 925 ff..

6 English translation: Eça de Queirós: The Sin of Father Amaro, transl. by Nan Flanagan. London: Max Reinhardt 1962; reprinted London: Transworld Publisher 1964.

7 The novel is translated into English as Eça de Queirós: The Maias, transl. by Patricia McGowan and Ann Stevens. London: Bodley Head 1965.

8 Cf. among others, Da Cal, Ernesto Guerra: Língua e Estilo de Eça de Queiroz. Coimbra: Livraria Almedina 1981.

When the novel opens she has been married for three years to a placid young engineer who works for the Ministry of Public Works. She lives an idle and contented existence, devoting her time to reading romantic literature and household tasks, in a state of happiness that is not overshadowed by the absence of children. This idyllic situation is threatened by two journeys in opposite directions; her husband leaves Lisbon for the provinces on business, and her cousin, and ex-fiancé, arrives from Brazil, where he has lived for some years. The main themes of the first part of the novel are infidelity and death and these are referred to in conversation, in musical and literary references, as well as on a symbolic level. If we note that the incompatibility between the mistress and her maid is made apparent from the start, we can see that the plot which is the basis of the novel is present *in nuce* from the first chapters. The second part of the narrative deals with Bazílio's wooing of his cousin, her seduction and the adultery, which will rapidly lead Luíza to a feeling of disillusionment. Bazílio turns out to be disrespectful, demanding, and less attractive than her own husband. A new phase of the narrative begins when Juliana, the maid, reveals that she has in her possession letters which Luíza had written to her lover; Juliana is bitter, spiteful and suffers from a serious heart condition; she makes ever-increasing blackmail demands on her mistress, subjecting her to humiliation after humiliation. On hearing of the blackmail demands, Bazílio flees to Paris and the heroine's despair increases, particularly when her husband returns and is surprised and angered at the special treatment the maid is given in the house. Juliana holds the upper hand in the duel with her mistress and increases her blackmail demands until she becomes her own victim. Her death is greeted with relief by the reader and the heroine alike, but does not lead to the happy ending the reader may have expected or even hoped for. Worn out by her troubles, Luíza becomes seriously ill with a "brain fever" and after a short period of convalescence, her condition deteriorates; she dies after two days of agony, which is described in great detail by the narrator.

Both this novel and *Effi Briest* relate the tragic fate of a young woman at the end of the last century, who allows herself to be seduced – in a more or less classic way – by a Don Juan figure who promises distraction from a tedious and idle life. Another similarity between the novels is the fact that both heroines are discovered and punished, and die as a result of this punishment. The main difference between the novels, and the point that I wish to analyse in more detail, lies in the attitude of the authors to what they are writing about, namely in the way each judges his heroine and her adulterous behaviour.

We cannot forget that we are dealing with an age in which the question of women's position in society was in vogue.[9] In Germany the works of positivist and determinist thinkers were popular, as were those of Schopenhauer and Nietzsche. They all saw women as inferior and subordinate to men. At the same time other thinkers such as August Bebel and the emancipation movement put forward a positive image of women, which led to frequent discussion of the situation of women in philosophical, legal and

---

9 Cf. Claudia Honegger: Die Ordnung der Geschlechter. Die Wissenschaften vom Menschen und das Weib: 1750-1850. Frankfurt a. M.: Campus 1991.

socio-political circles.[10] In Portugal, where women's movements were not yet organised, only a few writers dealt with this subject from a cultural point of view. Among the *Generation of 70* in particular, – under the influence of Michelet and Proudhon – we can find images of women which range from a euphoric and romanticised picture to a critical view which saw women as lesser beings, in need of protection.

Eça de Queirós's critical attitude towards women, and in particular towards urban middle-class women, a subject he wrote a lot about in non-fiction texts, is very different from that of Fontane.[11] In the few non-fiction texts that the German author wrote on the subject he shows a benevolent attitude to women, whom he appreciates because of their imperfections.[12] In the novels that I am comparing we can see that Fontane does not condemn his heroine, whereas Eça de Queirós censures not only his heroine but also the society in which she lives. These different attitudes affect the diegetic development of the novel and also the narrative techniques used.

We must first look at the different choice of events to be related and the effect that the textual economy has on the different stages of the narrative. To illustrate Elsbeth Hamann's comment on the symmetrical nature of Fontane's novel, I would like to note that Effi's seduction as she returns from a journey to the forester's house occurs almost in the middle of the novel, in the third of six narrative sequences, in the nineteenth chapter out of a total of thirty-six.[13] In the first two parts, the author presents the main character and the circumstances that have made her what she is, and by describing her evolution in detail gains the sympathy and the understanding of the reader for her behaviour. This kind of preparation does not exist in *O Primo Bazílio,* where we meet the heroine during the short seduction and then during the adultery itself and the process of blackmail. As we feel we do not know her well, we empathise less with her. In this connection it should be said that the initial description of the heroine in *O Primo Bazílio*, which is clearly disphoric, leads to a feeling of distance between the writer and Luíza, in contrast to what happens in *Effi Briest,* in which the initial description of the heroine is very positive.

To return to the structure of the novels, we can see that the Portuguese novel, like the German one, is practically symmetrical; however, its central point is not the seduction scene, but the scene in which Juliana begins to blackmail her mistress. Thus, in *O Primo Bazílio* the adultery and the blackmail are given equal weight and importance in the text. The structure of the novel leads the reader to see Luíza's

---

10 Cf. August Bebel: Die Frau und der Sozialismus. Stuttgart: Jubiläumsausgabe, 25th ed. 1895.

11 Eça de Queirós's opinions about women at this time are documented in the letters he wrote to Teófilo Braga, 12 March 1878, and Rodrigues de Freitas 30 March 1878, in which he comments on the ethical and aesthetic ideals in *O Primo Bazílio*. On this theme see also the review As Farpas, in particular the numbers of May 1871, March 1872 and September-October 1872.

12 As an example of the benevolent attitude of Fontane towards women, see his letter of 10 October 1895 to Colmar Grünhagen. In: Theodor Fontane: Fontanes Briefe in zwei Bänden, ed. by Gotthard Erler. Berlin, Weimar 1986, p. 382.

13 Cf. Elsbeth Hamann: Theodor Fontanes *Effi Briest* aus erzähltheoretischer Sicht. Bonn: Bouvier 1984, pp. 78-87.

punishment after the adultery as redressing the balance which had been disturbed by her mistake and, in this way, the punishment appears as a natural result of her previous behaviour.

An analysis of the narrative voice makes it clear that Fontane sympathises with his heroine, whereas Eça is harshly critical. In both novels a heterodiegetic narrator is present. In *Effi Briest* the narrator's presence is scarcely noticeable and dialogue is given a prime position, which allows the reader to see the action from various points of view. What is more, Fontane carefully selects the characters who are to be put in a focal position, giving a special place to the figure of the heroine, who thus gains the empathy of the reader. In *O Primo Bazílio*, which belongs to an earlier phase of narrative writing, the narrator's judgmental perspective is superimposed on the dialogue of the characters and the narrator can be interpreted as the voice of the author himself.[14] In the Portuguese novel, the narrator adopts the point of view of a number of characters, which may be Eça's way of giving us a rounded view of society; a special place is given to the heroine, although the effects are different from those in Fontane's text: Luíza is placed at a distance from the reader and unmasked by the author's strong, critical and ironic presence.[15]

To turn now to the external circumstances of the two heroines, we note that as well as the obvious difference in nationality, there are also great differences with regard to age and social position. Eça's heroine, Luíza, had come of age before marrying, whereas, at sixteen, Fontane's heroine typifies careless youth, which immediately reveals the position of the authors with regard to blame. Another important factor has to do with the marriages of these two girls; in neither case was it a marriage of love but rather a case of the heroine doing what society expected of her. In order for this to happen, girls were socialised and guided by their mothers, who were mainly responsible for their upbringing. In the German novel it is noteworthy that it is the mother who receives the marriage proposal and who communicates it to her daughter, producing a reaction for which Effi had long been prepared. In *O Primo Bazílio*, the proposal is made directly to the daughter, whose age and social class justify a greater autonomy; her first thought is, however, that her mother will be pleased and relieved by her acceptance of the proposal.

Although Effi is from a rural aristocratic background and is married to a Prussian civil servant and Luíza is only a middle-class woman from Lisbon, there are surprising social parallels between the two novels. In Portugal industrial development happened late, flooding the towns with cheap female labour, which allowed middle-class women to lead an idle life, leaving the work to maids.[16] In Germany this type of life was more typical of the aristocracy. In *Effi Briest*, in contrast to *O Primo Bazílio*, the woman is

---

14 On the evolution of perspectivisation in narrative writing, cf. Franz K. Stanzel: Theorie des Erzählens. Göttingen: Vandenhoeck & Ruprecht 1974, pp. 177-182.

15 Cf. Óscar Lopes: Efeitos de Queirosianos de polifonia vocal n' *O Primo Basílio*. In: Eça de Queirós "Os Maias". Actas do 1º Encontro Internacional de Queirosianos, ed. by Isabel Pires de Lima. Porto: Edições Asa 1990, pp. 109-115.

16 Cf. Teresa Martins de Oliveira: Dienstmädchengestalten in den Romanen *O Primo Bazílio* von Eça de Queirós und *Effi Briest*.

not denigrated for her idleness. Her ties with nature and open spaces, and her ambitions to project herself and to attain social brilliance, as well as her inability to adapt to closed and restricted spaces, are factors which do not lead us to see her in a negative light. In spite of the apparent similarity, there are differences in the way in which Luíza and Effi spend their time. They both play the piano, embroider and read. However Luíza's pastimes like those of Emma Bovary, are ultra-romantic;[17] if romanticism exists for Effi, it is the fantasy and mythology associated with being "a child of nature" and is not associated with the harmful influence that excessive romanticism has on the heroine in the Portuguese novel.

The most important trait that the two protagonists share is, however, a lack of strength of character. Effi's inner conflict, her attraction to opposites, to gambling and to danger, which is underlined by various symbols and allusions, is referred to not only by many characters in the novel, but also by Effi herself. Worried about her inconstant nature, and comparing herself to her future husband, Effi declares not long before her wedding:

> "And I think Niemeyer went on to say he's a man of principle. And that, I imagine, is a bit more. Oh, and I ...I haven't any."[18]

Luíza de Brito's potential inconstancy is discussed at the beginning by her husband, Jorge, on the eve of his departure for the Alentejo, when he asks a friend to watch over his wife. In his absence he does not want Luíza to entertain at home a female friend from her childhood, whom he considers to be a libertine:

> "Luíza is an angel, poor thing" ... "In some ways she is still a child! She can see no evil. She's so good, she just let's things happen. Just look at what happens with Leopoldina: they were brought up together, they were friends, so she doesn't have the courage to ask her to leave. She feels awkward about it, she's too kind. It's understandable! But you can't go through life like that!"
> [...]
> "So Sebastian, if you see her here while I'm away, if you find out that Leopoldina is coming here, say something to Luíza! Because that's the way she is, she doesn't stop to think: she puts things out of her mind and doesn't stop to think about them. She needs someone to warn her, someone to say to her: 'Come on, madam, this cannot be!' And then she is the first to agree! You come round and keep her company, play some music for her, and if you see any sign of Leopoldina, you say to her: 'Madam, this is not right.' She can be firm if she feels she's supported. Otherwise she's intimidated and lets her come. She's unhappy about it, but she simply does not have the courage to say to Leopoldina: 'I don't want you here, go away!' She doesn't have the courage for anything: her hands begin to shake, her mouth becomes dry... She's a woman, she's very much a woman!" [19]

---

17 On the affinities of the figures of Luiza de Brito and Emma Bovary, cf. among others, João Medina: O Bovarismo (Da Emma Bovary de Flaubert à Luíza de Eça) and Luíza ou a triste condição (feminina) portuguesa. (N'o Centenário de *O Primo Bazílio*). In: Eça de Queiroz e a Geração de 70, ed. by João Medina. Lisbon: Moraes Editores 1980, pp. 105-111 and 117.

18 Rorrison and Chambers: Theodor Fontane: Effi Briest, p. 25.

19 Translations into English are my own unless otherwise indicated.

In fact it is this tendency to "let things happen" which rules Luíza's life.[20] Before marrying, she has gone from the arms of Bazílio to those of Jorge in a theatrical but, at the same time practical, gesture and has got used to happiness. Once her husband has gone and Bazílio has returned, the latter has no difficulty in conquering her affections. The opinion that Frau Briest has of her daughter "She likes to be carried along"[21] is also applicable to Luíza. They both allow themselves to be guided by others and they are both attracted to the unknown. The attitude of the authors towards their heroines is, however, very different. Eça describes his heroine in positivist terms, explaining her behaviour by her background and the circle in which she lives; the society that formed and nurtured Luíza has turned her into an empty vessel, who reacts with her emotions to external events and who is ready to conform to what is expected of her. She is incapable of a moral thought, for which she substitutes mystical musings and in her trance-like state her degradation increases. Alongside this causal determinism, Eça de Queirós adopts a highly critical position; his criticism is aimed not only at his heroine but also at the society she belongs to, whose behaviour and interaction he unmasks.

In *Effi Briest*, on the other hand, the opposition between the aspirations of the heroine and society, lead to a positive view of the protagonist and the condemnation of society. Effi's volubility is seen not as a sign of emptiness, but rather as an indication of her inner wealth which is shown by her difficulty in adapting. Fontane's heroine is portrayed as a multi-faceted human being with a complex psyche, which justifies the contradictions that exist within her; she is at the same time a child of nature (*Naturkind*) and a member of society (*Gesellschaftsmensch*), Eve, Mary and Melusine.[22] Effi's inability to feel remorse is, more than anything a criticism of a

---

" – A Luíza é um anjo, coitada – mas tem coisas em que é criança! Não vê o mal. É muito boa, deixa-se ir. Como este caso da Leopoldina, por exemplo; foram criadas do pequenas, eram amigas, não tem coragem agora para a pôr fora. É acanhamento, é bondade. Ele compreende-se! Mas enfim as leis da vida têm as suas exigências! ....

– Por isso, Sebastião, enquanto eu estiver fora, se te constar que a Leopoldina vem por cá, avisa a Luíza! Porque ela é assim: esquece-se, não reflexiona. É necessario alguém que a advirta, que lhe diga: – Alto lá, isso não pode ser! Que então cai logo em si, e é a primeira! ... Vens por aí, fazes-lhe companhia, fazes-lhe música, e se vires que a Leopoldina aparece ao largo, tu logo: – Minha rica senhora, cuidado, olhe que isso não! Que ela, sentindo-se apoiada, tem decisão. Senão, acanha-se, deixa-a vir. Sofre com isso, mas não tem coragem de lhe dizer: Não te quero ver, vai-te! Não tem coragem para nada: começam as mãos a tremer-lhe, a secar-se lhe a boca ... É mulher, é muito mulher! ..." Eça de Queirós: O Primo Bazílio, p. 51.

20 Cf. Eduardo Lourenço de Faria: *O Primo Bazílio*: Structure vide ou structure remplie? In: Sillages, 4 (1974), pp. 57-68.

21 Rorrison and Chambers: Theodor Fontane: Effi Briest, p. 158.

22 The importance and the meaning to be given to the mythological and to the mythical elements in the characterisation of Effi Briest on the one hand and to the sociological and psychological elements on the other, vary according to the tendencies of the period and to the critical view of the analyst. Besides the sociological and psychological interpretation, of which the works of Müller-Seidel (cf. Walter Müller-Seidel: Theodor Fontane, Soziale Romankunst in Deutschland. Stuttgart: Metzler 1975, pp. 332-377, and of Hans-Heinrich Reuter: Fontane, vol. 2. Munich: Nymphenburg, 1968, pp. 640-647, are paradigmatic, we find interpretations that tend to accept a double motivation, that is both sociological and mythological (cf. Donald C. Riechel: *Effi Briest* and the Calendar of Fate.

society which imposes its own norms as moral norms. The opposition between "being
" and "seeming to be", which is mainly analysed in the novel through the conscience of
the character, reveals Effi's honest nature. This honesty does not signify total lucidity
and freedom. Although these characteristics are not entirely absent, as they are in *O
Primo Bazílio,* they are relativised. Although they do not lead to total justification of
Effi's behaviour – she cannot be said to be blameless – they do lead the reader to be
kindly disposed towards her.

In the same way, the main difference in the treatment of the theme of adultery is the
way in which the heroine herself is evaluated. In *Effi Briest,* the differences between
the couple, the disappointment which Effi feels concerning her marriage, the absence
of explicit references to the meetings between the lovers and the adultery itself, the
importance given to the heroine's inner thoughts, the fact that the relationship comes to
an end because of external factors and the way in which the lovers' flight is described,
all make the adultery itself appear less significant and help to preserve the dignity of
the female character.

On the other hand, in *O Primo Bazílio* the reader knows from the start that the
married couple have a good relationship, which makes the adultery appear more
shocking and the adultery itself is described in lengthy, almost sordid detail. Added to
this, the ease with which Luíza allows herself to be seduced by her cousin, and her
moral alienation, increase Luíza's guilt, though she is seen as a product of her
education and environment.

The way in which the two main characters behave after the discovery of the adultery
shows better than anything else Fontane's forgiving attitude towards his heroine, quite
unlike Eça's attitude to Luíza. Effi is banished, but her transfiguration before her
death is quite unlike Luíza's acceptance of her shameful and shaming punishment, and
her physical decline and death. The veiled tone of Fontane's criticism, which is both
typical of poetic realism and of a certain *fin-de-siècle* type of fatalism present in the
German novel, differs greatly from the radical tone of the Portuguese novel, in which
the satirical narrator places himself at a distance from the events narrated.

To conclude we can say that a common feature of the two novels is the careful
study of women and their situation in a society that does not permit them to develop in
an independent and responsible way. The indictment of Prussian social norms in *Effi
Briest* corresponds in *O Primo Bazílio* to the criticism of the heroine and of the society

---

In: Germanic Review, 48, (1973), pp. 189-211; and Peter Paul Schwarz: "Tragische Analyse" und
Schicksalsdeutungen in Fontanes Roman *Effi Briest.* In: Sprachkunst. Beiträge zur Literaturwissenschaft, 7, 2 (1976), pp. 247-260. It is commonly noted that the mythological and mythical
elements, allied to a complex web of motifs, contribute to creating a deeper social and psychological
dimension in the heroine (cf. Reinhart Thum: Symbol, motif and »Leitmotiv« in Fontanes »Effi
Briest«. In: Germanic Review 54 (1979), pp. 115-124; on the motif of Melusine in *Effi Briest*, cf.,
among others, Renate Schäfer: Fontanes Melusine-Motiv. In: Euphorion, 56 (1962), pp. 69-104;
Diethelm Brüggemann: Fontanes Allegorien. In: Neue Rundschau, 82, 2-3 (1971), pp. 290-310 and
pp. 486-505; and Hubert Ohl: Melusine als Mythos bei Theodor Fontane. In: Mythos und
Mythologie in der Literatur des 19 Jahrhunderts, ed. by Helmut Koopmann. Frankfurt a. M.:
Klostermann 1979, pp. 289-305.

in which she lives – Lisbon society towards the end of the last century, a society marked by ultra romanticism, by hollow politics and *petit-bourgeois* moralising. Eça de Queirós paints a clear, but sharply ironic picture of this society, which makes this novel, like *Effi Briest*, compulsory reading for anyone who wishes to learn more about the late nineteenth-century European realist novel.

Alexander Stillmark

Fontane and Turgenev:
Two Kinds of Realism

Placing Fontane and Turgenev side by side and reviewing their literary achievements as a whole would seem to show a broad pattern of correspondences as well as many striking similarities. They are all but exact contemporaries, Turgenev having been born but one year before Fontane. They both open their careers by writing verse (Fontane leaving behind a considerable body of poetry, including many celebrated ballads, whereas Turgenev is hardly known for any poetry other than *Parasha*); both later diversify into essayistic forms such as the physiological sketch and the literary review, though the novel figures early in Turgenev's output, whereas in Fontane it represents a form of mature culmination. For all their rootedness in, and devotion to their respective native landscape and culture, they both travel abroad extensively, spending long periods away from home and coming to view their respective societies from an extraneous perspective. Each of them becomes a discerning chronicler of social and cultural change in a Europe agitated by emergent nationalism and competing ideologies. Their focus on "the representative figure" in this scenario of transition shows evident parallels. Deriving from broadly comparable educational, if not social, backgrounds (Turgenev firmly turned his back on aristocratic status and privilege), their preferred milieu consisted largely of literary and artistic circles. Fontane was in touch with many important German men of letters, largely through the Berlin club "Der Tunnel über der Spree"; Turgenev spent many years at the centre of literary life in Paris and was in correspondence with most notable writers of his time. Both of them tend to be selective in their depiction of the social milieu and are remarkable for the prominent attention they give to the role of women in their fiction. Turgenev, rather than Fontane, permits a distinctive ideology to inform his social realism, and each, at some point, ventured into the realm of satire. By contrast to a Gogol, Dickens or Balzac, we find in Fontane's art detachment, reticence, the preservation of critical distance, clear-sighted tolerance touched by irony or resignation. In Turgenev there is less detachment, more emphasis on the conflict of ideas, and such as gave rise to repeated misconceptions and persistent polemics. If there is one distinguishing characteristic shared by these writers – it being understood that we are dealing with two distinctly individual styles – it is sustained technical finesse. Both authors achieve their particular artistic objectives by narrative strategies which depend on nuance, subtle accentuation, the calculated marshalling of minor detail, unobtrusive symbolism, oblique reference, deliberated composition, and fine tuning of verbal registers (especially in the writing of dialogue). In proposing such a range of partial and exact correspondences – as yet at the higher level of generality – it may surprise one to read Fontane's summary verdict on Turgenev as expressed in the letter of 24 July 1881 to his wife:

He observes everything wonderfully: nature, animals and people; he has something like a photographic gadget in eye and soul, but the added reflections, particularly where they are also meant to be poetic, are *not* of the highest. These stories are all 30 years old and it is quite evident that he then still lacked that maturity which he now has. Such maturity I do indeed find in "Smoke", which was written around 1865 or 1866, no less than in "Virgin Soil", yet I just can't relish this way of writing. I admire the sharp manner of observation and the high degree of unfussy art avoiding all silly trifles; but in fact, it bores me because, by contrast to the partly truly poetic, partly at least would-be poetic Huntsman's Tales, it reproduces things entirely *untransfigured*. Yet without such transfiguration there is no art as such, not even when the craftsman for all his skill as maker is truly an artist.[1]

Fontane habitually saw Turgenev in close proximity to Zola and the Naturalist camp as part of that consensus of radical realism whose forte lay in unsparing portrayal of the harsher aspects of social existence; "photographic fidelity" or "the greyness of our young realism" as he elsewhere called it.[2] Instead of viewing himself as cohort of the new European realism, he prefers to set himself apart from his contemporaries as one who is less tendentious, less pessimistic, and who cannot share their penchant for the seamy side of life. Writing of his early novella *L'Adultera* (*The Woman Taken in Adultery*), he declared it to be:

A chunk of life, without all ulterior motive or tendency. If I were but 10 years younger I would be quite sure to make my mark with it and succeed even better than Turgenev or Zola (though, of course, with less outward success), since my manner of writing is wholly free of two things: exaggeration in general, and above all exaggeration in matters of ugliness.[3]

---

1 "Er beobachtet alles wundervoll; Natur Tier und Menschen; er hat so was von einem photographischen Apparat in Aug' und Seele, aber die Reflexionszutaten, besonders wenn sie nebenher auch noch poetisch wirken sollen, sind *nicht* auf der Höhe. Diese Geschichten sind alle 30 Jahre alt, und es ist ganz ersichtlich, daß ihm damals noch die Reife fehlte, die er jetzt hat. Diese Reife find' ich denn auch wirklich in "Rauch", das etwa 1865 oder 1866 geschrieben wurde, gerade so wie in "Neuland", aber ich werde dieser Schreibweise nicht froh. Ich bewundere die scharfe Beobachtung und das hohe Maß phrasenloser, alle Kinkerlitzchen verschmähender Kunst; aber eigentlich langweilt es mich, weil es im Gegensatze zu den teils wirklich poetischen, teils wenigstens poetisch sein wollenden Jägergeschichten so grenzenlos prosaisch, so ganz *unverklärt* die Dinge wiedergibt. Ohne diese Verklärung gibt es aber keine eigentliche Kunst, auch dann nicht, wenn der Bildner in seinem bildnerischen Geschick ein wirklicher Künstler ist." Fontane to Emilie Fontane, 24 July 1881. In: Theodor Fontane: Briefe an seine Familie, vol.1, Berlin: F. Fontane 1905, p. 314. All translations into English are my own.

2 "[…] die photographische Treue"; Fontane: Holz/Schlaf: Die Familie Selicke; Kielland: Auf dem Heimwege. Causerien über Theater, NFA, XXII/2, 742. "Die Tristheit in unserem jungen Realismus"; Fontane: Hauptmann: Das Friedensfest. Causerien über Theater, NFA, XXII/2, 742.

3 "[…] ein Stück Leben, ohne jede Neben-Ansicht oder Tendenz. Wär ich nur 10 Jahre jünger, so wäre ich auch sicher, daß ich damit durchdringen und in so weit sogar besser als Turgenjew und Zola (wenn auch selbstverständlich mit geringerem äußerem Erfolg) reussieren würde, als meine Schreibweise von zwei Dingen völlig frei ist: von Übertreibungen überhaupt und vor allem von Übertreibungen nach der Seite des Häßlichen ist." Fontane to Martha Fontane, 5 May 1883, HFA, IV, 3, 243.

Though he would assert that he honoured and looked up to Turgenev as a master and model, he nonetheless publicly confessed to a deeper and persistent preference for the Romantic genre:

> I value all that is Romantic not just very highly, it remains my favourite genre in literature, and all the artistic delight which I owe to the Realist school, the admiration with which I have read Zola, Turgenev, Tolstoy and Ibsen, pales beside the sublime joy which Romantic writing has offered me throughout an entire life.[4]

The inner dichotomy (which incidentally reminds one of Heine), appears as a conflict between aesthetic and intellectual loyalties in a writer who knew full well where the road to modernity lay, yet could not forswear the high achievements of Weimar and Jena: "The victory of Realism only rids the world of false Romanticism, of a Romanticism unworthy of the name."[5] Fontane perceived with absolute clarity that Romanticism and Realism were not incompatible but could complement and reinforce one another, as may amply be attested historically. His objection was to over-accentuation, to one-sidedness, in all forms of literature and art; to the loss of equilibrium. This is what he seized on in reviewing Turgenev's play *Natalie* (*A Month in the Country*):

> I am, in principle, against dramas and novels which view that many-faceted thing called life purely from the point of view of love. The life also led by those who are in love is not played out exclusively in love scenes, and the neglect of this, if you will, prosaic fact produces an image of life lacking the full reality.[6]

There is a refreshing directness and sobriety in all Fontane's critical verdicts which, far from over-simplifying the problem considered, help to dispel the fog of pedantic complexity by the clear light of pragmatic counsel. Fontane as critic and artist incessantly wrestled with the problem of the peripheral ("das Nebensächliche") and the central, with the relationship of detail to totality, of art ("Kunst") to the artificial ("Gekünsteltes"), of truth ("Wahrheit") to effect ("Wirkung"). What he perceived as a surfeit of love-making ("das Liebes-Zuviel") in Turgenev's play, seemed an artificial distortion, and thus a weakness, which, like all exaggeration, tends to fatigue. What he could not fail to admire were Turgenev's powers of psychological exploration: "in the

---

4 "Ich stelle das Romantische nicht nur sehr hoch, es bleibt auch meine Lieblingsgattung in der Dichtung, und aller künstlerischen Genuß, den ich der realistischen Schule verdanke, die Bewunderung mit der ich Zola Turgenjew, Tolstoi, Ibsen gelesen habe, verschwindet neben der erhabenen Freude, die mir, durch ein ganzes Leben hin, romantische Dichtungen [...] gemacht haben." Fontane: Richard Voss, Brigitta. Causerien über Theater, NFA, XXII/2, 638.
5 "Der Sieg des Realismus schafft nur die falsche Romantik aus der Welt, die Romantik, die keine ist." Fontane: Richard Voss, Brigitta, p. 638.
6 "Ich bin im Prinzip gegen Dramen und Romane, die das vielgestaltete Ding, das man Leben heißt, nur unter dem Liebesgesichtspunkt zu sehen. Auch das Leben, das Verliebte führen, verläuft nicht ausschließlich in Liebesszenen, und die Mißachtung dieser meinetwegen prosaischen Tatsache, schafft ein Lebensbild, das der vollen Realität entbehrt." Fontane: Iwan Turgenjew, Natalie. Causerien über Theater, NFA, XXII/ 2, 632.

exploration of the human heart, especially female hearts, and more especially the hearts of young women."[7]

The crucial question "what is the aim of the modern novel?" posed in Fontane's late review of Gustav Freytag's *Die Ahnen*, is answered succinctly and confidently from a premise he has made his own: "the modern novel ought to be an image of the times, an image of its own time." More precisely: "the novel ought to be an image of the times to which we ourselves belong, at least the reflection of a life at whose borders we ourselves have stood, or of that our parents still told us about."[8] Not that Turgenev had failed to fulfil this condition; he had, in Fontane's eyes, fulfilled it too narrowly and too starkly. The terms "unverklärt" (untransfigured) and "unpoetisch" (unpoetic) from the earlier critique, are ever tacitly present as the latent flaw. However if we turn to the pronouncements made by both novelists in their theoretical essays, we find them in close accord. Fontane, in his seminal essay *Unsere lyrische und epische Poesie seit 1848* (Our lyric and epic poetry since 1848) (1853), offers us his fullest considered views on the nature of realism as the very badge and essence of contemporary art and literature. In its assertive tone of conviction it reads like a manifesto. In it, he goes so far as to identify realism as the supreme aesthetic principle: "Realism in art is as ancient as art itself, indeed: it is art."[9]

In tracing out the resurgence of a basic artistic trend which, though perennial, had again triumphed in his day, he sees it as a victory for genuine art over the unnatural, over mendacity, mannerism, vagueness, and rigidity of form. He equally condemns the exclusive bias towards the ugly and tendentious:

This trend relates to genuine realism as crude ore does to metal: purification is lacking. True, the motto of realism is the Goethean exhortation:

'Take hold of the fullness of human life,
Wherever you grasp it, there interest lies.'

But just the same, the hand that grasps must needs be artistic.[10]

---

7 "[...] in der Aufschließung des Menschenherzens, besonders weiblicher Herzen, und ganz besonders der Herzen junger Frauen." Fontane: Iwan Turgenjew, Natalie. Causerien über Theater, NFA, XXII, 2, 633.

8 "[...] der moderne Roman soll ein Zeitbild sein, ein Bild seiner Zeit." "Der Roman soll ein Bild der Zeit sein, der wir selber angehören, mindestens die Wiederspiegelung eines Lebens, an dessen Grenze wir selber noch standen, oder von dem, was unsere Eltern noch erzählten." Fontane: Gustav Freytag, Die Ahnen. Literarische Essays und Studien, NFA, XXI/1, 242.

9 " [...] der Realismus in der Kunst ist so alt wie die Kunst selbst, ja, noch mehr: er ist die Kunst." Fontane: Unsere lyrische und epische Poesie seit 1848. Literarische Essays und Studien, NFA, XXI/1, 9.

10 "Diese Richtung verhält sich zum echten Realismus wie das rohe Erz zum Metall: Die Läuterung fehlt. Wohl ist das Motto des Realismus der Goethesche Zuruf:
Greif nur hinein ins volle Menschenleben,
Wo du es packst, da ist's interessant,
Aber freilich die Hand, die diesen Griff tut, muß eine künstlerische sein."
Fontane: 'Unsere lyrische und epische Poesie seit 1848', p. 12.

It was Turgenev's artistic hand which later wrote the following words in defence of his most carefully crafted and also most contentious novel, *Fathers and Sons*:

> And so, my youthful brothers, it is to you that my words are addressed.
>
> 'Take hold of the fullness of human life!'
>
> I would say to you in the words of our common mentor Goethe:
>
> 'Though each one lives it – yet not many know,
> Wherever you grasp it, there interest lies!'[11]

In choosing to quote the selfsame lines as a pointer towards that Goethean breadth of vision, that boldness of grasp, which is to serve the realist novelist as guiding principle, Fontane and Turgenev are seen to be making common cause. Fontane's critical response to the Russian's art appears unable to register its luminous style, its refined poetic texture, or yet its partly submerged ideality (in which censorship played its part); that is to say, its essentially Russian features, which translation is likely further to obscure.

Yet Fontane never failed to appreciate Turgenev's powers of evocative description; that technique of recapturing sensuous experience and fleeting moods, later known as Impressionism. Turgenev has, among the many other traits linking him to Fontane, the gift of portraying in his fiction "the representative figure", the character who incorporates essential elements of the Zeitgeist. This is not to say that their fictive characters are artificial repositories of ideas (a flaw to which Hebbel was prone), but that they are wholly plausible and convincing human portraits in whom the prevailing trends and temper of the age subtly manifest themselves. It is for reasons of conviction and contemporaneity that the figures Bazarov, Insarov or Lavretsky gave rise to the most heated public debates (reactions which largely persuaded Turgenev to leave Russia). Fontane too repeatedly endured bigoted remonstrations over such largely emancipated figures as Melanie, Effi, Cécile or Lene. One has only to recall the voice of outrage during the serialisation of Lene's and Botho's affair as addressed to the chief editor of the *Vossische Zeitung*: "Isn't this horrid tale of a whore going to end soon?"[12] The challenges contained within the novels of both writers to the predominantly conservative ideological and ethical culture were such as to arouse strong public reaction.

The figure which constantly preoccupied Turgenev, and which appeared in various transformations throughout his work from Rudin to Nezhdanov in *Virgin Soil*, is that

---

11 Turgenev quoted Goethe's lines from Faust more accurately than Fontane:
   "Greift nur hinein in's volle Menschenleben!
   Ein jeder lebt's – nicht vielen ist's bekannt,
   Und wo ihr's packt da ist's interessant!"
   Ivan Turgenev, Polnoye Sobranie Sotchinenii i Pisem v 28 Tomakh. Leningrad: Izdatel'stvo Nauka, 1960 ff., XIV, 106.
12 "Wird denn die gräßliche Hurengeschichte nicht bald aufhören?" HFA, I, 2, 910.

of "the superfluous man"; that sensitive, indecisive, ineffectual, ruminating *flâneur* whose prototype was Hamlet, and who haunts the pages of nineteenth-century Russian fiction and drama from Pechorin to Platanov. The intellectual stranglehold that this so-called "Hamletism" had on Russian cultural life is familiar enough not to require elaboration. In his Shakespeare speech of 1864, Turgenev claimed that the figure of Hamlet stood closer to the Russians than to the French or even to the English. Significantly, while still in his early twenties, Fontane chose in particular to translate Hamlet. Turgenev, in his well-known essay *Hamlet and Don Quixote* (1860) elaborates his dualistic theory of human typology in which Hamlet, the representative of analysis, egoism and unbelief, is contrasted with Don Quixote who stands for idealism, faith an moral strength. He there argues that these dual powers of inertia and movement, conservatism and progress, inherent in mankind, are the most significant forces in all being; that they can even offer the key to our understanding of both biological and human development.

These speculations merit attention less for any philosophical truth they may contain, than for the light they throw on the novelist's mode of perception and thought; for the perspective to be gained on the relationship of figure to idea. It seems to me a striking feature that Turgenev and Fontane both adopt a similarly pronounced bias in their treatment of the sexes, which in point of fact amounts to an inversion of their conventional roles. The repeated pattern shows the male figures as passive, more conformist, less determined and lacking in will, much more inclined to compromise and resignation. What stands out as a common weakness in the aristocratic characters Rudin, Lavretsky, Litvinov, Nezhdanov, is the effective loss of a sense of purpose; they are all given to brooding and aimless passivity, and in this they are inescapably products of their social conditioning. Character and the social whole are indissolubly linked. This is not just implicit in Turgenev's representation but forms part of the ongoing debate in Russia with that baneful brake on Russian progress, Oblomovism, most famously analysed by Dobrolyubov in his essay of 1859: "What is Oblomovshchina?"[13] The "consciously heroic natures", as Turgenev called them – Bazarov and Insarov – are deliberately drawn as atypical "outsiders" to the norm by virtue of character, class and culture, since they are conceived as models for radical social change. But these are the rare exceptions in his oeuvre, and their premature deaths also throw into doubt the whole question of the plausibility of their success. Turning to Turgenev's female counter-figures – Natalya, Lisa, Irina, Elena and Marianna – these are, though finely executed individual portraits, all more energetic, self-possessed, strong-minded women, than the men who enter their lives and whom they attempt to inspire. In Natalya, Elena and Marianna specifically, he has created figures who are prepared to risk all, to make personal sacrifices, to cast their past existences from them and move forward into an uncertain future, and they remain staunchly loyal to their feelings and convictions. Significantly Natalya's mother in

---

13 N. A. Dobrolyubov: Selected Philosophical Essays, translated by J. E. Fineberg. Moscow: Foreign Publishing House 1948, pp. 174-218.

Rudin jokingly calls her "mon honnête homme de fille".[14] Fontane's leading female figures can equally, and without distortion, be viewed in a parallel sequence of strong personalities, resilient even in defeat, possessing firmness of will and determination to effect change in their lives; to defy rather than to submit.

Melanie, Cécile and Effi variously rebel against the mendacity of a loveless match; the irrepressible Jenny Treibel emerges triumphant as the undefeated "Frau Bourgeoise", Christine remains loyal and stoic throughout her years of suffering, and Mathilde Möhring's final words "It'll come right" stand in testimony to her indomitable spirit.[15]

Yet the true issue is, how skilfully the novelist is able to convey and explore ideas through the figures he has created and how close he is to the pulse of the times. In Turgenev's *Sketches from a Huntsman's Album*, the work which first established his European reputation, the technique of deftly introducing critically slanted detail is already developed. The miniature portraits he offers in *Two Landowners* of Khvaynsky and Stepunov are sharply observed assessments of personality in its visible and also invisible facets, which tread a fine line between objectivity and satire:

> He is a most kindly man yet with some rather strange notions and habits. For example, he can never treat impoverished noblemen or those without standing as his equals. Conversing with them, he usually looks at them sideways, propping his cheek firmly against his stiff white collar, and then suddenly fixes them with a sharp, unwavering stare, stops talking and starts twitching the skin over his whole scalp […]
>
> He is a terrible fuss-pot and a miser but a dreadful manager of his own affairs, having taken on as administrator of his estate a retired sergeant-major, a Little Russian, who is an unusually stupid man.[16]

The personal idiosyncrasies are to be read as signs of managerial ineptitude and social stagnancy; instead of strictness of system we have arbitrariness and chaos. The rotund, genial Stepunov with his five hundred serfs, is contrasted in physical terms but his opulence shows every sign of waste and neglect. His domestic interior is the objective correlative of Russia's social and political ills:

> Mardary Appollonych lives completely in the old style. Even his house is of antiquated construction: in the hall, as one would expect, it smells of kvas, tallow candles and leather; on the right stands a sideboard filled with pipes and hand-towels; in the dining room are the family portraits, flies, a large tub of geraniums and some ramshackle pianos; in the drawing room there are three sofas, three tables, two mirrors and a wheezy clock of blackened enamel with bronze fretted hands; the study contains a table piled high with papers, a screen of a bluish colour plastered with pictures cut from various works of the last century, cupboards filled with stinking

---

14 Ivan Turgenev: Rudin. In: Polnoye Sobranie Sitchinenii I Pisem, VI, p. 280.

15 "Es wird schon." Fontane: Mathilde Möhring, NFA, VI, 309.

16 Ivan Turgenev: Two Landowners. In: Polnoye Sobranie Sotchinenii i Pisem v 28 Tomakh. Leningrad: Izdatel'stvo Nauka 1960 ff., IV, p. 176.

tomes, spiders and black dust, a stuffed armchair, and an Italian window as well as a door leading to the garden which was nailed fast ... in a word, everything as it should be.[17]

Though the state of the study may not appear unusual to academics, the all-over picture is full of clear pointers that the management of this large estate is not in the best of hands. Stepunov creates a torpor of apathy among his guests "thanks to the stupefying properties of Russian cookery", and allows his affairs to be run by an aged bailiff picked from his peasants. This is also to be read as a political metaphor. The sentence "But we still have a good few such landowners in Russia" is cunningly slipped into this passage almost in passing; yet it encapsulates the true heart of the matter. This subversive undercurrent of social criticism is to be found in varying degrees of explicitness throughout the collection of sketches. They stop short of forthright satire in the manner of Gogol or Saltykov-Shchedrin, but most sketches like *Khor and Kalinych* or *Bailiff* leave the reader in no doubt as to the abuse and neglect of authority or the absence of freedoms under the prevailing system of serfdom. The submerged sophistry of the narrator's point of vantage may be seen to break cover when he allows the landowner Radilov to say, "all's for the best in the best of all possible worlds", in total innocence of the satirical purport of Voltaire's dictum.

The novel in which Fontane most fully engages in satirical treatment of contemporary society is *Frau Jenny Treibel* (*Jenny Treibel*), and in this he could scarcely help himself in view of his ardent contempt for the bourgeois. "I hate all that is bourgeois as passionately as if I were a fully signed-up Social Democrat", he wrote during his work on the novel.[18] His novelistic treatment does not, however, measure up to the passion privately expressed. Unlike a Thomas Love Peacock or a Samuel Butler, who espouse the genre consummately, moulding the novel form to their satirical purpose and adopting a manner and tone which carry the critical message surely to its target, Fontane retains the aloof and objective narrative voice of the realist; yet one which cannot quite contain its vitriolic irony. The brash optimism of nineteenth-century materialism is amply exposed in the avid social climber Jenny (née Bürstenbinder), sprung "from a humble fruiterer's shop in the Spreegasse"[19] and ascended into the luxury of Kommerzienrat Treibel's villa. Though she surrounds herself with the ostentatious trappings of wealth and status, (which include the obligatory Maltese spaniel, two impoverished titled ladies, and a tenor past his prime) she affects to retain "a heart for the poetic"[20] as sterling proof of her higher sense of values. The satire is concentrated particularly on this glaring disparity between the snobbishness that derives from wealth and the charade of pretended loyalty to immaterial, spiritual values. Fontane makes this charade transparent both through what we discover of the real, predictable Jenny through her former lover Schmidt, through accurately observed satirical touches (such as the uses of a tradesman's entrance,

---

17 Ivan Turgenev: Two Landowners. In: Polnoye Sobranie Sotchinenii i Pisem, IV, p. 180f.

18 "Ich hasse das Bourgeoishafte mit einer Leidenschaft, als ob ich ein eingeschworener Sozialdemokrat wäre." Fontane to Martha Fontane, 25 August 1891, HFA, IV, 4, 148.

19 "[…] aus einem Obstkeller in der Spreegasse." Fontane: Frau Jenny Treibel, NFA, VII, 8.

20 "[…] das Herz für das Poetische." Fontane: Frau Jenny Treibel, NFA, VII, 11.

ceremonial music-making, Jenny's "obligatory tear", or the air cushion under her seat, designed to raise her above her guests) and then especially through her own affected, would-be sentimental posturing:

> My mother, and I thank her in her grave for it, was always for the better classes. And that's what every mother should be, for it's decisive for our pathway in life. All that's low and vulgar can't reach us then and remains behind.[21]

The sustained make-believe uncovered in this portrayal, especially in Chapter 10 where Schmidt and Jenny discourse on the illusoriness of happiness, consists in exposing the spoken word to critical doubt and allowing that doubt to persist as irony. The hypocrisy pilloried in Jenny is most pointedly tested in relation to the verses Schmidt composed for her in her youth and which he now casually dismisses as "a heavenly trifle".[22] This clichéd parody of itself is cherished by Jenny as her "Lebenslied", since for her it expresses the essence of her ideals. Schmidt's more sober verdict on Jenny as this "type of a bourgeoise"[23] carries fuller weight of conviction: "gold is trumps, and that's about it".[24] The obliqueness of Fontane's satirical approach produces a wealth of nuances (too numerous to do justice to here) which result in that diverse, differentiated image of the chosen sector of society which firmly establish its credentials as social realism.

Turgenev's technique of satirical narration differs from Fontane's principally by virtue of its forthrightness. His is much more in line with Gogol's full-blooded approach, as one which relentlessly exposes to ridicule and does not stop short of caricature. The opening pages of *Smoke* which depict the aristocratic Russian visitors in pursuit of pleasure in Baden-Baden, are distinguished by their undisguised acidic tone of mockery and disdain:

> By the Russian tree – à l'Arbre Russe – there habitually gathered our endearing fellow-countrymen and women; they approached in their splendour, nonchalant, elegant, greeted one another grandly, with familiarity and charm as befits beings who stand on the very summit of education; but having come together and sat down, they simply did not know what to say to one another ... [25]

A whole gallery of grotesques, flaunting themselves and posing, each qualified by a few cutting comments, run the gauntlet of the author's castigation. Turgenev the Westerner is all too clearly engaging in that ever vital polemic against the self-important ambassadors of Russian civilisation who parade their petty nationalism abroad. It was over this issue that the rift with the Slavophile Dostoevsky originated.

---

21 " Meine Mutter, wofür ich ihr noch im Grabe danke, war immer für die besseren Klassen. Und das sollte jede Mutter, denn es ist bestimmend für unseren Lebensweg. Das Niedere kann dann nicht heran und bleibt hinter uns zurück. " Fontane: Frau Jenny Treibel, NFA, VII, 26.

22 "eine himmlische Trivialität" Fontane: Frau Jenny Treibel, NFA, VII, 71.

23 "Typus einer Bourgeoise" Fontane: Frau Jenny Treibel, NFA, VII, 70.

24 "Gold ist Trumpf und weiter nichts". Fontane: Frau Jenny Treibel, NFA, VII, 71.

25 Ivan Turgenev: Smoke. In: Polnoye Sobranie Sotchinenii i Pisem, IX, p. 144.

Turgenev had touched a sensitive nerve with this topical subject and the swift reflex this provoked said something about his unerring eye. The satire in *Smoke* is not consistent but intermittent, the love interest involving the lethargic Russian male who wavers between two women gradually taking centre stage. And again a contrast between the two novelists may be noted: to set Litvinov's agonising and indecision in matters of the heart beside Woldemar Stechlin's tolerable quandary in choosing between Melusine and Armgard, is to appreciate Fontane's more dispassionate and lighter touch. The Russian novelist delves into the passions; the German favours ironic distancing. One can, however, discover some telling parallels in socially critical writing between the two late novels. In Chapter 10 of *Smoke*, where the young Russian generals are described in their display of self-importance, the author's accompanying comments are biting:

> Litvinov found himself on a picnic with the young generals, personages of the highest social circles and of considerable importance. Their importance was expressed in all things: in their measured familiarity, in their graciously magisterial smiles, in the strained distraction of their glances, their effeminate twitching of the shoulders, their swaying posture and flexing of knees; it was expressed in the very tone of voice, as though thanking a crowd of subordinates courteously yet with an air of disgust. All these warriors were superbly washed, shaven, and thoroughly perfumed with some truly gentrified fragrance of the Guards, with a mixture of the choicest cigar smoke and the most exquisite patchouli. Their hands were all gentrified, white, large, with strong nails as though of ivory; their whiskers were all glossy, their teeth gleamed, and the delicate skin cast a flush over their cheeks, and a delicate blue upon their chins. Several of the young generals were playful, others were pensive; but all bore the stamp of excellence and propriety. Each, it appeared, was profoundly conscious of his own worth, of the importance of his future role in the state, and bore himself both correctly and easily, with a slight touch of that abandon, that "may the devil take me" which so naturally arises during trips abroad. [26]

Fontane's comparable portrayal of the idle Junkers during the local elections in Chapter 19 of *Der Stechlin* (*The Stechlin*) tends rather towards humorous ridicule, but ridicule nonetheless:

> Those who were sitting there and out of sheer boredom debating the merits of Allasch and Chartreuse were Messrs. von Molchow, von Krangen and von Gnewkow, and in addition Baron Beetz and one Baron von der Nonne, whom nature appeared to have fashioned with special regard to his name. He sported a high black cravat, upon which squatted his decrepit little head, and when he spoke it sounded like the whistling of mice. He was the comic figure of the circle and was goaded and teased but did not take it amiss, since his mother was a Silesian countess whose name ended in '-inski'; a fact which to his mind secured him such a great advantage that he was at any time prepared, like Frederick the Great, "to let the occasional caricature be hung lower for all to see".[27]

---

26 Turgenev: Smoke. In: Polnoye Sobranie Sotchinenii i Pisem, IX, p. 198.

27 "Die da saßen und aus purer Langeweile sich über die Vorzüge von Allasch und Chartreuse stritten, waren die Herren von Molchow, von Krangen und von Gnewkow, dazu Baron Beetz und ein Freiherr von der Nonne, den die Natur mit besonderer Rücksicht auf seinen Namen geformt zu haben schien. Er trug eine hohe, schwarze Krawatte, drauf ein kleiner vermickerter Kopf saß, und wenn er sprach,

Both works are *Zeitromane* in the fullest sense, in that they not only embrace a wealth of contemporary reference, consisting of tell-tale physical detail as well as topical intellectual content sufficient to give them status akin to social histories; but more importantly, they enter into a purposeful discourse with the world depicted. A small but significant part of that discourse is satirical; for the rest Fontane especially resorts to certain finer, oblique forms of reference which challenge the reader to uncover their meaning. In Turgenev's novels the discourse is conducted at an altogether more overt level, as characters debate ideas and the narrative voice is made more prominent.

A somewhat neglected aspect of Fontane's "two-tiered realism"[28] as it has been called, is highlighted by the centennial exhibition "Fontane and the Fine Arts" which was mounted in Berlin and subsequently in Munich.[29] The great importance of the visual arts as one further aid to our understanding of his particular mode of realism was there persuasively portrayed and commentated. It seems evident that the qualities he admired in the Pre-Raphaelites, ("the poetic painters of reality" as they have been called)[30] showed recognition of that combination of Realism and Ideality which he perceived to be their major achievement. The subtle ambiguities of this "non-explicit realism full of ambivalent poetry"[31] with its abundance of allegorical and symbolic sign language, are still actively being explored by scholarship. Moritz Wullen, who speaks of "this pictorial tendency of visual processes ever again brought into play by Fontane", sees it as a pervasive feature not just of the novels, but of his correspondence and diaries also.[32] Fontane notably looked back to Hogarth as the father of modern English painting and as begetter of that abundant realism which consisted in "transparency of composition coupled with infinite fullness of detail",[33] and he derived many fertile insights from his early years as art critic which later entered into his writing.

The tendency to create *tableaux vivants* at significant points of a narrative is an individual feature of Fontane's quasi-painterly technique. These meaningful "stills", though unobtrusive as part of description, are nonetheless carefully gauged compositions serving a narrative function. There is, for example, the poignant scene in

---

war es, wie wenn Mäuse pfeifen. Er war die komische Figur des Kreises und wurde gehänselt, nahm es aber nicht übel, weil seine Mutter eine schlesische Gräfin auf '-inski' war, was ihm in seinen Augen ein solches Übergewicht sicherte, daß er, wie Friedrich der Große, jeden Augenblick bereit war, "die sich etwa einstellenden Pasquille niedriger hängen zu lassen." Fontane: Der Stechlin, NFA, VIII, 171.

28 The phrase "doppelbödigen Realismus" is employed by Peter-Klaus Schuster in his revealing essay Die Kunst bei Fontane. In: Fontane und die bildende Kunst, ed. by Claude Keisch, Peter-Klaus Schuster and Moritz Wullen. Berlin: Henschel 1998, p. 19.

29 "Fontane und die bildende Kunst".

30 "[…]"die dichterischen Maler der Wirklichkeit." Peter-Klaus Schuster: Die Kunst bei Fontane, p.19.

31 "[…] nicht eindeutigen Realismus voll vieldeutiger Poesie" Peter-Klaus Schuster: Die Kunst bei Fontane, p. 19.

32 "Diese von Fontane immer wieder beschworene Bildtendenz visueller Prozesse […]" Moritz Wullen. In: Fontane und die bildende Kunst, p. 260.

33 "Durchsichtigkeit der Komposition bei endloser Fülle von Details. Peter-Klaus Schuster, Die Kunst bei Fontane, p. 14.

Chapter 16 of *Irrungen, Wirrungen* (*Delusions, Confusions*) where Lene, close to swooning on unexpectedly seeing Botho with his new wife, sinks down on some veranda steps and is intently observed from the flower beds by "a half-grown girl" and also by "an aged nurse" from the veranda; three generations of womankind are brought together in this moment of personal anguish: "and it was almost as if the first notion of life's pain had dawned in the heart of the child".[34] Then the "picture" with which Chapter 2 of *Effi Briest* closes, shows us an open window symbolically over-shadowed "by virginia creeper"; a nervous, trembling Effi stands by the stiff formal figure of Innstetten, to whom she has just become engaged, while the two carefree young girls call her back to childhood games from the garden: "Effi, come".[35] Other illustrations of this technique may be found in Chapters 13 and 14 of *Irrungen, Wirrungen* in set pieces such as that showing the maid kneeling as she cleans her pots and pans and interpreted by Lene as a sign to her; or the idyllic scene where Botho observes workers and their wives happily sharing a lunch break and summarised by him in the words "labour and daily bread and order". There is more than a touch of Victorian genre painting in these and many another significantly composed scene in Fontane where image and idea are seen to interact. To such must be added his deliberate and subtle use of the traditional language of flowers. Just the name of "Effi", playfully linked by her father to "Efeu" (ivy), which signifies fidelity, and the aloes (grief) growing in front of the house, function as anticipatory motifs. Fontane is thus inclined to hint at meanings much in the manner of Pre-Raphaelite painters like Millais, Hunt and Rossetti. Turgenev too, occasionally but more sparingly, employs the emblematic meaning of flowers such as the heliotrope (signifying devotion and faithfulness in *Smoke*, Chapters 6 and 8) first sent to Litvinov by Irina as a token, later presented by him as a sign to her of his unaltered feelings.

An important distinction between Turgenev and Fontane as novelists is that in the Russian a recognisable world view clearly informs and remains apparent in his writing. His six novels are *Zeitromane* with a pronounced polemical tendency which did more than mirror the times; they instigated intellectual debate by the boldness of their challenge. The *Sketches from a Huntsman's Album* even helped to bring about social change in furthering the cause of the liberation of the serfs. In Fontane's art the personality of the writer is to a greater extent withdrawn and his personal conviction held in reserve. It has been said that "Turgenev's entire philosophy of history is contained in Solomin's conversation with Marianna about work".[36] In tsarist Russia, literature as a whole, and the novel in particular, largely took the place of a Parliament as the chief debating chamber of a liberal intelligentsia who sought solutions to Russia's ills. Turgenev's search for the Russian hero, the tribune of the people who could break with the past and help build a just and free society, produced that

---

34 "[…] und es war fast, wie wenn in dem Kinderherzen eine erste Vorstellung von dem Leid des Lebens gedämmert hatte. " Fontane: Irrungen, Wirrungen, NFA, III, 181.

35 "Effi komm.", Fontane: Effi Briest, NFA, VII, 181.

36 Thomas Garrigue Masaryk: The Spirit of Russia, transl. by Robert Bass. London: George Allen and Unwin 1967, p. 269.

prominent series of portraits from Rudin to Nezhdanov in which contemporary society at once recognised facets of itself. Yet since it was part of Turgenev's natural disposition, as well as a feature of his realism, to include the paradoxical and the pessimistic in his portraiture, these figures gave rise to a host of contrary reactions and interpretations. The figure of Bazarov in particular offended both the younger generation and displeased the older revolutionary democrats. Fontane's much more reserved stance is made present in his uniquely subtle manipulation of conversation. He developed into a fine art the technique of disguising his major themes in minor detail and in seemingly desultory dialogue. In the middle of a relaxed conversation in *Frau Jenny Treibel* about the relative importance of historical event, Distelkamp says to his friend Schmidt:

> "You were always for the anecdotal, for the genre-like. For me what matters in history is only what is great, not the petty, the peripheral."
> "Yes and no, Distelkamp. The peripheral is of no value, that's true. If it is only peripheral, if it has nothing to offer. But if it does have something to offer, then it's the very core, for then it always shows one the essentially human issue."[37]

Little can more fittingly convey the essence of Fontane's realism than these words.

---

37 "'[…] Du warst immer fürs Anekdotische, fürs Genrehafte. Mir gilt in der Geschichte nur das Große, nicht das Kleine, das Nebensächliche.'
'Ja und nein Distelkamp. Das Nebensächliche, so viel ist richtig, gilt nichts, wenn es bloß nebensächlich ist, wenn nichts drinsteckt. Steckt aber was drin, dann ist es die Hauptsache, denn es gibt einen dann immer das eigentlich Menschliche.'" Fontane: Frau Jenny Treibel, NFA, VII, 62.

Godela Weiss-Sussex

Fontane's and Georg Hermann's Berlin:
Relationships with Contemporary Berlin Painting

This paper is concerned with the relationship between Fontane's work and that of Georg Hermann. The German-Jewish writer Georg Hermann was born in Berlin in 1871 and died in Auschwitz in 1943. In the first decades of the twentieth century, his novels were much read, translated into many languages and reprinted many times. Banned under the National Socialist regime, his work was subsequently neglected by readers and Germanists for a long time. However, since the mid-1980s, attention has begun to turn to Hermann as a writer standing on the threshold between tradition and modernity.[1]

Hermann has often been described as a writer in Fontane's tradition, especially in regard to the Realist narrative structures of his novels.[2] Like Fontane, Hermann was deeply rooted in Berlin and he devoted many of his novels to the literary portrayal of the city and its inhabitants. This paper examines to what extent the evaluation of Hermann as a pupil of Fontane's can be verified in the specific context of the representation of Berlin. Analogies between the representations of Berlin in the two novelists' works and those in contemporary painting will be used to support the argument. This approach is particularly appropriate, as both Fontane and Hermann had worked as art critics before they found success as novelists and thus they were certainly aware of the aesthetics of city representation in the visual arts. Furthermore, depictions of localities in both their works have been characterised by literary critics as strikingly close to those in painting.[3] With the help of analogies between Hermann's

---

1 See Hans-Otto Horch: Über Georg Hermann. Plädoyer zur Wiederentdeckung eines bedeutenden deutsch-jüdischen Schriftstellers. In: Bulletin des Leo Baeck Instituts, 77 (1987), pp. 73-95; Gert and Gundel Mattenklott: Georg Hermann - ein Porträt. In: Georg Hermann. Werke und Briefe in 21 Bänden. Ankündigung, publisher's prospectus, Berlin: Das Neue Berlin 1996, pp. 10-21.

2 See for example Peter Härtling: Ein verlassener Held. Über Georg Hermanns *Kubinke*. In: Härtling: Zwischen Untergang und Aufbruch. Aufsätze, Reden, Gespräche, ed. by Günther Drommer. Berlin, Weimar: Aufbau 1990, pp. 131-135; Cornelis Geeraard van Liere: Georg Hermann. Materialien zur Kenntnis seines Lebens und seines Werkes, Dissertation, University of Leiden. Amsterdam: Rodopi 1974.

3 For Fontane, see Wilfried Richter: Das Bild Berlins nach 1870 in den Romanen Theodor Fontanes, unpublished dissertation, Freie Universität Berlin 1955; Hubert Ohl: Bild und Wirklichkeit. Studien zur Romankunst Raabes und Fontanes, Heidelberg: Stiehm 1968. For specific reference to Fontane's Berlin depictions, see Charlotte Jolles: Weltstadt – verlorene Nachbarschaft. Berlin-Bilder Raabes und Fontanes. In: Jahrbuch der Raabe-Gesellschaft, (1988), pp. 52-75. For Hermann, see Peter Härtling: Nachwort. In Hermann: Kubinke. Frankfurt a. M.: Fischer 1974, pp. 289-294; Siegfried Jacobsohn: Alt-Berlin. In: Die Schaubühne, 11 (1915), p. 515f.; Hans Kohn: Der Roman des Entwurzelten. Georg Hermann: *Die Nacht des Doktor Herzfeld* . In: Juden in der

and Fontane's representations of Berlin and those in contemporary painting, the basic aesthetic principles of the novelists' representations will be determined.[4] The legitimacy of this approach is supported by Fontane himself, who postulated in the literary sketch *Hans und Grete* of 1884, "The same laws apply to the narrative arts as to the visual arts and there is no difference between representation in words and in paint".[5]

Turning first to one of Fontane's depictions of the city:

> Duty at the barracks was over at twelve, and Botho von Rienäcker strolled down the Unter den Linden towards the Brandenburg Gate, merely intending to fill the hour until his appointment at Hiller's as well as possible.[6]

After making the reader part of Botho's ruminations on the Achenbach brothers' paintings, some of which are displayed in a shop window, Fontane continues:

> Lost in such reflections, he stood a while in front of Lepke's window. Then crossing the Pariser Platz he proceeded toward the Gate and the Tiergartenallee, which ran diagonally to the left, until he came to a stop in front of Wolff's *Lion Group*.[7]

It is striking in this passage how concerned Fontane is with the precise description of route, a detail that is quite irrelevant to an understanding of the novel. The route taken by Botho can be followed with great exactness on the city map. Any evocation, however, of the atmosphere of the scene, the traffic, the noise, the other passers-by, is omitted. This emphasis suggests a comparison with Berlin paintings of the 1830s and

---

deutschen Literatur. Essays über zeitgenössische Schriftsteller, ed. by Gustav Krojanker. Berlin: Welt 1922, pp. 27-40.

4   I thereby follow Ulrich Weisstein's theoretical framework, as most recently summarised in his introduction to Literatur und bildende Kunst. Ein Handbuch zur Theorie und Praxis eines komparatistischen Grenzgebietes, ed. by Ulrich Weisstein, Berlin: E. Schmidt 1992, pp.11-31, 'Einleitung. Literatur und bildende Kunst: Geschichte, Systematik, Methoden'. Among a number of potentially fruitful types of analysis, Weisstein includes that of "literary works seeking to reproduce movement styles in the visual arts." This category of analysis looks at the "transliteration" of a complex movement style and is based on, but goes beyond, merely looking at the transfer of particular techniques from the visual arts into literature.

5   "Es gelten für die erzählende Kunst dieselben Gesetze wie für die bildende Kunst und zwischen der Darstellung in Worten und in Farben ist kein Unterschied." Theodor Fontane: Hans und Grete, NFA, XXIV, 298. Unless otherwise indicated, translations into English are my own.

6   "Um zwölf war der Dienst in der Kaserne getan, und Botho von Rienäcker ging die Linden hinunter aufs Tor zu, lediglich in der Absicht, die Stunde bis zum Rendezvous bei Hiller, so gut sich's tun ließ, auszufüllen." Theodor Fontane, Irrungen, Wirrungen, NFA, III, 122f. The English quotation is taken from Theodor Fontane: Delusions, Confusions and The Poggenpuhl Family, ed. by Peter Demetz; Foreword by J. P. Stern; with an Introduction by William L. Zwiebel, The German Library, vol. 47. New York: Continuum 1984, p. 36. Delusions, Confusions is translated by Zwiebel; The Poggenpuhl Family is translated by Gabriele Annan.

7   "Unter solchen Betrachtungen stand er eine Zeitlang vor dem Lepkeschen Schaufenster und ging dann, über den Pariser Platz hin, auf das Tor und die schräg links führende Tiergartenallee zu, bis er vor der Wolfschen Löwengruppe Halt machte." Fontane: Irrungen, Wirrungen, NFA, III, 123; Zwiebel: Fontane: Delusions, Confusions, p. 36.

40s by artists such as Wilhelm Brücke and Eduard Gaertner, who produced detailed and panoramic representations of the city's architecture and topography.[8] In the catalogue for the exhibition "Fontane und die bildende Kunst", staged in autumn 1998 in Berlin, Peter-Klaus Schuster expresses surprise that Gaertner's paintings of the city receive no mention in Fontane's works.[9] He finds this all the more striking as the dust jackets of recent critical literature on Fontane have repeatedly displayed pictures of Berlin from the 1830s and 40s. Considering the importance of the references to topographical reality in both Fontane's and Gaertner's work, Schuster certainly has a point here.

However, the differences between Fontane's depictions of the city and those by the city painters of the 1830s and 40s should not be overlooked. The latter were mostly commissioned by the Prussian King and thus concentrated on the depiction of representative official buildings, squares and avenues in the centre of Berlin. From the description of Botho's route quoted above, by contrast, it is clear that Fontane is not interested in the representation of the Berlin city centre for its own sake. Rather, the exactness of his description serves to anchor the fictional world of the novel in reality. It is sufficient for this purpose to refer to certain points of orientation within the co-ordinate system of the city (Linden, Hiller, Lepke, Pariser Platz), without describing these in any further detail. Fontane uses the depiction of the city to support the characterisation of his protagonists or to indicate particular social constellations in his novels. In the case of *Irrungen, Wirrungen* (*Delusions, Confusions*), the co-ordinates mentioned in the excerpt above define Botho's world: the world of the aristocracy, of the higher ranks of the military, of the centre of the Prussian capital. This social world stands in contrast to the suburban environment that his sweetheart Lene inhabits in Wilmersdorf on the outskirts of Berlin.[10]

Furthermore, the description of the boulevard Unter den Linden is a rather rare exception in Fontane's work. He is usually less interested in the central public areas of the capital than in the spheres of life that his protagonists inhabit as private individuals. His depictions of the Invalidenstraße (*Stine*), the Georgenstraße (*Mathilde Möhring*) or the Kronprinzenufer (*Der Stechlin* (*The Stechlin*)) are all cases in point. In this regard Fontane's view of Berlin is close to that of Adolph Menzel's. Both have depicted Berlin as a living environment away from the imposing facades of the city

---

8 For further information on Brücke and Gaertner, see Sybille Gramlich: Königliches Spree-Athen. Berlin im Biedermeier. In: Stadtbilder. Berlin in der Malerei vom 17. Jahrhundert bis zur Gegenwart, exhibition catalogue, Berlin Museum. Berlin: Nicolai 1987, pp. 95-172; Irmgard Wirth: Eduard Gaertner. Der Berliner Architekturmaler. Frankfurt a. M., Berlin, Vienna: Propyläen 1979.

9 Peter-Klaus Schuster: Die Kunst bei Fontane. In: Fontane und die bildende Kunst, exhibition catalogue, Staatliche Museen zu Berlin, Nationalgalerie, ed. by Claude Keisch, Peter-Klaus Schuster and Moritz Wullen. Berlin: Henschel 1998, p. 22f.

10 For the function of the social definition of locations, see Peter Demetz: Formen des Realismus: Theodor Fontane. Munich: Hanser 1964; Marilyn S. Fries: The Changing Consciousness of Reality. The Image of Berlin in Selected German Novels from Raabe to Döblin. Bonn: Bouvier 1980.

centre. Both have shown an interest in the detail of everyday life. In *Irrungen, Wirrungen*, for instance, Fontane describes what he calls a "peculiar sort of suburban activity":[11]

> On one of these paths all sorts of sheds could be seen, between which stood scaffolds, seemingly intended for gymnasts. Botho's curiosity was awakened. Before he could ask what it really was, however, the activity in the distance answered his question. Across the scaffoldings, rugs and carpets were spread and in that instant such a knocking and beating with large cane paddles started up that the path soon lay hidden in a cloud of dust. [12]

In terms of its subject matter, this description is reminiscent of paintings by Menzel, especially those of his earlier years. In *Hinterhof und Haus* (1844) (Illustration 1), for instance, building materials, bushes and a water pump are depicted on an otherwise empty plot of land. The centre of the composition remains vacant. Other paintings by Menzel, especially from the 1840s, indicate by their titles the unspectacular nature of their subjects: rear buildings in *Hinterhäuser* and *Hinterhäuser im Schnee* (both 1847) and a building plot in *Bauplatz mit Weiden* (1846). In *Stadtbahn Berlin-Potsdam* (Berlin-Potsdam railway) (1847) (Illustration 2), the area on the city's edge was for the first time used as a subject in Berlin painting.

It is not only the choice of subject that links Fontane and Menzel.[13] They also share an understanding of Realism as an aesthetic that aims to concentrate and poeticise ("verklären") reality, without abandoning its close and detailed representation.[14] *Stadtbahn Berlin-Potsdam*, the first of Menzel's works bought by the National Gallery in Berlin, in 1899, illustrates this Realist aesthetic. Menzel shows the area for what it was – fallow land at the edge of Berlin, building land for the future development of the city. But the picture is dominated by the dynamism of the railway line. This

---

11 "[…]ein eigentümliches Vorstadtleben". Fontane: Irrungen, Wirrungen, NFA, III, 134; Zwiebel: Fontane: Delusions, Confusions, p.50.

12 "An dem einen dieser Wege befanden sich allerlei Schuppen, zwischen denen reckartige, wie für Turner bestimmte Gerüste standen und Bothos Neugier weckten; aber ehe er noch erkunden konnte, was es denn eigentlich sei, gab ihm das Tun drüben auch schon Antwort auf seine Frage: Decken und Teppiche wurden über die Gerüste hin ausgebreitet, und gleich danach begann ein Klopfen und Schlagen mit großen Rohrstöcken, so daß der Weg drüben alsbald in einer Staubwolke lag." Fontane: Irrungen, Wirrungen, NFA, III, 134; Zwiebel: Fontane: Delusions, Confusions, p. 50.

13 For further analysis of analogies between Menzel's and Fontane's work, see Kurt Ihlenfeld: Kameraden der Realität. In: Neue deutsche Hefte, 16 (1969), pp. 108-126; Donald C. Riechel: Theodor Fontane and the Fine Arts: A Survey and Evaluation. In: German Studies Review, 7 (1984), pp. 39-64 and Claude Keisch: "Ja, wer ist Menzel?" In: Fontane und die bildende Kunst, pp. 200-213.

14 The principle is clearly formulated by Fontane: "Darauf kommt es an, daß zwischen dem erlebten und erdichteten Leben kein Unterschied ist als der jener Intensität, Klarheit, Übersichtlichkeit, die die verklärende Aufgabe der Kunst ist."; "What matters is that there is no other difference between life lived and life described in fiction than that of the intensity, clarity, distinctness, which is the poeticising task of art." In: Theodor Fontane, Schriften zur Literatur, ed. by Hans-Heinrich Reuter, Berlin: Aufbau-Verlag 1960, p. 109.

composition concentrates and poeticises the view. The silhouette of Berlin in the background further contributes to the poeticisation of the scene, underlining the peripheral character of the location and drawing the observer's eye to the beauty in the distance.[15]

How does this principle of *Verklärung* (literally: "transfiguration") manifest itself in Fontane's depictions of the city? Firstly, city life is generally seen from a distance. Often, it is a view from a window, which enables the onlooker to enjoy the bustle of the Berlin streets without being engulfed in it. The uncle in *Die Poggenpuhls* (*The Poggenpuhl Family*) thus enjoys observing the busy streets around his residence in town, the Hotel Fürstenhof, while lounging at his window "with a sofa cushion under each elbow".[16] In several instances, Fontane uses a further technique to give his depictions of the city a dimension of *Verklärung*. In these cases, the city is not viewed directly, but through a filter which affects the vision. Widow Pittelkow looks at Invalidenstraße reflected in a window mirror and comments:

> When I look in the mirror and see all those people and horses in it, then it seems to me that it is different from seeing things with the naked eye. And it really is a little different. I think, the mirror makes everything smaller, and making things smaller is almost as good as making them prettier.[17]

In a similar way, Fontane compares the distant view of the city with seeing it via a *camera obscura*. Looking from the Bellevuestraße over to the Tiergarten, Botho observes how, "as if on the screen of a *camera obscura*, people and vehicles silently moved back and forth"[18], and comments with satisfaction, "How beautiful. Really, I

---

15 Especially in the comparison with J. M. W. Turner's *Rain, Steam and Speed*, a very different rendering of a similar subject matter, painted only three years before Menzel's *Stadtbahn Berlin – Potsdam*, the Realism of Menzel's depiction stands out. For further analysis of this painting, see Claude Keisch: Le Chemin de fer Berlin – Potsdam. In: Menzel 1815 – 1905. La névrose du vrai, exhibition catalogue, Musée d'Orsay. Paris: Éditions de la Réunion des musées nationaux 1996, pp. 211-214.

16 "[…] links und rechts ein Sofakissen unterm Arm". Fontane: Die Poggenpuhls, NFA IV, 316. The translation is Annan's, from Demetz (ed.): Fontane: Delusions, Confusions and The Poggenpuhl Family, p. 205.

17 "Wenn ich in den Spiegel kucke und all die Menschen und Pferde drin sehe, dann denk ich, es is doch woll anders als so mit bloßen Augen. Un ein bißchen anders is es auch. Ich glaube, der Spiegel verkleinert, und verkleinern is fast ebenso gut wie verhübschen." Fontane, Stine, NFA, III, 240. See Klaus Scherpe's interpretation of the window mirror as "[…] optischer Vermittler zwischen dem kleinbürgerlichen Interieur und Handlungsraum und der großstädtischen Außenwelt der Straßen-szene"; "[…] optical mediator between the petit bourgeois interior that is the setting of the novel's action and the metropolitan outer world of the street scene." In: Nonstop nach Nowhere City? Wandlungen der Symbolisierung, Wahrnehmung und Semiotik der Stadt in der Literatur der Moderne. In: Klaus Scherpe (ed.), Die Unwirklichkeit der Städte. Großstadtdarstellungen zwischen Moderne und Postmoderne, Reinbek: Rowohlt 1988, p. 139.

18 "wie auf einem Camera obscura-Glase, die Menschen und Fuhrwerke sich geräuschlos hin- und herbewegen"; "Wie schön. Es ist doch wohl eine der besten Welten." Fontane: Irrungen, Wirrungen, NFA, III, 122. Demetz (ed.): Fontane: Delusions, Confusions, p. 35.

suppose it probably is one of the best possible worlds". The city seen in the mirror and the comparison with the *camera obscura* correspond to a representation which contains a realistic reflection of the city environment, but at the same time concentrates the view and distances the reader from it. Concentration and poeticisation are the main functions of this kind of representation, which structures the observed reality and thus wards off the chaos of city life.

How far does Fontane go in taking up in his representations of Berlin the new aesthetic movements of the 1880s and 90s? Wolf J. Siedler claims that Fontane completely ignored contemporary developments. In his letter to Schuster, declining an invitation to contribute to the catalogue to the exhibition "Fontane und die bildende Kunst", Siedler claims:

> Of course it would be possible to offer some comments on Fontane and the art of his epoch, but in the end this would boil down to an embarrassed astonishment at the seclusion of the artist in his own world.[19]

Indeed, the accusatory social criticism of Naturalist art is absent from Fontane's writing, as it contradicts the principle of *Verklärung* which forms the basis of his concept of Realism. However, Siedler's rather sweeping judgement must be revised where the development of Impressionism is concerned. "Fontane was well aware of the triumphant advance of Impressionism in Berlin", as Schuster claims and proves in the exhibition catalogue.[20] In the context of this essay it is therefore interesting to investigate the influence of Impressionism in Fontane's depictions of the city.

In Berlin, the Impressionist aesthetics of the city were formulated in the 1890s. Heinrich Schackow's essay "Berolina. Eine Großstadt-Ästhetik", appeared in 1896 in the journal *Neue deutsche Rundschau*, and in 1908 August Endell published his treatise *Die Schönheit der großen Stadt*.[21] Both Schackow and Endell see the beauty of the city in its specifically modern aspects: in the rhythmical movement of crowds, in the incessant traffic and in the abstract forms of the industrial landscape. They emphasise the transfiguration of objective reality through light and, Endell especially, through the effect of veils produced by mist, fog, dust or even darkness. Fundamental to the Impressionist concept of the beauty of the city is a process of aestheticising abstraction in which beauty is created by the veiling of reality. This creates "a new world of wonders"[22] that can only be perceived by the onlooker who does not attempt

---

19 "Natürlich könnte man einige Bemerkungen über Fontane und die Kunst seiner Epoche machen, aber im Grunde würde das auf das verlegene Staunen über die Eingeschlossenheit des Künstlers in seine eigene Welt hinauslaufen." Wolf J. Siedler: Nachdenkliche Absage. In: Fontane und die bildende Kunst, p. 10.

20 "Fontane ist dieses Siegeszuges des Impressionismus in Berlin sehr wohl gewahr geworden." Schuster: Die Kunst bei Fontane, p. 23.

21 Heinrich Schackow: Berolina. Eine Großstadt-Ästhetik. In: Neue deutsche Rundschau, 7 (1896), pp. 386-390; August Endell: Die Schönheit der großen Stadt. In: August Endell, der Architekt des Photoateliers Elvira, exhibition catalogue Villa Stuck, Munich, ed. by Klaus J. Sembach et al.. Munich 1977, pp. 88-120.

22 "[...]eine neue Wunderwelt"; Endell: Die Schönheit der großen Stadt, p. 103.

to pierce the veil. Details disappear. What remains is the abstracting veil itself; the pure visual impression is primary, rather than the object that is seen.

To what extent does this new aesthetic find expression in Fontane's representations of Berlin? There are passages, especially in *Der Stechlin*, in which Fontane extols the beauty of the specifically modern aspects of the city. Comparing the location of the Berchtesgadens' dwellings in Lennéstraße to that of her own on Kronprinzenufer, Melusine praises the urban character of the latter:

> When I sit in our niche, with the long rows of approaching Stadtbahn[23] cars before me, not too close, but not too far either, and when I see how the evening twilight glows through the smoke of the locomotives and shimmers in the filigree trim of the little exhibition park tower, what can that wall of Tiergarten greenery of yours offer to match that?[24]

In a similar vein, when evoking the evening atmosphere on the excursion to the "Eierhäuschen", Fontane describes not the setting sun, but the faraway lights of the city and the multicoloured signals on the railway lines on the opposite bank of the river Spree.[25] He thus emphasises the functional, modern elements of the landscape. These elements are transfigured by the evening light and shown to have their own specific beauty.

With this kind of description, Fontane adopts motifs which are typical of the city paintings of the French Impressionists. Illuminated cityscapes by night and, as painted by Monet and Pissarro, railway stations have become symbols of the period. In the field of Berlin painting, Franz Skarbina's work is comparable. Especially in the two decades around the turn of the century, Skarbina painted a whole series of sensitively observed depictions of Berlin. *Gleisanlagen im Norden Berlins*, painted circa 1895, may serve as an example here. Depicted is a working-class couple, bent over with fatigue, on their way home from work. The background, however, draws away the observer's attention away from their suffering to revel in the sea of lights of the city, foremost of which are the railway signals. The beauty of this sight is created by the contrast of the electrical lights against the nocturnal darkness and is compounded by the veiling effect of the locomotives' steam.

Skarbina, a founding member of the "Gruppe der XI"[26] and, subsequently, of the "Secession"[27], is not only referred to in *Der Stechlin*, but the evocation of his art is

---

23 Berlin's elevated tramway. This annotation is William L. Zwiebel's in Fontane: The Stechlin, transl. with an introduction and notes by William L. Zwiebel, Columbia, SC: Camden House 1995, p. 89. All English translations are taken from this text.

24 "Wenn ich in unsrer Nische sitze, die lange Reihe der herankommenden Stadtbahnwaggons vor mir, nicht zu nah und nicht zu weit, und sehe dabei, wie das Abendrot den Lokomotivenrauch durchglüht und in dem Filigranwerk der Ausstellungsparktürmchen schimmert, was will Ihre grüne Tiergarten-wand dagegen? " Fontane: Der Stechlin, NFA, VIII, 101. Zwiebel: Fontane: The Stechlin, p. 89.

25 Fontane: Der Stechlin, NFA, VIII, 138f.; Zwiebel: Fontane: The Stechlin, p. 123f.

26 This association of Berlin artists, established on 5 February 1892 under the leadership of Max Liebermann and Walter Leistikow, was the first to oppose the official, academic and traditionalist, policy for the arts under Emperor Wilhelm II.

used by Fontane in the description of a city scene. Baroness Berchtesgaden reports on the Berlin city centre on a foggy day: " [...] at the Brandenburg Gate with those big chandeliers in between, it almost looked like a picture by Skarbina."[28] Specifically emphasising the motif of gas lights in the fog, Fontane may well have had paintings by Skarbina such as *Droschkenhalteplatz* (undated) (Illustration 3) in mind. In its emphasis on atmosphere, *Droschkenhalteplatz* clearly shows elements of the Impressionist aesthetics as formulated by Schackow and Endell. Skarbina captures a hazy cold winter's night in the city, illuminated by shop windows and street lights. Yet he does not subordinate his subject matter to the depiction of atmosphere and light and thus firmly remains within the representational tradition of Menzel. As another of Skarbina's nocturnal city pictures, *Café Bauer* (ca. 1893) (Illustration 4) shows more clearly *Droschkenhalteplatz*, delineation and detail maintain their importance next to the abstract play of light and haze. The detailed representation of reality remained Skarbina's foremost principle, even if he advanced the heightening of atmosphere by veiling his city views.[29]

How does this way of representing the city compare with Fontane's descriptions of Berlin? To what extent does Fontane incorporate the Impressionist principle of abandoning detail and instead veiling the view of the city? In *Der Stechlin*, the view from the river Spree towards the city in the distance is described as follows:

> The weather was splendid. Upstream all was clear and sunlit, while a thin haze lay over the city. They seated themselves on chairs and benches at both sides of the stern deck and from there looked back on the veiled outline of the city.[30]

Fontane does not go beyond this brief description of the scene, however, and most significantly, it is not the effect of the veiling mist that is stressed. On the contrary: what follows is an enumeration of the church spires that can be seen *through* the transfiguring and abstracting veil. The analogy of Fontane's depiction with Skarbina's, which is still on the threshold between Menzel's interest in detail and the Impressionist emphasis on the atmospheric influences of light and air, is thus more apt than the reference to Impressionist aesthetics as formulated by Schackow and Endell. Even

---

27 The "Secession" was founded on 2 May 1898, again on the initiative of Leistikow and with Liebermann as president. It followed the principles of the "Group of XI" to promote avant-garde art in Berlin, extended its membership and power and began to stage annual exhibitions.

28 "Am Brandenburger Tor, mit den großen Kandelabern dazwischen, sah es beinah aus wie ein Bild von Skarbina." Fontane: Der Stechlin, NFA, VIII, 211. Zwiebel: Fontane: The Stechlin, p. 190.

29 For a similar evaluation of Skarbina's art, see Margrit Bröhan: Franz Skarbina, exhibition catalogue Bröhan-Museum. Berlin: Ars Nicolai 1995.

30 "Das Wetter war prachtvoll, flußaufwärts alles klar und sonnig, während über der Stadt ein dünner Nebel lag. Zu beiden Seiten des Hinterdecks nahm man auf Stühlen und Bänken Platz und sah von hier aus auf das verschleierte Stadtbild zurück." Fontane: Der Stechlin, NFA, VIII, 126; Zwiebel: Fontane: The Stechlin, p. 112.

though Fontane uses Impressionist stylistic devices, his depictions of the city of Berlin remain focussed on the details of the view.[31]

Essential elements of the Impressionist city aesthetic, such as the experience of the *flâneur*, the enjoyment of drifting in the urban multitude, and the fleeting encounters that occur between city dwellers, are motifs that find no place in Fontane's writing. We can find in Fontane's novels an enjoyment of the city environment but, as described above, the enjoyment is that of the observer who is not directly involved in the bustle of city life, but rather remains detached and observes from a distance. Rather than describing them in detail, Fontane often merely refers to the tumult of busy street scenes in concentrated allusions such as "the bustle" or "the colorful commotion".[32] In the crowded cafés, that are often the end points of Fontane's protagonists' excursions into the Berlin environs, his characters often appear to be the only customers. Even the city streets often seem devoid of people. When Lene, for example, walking down Lützowstraße, spots Botho and Käthe coming towards her, there seems to be no one else on this busy road.[33]

In Fontane's novels, the depictions of the city environment derive their significance from their referential function, not as subjects in themselves. Hence, Fontane's city views typically take the form of concentrated sketches with a few references rather than a full description. The evocation of atmosphere is part of the rendering of this concentrated city depiction and as such is only hinted at rather than being developed in any depth.

How do the Berlin depictions in the novels of Georg Hermann compare to Fontane's? To what extent does Hermann take up the tradition established by Fontane in his representations of the city, and to what extent does he develop it further? Hermann's adoption of Fontane's brand of Realism is most obvious in his novel *Jettchen Gebert* (1906) set in Biedermeier Berlin. The opening paragraph of *Jettchen Gebert* establishes the time and location of the story:

---

31 Fontane's attitude to Impressionism is still a matter of scholarly debate. Referring to an essay by Fontane entitled "Über das Gemeinsame im Realismus und Idealismus der modernen Kunstbestrebung", NFA, XXIII/2, 171, Schuster claims that Fontane shows a positive attitude towards Impressionism (see Peter-Klaus Schuster: Theodor Fontane: Effi Briest – Ein Leben nach christlichen Bildern. Tübingen: Niemeyer 1978, p. 183f.. Riechel, however, points out that Fontane's "receptivity to the new in art" as expressed in this essay, "is an ethical endorsement" of an art form that "brings fresh perspectives and new understanding" (Riechel: Theodor Fontane and the Fine Arts, p. 56), rather than an aesthetic statement. " [...] one is bound to suspect", Riechel concludes with reference to Fontane's criticism of Turner's later works, "that wherever Impressionism tends toward fragmentation of the objective world, [...] Fontane would warn against a loss of *Zusammenhang*." (Riechel: Theodor Fontane and the Fine Arts, p. 61)

32 "das Treiben"; "das bunte Durcheinander"; Fontane: Irrungen, Wirrungen, NFA, III, 106; Zwiebel: Fontane: Delusions,Confusions, p. 103.

33 Fontane: Irrungen, Wirrungen, NFA, III, 106f.; Zwiebel: Fontane: Delusions, Confusions, p. 103.

> Hardly anyone will now be able to remember Jettchen Gebert walking along Königsstraße. Clouds of dust were blown by the wind from Alexanderplatz into Königsstraße; for it was the first really beautiful blue spring day of the year. Between the "dolls" of the "Königskolonnaden" up on the roof, between the busy stone figures, small white clouds were moving in the sky. In the Neue Friedrichstraße, in the gardens behind the wall, the trees were just emerging in red and brown; catkins were quivering on the poplars and dabs of blossom covered even the finest twigs of the elm trees.[34]

Hermann uses here the technique of a storyteller engaging his audience. By evoking a potentially common experience, Hermann creates a feeling of integration and identification. Like Fontane, Hermann sets exact geographical coordinates.[35] Street names and details of the city's architecture are mentioned but not described. Hermann's reference, for instance, to the "dolls" of the "Königskolonnaden" must remain enigmatic to the reader who is unfamiliar with Berlin. As in Fontane's novels, the reader's knowledge of the city is assumed. Whereas Fontane uses this knowledge to indicate the social status of his characters by their addresses,[36] Hermann uses it to engage the reader by a process of identification based on a common history.

Another example of the structural and functional similarities between Hermann's representations of the city and Fontane's will suffice. At one point in *Jettchen Gebert*, the "Scheunenviertel", one of the oldest parts of central Berlin, through which Jettchen and her suitor Kößling are walking, is described as follows:

> Outside their doors, men sat with their wives and children and looked out from the darkness of the narrow alleys over the roofs opposite, up into the bright, white spring sky. From each doorway came a different smell. Here, it smelt of freshly tanned leather, here of cotton bales, here it smelt of coffee and nutmeg and here of stables or cows. And many of the people, who sat there enjoying their evening after a day's work, greeted Jettchen [...].[37]

---

34 "Es kann sich wohl kaum noch einer erinnern, wie damals Jettchen Gebert die Königstrasse entlangging. Staubwolken blies der Wind vom Alexanderplatz in die Königstrasse hinein; denn es war so der erste wirklich schöne blaue Frühlingstag im Jahre. Gerade zwischen den Puppen der Königskolonnaden oben auf dem Dach, zwischen den hastig bewegten Steinfiguren, zogen am Himmel weiße Wölkchen hin. In der Neuen Friedrichstrasse, in den Gärten hinter der Mauer, wurden eben die Bäume rot und braun; Kätzchen pendelten an den Pappeln und Blütentupfen überzogen selbst die feinsten Ästchen der Ulmen." Georg Hermann: Jettchen Gebert. Reinbek: Rowohlt 1989, p. 7.

35 In the same way as Fontane's depictions of place are in many cases prepared by the geographical and historical study that went into his Wanderungen durch die Mark Brandenburg, Hermann's description of Biedermeier Berlin was prepared by detailed study of the period. His studies found expression in *Das Biedermeier im Spiegel seiner Zeit* (1913), an anthology introduced by a historical essay. In his anthology, Hermann collects extracts from a wide variety of historical and contemporary Biedermeier sources to collate a multi-faceted picture of the period.

36 See Demetz' description of Fontane's literary geography as "die 'Welt der richtigen Adresse'" Demetz: Formen des Realismus, p. 117.

37 "Neben den Türen saßen die Bürger mit Frauen und Kindern und sahen aus dem Dunkel der schmalen Gassen über die Dächer von drüben zu dem weißen, lichtstrahlenden Frühlingshimmel. Aus jedem Hausflur kamen andere Gerüche. Hier von frisch gegerbtem Leder und hier von

The depiction of the city is used, as in Fontane's novels, to characterise the protagonists through their social environment. Note that it is only Jettchen who is greeted. Kößling, by contrast, clearly a stranger here, is merely stared at. Hermann emphasises the down-to-earth native Berliner Jettchen's sense of belonging in this idyll of old town Berlin, and contrasts this with the foreignness of Kößling, the intellectual from provincial Brunswick.

This depiction also illustrates how Hermann shares not only Fontane's interest in the living environment of the ordinary city dweller but also the precision of his observations. As in Fontane's novels, the realistic description of specific city views is combined with the poeticisation of the scene. Both authors at times transform city views into idylls, while at the same time exposing the process and thereby questioning the idyll. Fontane shows this "ambivalent empiricism" (Demetz's term) in the first two chapters of *Irrungen, Wirrungen*, in which he describes the Dörr's nursery first in poetic and then in prosaic terms.[38] Hermann uses the same strategy of building up and then questioning an idyll both in the depiction of Old Berlin in *Jettchen Gebert*[39] and in that of the Kurfürstendamm in *Die Nacht des Doktor Herzfeld*. The passage from *Jettchen Gebert* quoted above also shows, however, that with his careful description of the sensual impressions left by the scene, Hermann clearly goes beyond Fontane. Apart from the contrast of darkness and light between the alleyways and the sky above, the mixture of different smells, which characterises this part of town, is evoked.

A comparison with Adolph Menzel's paintings is again instructive at this point. Hermann's interest in everyday life and the eye for detail inherent in his realistic depictions are again reminiscent of Menzel's Berlin paintings. The painter Max Liebermann also noticed this similarity. He commented on another of Hermann's novels, *Grenadier Wordelmann* (1930), thus: "This is a Menzel".[40] I have already noted that Fontane also shares this interest in realistic detail and in portraying daily life. However, the stress on the atmospheric that is clearly visible in Menzel's early paintings and gouaches of Berlin scenes, is a concern that the painter shares more obviously with Hermann than with Fontane.

Kattunballen, hier roch es nach Kaffee und Muskat und hier nach Pferdeställen oder Kühen. Und viele der Leute, die da ihre Feierstunde hielten, grüßten Jettchen [...]". Hermann: Jettchen Gebert, p. 117.

38 For an interpretation of *Irrungen, Wirrungen* in this context, see Karl-Gert Kribben: Großstadt- und Vorstadtschauplätze in Theodor Fontane's Roman *Irrungen, Wirrungen*. In: Studien zur deutschen Literatur. Festschrift für Adolf Beck zum 70. Geburtstag. Heidelberg: Winter 1979, pp. 225-244.

39 See Godela Weiss-Sussex, Ein "kleinstädtisches Großstadtsujet"? Zur Darstellung Berlins in *Jettchen Gebert*. In: "... und ihr Ruf verhallt ins Leere hinein." Der Schriftsteller Georg Hermann (1871 Berlin – 1943 Auschwitz). Aufsätze und Materialien, ed. by Kerstin Schoor. Berlin: Weidler 1999, pp. 87-121.

40 "Det is'n Menzel." Max Liebermann to Georg Hermann, 3 October 1930, held in the Georg Hermann Collection, Leo Baeck Institute, New York, section AR-B. 342 3109. On the similarity of interiors in Hermann's novels and Menzel's early works, see also Mario Krammer: Berlin im Wandel der Jahrhunderte. Eine Kulturgeschichte der deutschen Hauptstadt. Berlin: Rembrandt 1956, p. 213.

Given the resonances between Fontane's and Hermann's novels and Menzel's paintings, it is worth following up the relationships between the writers and Menzel. A look at Hermann's and Fontane's evaluations of Menzel's paintings elucidates the parallels and differences in the two writers' aesthetics and especially in their attitudes to the representation of Berlin. Above all, Fontane emphasises the merging of Realist faithfulness and artistic poeticisation in Menzel's paintings.[41] But there are other aspects, too, that he appreciates in Menzel's work. In an essay written in 1895 on the occasion of Menzel's eightieth birthday, Fontane considers the artistic innovations wrought by Menzel, especially in the representation of light and the use of colour. He praises the painter as a man "[...] who found his ideal in continually inventing new techniques and at the same time solving a never-ending stream of new problems".[42] However, this should not be read as condoning a kind of painting that is based merely on the interaction of colours. Fontane's attitude to this kind of "Kolorismus" was very critical indeed. In a biographical sketch on Eduard Hildebrandt, he claims: "*In the long run*, an intention to paint nothing but air and light was bound to lead artists astray [...]."[43] Repeatedly, Fontane stresses the importance of line over colour and the need for well executed detail in painting. His ideal, which he sees realised in Menzel's work, is "the combination of genius and painstaking conscientiousness".[44] The moral approach to art criticism that is apparent in this judgement is even more marked in the essay Fontane wrote to honour Menzel on his eightieth birthday. Here, he emphasises the self-control, diligence, sense of duty and courage of the painter, qualities which, in Fontane's opinion, made him a "true Prussian".[45]

A comparison with two essays written about Menzel by Hermann – an obituary from 1905 and another essay from 1908 – shows that Hermann's evaluation of the painter in some areas corresponds to that voiced by Fontane. Hermann too highlights the Prussian element in Menzel's character and work. Hermann means by this a

---

41 See Theodor Fontane, Das Krönungsbild von Adolf Menzel, NFA, XXIII/1, 260 "Die Haupt-schwierigkeit aber bleibt immer die: etwas ganz bestimmt Gegebenes in realistischer Treue und zugleich in künstlerischer Verklärung darzustellen. Erst wo diese Verschmelzung glückt, da wird aus dem bloßen Tableau ein historisches Bild. Ein solches haben wir hier." "The main difficulty always remains this: to represent something definitely given while remaining simultaneously faithful to reality and contriving to achieve its artistic transfiguration. It is only where this fusion succeeds that the tableau is transformed into a historical painting. This is such a painting."

42 "[...], der in der Erfindung immer neuer Techniken und zugleich in der Lösung immer neuer Probleme sein Ideal fand. ". Fontane: Adolf Menzel, NFA, XXIII/1, 518.

43 "*Auf die Dauer* mußte es auf Irrwege führen, nur Luft und Licht malen zu wollen." Fontane: Eduard Hildebrandt, NFA, XXIII/1, 496. On Fontane's critical attitude to "Kolorismus", see Claude Keisch: Aus der Werkstatt des Kunstkritikers. Fontanes Notizen aus Berliner Kunstausstellungen. In: Fontane und die bildende Kunst, pp. 279-291.

44 "die Verquickung von Genius und peinlicher Gewissenhaftigkeit" Fontane: Das Krönungsbild von Adolf Menzel, NFA, XXIII/1, 261.

45 See Fontane: Adolf Menzel, NFA, XXIII/1, 519: " [...] ist er doch zugleich ein Mann der Freiheit und als solcher immer da zu finden, wo von alter Zeit her die richtigen Preußen, die Leute von festem Rückgrat, gestanden haben. "; "[...] at the same time he is a man of freedom and as such is always to be found where the true Prussians, the people with backbone, have always stood."

rational approach to art, an exactness of observation and detailed representation.[46] In contrast to Fontane, however, Hermann does not regard the exactness and the wealth of detail in Menzel's pictures with unqualified approval. Rather he criticises these aspects of Menzel's work as too cerebral. Thus he writes about Menzel's portrait of Clara Ilgner:

> This work by the young Menzel shows a unity of style that the later Menzel would no longer achieve, for he killed the soul with the sharpness of his intellect and endangered the whole by his attention to the constituent parts.[47]

Most importantly however, Hermann praises Menzel as an "innovator and precursor of modern art". In this respect Hermann goes far beyond Fontane's appreciation of the innovative elements in Menzel's art, so far, indeed, that he claims that Menzel "anticipated everything that was later to be achieved in art".[48] Particularly in Menzel's depictions of Berlin city streets, Hermann sees the anticipation of Impressionism.[49] It is clear that in comparison to Fontane's judgement of Menzel's art, Hermann's has already moved much closer to the evaluation shared by most art historians today. One need only think of the exhibition of Menzel's work shown in Paris, Washington and Berlin in 1996/97, in which Menzel was celebrated as a precursor of Modernism.[50]

Fontane's and Hermann's differing judgements may be due to the fact that most of Menzel's alla prima paintings, which are valued so highly today, were not shown to the public until 1905, when the Nationalgalerie in Berlin staged a memorial exhibition of Menzel's work. Fontane, thus, may never have seen them. However, as Fontane and Menzel were well acquainted, it is possible, but by no means certain, that Fontane saw these pictures privately.[51] A second, more important, explanation for the difference

---

46 See Georg Hermann: Adolf von Menzel. In: Berliner Zeitung, 9 February 1905.

47 Georg Hermann: Adolf von Menzel: Fräulein von Knobelsdorf. In: Nord und Süd, 373 (1908), p. 159. "Diese Arbeit des jungen Menzel ist von einer Einheitlichkeit, die dem Menzel von später nicht mehr gegeben war, der mit der Schärfe des Verstandes die Seele totschlug und durch Einzelnes das Ganze gefährdete."

48 "Neuerer und Vorahner der modernen Kunst." "Und doch hat [...] dieser Mann alles antizipiert, was die spätere Kunst erreicht hat." Hermann: Adolf von Menzel (1905).

49 "Die bunte Bewegtheit, die er in seinen Straßenbildern aus den sechziger Jahren von Berlin und Paris gibt, nimmt eigentlich alles vorweg, was der Impressionismus der Franzosen eines Pissarro später glücklicher bewältigte"; "The colourful animation of his street scenes from the 1860s of Berlin and Paris really anticipate everything that the French Impressionism of, say, Pissarro was later to achieve more successfully." Hermann: Adolf von Menzel (1905).

50 See Menzel (as in footnote 15). Especially relevant in this context are the contributions by Françoise Foster-Hahn: 'Adolph Menzel: peintre de Frédéric le Grand et précurseur de l'impressionisme?' pp. 103-112, and Peter-Klaus Schuster: La modernité de Menzel, pp. 137-160.

51 For two contrasting views on this speculation see Rolf Hochhuth: Menzel. Maler des Lichts Frankfurt a. M.: Insel 1991, and Keisch: "Ja, wer ist Menzel?". Hochhuth claims that "Fontane kann [Menzels Bleistiftzeichnungen und Pastelle junger Mädchen und Frauen], [...] [im Jahre 1895] so wenig schon gekannt haben, wie die frühen impressionistischen Meisterwerke, etwa 'Weiden mit Bauplatz' oder 'Das Balkonzimmer' [...]"; "[In 1895], Fontane cannot possibly have known either [Menzel's pencil drawings and watercolours of young girls and women] or his early Impressionist

between Fontane's and Hermann's evaluations of Menzel is that the two writers' judgements reflect their own different aesthetic positions. Each sees in different aspects of Menzel's work the painterly realisation of his own artistic approach. Hermann's evaluation of Menzel is not morally motivated, the painter's exactness of execution no longer has the same importance to him that it had for Fontane. There is no need, in the first years of the twentieth century, when Hermann expressed his views, to specifically emphasise or even defend Menzel's Realism. By contrast, the two aspects that Hermann most stresses and applauds in Menzel's works are their unity of mood and their foreshadowing of Impressionism. Both of these aspects are important elements of Hermann's own aesthetics.

The first aspect, the importance that Hermann accorded to mood, can be detected in the introductory passage to *Jettchen Gebert* quoted above. Like Fontane, Hermann is concerned in this description of the Berlin setting to anchor his fiction in reality. Of equal importance however is the creation of a consistent mood for the narrative. The Old Berlin city centre is evoked as a place of perfect integration and harmony between city and nature. Hermann describes in some detail the atmosphere, weather conditions and colours of the spring day (clouds of dust, blue sky, little white clouds, red and brown trees and the colourful dabs of blossom). In the novel as a whole, the exact description of historical reality is combined with a nostalgic, elegiac mood. This mood serves to poeticise reality and thus create a depiction that is based on the same Realist aesthetic as Fontane's writing. The following quotation from *Henriette Jacoby* (1908), the sequel to *Jettchen Gebert*, makes this reliance on the principle of poeticisation explicit:

> Formerly, when I was young and more cheerful than now, I thought that it would be right and strong to depict life without pity, to tear off the mask from this beautiful beast that mauls us and to show its mouth dripping with blood. Now that I am less cheerful and really know this beast, I am only too willing to put the mask back in front of its face, and I take care to make it up to look rosy and delicate, in order to forget the mouth dripping with blood.[52]

The importance of mood in Hermann's depictions goes beyond the poeticisation of reality, however. It becomes an end in itself. Hermann's concern with an all-pervading

---

masterpieces such as 'Willows and Building Plot' or 'The Balcony Room' [...]." Hochhuth: Menzel, p. 41; Keisch, on the contrary, argues that "Menzels malerisches Frühwerk kann Fontane nicht ganz entgangen sein, doch er registriert es nur als Hintergrund für das 'eigentliche', öffentliche Werk"; "Menzel's early work cannot entirely have escaped Fontane's notice, but he only registers it as background to the 'proper', public work." Keisch: "Ja, wer ist Menzel?" p. 201. Riechel, too, "assumes that Fontane saw the paintings [of "the other Menzel"] particularly of the 1840s". In: Riechel: Theodor Fontane and the Fine Arts, p. 53.

52 "Früher, als ich jung war und heiterer denn heute, da meinte ich, daß es richtig und stark wäre, das Leben so mitleidlos zu schildern, dieser schönen Bestie, die uns zerfleischt, die Maske herunterzureißen und ihr bluttriefendes Maul zu weisen. Heute, da ich weniger heiter bin und diese Bestie nun wirklich kenne, da setze ich nur zu gern ihr die Maske wieder vors Gesicht, und ich bemühe mich, sie noch rosig und zart zu schminken, nur um das bluttriefende Maul zu vergessen." Georg Hermann: Henriette Jacoby. Reinbek: Rowohlt 1990, p. 283.

and unifying atmosphere is expressed in the autobiographical novel *Der kleine Gast* (The little visitor) (1925), in which he records the process of writing *Jettchen Gebert*. In analogy to the composition of a work of music, Hermann says it is one of his main concerns to maintain the same mood "without losing the harmony, even for a single second, for a single line".[53] The placing of such importance on the general atmospheric impression is scathingly described by Richard Hamann and Jost Hermand as an element of the decadent and deliberately aestheticising movement of *Neuromantik* (Hamann and Hermand call it "Neuro-Mantik").[54] The importance Hermann accords to mood thus mixes the Realism in his depictions with influences from turn-of-the-century aesthetics.

The second main aspect of Hermann's aesthetics, the influence of Impressionism, is evident in all of his novels. For example, the evocation of the spring day complete with dabs of blossom in the introductory passage from *Jettchen Gebert* clearly refers to the Impressionist practice of emphasising the fleeting impression of colour over precision of form. The Impressionist aesthetic is to be seen particularly, however, in Hermann's later Berlin novels, most clearly in *Kubinke*, published in 1910. Going far beyond mere pictorialism, Hermann here uses Impressionist literary conventions which were being developed in parallel to those in painting. A longer quotation from *Kubinke* exem-plifies this in the particular context of the representation of the city:

> And darkness fell, a warm, mild darkness. Above lay the night with a soft haze and faint, glimmering stars; and below the electric streetlights gained power over the street and shone over the lady with Hermes' staff sitting above the portal, and sketched the branches and twigs of the trees onto the pavement. And into the dust from all those trams and from the moving cars, something of the fresh, bitter smell of the rising sap in the elms and lime trees was mixing. The street had not been this lively all day. [...] Whereas earlier tram had followed tram after a long pause, now the illuminated boxes seemed to be rolling along in fours, in sixes; and empty builders' carts were clattering alongside them with yelling coachmen; and cabs finishing their shift for the night were trotting with tired horses very slowly home; and the others who were only starting now, were coming to meet them. [...]
>
> The tingling breath of adventure hovered in the air [...]. And even the dignified husbands sitting in the trams could not tear their gazes away from the beautiful women sitting next to them, and time and time again, over the rims of their newspapers, their eyes sought those of their neighbours. And they travelled on for one, two, three stops, before yanking themselves up with an effort and staggering off.[55]

---

53 "[...] keine Sekunde, keine Zeile, die Tonlage aus dem Ohr verlieren". Georg Hermann: Der kleine Gast. Stuttgart, Berlin, Leipzig: Deutsche Verlagsanstalt 1925, p. 277.

54 Cf. Richard Hamann and Jost Hermand: Impressionismus (Epochen deutscher Kultur von 1870 bis zur Gegenwart, vol. 3.). Munich: Nymphenburg 1972, p. 308.

55 "Und die Dunkelheit brach herein, eine warme, milde Dunkelheit. Oben lag die Nacht mit weichem Dunst und matten, flimmernden Sternen; und unten gewannen die elektrischen Bogenlampen die Macht über die Straße und überglänzten die Dame mit dem Merkurstab, die über dem Portal saß, und zeichneten die Äste und Zweige der Bäume auf dem Bürgersteig ab. Und in den Staub von all den Straßenbahnen und von den rollenden Wagen mischte sich doch etwas von dem frischen, bitteren Geruch der steigenden Säfte in den Ulmen und Linden. So belebt aber war die Straße den

On the basis of a detailed, Realist perception of the street scene, Hermann here gives a purely sensual impression of the city environment. This is conveyed through the accumulation of adjectives, personifications, onomatopoetic verbs and participles, through parallel constructions, the inversion of syntactic pattern (giving first the description, then the object) and clauses beginning with "and", conveying the idea of juxtaposition rather than causality.[56] The sensual impression always takes precedence over the naming of individual objects and elements in the scene. Hermann goes furthest in this abstraction of form from content when describing tram cars simply as illuminated boxes. The visual impression dominates here, consisting of light and colour, rather than the object itself. In comparison with Fontane's description of Unter den Linden from *Irrungen, Wirrungen* quoted at the beginning of this essay, as well as with his depictions of Invalidenstraße in *Stine* or the Berlin city centre in *Die Poggenpuhls*, the innovative Impressionist elements of Hermann's depiction of the city street are apparent. There is also a second respect in which Hermann's representation of the city goes beyond that of Fontane: he links the description of the busy street scene with a reflection on the city inhabitants' psychological make-up. He writes about the tingling breath of adventure ("prickelnden Hauch von Abenteuern") and addresses the tension and attraction between strangers, which builds up and discharges in fleeting encounters and noncommittal flirtations.

In Hermann's depictions of the city in *Kubinke*, it is not the geographical co-ordinates that dominate, but the rhythm and atmosphere of city life – elements that play an important role in the Impressionist city aesthetics of August Endell noted above. The individual's experience of the city becomes a literary subject in itself and is thus considered worthy of sensitive and detailed description. In this respect, by exploring individual experience, Hermann departs from the allusive style that we know from Fontane's descriptions of the city and goes beyond simply concentrating on those aspects that are relevant to the characterisation of the novels' protagonists or constellations of characters.

---

ganzen Tag nicht gewesen. [...] Und wenn ehedem in langen Pausen Bahn auf Bahn gefolgt war, so schienen jetzt ihre erhellten Kästen gleich zu vieren, zu sechsen hintereinander heranzurollen; und leere Bauwagen klapperten mit johlenden Kutschern nebenher; und Droschken, die für die Nacht Schicht machten, trotteten mit müden Pferdchen ganz langsam nach Hause; und die anderen, die jetzt erst begannen, kamen ihnen entgegen. [...] Es schwebte der prickelnde Hauch von Abenteuern in der Luft [...]. Und selbst die würdigen Eheherren, die in der Bahn saßen, konnten ihre Blicke nicht von der schönen Nachbarin losreißen, und immer wieder suchten ihre Augen über die Zeitung fort die Augen der Nachbarin. Und sie fuhren ein, zwei, drei Haltestellen weiter, ehe sie sich ganz mühselig hochrissen und herauswankten." Georg Hermann: Kubinke. Berlin: Das Neue Berlin 1951, p. 48f..

56 All of these have been described by Hartmut Marhold as techniques fundamental to the development of an Impressionist style in literature. See Hartmut Marhold: Impressionismus in der deutschen Dichtung. Frankfurt a. M.: Lang 1985. On their own, they may not have a great impact, but combined, as they appear in the extract analysed here, they contribute to the text's quality of immediacy and give the reader an unadulterated impression of the colours, forms and atmosphere that constitute the scene described.

In *Kubinke* and to an even greater degree in *Die Nacht des Doktor Herzfeld*, published in 1912, Hermann aestheticises the city in a way very similar to that put forward in Endell's essay on the beauty of the city. The city environment is described as beautiful when perceived through the abstracting veil of fog, mist, or darkness, as in the following description of the Kurfürstendamm at night, taken from *Die Nacht des Doktor Herzfeld*:

> Towards evening, however, I cannot imagine anything more delicious than to be walking along here. All this stupid stucco, all these wild oriels and gables, covered with gold stripes, then disappear and what remains are high, dark and deeply coloured lines of houses, on whose many jagged points and cliffs changing lights flicker and play fantastically. Every detail vanishes; only chains of broad reflecting windows remain, in which the illuminated ones alternate so gaily with the dark ones as though a jeweller had made them with glittering colourful gems and dark, cloudy stones.[57]

In contrast to Fontane's depiction of the cityscape through the mist in *Der Stechlin*, it is not the detail but rather its disappearance that is stressed here.

Hermann's Impressionist representations of Berlin find their pictorial counterparts in the works of the Berlin painter Lesser Ury. Especially in the period 1887 to 1905, Ury, who is today credited by many with having discovered the modern city of Berlin for painting,[58] depicted the growing capital again and again. Ury's art concentrates on an exploration of the effects of light and colour. These are given priority over form and traditional composition. Objects dissolve to bring the atmosphere of the city environ-ment to the fore. An excellent example of Ury's art is his painting of *Leipziger Straße* from 1889 (Illustration 5). Here, Ury is evidently not interested in the exact representation of the topography, he does not even explore in naturalistic detail the reflection of the lights on the wet street surface. As the art critic Cornelius Gurlitt put it in a review in *Die Gegenwart* in 1890, the painting shows "a collection of white splashes on a predominantly black hotchpotch of colours".[59] However, as Gurlitt himself was the first to concede, the *atmosphere* of the city night is conveyed sensitively and to great effect by this "daub"[60]. Whereas Skarbina, like Fontane, still depicted details of the city environment through an atmospheric mist, the magic of

---

57 "Aber gegen Abend kann ich mir kaum etwas Köstlicheres denken, als hier entlang zu gehen. All der blöde Stuck, all die wilden Erker und Giebel, mit Goldstreifen überzogen, verschwinden dann, und es bleiben hohe, dunkle und tieffarbige Häuserketten, die mit ihren vielen Zacken und Klippen phantastisch von wechselnden Lichtern überflackert und überspielt sind. Jede Einzelheit verschwindet; es bleiben nur Ketten breiter Spiegelfenster, in denen so lustig die erleuchteten mit den dunklen wechseln, als hätte es ein Juwelier mit blitzenden farbigen und tiefen blinden Halbedelsteinen ersonnen. " Georg Hermann: Die Nacht des Doktor Herzfeld. Berlin: Fleischel 1912, p. 24f..

58 See, for example, Adolph Donath: Lesser Ury. Seine Stellung in der modernen deutschen Malerei. Berlin: Perl 1921.

59 "eine Reihe von weißen Klexen, auf einem vorwiegend schwarzen Farbenragout." Cornelius Gurlitt, quoted in Der künstlerische Nachlaß von Lesser Ury, exhibition catalogue, Paul Cassirer. Berlin 1932, p. 11.

60 "Schmiererei". Gurlitt: Der künstlerische Nachlaß von Lesser Ury, p. 11.

Ury's city depiction, as well as that of Hermann in his contttemporary Berlin novels *Kubinke* and *Die Nacht des Doktor Herzfeld*, consists in a far ımore abstract way in the veiling itself.

What conclusions can be drawn from this investigation? It hæas been shown that with regard to the representation of Berlin, Hermann follows the» Realist tradition established in the novels of Fontane. Especially in *Jettchen Gebert*, the style and function of his depictions of the city correspond closely to those in Fontttane's novels. Hermann's representations of Berlin, as Fontane's, fulfil the functiomm of characterising the individuals in his novels and their social constellations, and combine detailed descriptions with poeticisation of the scenes described.

The span of fifteen years, however, that lies between Fomtane's *Der Stechlin* and Hermann's *Die Nacht des Doktor Herzfeld* has created diffîèerent conditions for the artistic depiction of Berlin. In those of Hermann's novels which are set in contemporary Berlin (such as *Kubinke* and *Die Nacht des Doktor ıiHerzfeld*), the author can no longer refer to the city as a known and shared space to the» same extent as Fontane could. The stability of the city environment has been shnaken by Berlin's rapid development around the turn of the century. The system of coɔncise references used in Fontane's representations of Berlin, is thus no longer applicaĺible. The function of the city as a system of social stratification has been weakened. ÎÎʹhe referential power of depictions of the city recedes, making room for more extensiìive portrayals of the city environment. The city space becomes a literary subject in itse»ːlf. Hermann stresses the changes in the city environment; and he does so not only⁄⁄ with respect to social stratification and mobility, as Fontane did, but also in terms of the physical transformation of the metropolis and its psychological effect «on the city dweller. This change in focus necessitates a new approach to literary rɾepresentation and leads Hermann to experiment with new aesthetic concepts and techmniques, especially those offered by Impressionism.

The use of Impressionist techniques that we see in its initiaĺll stages in Fontane's city representations – especially in later novels such as *Der Stecːːhlin* – is reinforced and developed further by Hermann. After using a literary Realismm in *Jettchen Gebert* that is interspersed with Impressionist depictions, he goes on to» present in *Kubinke* an essentially Impressionist city novel in which he sketches aau kaleidoscopic view of Berlin around 1910. The novel's plot is so much reduced in immportance that it becomes a mere frame for long, detailed and intensely atmospheric descriptions of the city environment.

Fontane and Hermann share what Friedrich Sengle termedll "the unprejudiced view of the city".[61] This lack of bias in their representations of B이erlin distinguishes them from many of their contemporaries. If Fontane, according ttto Sengle, was the first novelist to show this openness towards Berlin, Hermann wɾɾas the novelist who re-awakened this attitude, albeit to a changed city and with diiifferent means, after the

---

61 "die unbefangene Sicht der Großstadt". Friedrich Sengle: Wunschbild Land und Schreckbild Stadt.
  In: Studium Generale, 16 (1963), p. 627

intervening period of Naturalist criticism of Berlin as a "moloch".[62] Charlotte Jolles once described Fontane as the "interpreter of the capital of the new empire".[63] The title I would propose for Hermann, who built on Fontane's Realism but developed his representation of Berlin in the direction of literary Impressionism, is that of "interpreter of the new metropolis" ("Gestalter der neuen Großstadt").

---

62 For this evaluation of Hermann's writing on Berlin, compare Theodor Heuß: Berliner Romane: "Kubinke". In: Das literarische Echo, 13 (1910/11), 711f..

63 "Fontane wurde erst der Gestalter Berlins, als es zur Hauptstadt des neuen Kaiserreichs geworden war [...]." Jolles: Weltstadt – verlorene Nachbarschaft. Berlin-Bilder Raabes und Fontanes, p. 66.

Illustration 1: Adolf Menzel: Hinterhof und Haus

Illustration 2: Adolf Menzel: Stadtbahn Berlin-Potsdam

Illustration 3: Franz Skarbina: Droschkenhalteplatz

Illustration 4: Franz Skarbina: Café Bauer

Illustration 5: Lesser Ury: Leipziger Straße

Maite Zubiaurre

Panoramic views in Fontane, Galdós and Clarín: an Essay on Female Blindness

German and Spanish realism share a number of significant traits. First of all, they are latecomers, in comparison to the French model. Thus, German and Spanish writers of the second half of the nineteenth century are already experienced connoisseurs of the realist mode and, not surprisingly, their fictions clearly show that knowledge and experience. Sometimes, this knowledge manifests itself in narrative irony and self-conscious meta-fiction. But, most importantly, both German and Spanish realism acquire a relatively new air of intensified spiritualism, as opposed to the materialism and naturalism so strongly present in French fiction. In Germany, this particular literary period is generally known as "Poetischer Realismus"; in Spain, critics consistently refer to the "realismo espiritual" of Pérez Galdós, Pardo Bazán and Clarín. But, beside these obvious similarities, which in each country follow different historical and cultural paradigms, there are other less well known traits equally shared by both countries, and by European realism in general. One of these features is the stereotyped as well as revealing manner in which realist novels depict landscape and setting. There has been, in recent years, an increasing interest in the narrative representation of space. Bobes Naves, Gullón, Hillebrand, López-Landy, Weisgerber, and Zumthor are among the scholars who have written substantially on the subject.[1] Nevertheless, not even their extensive accounts of setting and landscape in the novel refer to the gendered nature of space in the novel. The following pages will partially fill this critical gap by discussing the spatial theme of the panoramic vision as a predominantly male chronotope in realist fiction.

Realist narratives show a strong preference for the domestic setting. Interiors are, indeed, the true discovery of the realist novel. These settings, however, are always integrated in a more ample exterior space, which is very often depicted in a panoramic view. Realism still derives its meaning from the antagonistic relationship between settings (especially, between the public sphere and the domestic domain), or, as Brüggemann puts it, from a particular dialectic of showing and hiding, which is of great importance in the realm of urban space and the literary experience of the city.[2]

---

1   María del Carmen Bobes Naves: Teoría general de la novela. Semiología de *La Regenta*. Madrid: Gredos 1985; Ricardo Gullón: Espacio y novela. Barcelona: Bosch 1980; Bruno Hillebrand: Mensch und Raum im Roman. Studien zu Keller, Stifter, Fontane. Munich: Winkler 1971; Ricardo López-Landy: El espacio novelesco en la obra de Galdós. Madrid: Ediciones Cultura Hispánica 1979; Jean Weisgerber: L'Espace romanesque. Lausanne: Éditions l'Age d'Homme 1978; Paul Zumthor: La mesure du monde. Représentation de l'espace au Moyen Âge. Paris: Éditions du Seuil 1993.

2   Heinz Brüggemann: "Aber schickt keinen Poeten nach London!" Großstadt und literarische Wahrnehmung im 18. und 19. Jahrhundert. Texte und Interpretationen. Hamburg: Rowohlt 1985.

Thus, in classical realist narratives, a large panorama leads almost always to a narrower focus. The public space inevitably advances toward the privacy of a domestic setting, as if the narrator were using an imaginary telescope to bring a certain section of the space closer to his view, in order to reproduce it with all its otherwise invisible peculiarities. The urban landscape, especially, is fertile terrain for the expectations of the reader, and his or her longing for details and the multiplicity of spatial surroundings. At the same time, however, urban settings very often are a threat to the realist author, who sees in the cohabitation of so many spaces the hidden danger of dispersion and chaos. For this reason, the realist novel tends to depict an urban landscape in the very same way it depicts nature, namely, by means of the panoramic view. Panoramic perspectives (from above or from a distance) offer a landscape seen as a harmonious whole. Very often, the urban ensemble appears inserted in a natural landscape, and even contributes to its enhancement. Thus the city, when transformed into a poetic image or painting, becomes part of the natural landscape and passively ("feminine") surrenders to nature. Susan Stewart calls it the "pastoralising of the city": "If we attempt to describe the city from a distanced and transcendent position, to thereby miniaturise it, the tendency is to naturalise the city landscape".[3] Perhaps we should rephrase Stewart's quotation, for the sake of greater precision: "If we attempt to describe the city from a male transcendent position, to thereby miniaturise it, the tendency is to feminise it." The pastoralising of the city and its transformation into a female character is also a way of imposing a restrictive as well as reassuring frame on reality. "The typical view of the city is through the window – a view within a definite frame and limited perspective, mediated and refracted through the glass of the city's abstraction of experience."[4]

The ordering of reality through frames, spatial boundaries and various *mise en abîmes* is a common practice in realist fiction, as I note and exemplify elsewhere.[5] *La Regenta*, certainly, is no exception to that rule. The panoramic view from the cathedral tower shows the green belt of lush natural landscape embracing the city of Vetusta. The city itself, conveniently bounded by nature, keeps decomposing into different neighbourhoods. Finally, one of these environs, *La encimada*, where the homes of rural aristocracy are grouped under the shade of the imposing cathedral, will suffer further "cuttings" and framings:

> Celedonio had peeped once or twice through the canon's spyglass when its master had left it behind, and he knew that it was a powerful device: from the tower's upper gallery, which was far above the belfry, he had once had a clear view of the judge's wife, a very pretty lady, as she walked, reading a book, in her back garden, known as Ozores Park. Yes, he'd seen her close enough to touch, even though her house was in the corner of the Plaza Nueva, quite a long way from the cathedral tower [...]. What else? Through that spyglass you could see part of the

3 Susan Stewart: On Longing. Narratives of the Miniature, the Gigantic, the Souvenir, the Collection. Durham: Duke University Press 1993, p. 78.
4 Susan Stewart: On Longing, p. 79.
5 Maria Teresa Zubiaurre: El espacio en la novela realista: Paisajes, miniaturas, perspectivas. Mexico: Fondo de Cultura Económica. [Forthcoming].

billiards room in the Gentlemen's Club, next to St. Mary's Church; and he, Celedonio, had seen the ivory balls rolling over the table.[6]

As expected, the telescope suddenly turns into a microscope: after having captured the scene of a woman in her garden, it tries to get a similar tangible hold on the public scenery of the casino, depicting the billiard table and even the rolling of the ball. The garden is, again, another boundary, designed to both mirror and contain Ana Ozores's beauty. At the same time, her beauty seeks the even smaller refuge of the open book and the reassuring frame of its pages. The billiard room also suffers two spatial reductions. The frame of the window sets limits to the frame of the billiard table. In the middle of the frantic process of endless framing and meticulous space cutting, the book remains the symbol of the intimacy and solitary confinement of the female character and her domestic realm, while the billiard table is clearly a metaphor for the male universe and the public domain.

It is worthwhile stressing that the passion for miniatures and the increasing reduction and concentration of settings threatens to become a seemingly endless process, not only in Spanish realism, but in German realist novels as well. In Fontane's *Stine*, for example, the "framing" abilities of the window serve as the grounds for the installation of another instrument used to reduce and miniaturise reality. The female protagonist looks into a moveable "street mirror" ("ein Dreh-und Straßenspiegel"), meant to discreetly reflect what is happening on the street. It brings inside what is outside and converts the chaotic urban scene into a small and innocent decorative painting: "I believe, the mirror miniaturises everything, and to miniaturise is almost the same as to embellish."[7] In Raabe's *Die Chronik der Sperlingsgasse*, (The Chronicle of Sparrow Lane) on the other hand, the gaze of the narrating character finds an ingenious way to enter the domestic space of her beautiful neighbour and bring it closer to him, since his window has a small imperfection in the form of a bubble that functions as a magnifying glass. Due to this circumstance, a fragment of reality is able, once again, to convey the impression of totality: "I understood that the whole world could be con-centrated in one point."[8]

---

6 Leopoldo Alas Clarín: La Regenta, translated with an introduction by John Rutherford. Athens GA: The University of Georgia Press 1984 p. 28. All translated quotations are from this edition and further references are given in the text. "Celedonio que en alguna ocasión, aprovechando un descuido, había mirado por el anteojo del Provisor, sabía que era de poderosa atracción; desde los segundos corredores, mucho más altos que el campanario, había él visto perfectamente a La Regenta, una guapísima señora, pasearse, leyendo un libro, por su huerta que se llamaba el Parque de los Ozores; sí, señor, la había visto como si pudiera tocarla con la mano, y eso que su palacio estaba en la rinconada de la Plaza Nueva, bastante lejos de la torre [...].¿Qué más? Con aquel anteojo se veía un poco del billar del casino, que estaba junto a la iglesia de Santa María; y él, Celedonio, había visto pasar las bolas de marfil rodando por la mesa." Leopoldo Alas Clarín: La Regenta, edición, introducción y notas de Gonzalo Sobejano. Madrid: Castalia 1981, p. 105.

7 "Ich glaube, der Spiegel verkleinert, und verkleinern ist fast ebensogut wie verhübschen." Fontane: Stine, NFA, III, 240. Translations into English are my own unless otherwise indicated.

8 "Ich begriff, daß das Universum sich in einem Punkt konzentrieren könne", Wilhelm Raabe: Die Chronik der Sperlingsgasse. Munich: Winkler 1961, pp. 15-16.

The centre of a great many of these "miniaturised" and highly concentrated totalities is usually inhabited by women, as exemplified in *La Regenta*, and in *Die Chronik der Sperlingsgasse*. Thus, female characters are irrevocably located inside a landscape, while men persistently watch them from the outside.[9] Not surprisingly, in *La Regenta*, the three "outside" characters in charge of cutting space into settings, and, ultimately, of conquering both a city (Vetusta) and a woman (Ana Ozores) are male. The first perspective is offered by Celedonio, the half-witted acolyte, whose vertical look from the tower is only able to grasp what lies closest to the cathedral. The second point of view, that of the omniscient narrator, avoids the city altogether and concentrates instead on a careful depiction of the natural landscape around Vetusta. The description of the urban setting, finally, is Don Fermín's exclusive responsibility. The ambitious priest, like L'abbé Faujas in Zola's *Conquête de Plassans*, wants to visually conquer the city, as a first step that symbolically refers to a later and more real conquest. It is important to note that the canon moves in the opposite direction from the acolyte. While Celedonio looks only at specific details, shortsightedly ignoring broader views, Don Fermín always proceeds from the general to the particular. He carefully organises space and looks for the abstract and geometric features of urban cartography. Only after doing so, is he willing to adorn the city map with tangible scenes and objects, as well as with female beauty. Don Fermín is first of all demiurge and only after that, *voyeur*, while Celedonio is never anything more than a pathetic peeping Tom. In either case, both Vetusta and Ana Ozores become the main targets of male voyeurism and desire.

So far, sight has proven to be strongly male, and an indisputable *tour de force* in the realm of realist fiction. According to Jenks, "vision, in Western Culture, is lionised among the senses and treated as wholly autonomous, free and even pure".[10] Thus in *La Regenta*, the "free vision" of Don Fermín, a precise metaphor for "pure knowledge", is at odds with Ana Ozores's confused senses and the "impure" conscience of sexual temptation. In a telling scene, Ana's religious reflections while waiting for her maid at a fountain in the countryside remind her of the visions of her childhood, so close, in her words, to "true religion". However, her present meditations do not culminate, as then, in "mystical terror" (p. 96). The open sexuality of the maid, who returns sweating and agitated from a short visit paid to her cousin, is symbolised in the "strident choir of frogs" and its comparison with "a hymn sung by pagan savages to the darkness approaching from the east" (p. 190). From this point on, the allusions to sexuality will multiply and find easy access to Doña Ana's disturbed conscience. Lust, however, does not stop at the environs of Vetusta. Nature, felt for the first time by Ana Ozores as a vigorous erotic energy, blends with the city and the neighbourhoods of the poor.

---

9 Even nineteenth-century female travellers who wrote travel literature seem to conform to the gendered stereotype, for they symptomatically prefer to locate themselves within the landscape, instead of outside of it. See: Alison Blunt: Travel, Gender and Imperialism. Mary Kingsley and West Africa. New York: The Guilford Press 1995, p. 96. Naturally, panoramic visions are sparse in their narratives, and tend to avoid the presumed "objectivity" of external perspectives.

10 Chris Jenks (ed.): Visual Culture. London: Routledge 1995, p. 1.

> The judge's wife had come this way once or twice before at nightfall. But it was only now that she thought she could see and sense in this mass of dirty clothes – even in the acrid smell of the riff-raff, in the hubbub made by the rabble – a manifestation of the delights of love: love was, it seemed, a universal necessity. (p. 193) [11]

"Seeing", in the paragraph above, is equivalent to "sensing" or "feeling" ("she could see and sense"). At the same time, the verb "to feel" includes the senses of smell, ("the acrid smell of the riff-raff"), of hearing ("in the hubbub made by the rabble") and of touch, as the memorable ending of Clarín's novel only too cogently shows:

> A wretched desire stirred in Celedonio: a perversion of his perverted lust. To enjoy a strange pleasure, or perhaps to discover whether he would enjoy it, he bent over and brought his vile face close to the face of the judge's wife and kissed her mouth. Ana returned to life, overcome by nausea and tearing at the mists of delirium. For she thought she had felt on her lips the cold and slimy belly of a toad. (p. 715) [12]

It is not by chance that in *La Regenta's* last paragraph Ana Ozores and Celedonio appear in promiscuous reunion. After all, they look very much alike: according to the discriminatory interpretation that realist fiction makes of the sense of sight, both characters are rendered shortsighted, if not totally blinded by either social condition or gender. The privileged point of view of a high tower is of no help to Celedonio: he still sees only a small and unimportant portion of reality. Ana Ozores's perception is no less impoverished and biased: her senses get so hopelessly confused by her close surroundings and her own feelings and inner world, that a broader and more ambitious perspective becomes utterly impossible. Thus, while Clarín's novel starts very forcefully with superior sight and male knowledge as a way to conquer a feminised city, it unhappily ends with irrational instinct and the lower and "feminine" sense of touch reigning over masculine intellect.

Fontane also insists on stereotyped female blindness. He consciously plays with the inherent contradiction of a panoramic view that leads nowhere, when writing down with keen irony the following dialogue in *Frau Jenny Treibel* (*Jenny Treibel*):

> "Well, dear friends," Treibel began, [...] "are you for climbing the tower and do you feel an urge to see this wonderworld in which no human eye has yet been able to discover a fresh blade of grass – do you feel an urge, I say, to see this great desert panorama interspersed with asparagus beds and railway embankments spread out at your feet?"

---

11 "Alguna vez había pasado la Regenta por allí a tales horas, pero en esta ocasión, con una especie de doble vista, creía ver, sentir allí, en aquel montón de ropa sucia, en el mismo olor picante de la chusma, en la algazara de aquellas turbas una forma del placer del amor; del amor que era por lo visto una necesidad universal." Leopoldo Alas Clarín: La Regenta, edición, introducción y notas de Gonzalo Sobejano, p. 352.

12 "Celedonio sintió un deseo miserable, una perversión de la perversión de su lascivia; y por gozar un placer extraño, o por probar si lo gozaba, inclinó el rostro asqueroso sobre el de la Regenta y le besó los labios. Ana volvió a la vida rasgando las nieblas de un delirio que le causaba náuseas. Había creído sentir sobre la boca el vientre viscoso y frío de un sapo." Leopoldo Alas Clarín: La Regenta, p. 537.

"I think", said Frau Felgentreu [...], "I think, dear Treibel, we'll stay where we are. I'm not for climbing, and besides I think one should always be satisfied with what one happens to have."
"Good then", Treibel continued, "we'll stay below. Why strive for the higher. One must be satisfied with what fate has determined, as my friend Felgentreu has just declared. In other words: 'Enjoy happily what you have'." [13]

There is an evident meta-fictive purpose in this concrete reference, deliberately put into the mouth of a *petit bourgeois*, to the "wonderworld" watched from the height of a tower, as well as in the later commentary about a space never seen and still unexplored. The German author intentionally re-establishes the link with the long tradition of the *Bildungsroman*, a genre built on the adventurous spirit of the protagonist and prone to identify the still unknown facets of human existence with breathtaking panoramic views and the promising mystery of unfamiliar spaces. But at the same time he recognises, with nostalgic sarcasm, the impossibility of a perpetuation of the daring spirit of Romanticism during the second half of a century marked by prosaic thoughts and a rapid process of industrialisation. Therefore, it is not surprising that this reference to a space never seen ends with an ironic twist: "In which no human eye has yet been able to discover a fresh blade of grass." When Treibel decides, in agreement with his friend's wishes, to remain on the ground and to renounce any height or elevation, the irony becomes even more intense. The bourgeois dogma of "down-to-earthness" and its reluctance to leave the familiar site ("I think we'll stay where we are"), and to aspire to more ("Enjoy happily what you have") materialises in the dialogue between the two friends. "To stay" and "to have" convey a strictly materialist meaning. This materialism is so widespread among the bourgeoisie that there is no longer any space for spiritual ascension. Treibel's proposal to climb the tower and to enjoy the view would have functioned, in different circumstances, as a meaningful symbol for the spiritual climbing of the soul. In *Frau Jenny Treibel*, however, the landscape remains predictable, regardless of the perspective or height from which it is perceived.

The bounded and domesticated geography of railways and agriculture seems to contradict, one by one, the daring traits that cultural tradition has attributed to the panoramic view. The truth, however, is that coherence is very soon re-established. Fontane's narrative remains faithful to the strict androcentric code of realist fiction, for

---

13 Fontane: Jenny Treibel, translated, with introduction and notes, by Ulf Zimmermann, New York: Ungar 1976, p. 115f. "Nun, liebe Freunde", nahm Treibel das Wort, [...] "sind Sie für Turm-besteigung und treibt es Sie, diese Wunderwelt, in der keines Menschen Auge bisher einen frischen Grashalm entdecken konnte, treibt es Sie, sag ich, dieses von Spargelbeeten und Eisenbahndämmen durchsetzte Wüstenpanorama zu Ihren Füßen ausgebreitet zu sehen? "
"Ich denke", sagte Frau Felgentreu [...],"ich denke, lieber Treibel, wir bleiben, wo wir sind. Ich bin nicht für Steigen, und dann mein ich auch immer, man muß mit dem zufrieden sein, was man gerade hat."
"Gut denn", fuhr Treibel fort, "wir bleiben also in der Tiefe. Wozu dem Höheren zustreben? Man muß zufrieden sein mit dem durch Schicksalsbeschluß Gegebenen, wie meine Freundin Felgentreu soeben versichert hat. Mit anderen Worten: Genieße fröhlich, was du hast." Fontane: Frau Jenny Treibel, NFA, VII, 99.

he very obediently pictures a woman – Frau Felgentreu – refusing to climb a tower. Why on earth should she engage in such meaningless activity? After all, she knows, and readers do too, that female characters, as well as *petit bourgeois* and other half-witted beings, like Celedonio in *La Regenta*, are not allowed to enjoy any panoramic view whatsoever.

Female blindness is equally present and persistent in *Der Stechlin* (*The Stechlin*), Fontane's last novel. As in *La Regenta*, the first image of Stechlin (situated in the Mark Brandenburg) is a cartographic and aerial depiction of its geography (NFA, VIII, 5-6), introduced, once again, through the impersonal voice of the omniscient narrator. The second impression comes from Woldemar, the retired major's son, and two of his friends. The perspective during this second view is equally panoramic; instead of coming from above, though, it is now approximately on the same level as the depicted space, since the three friends enjoy the view as they ride their horses (NFA, VIII, 4-5). Yet another viewpoint comes through the eyes of the two countesses Barby. Although readers recognise the landscape they already saw on two different occasions, now they watch it from an even closer standpoint. It is no longer a panoramic ensemble but a harmonious collection of meticulously observed details, and of the playful occurrences of nature. One of the two countesses, for example, delights in "the sight of two squirrels playing above them, leaping from tree to tree in a constant game of tag".[14] The narrator tells the reader that "Armgard could not take her eyes from the scene, laughing as the little creatures, who disappeared momentarily, reappeared again in a flash."[15] Melusine, on the other hand, also seems to be more appreciative of the beauty embedded in what is small and unimportant, and unabashedly shows her *ennui* when confronted with the panoramic view of the infamous lake of Stechlin: "Well, now […], so this is the great moment. I'm fully informed. But as is always the case with something grand, I nevertheless do feel a touch of disappointment too".[16]

It is no accident that the ultimate exercise in decomposing the setting and carefully analysing its smallest components is carried out by female characters. The attribution of superior skills of abstraction to male characters and of the fondness of what is tangible to their female counterparts, stands out among the multiple spatial stereotypes of the realist novel. Thus, the female mode of perception remains conventional, and shows an evident interest in conforming to the male perspective. The usage of stereotypes and conventions for the depiction of a setting reinforces the impression of a "frozen" reality, doomed to remain static. A landscape which remains unchanged,

---

14 Fontane: The Stechlin, transl. with an introduction and notes by William L. Zwiebel, Columbia SC: Camden House 1995, p. 222. "[Sie] gewahrten, wie zwei Eichhörnchen über ihnen spielten und in beständigem Sichhaschen von Baum zu Baum sprangen." Fontane: Der Stechlin, NFA, VIII, 274.

15 Zwiebel: The Stechlin, p. 222. "Armgard mochte sich von dem Schauspiel nicht trennen, lachte, wenn die momentan verschwundenen Tierchen mit einem Male wieder zum Vorschein kamen." Fontane: Der Stechlin, NFA, VIII, 274.

16 Zwiebel: The Stechlin, p. 222. "Ja […], das ist nun also der große Moment. Orientiert bin ich. Aber wie das mit allem Großen geht, ich empfinde doch auch etwas von Enttäuschung." Fontane: Der Stechlin, NFA, VIII, 275.

despite having been contemplated and depicted from three different angles, adds emphasis to the sensation of a world already created and of a horizon that narrows the perspective instead of widening it. Koschorke, in agreement with Hillebrand's and Glaser's conclusions, talks about "the new closing of the world" as an essential trait of the bourgeois spirit and its settings.[17] Once again, however, critics are telling only part of the truth. Not only the bourgeoisie but especially female characters and their obstinate blindness have to be made responsible for a world that closes up again, and leaves behind the limitless horizons of the Renaissance.

Female characters in *La Regenta*, *Frau Jenny Treibel*, and *Der Stechlin* remain hopelessly shortsighted. Their eyes and attention get caught only by what is near and graspable. Touch, certainly, tends to be the most developed sense among female characters in the realist novel. Rosalía, in Galdós's novel *La de Bringas*, spends many hours of her leisurely time enjoying the lavish texture of rich fabrics imported from France. Surrounded by textile chaos and carried away by the intoxicating touch, smell and close sight of so many pieces of expensive clothing, as well as of all sorts of delicate trimmings, she fails to notice how speedily complete financial disaster and bankruptcy are approaching her home and family. So far, Galdós's plot remains within the limits of narrative orthodoxy. Disorder, in realist fiction, is most often blamed on female characters and their blurred vision of the real world. What is new, however, is the absence, in *La de Bringas*, of a strong male character, designed to re-establish order and to effectively control female chaos. In Flaubert's *L'Education sentimentale*, the reader finds in Rosannette's *boudoir* an anarchical world of little things and frivolous adornments very similar to Rosalía's textile pandemonium. Nevertheless, the French novel imposes on Rosannette's disorder the regulating force of Frédéric's gaze. Although Frédéric confesses to being alternately appalled and fascinated by his mistress's existential as well as domestic commotion, his oscillating feelings never make him shortsighted. His moral sense of order somehow prevails and helps the reader in putting limits to female turmoil. These limits, precisely, are missing in *La de Bringas*, for there is no controlling force watching over chaos: the male protagonist is as blind and lost in confusion as female characters usually are. Galdós's sexist message to the reader has to be understood as follows: female disorder certainly, is always dangerous. But it turns out to be fatal if a male character fails to see it and to intervene without delay. Ironically enough, blindness and infirmity befall Don Francisco Bringas, the main character, during the second half of the novel. His "real" blindness, however, besides being strongly sarcastic, is mostly redundant, and adds up to the long list of synonyms and repetitions so dear to realist narrative. Don Francisco, truly enough, is blind already from the first chapter on, because of his innate incapability of visually and intellectually embracing a broad panorama. His "feminine" fixation with

---

17 "die Wiederverschlossenheit der Welt". Albrecht Koschorke: Die Geschichte des Horizonts. Grenze und Überschreitung in literarischen Landschaftsbildern. Frankfurt a. M: Suhrkamp 1990, p. 30. Hermann Glaser, 'Psychodrom und Ver-rückter Garten. Zwei Topoi industrieller Umbruchzeit'. In: Literatur in einer industriellen Kultur, ed. by Klaus Götz Gross and Eberhard Lämmert. Stuttgart: Cotta 1989.

minute details and childish trifles tragically keeps him from seeing reality, both domestic and national. Not unlike Rosalía, who is equally shortsighted and unaware of tragedy, Don Francisco happily dwells among the "harmless" upheaval of very small things. The first paragraph of the novel describes:

> an elegant and highly ornate funereal artefact of great architectural daring and grandiose design. Some parts of it were done in the austere, straight lines of the Vignola school, while others were soaring, undulating and ethereal in the Gothic mode, with lurking touches of the Plateresque, topped off with intricate cresting reminiscent of the Tyrolean style so popular on those oriental pavilions you see in the parks these days. It boasted a pyramidal staircase, Greco-Roman plinths, buttresses, pointed arches, pinnacles, gargoyles and canopies. There was a profusion of torches, urns, bats, amphorae, owls, wreaths of everlastings, winged waterclocks, scythes, palm fronds, coiled serpents and other symbols of death and life eternal on all sides.[18]

Only at the very end of the first chapter, is the reader told that what appears to be an arbitrary sum of unconnected objects, is, indeed, a whole ensemble meant to depict a funeral monument, a miniaturesque sepulchral artifice made out of human hair. Because of the way the "piece of capillary art" has been described, readers are forced to conform to Don Francisco's limited vision. Their visual perception, not unlike the perception of Celedonio and Ana (*La Regenta*), of Rosalía (*La de Bringas*), and of the countesses Barby (*Der Stechlin*), gets confused with details and has difficulty in grasping a more general meaning or setting. Thus, both the reader and Don Francisco suddenly show some of the behaviour and psychological traits usually attributed to female characters in realist fiction. Don Francisco is described as having, besides a weak character, "a monkish precision, sure hands" (p. 4), great dexterity and a overwhelming passion for manual work, as well as the wish to "create the overall effect by means of an accumulation of details" (p. 5). Even Rosalía knows how to read the sexist code of realism, and recognises in these qualities her husband's feminine personality. With profound disdain she wonders "how that dummy had made her the mother of four children" (p. 104).

Fontane too plays in *Effi Briest* with the stereotypes of female blindness and disorder, as well as with the dangerous fall of a male character into feminine chaos and shortsightedness. In *Effi Briest*, to impose order and discipline on the female protagonist becomes Geert von Innstetten's obsessive target. Not surprisingly, like

---

18 Benito Pérez Galdós: That Bringas woman, transl. and edited by Catherine Jagoe, London: Everyman 1996, p. 3. All translated quotations are from this edition and further references are given in the text. "Un gallardo artificio sepulcral de atrevidísima arquitectura, grandioso de traza, en ornamentos rico, por una parte severo y rectilíneo a la manera viñolesca, por otra movido, ondulante y quebradizo, a la usanza gótica, con ciertos atisbos platerescos donde menos se pensaba; y por fin cresterías semejantes a las del estilo tirolés que prevalece en los quioscos. Tenía piramidal escalinata, zócalos grecorromanos, y luego machones y paramentos ojivales, con pináculos, gárgolas y doseletes. Por arriba y abajo, a izquierda y derecha, cantidad de antorchas, urnas, murciélagos, ánforas, búhos, coronas de siemprevivas, aladas clepsidras, guadañas, palmas, anguilas enroscadas y otros emblemas del morir y del vivir eterno". Benito Pérez Galdós, La de Bringas, edición de Alda Blanco y Carlos Blanco Aguinaga. Madrid: Cátedra 1985, p. 3.

Charles, in *Madame Bovary*, or Frédéric, in *L'Education sentimentale*, he cherishes the rare moments of domestic bliss and well structured happiness:

> Innstetten was relaxed and jolly and seemed to revel in the joys of domesticity, lavishing much attention on the child. [...] Effi, too, spoke and laughed a lot; but none of it came from her innermost soul. She felt depressed, and did not know who to hold responsible for it, herself or Innstetten.[19]

Order and domestic happiness, thus, tend to be deceitful and misleading in realist fiction. Behind an apparent harmony lurks the ghost of female unfulfillment and moral disorder, a ghost that forces Charles Bovary to seek consolation in his famous sentence ("C'est la faute de la fatalité"), that makes Innstetten repudiate his wife and that compels Frédéric to compare the female heart to an empty chest of drawers.

In the two first novels, especially, a male surveying figure watching over female chaos is consistently missing. We saw how in *La de Bringas*, male shortsightedness becomes a welcome excuse for merciless irony: the ignoble and daily spectacle of Don Francisco's lack of vision and his childish obsession with hair pictures, forces the reader to favour Rosalía and to even prefer her boundless squandering of money and her no less extravagant passion for clothes.

In other instances, the irony gives way to sombre reproaches and moral condemnation. Effi's feverish fantasy and her infantile fears, perfectly justifiable in a woman who only recently left childhood, are cruelly misused and manipulated by her husband. The young, recently married woman believes – has been forced to believe – she inhabits a haunted mansion. Her husband, far from denying it and restoring her peace of mind, feigns to be also a victim of the same superstition. The narrator, certainly, shows his pity for Effi as well as profound contempt for Innstetten's morally despicable methods:

> For Innstetten to muster a ghost so as not to live in an absolutely ordinary house might pass at a pinch, that fitted in with his desire to distinguish himself from the crowd; but the idea of using the ghost to improve her, that was really too much, it was almost insulting. And "improvement ", that much was clear to her, was only half the story, the lesser half; what Crampas had meant was more, much more, it was a kind of device calculated to frighten her. Here was a total lack of goodness of heart, verging on cruelty. The blood rushed to her head and she clenched her little fingers, suddenly determined to make plans [...] [20]

---

19 Fontane: Effi Briest, transl. by Hugh Rorrison and Helen Chambers, London: Penguin Books 2000, p. 108. "Innstetten, unbefangen und heiter, schien sich seines häuslichen Glücks zu freuen und beschäftigte sich viel mit dem Kinde. Auch Effi sprach viel und lachte viel, aber es kam ihr nicht aus innerster Seele. Sie fühlte sich bedrückt und wußte nur nicht, wen sie dafür verantwortlich machen sollte, Innstetten oder sich selber." Fontane: Effi Briest, NFA, VII, 296.

20 Rorrison and Chambers: Effi Briest, p. 98. "Daß Innstetten sich seinen Spuk parat hielt, um nicht ein ganz gewöhnliches Haus zu bewohnen, das mochte hingehen, das stimmte zu seinem Hange, sich von der großen Menge zu unterscheiden; aber das andere, daß er den Spuk als Erziehungsmittel brauchte, das war doch arg und beinahe beleidigend. Und "Erziehungsmittel", darüber war sie sich klar, sagte nur die kleinere Hälfte; was Crampas gemeint hatte, war viel, viel

In realist fiction, blindness and lack of vision are usually considered female flaws. Accordingly, male characters who do not "see" with keen eyes and a powerful intellect turn into weak women disguised as men. Innstetten, like Don Francisco, appears as a "feminised" character, for he too is unable to grasp the panoramic view of his marriage. Instead, he consistently gets obsessed with trifles. Spending much of his time at home, as Don Francisco and female characters usually do, he limits all his efforts to imposing ludicrous domestic rules on his wife. Don Francisco seeks order through manual work, like so many female characters in realist fiction. Geert von Innstetten, on the other hand, tries to fight domestic and moral chaos through what are considered to be predominantly feminine practices, namely, gossip and belief, both real and feigned, in absurd superstitions.

Critics have stressed the strong meta-fictional tendency of *La de Bringas* in connection with the narrator. With striking easiness, he renounces omniscience, becomes a mere witness and promiscuously mixes with the characters. He even confesses to having had an affair with Rosalía! But meta-fiction is present also in Innstetten's and Don Francisco's "artificial" feminine traits. To write meta-fictionally means to be aware of certain literary conventions. Certainly, both Fontane and Galdós, being late realists, are more than familiar with European realism and its leading French model; therefore, it is not difficult for them to apply ironically the recipe of female psychology and its telling relationship with objects and space to male characters, and to disdainfully call them limited, short-sighted women.

Meta-fictional resources mean that certain clichés have been somehow overcome. But, ironically, they also help in establishing them even more firmly. Certainly, the spatial stereotypes of male panoramic visions and of female blindness are still present in contemporary literature, cinema and art. What Jenks calls "the centralism of the western eye", should be more appositely rephrased as "the centralism of the male eye".[21] Women do not see, therefore blind men become women. In realist fiction, panoramic views remain the responsibility and privilege of "truly" male characters and narrators.

---

mehr, war eine Art Angstapparat aus Kalkül. Es fehlte jede Herzensgüte darin und grenzte schon fast an Grausamkeit. Das Blut stieg ihr zu Kopf, und sie ballte ihre kleine Hand und wollte Pläne schmieden [...]" Fontane: Effi Briest, NFA, VII, 283.

21 Jenks: Visual Culture, p. 14.

List of Illustrations

Illustration 1: Adolph Menzel: Hinterhof und Haus (about 1845). Oil on canvas. Reproduced by permission of the Alte Nationalgalerie, Berlin.

Illustration 2: Adolph Menzel: Stadtbahn Berlin-Potsdam. Oil on canvas. Reproduced by permission of the Alte Nationalgalerie, Berlin.

Illustration 3: Franz Skarbina: Droschken-Halteplatz. Oil on canvas. Private collection. Reproduced by permission of Dr Margit Bröhan.

Illustration 4: Franz Skarbina: Café Bauer – Unter den Linden/Ecke Friedrichstraße (about 1893). Watercolour on cardboard. Private collection. Reproduced by permission of Dr Margit Bröhan.

Illustration 5: Lesser Ury: Leipzigerstraße, (1889). Oil on canvas. Private collection. Reproduced by permission of Berlinsche Galerie.

Professor Norbert Bachleitner is Professor of Comparative Literature at the University of Vienna. His research interests include the reception of English and French literature in German-speaking countries, translation studies, and the social history of literature, particularly of book-selling and censorship. Selected publications include: *Der englische und französische Sozialroman des 19. Jahrhunderts und seine Rezeption in Deutschland.*Amsterdam, Atlanta/Ga: Rodopi 1993; *Kleine Geschichte des deutschen Feuilletonromans.* Tübingen: Narr 1999; (as editor) *Beitrage zur Rezeption der britischen und irischen Literatur des 19. Jahrhunderts im deutschsprachigen Raum.* Amsterdam, Atlanta/Ga: Rodopi 2000; (as co-author) *Geschichte des Buchhandels in Osterreich.* Wiesbaden: Harrassowitz 2000.

Professor Renate Böschenstein taught German literature at the University of Geneva from 1971 to 1998. Her publications have focussed on bucolic/idyllic poetry; nineteenth-century literature; the reception of Greek mythology in modern writing. She is currently working on a book on Fontane.

Dr. Peter James Bowman has recently been awarded a Ph.D. by the University of Cambridge for a thesis entitled *Dialogue and Identity: Characterization in the Novels of Theodor Fontane*; he has published on Fontane's *Cécile* in German Life and Letters, 53,1, 2000.

Professor Helen Chambers is Professor of German at St Andrews University. Her publications focus on narrative fiction in German and reception history. They include *Supernatural and Irrational Elements in the Works of Theodor Fontane.* Stuttgart 1980, and *The Changing Image of Theodor Fontane.* Columbia SC 1997.

Professor Yves Chevrel teaches Comparative Literature at the University of Paris-Sorbonne (Paris-IV). His main publications are *Le Naturalisme. Étude d'un mouvement littéraire international.* Paris, 2nd ed., 1993; *La Littérature comparée.* Paris, 4th ed., 1997; American translation: *Comparative Literature Today.* T. Jefferson U.P. 1995; *La recherche en littérature.* Paris 1994.

Dr Hans Ester teaches German studies and Comparative Aesthetics at the Catholic University of Nijmegen. He has written extensively on Fontane, in particular on aspects of reception. His most recent publications include (as co-editor with Jattie Enklaar) *Von Goethe war die Rede.* Amsterdam: Atlanta 1999; (as co-editor with Jattie Enklaar) *Das Jahrhundert Berlins.* Amsterdam: Atlanta 2000; (as co-editor with Meindert Evert.) *Nietzsches Wirkung auf Dichter und Denker des zwanzigsten Jahrhunderts.* Nijmegen 2000.

Dr Barbara Everett has held Fellowships and Lectureships at both the Universities of Oxford and Cambridge, and is now Senior Research Fellow at Somerville College, Oxford. She has delivered the Lord Northcliffe Lectures at University College, London and the Clarke Lectures at Trinity College, Cambridge. She has published on a wide variety of subjects. Her Shakespeare editions include *Antony and Cleopatra* (Signet) and *All's Well That Ends Well* (New Penguin). Her most recent books are *Poets in Their Time: Essays on English Poetry from Donne to Larkin*. Faber 1986 (hardback); OUP 1991, (paperback) and *Young Hamlet: Essays on Shakespeare's Tragedies*. OUP 1989 (hardback) and 1990 (paperback).

Professor Inga-Stina Ewbank is Emeritus Professor of English Literature, University of Leeds. She has written extensively on Shakespeare and early modern drama, the Brontës, Scandinavian drama, etc., and has translated plays by Ibsen and Strindberg. Her most recent (co-edited) book is *Anglo-Scandinavian Cross-Currents*. Norvik 1999.

Professor Dr. Phil. Hans Vilmar Geppert has held the Chair of German and Comparative Literature at the University of Augsburg since 1984. His main areas of interest are the novel and the poetry of the nineteenth and twentieth centuries. His most recent main publications include *Der realistische Weg,* on European Realism from Balzac to Raabe and Hardy (1994), essays on Bert Brecht's poetry, the theme of exile in literature, Faulkner and the German post-war novel, the reception of Walter Scott in Germany, the semiotics of Realism and Postmodernism. Forthcoming publications include: *Literatur im Dialog der Medien. Bert Brecht, Heinrich Mann, Alfred Döblin u.a.* and *Der historische Roman. Traditionen – Strukturen – Vergleiche*.

Professor Rüdiger Görner is Director of the Institute of Germanic Studies, University of London, and Professor of German at Aston University in Birmingham. His recent publications include *Theodor Fontane. Ausgewählte Gedichte*. Frankfurt/Leipzig 1998; *Mauer, Schatten, Gerüst. Kulturkritische Essays*. Tübingen 1999; *Nietzsches Kunst. Annäherungen an einen Denkartisten*. Frankfurt, Leipzig 2000.

Professor Barbara Hardy is Emeritus Professor of English, University of London. She has written critical studies of Shakespeare, Austen, Thackeray, Charlotte and Emily Brontë, Dickens, Eliot, Hardy, and Henry James; on lyric, narrative and the presentation of feeling in fiction; many articles including a collection, *Novelists and Narrators*; a memoir, *Swansea Girl*, and a novel, *London Lovers*. Her most recent book is *Dylan Thomas: An Original Language* and her next will be *Severn Bridge*, a collection of poetry.

Dr. Patricia Howe is Senior Lecturer in German at Queen Mary and Westfield College, University of London. Her research interests are narrative fiction and travel-writing in the nineteenth and early twentieth centuries. She has written on Fontane, Saar, Storm, Hofmannsthal and Schnitzler, and on women writers.

Dr Helmut Kuzmics is Professor of Sociology at the University of Graz, Austria. He is currently working on the relationship between fiction and sociology. His publications include *Der Preis der Zivilisation*. Frankfurt am Main and New York 1989; and (with Roland Axtmann) *Autorität, Staat und Nationalcharakter. Der Zivilisationsprozeß in Österreich und England 1700-1900*. Opladen 2000.

Professor Jacques Legrand is a translator; he has been Lector in French at the University of Heidelberg, and has taught French at the French Institutes in Innsbruck and Hannover and at grammar schools in Vienna and Saarbrücken. His translations include works by Fontane, Rilke, Trakl, Johannes Urzidil, Ludwig Harig, Stefan Zweig.

Professor W.J. Mc Cormack is Professor of Literary History at Goldsmiths College, University of London. *Fool of the Family*, his biography of J. M. Synge, was published by Weidenfeld and Nicolson in 2000. He is currently working on a 'prequel', provisionally called *The Death of Sam M'Cracken and the Birth of Anglo-Ireland*. Under the nom-de-plume, Hugh Maxton, he has published poetry for over thirty years, the latest collection being *Gubu Roi*. Lagan Press 2000

Dr. Teresa Martins de Oliveira teaches at the Instituto de Estudos Germanísticos, University of Porto. She has published a comparative study of Fontane and Eço de Queirós entitled *A Mulher e o Adultério nos romances Effi Briest de Theodor Fontane e O primo Bazilio de Eço de Queirós*. Oporto 1998.

Professor Domenico Mugnolo teaches at Universita degli Studi di Bari. His research interests include German theatre of the Age of Enlightenment, the nineteenth-century German novel, and contemporary German literature. He has published on Lessing, Fontane, Gregorovius, de Bruyn, Jurek Becker, and Volker Braun.

Hugh Rorrison is a freelance writer and translator. He has published extensively on modern German theatre. Among his translations are Wedekind's *Lulu Plays*, Pavel Kohout's *Maple Tree Game*. Heiner Müller's *Road to Volokolamsk* (for BBC Radio 3), Brecht's *Berlin Stories* and *Journals 1934-55*, Piscator's *The Political Theatre*. He has adapted *Effi Briest* for BBC Radio 4 and is co-translator, with Helen Chambers, of *Effi Briest*. Penguin Classics 2000.

Alexander Stillmark is Emeritus Reader, University College London. His publications are principally in the area of comparative literature of the nineteenth and twentieth centuries. He is co-editor of the following: (with J. Lachinger) *Adalbert Stifter heute*. Linz, London 1985; (with H. Castein) *Deutsche Romantik und das 20. Jahrhundert*. Stuttgart 1986; *Erbe und Umbruch in der neueren deutschsprachigen Komödie*. Stuttgart 1990: (with F. Wagner) *Lenau zwischen Ost und West*. Stuttgart 1992; (with P. Kirschner) *Between Time and Eternity. Nine Essays on W.B.Yeats and his Contemporaries Hofmannsthal and Blok*. Amsterdam 1992; *Joseph Roth. Der Sieg über die Zeit*. Stuttgart 1996; (with T. J. Reed) *Heine und die Weltliteratur*. Oxford

2000. In 2001 he will publish *Georg Trakl, Poems and Prose*. Translated and with an Introduction and Notes.

Dr. Godela Weiss-Sussex is Senior Lecturer in German, De Montfort University. Her publications include: Naturalist Metaphor of Destruction or Impressionist Panorama? A Re-evaluation of Georg Hermann's Berlin Novel Kubinke. In: Comparative Literature Studies, 35,4 1998, and *Metropolitan Chronicles. Georg Hermann's Berlin Novels 1897 to 1912*, Stuttgart 2000.

Professor Maite Zubiaurre is Assistant Professor of Spanish and Portuguese and Comparative Literature at the University of Southern California, Los Angeles. She has published extensively on the representation of gender, sexuality and space in modern European, Spanish, and Latin American fiction. She is the author of the forthcoming book *El espacio en la novela realista. Paisajes, miniaturas, perspectivas*. Mexico: El Fondo de Cultura Económica.